NEIL GAIMAN

The View from the Cheap Seats

SELECTED NON FICTION

headline

First published in Great Britain in 2016 by
HEADLINE PUBLISHING GROUP

1

Cataloguing in Publication Data is available from the British Library

ISBN 978 1 4722 0799 9 (Hardback)
ISBN 978 1 4722 0801 9 (Trade paperback)

Typeset in Zapf Elliptical by Palimpsest Book Production Limited,
Falkirk, Stirlingshire

Printed and bound in Great Britain by Clays Ltd, St Ives plc

Headline's policy is to use papers that are natural, renewable and recyclable
products and made from wood grown in sustainable forests. The logging
and manufacturing processes are expected to conform to the environmental
regulations of the country of origin.

HEADLINE PUBLISHING GROUP
An Hachette UK Company
Carmelite House
50 Victoria Embankment
London EC4Y 0DZ

www.headline.co.uk
www.hachette.co.uk

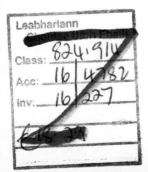

The View from
the Cheap Seats

By Neil Gaiman and published by Headline

The View from the Cheap Seats
Trigger Warning
The Ocean at the End of the Lane
Fragile Things
Anansi Boys
American Gods
Stardust
Smoke and Mirrors
Neverwhere

How the Marquis Got His Coat Back
(A Neverwhere short story)

The Truth is a Cave in the Black Mountains
(illustrated by Eddie Campbell)

Mirror Mask: The Illustrated Film Script
(with Dave McKean)

For Ash, who is new,
for when he is grown.

These were some of the things
your father loved and said
and cared about and believed,
a long time ago.

Contents

Introduction   1

I SOME THINGS I BELIEVE

Credo   7

Why Our Future Depends on Libraries,
Reading and Daydreaming: The Reading
Agency Lecture, 2013   9

Telling Lies for a Living . . . and Why We Do It:
The Newbery Medal Speech, 2009   21

Four Bookshops   31

Three Authors. On Lewis, Tolkien and Chesterton:
The MythCon 35 Guest of Honor Speech   38

The Pornography of Genre, or the Genre
of Pornography   44

Ghosts in the Machines: Some Hallowe'en
Thoughts   54

Some Reflections on Myth (with Several Digressions
onto Gardening, Comics and Fairy Tales)   59

How Dare You: On America, and Writing
About It   69

All Books Have Genders   72

The PEN Awards and *Charlie Hebdo*   78

What the [Very Bad Swearword] Is a Children's
Book, Anyway? The Zena Sutherland Lecture   82

II SOME PEOPLE I HAVE KNOWN

These Are Not Our Faces   99
Reflections: On Diana Wynne Jones   101
Terry Pratchett: An Appreciation   106
On Dave McKean   112
How to Read Gene Wolfe   117
Remembering Douglas Adams   120
Harlan Ellison: *The Beast That Shouted*
   Love at the Heart of the World   123
Banging the Drum for Harlan Ellison   131
On Stephen King, for the *Sunday Times*   135
Geoff Notkin: Meteorite Man   147
About Kim Newman, with Notes on the Creation
   and Eventual Dissolution of the Peace
   and Love Corporation   150
Gumshoe: A Book Review   156
SimCity   160
Six to Six   162

III INTRODUCTIONS AND MUSINGS:
SCIENCE FICTION

Fritz Leiber: The Short Stories   171
Hothouse   175
Ray Bradbury, *Fahrenheit 451* and What
   Science Fiction Is and Does   183
Of Time, and Gully Foyle: Alfred Bester
   and *The Stars My Destination*   189
Samuel R. Delany and *The Einstein Intersection*   193
On the Fortieth Anniversary of the Nebula
   Awards: A Speech, 2005   198

IV FILMS AND MOVIES AND ME

The Bride of Frankenstein   207
MirrorMask: An Introduction   211
MirrorMask: A Sundance Diary   218
The Nature of the Infection: Some Thoughts on
   Doctor Who   223
On Comics and Films: 2006   228

V ON COMICS AND SOME OF THE PEOPLE WHO MAKE THEM

Good Comics and Tulips: A Speech   235
A Speech to Professionals Contemplating
   Alternative Employment, Given at ProCon,
   April 1997   245
'But What Has That to Do with Bacchus?' Eddie
   Campbell and *Deadface*   261
Confessions: On *Astro City* and Kurt Busiek   265
Batman: Cover to Cover   271
Bone: An Introduction, and Some Subsequent
   Thoughts   279
Jack Kirby: King of Comics   282
The Simon and Kirby Superheroes   285
The Spirit of Seventy-Five   289
The Best of the Spirit   293
Will Eisner: New York Stories   297
The Keynote Speech for the 2003 Eisner
   Awards   301
2004 Harvey Awards Speech   307
The Best American Comics 2010   315

VI INTRODUCTIONS AND CONTRADICTIONS

Some Strangeness in the Proportion:
   The Exquisite Beauties of Edgar Allan Poe   323
On *The New Annotated Dracula*   328
Rudyard Kipling's Tales of Horror and Fantasy   333
From the Days of Future Past: *The Country*
   of the Blind and Other Stories by H. G. Wells   335
Business as Usual, During Alterations:
   Information Doesn't Want to Be Free by
   Cory Doctorow   346
The Mystery of G. K. Chesterton's Father Brown   350
Concerning Dreams and Nightmares: The
   Dream Stories of H. P. Lovecraft   353
On *The 13 Clocks* by James Thurber   359
Votan and Other Novels by John James   362
On *Viriconium:* Some Notes Toward an
   Introduction   367
So Long, and Thanks for All the Fish: An
   Introduction   373
Dogsbody by Diana Wynne Jones   379
Voice of the Fire by Alan Moore   383
Art and Artifice by Jim Steinmeyer   387
The Moth: An Introduction   390

VII MUSIC AND THE PEOPLE WHO MAKE IT

Hi, by the Way: Tori Amos   395
Curious Wine: Tori Amos II   397
Flood: Twenty-Fifth Anniversary Edition,
   They Might Be Giants   400
Lou Reed, in Memoriam: 'The Soundtrack to
   My Life'   403

Waiting for the Man: Lou Reed   408
Afterword Afterword: Evelyn Evelyn   423
Who Killed Amanda Palmer   427

VIII ON *STARDUST* AND FAIRY TALES

Once Upon a Time   431
Several Things About Charles Vess   438
The King of Elfland's Daughter, Lord Dunsany   441
Lud-in-the-Mist   444
The Thing of It Is: *Jonathan Strange & Mr Norrell*   446
On Richard Dadd's *The Fairy-Feller's Master-Stroke*   451

IX MAKE GOOD ART

Make Good Art   459

X THE VIEW FROM THE CHEAP SEATS:
REAL THINGS

The View from the Cheap Seats   471
A Wilderness of Mirrors   478
The Dresden Dolls: Hallowe'en 2010   485
Eight Views of Mount Fuji: *Beloved Demons*
   and Anthony Martignetti   492
So Many Ways to Die in Syria Now: May 2014   501
A Slip of the Keyboard: Terry Pratchett   508

Credits   513
Index   521

Introduction

Ifled, or at least, backed awkwardly away from journalism because I wanted the freedom to make things up. I did not want to be nailed to the truth; or to be more accurate, I wanted to be able to tell the truth without ever needing to worry about the facts.

And now, as I type this, I am very aware of a huge pile of paper on the table beside me, with words written by me on every sheet of the paper, all written after my exit from journalism, in which I try very hard to get my facts as right as I can.

I fail sometimes. For example, I am assured by the Internet that it is not actually true that the illiteracy rates of ten- and eleven year olds are used as a measure by which future prison cells are built, but it is definitely true that I was told this at an event at which the then-head of education in New York assured us that this was the case. And this morning, listening to the BBC news, I learned that half of all prisoners in the UK have the reading age of an eleven-year-old, or below.

This book contains speeches, essays and introductions. Some of the introductions made it into this volume because I love the author or the book in question, and I hope my love will be contagious. Others are here because, somewhere in that introduction, I did my best to explain something that I believe to be true, something that might even be important.

The authors from whom I learned my craft, over the years,

were often evangelists. Peter S. Beagle wrote an essay called 'Tolkien's Magic Ring', which I read as a small boy and which gave me Tolkien and *The Lord of the Rings*. A few years later H. P. Lovecraft, in a long essay, and after him Stephen King, in a short book, both told me about authors and stories that had shaped horror, and without whom my life would be incomplete. Ursula K. Le Guin wrote essays, and I would track down the books she talked about to illustrate her ideas. Harlan Ellison was a generous writer, and in his essays and collections he pointed me at so many authors. The idea that writers could enjoy books, sometimes even be influenced by them, and point other people at the works that they had loved, seemed to me to make absolute sense. Literature does not occur in a vacuum. It cannot be a monologue. It has to be a conversation, and new people, new readers, need to be brought into the conversation too.

I hope that, somewhere in here, I will talk about a creator or their work – a book, perhaps, or even a film or a piece of music – that will intrigue you.

I am writing this in a notebook, with a baby on my lap. He grunts and squeaks in his sleep. He makes me happy, but he also makes me feel vulnerable: old fears, long forgotten, creep out from shadowy places.

Some years ago a writer not much older than I am now told me (not bitterly, but matter-of-factly) that it was a good thing that I, as a young writer, did not have to face the darkness that he faced every day, the knowledge that his best work was behind him. And another, in his eighties, told me that what kept him going every day was the knowledge that his best work was still out there, the great work that he would one day do.

I aspire to the condition of the second of my friends. I like the idea that one day I'll do something that really works, even if I fear that I've been saying the same things for over thirty years. As we get older, each thing we do, each thing we write reminds us of something else we've done. Events rhyme. Nothing quite happens for the first time any more.

I have written many introductions to books of my own. They are long, and describe the circumstances under which the pieces in the book were written. This, on the other hand, is a short introduction, and most of these pieces will stand alone, unexplained.

This book is not 'the complete non-fiction of Neil Gaiman'. It is, instead, a motley bunch of speeches and articles, introductions and essays. Some of them are serious and some of them are frivolous and some of them are earnest and some of them I wrote to try and make people listen. You are under no obligation to read them all, or to read them in any particular order. I put them into an order that felt like it made some kind of sense – mostly speeches and suchlike at the beginning, more personal, heartfelt writing at the end. Lots of miscellaneous writing, articles and explanations, about literature, film, comics and music, cities and life, in the middle.

There is writing in here about things and people that are close to my heart. There's some of my life in here, too. I tend to write about things from wherever I am standing, and that means I include possibly too much me in the things I write.

And now, before we close and I leave you to the words, a few thank-yous.

Thank you to all the editors who commissioned these pieces. *Thank you* isn't a big enough expression of gratitude for Kat Howard, who went through so many of my articles and introductions, and decided which ones would make it into this book and which ones would be thrust into darkness, who put them into some kind of sensible order a dozen times just so that I could say, 'I have another idea . . .' (I also complicated things for her every time she was certain she had everything she needed by saying, 'Well, I already wrote about that in my essay about . . .' and rummaging around on the hard disk or clambering up dusty shelves until we found it.) Kat is a saint (probably Joan of Arc come round again). Thank you to Shield Bonnichsen, who found an essay we didn't have a copy of anywhere else. Thank you to Christine DiCrocco and Cat Mihos for finding things, typing them and generally helping and being wonderful.

Thank-yous also in abundance to Merrilee Heifetz, my agent; Jennifer Brehl, my American editor; to Jane Morpeth, my UK editor; and, ever and always, to Amanda Palmer, my remarkable wife.

Neil Gaiman

I

SOME THINGS I BELIEVE

'I believe that in the battle between guns and ideas, ideas will, eventually, win.'

Credo

I believe that it is difficult to kill an idea because ideas are invisible and contagious, and they move fast.

I believe that you can set your own ideas against ideas you dislike. That you should be free to argue, explain, clarify, debate, offend, insult, rage, mock, sing, dramatise and deny.

I do not believe that burning, murdering, exploding people, smashing their heads with rocks (to let the bad ideas out), drowning them or even defeating them will work to contain ideas you do not like. Ideas spring up where you do not expect them, like weeds, and are as difficult to control.

I believe that repressing ideas spreads ideas.

I believe that people and books and newspapers are containers for ideas, but that burning the people who hold the ideas will be as unsuccessful as firebombing the newspaper archives. It is already too late. It is always too late. The ideas are already out, hiding behind people's eyes, waiting in their thoughts. They can be whispered. They can be written on walls in the dead of night. They can be drawn.

I believe that ideas do not have to be correct to exist.

I believe you have every right to be perfectly certain that images of god or prophet or human that you revere are sacred, and undefilable, just as I have the right to be certain of the sacredness of speech, and of the sanctity of the right to mock, comment, to argue and to utter.

I believe I have the right to think and say the wrong things. I believe your remedy for that should be to argue with me or to ignore me, and that I should have the same remedy for the wrong things that I believe you think.

I believe that you have the absolute right to think things that I find offensive, stupid, preposterous or dangerous, and that you have the right to speak, write or distribute these things, and that I do not have the right to kill you, maim you, hurt you or take away your liberty or property because I find your ideas threatening or insulting or downright disgusting. You probably think some of my ideas are pretty vile too.

I believe that in the battle between guns and ideas, ideas will, eventually, win. Because the ideas are invisible, and they linger, and, sometimes, they can even be true.

Eppur si muove: and yet it moves.

Parts of this were first published in the 19 January 2015 issue of the *Guardian,* with accompanying illustrations by Chris Riddell. It was first published in its complete form in the *New Statesman* of 27 May 2015, illustrated by Dave McKean.

Why Our Future Depends on Libraries, Reading and Daydreaming: The Reading Agency Lecture, 2013

I t's important for people to tell you what side they are on and why, and whether they might be biased. A declaration of member's interests, of a sort. So, I am going to be talking to you about reading. I'm going to tell you that libraries are important. I'm going to suggest that reading fiction, that reading for pleasure, is one of the most important things one can do. I'm going to make an impassioned plea for people to understand what libraries and librarians are, and to preserve both of these things.

And I am biased, enormously and obviously: I'm an author, often an author of fiction. I write for children and for adults. For about thirty years I have been earning my living through my words, mostly by making things up and writing them down. It is obviously in my interest for people to read, for them to read fiction, for libraries and librarians to exist and help foster a love of reading and places in which reading can occur.

So I'm biased as a writer.

But I am much, much more biased as a reader. And I am even more biased as a British citizen.

And I'm here giving this talk tonight, under the auspices of the Reading Agency: a charity whose mission is to give everyone an equal chance in life by helping people become confident and enthusiastic readers. A charity which supports literacy programmes, and libraries and individuals, and nakedly and wantonly encourages the act of reading. Because, they tell us, everything changes when we read.

And it's that change, and that act of reading, that I'm here to talk about tonight. I want to talk about what reading does. What it's good for.

Once in New York, I listened to a talk about the building of private prisons – a huge growth industry in America. The prison industry needs to plan its future growth – how many cells are they going to need? How many prisoners are there going to be, fifteen years from now? And they found they could predict it very easily, using a pretty simple algorithm, based about asking what percentage of ten- and eleven-year-olds couldn't read. And certainly couldn't read for pleasure.

It's not one-to-one: you can't say that a literate society has no criminality. But there are very real correlations.

And I think some of those correlations, the simplest, come from something incredibly simple. Literate people read fiction, and fiction has two uses. Firstly, it's a gateway drug to reading. The drive to know what happens next, to want to turn the page, the need to keep going, even if it's hard, because someone's in trouble and you have to know how it's all going to end . . .

. . . that's a very real drive. And it forces you to learn new words, to think new thoughts, to keep going. To discover that reading per se is pleasurable. Once you learn that, you're on the road to reading everything. And reading is key. There were noises made briefly, a few years ago, about the idea that we were living in a postliterate world, in which the ability to make sense out of written words was somehow redundant, but these days, those noises are gone: words are more important than they ever were. We navigate the world with words, and as the world slips onto the Web, we need to follow, to communicate and to comprehend what we're reading.

People who cannot understand each other cannot exchange ideas, cannot communicate, and translation programs only get you so far.

The simplest way to make sure that we raise literate children is to teach them to read, and to show them that reading is a pleasurable activity. And that means, at its simplest, finding books that they enjoy, giving them access to those books and letting them read them.

I don't think there is such a thing as a bad book for children. Every now and again it becomes fashionable among some adults to point at a subset of children's books, a genre, perhaps, or an author, and to declare them bad books, books that children should be stopped from reading. I've seen it happen over and over; Enid Blyton was declared a bad author, so was R. L. Stine, so were dozens of others. Comics have been decried as fostering illiteracy.

It's tosh. It's snobbery and it's foolishness.

There are no bad authors for children, that children like and want to read and seek out, because every child is different. They can find the stories they need to, and they bring themselves to stories. A hackneyed, worn-out idea isn't hackneyed and worn out to someone encountering it for the first time. You don't discourage children from reading because you feel they are reading the wrong thing. Fiction you do not like is the gateway drug to other books you may prefer them to read. And not everyone has the same taste as you.

Well-meaning adults can easily destroy a child's love of reading: stop them reading what they enjoy, or give them worthy-but-dull books that you like, the twenty-first-century equivalents of Victorian 'improving' literature. You'll wind up with a generation convinced that reading is uncool and, worse, unpleasant.

We need our children to get onto the reading ladder: anything that they enjoy reading will move them up, rung by rung, into literacy.

(Also do not do what this author did when his eleven-year-old daughter was into R. L. Stine, which is to go and get a copy of Stephen King's *Carrie,* saying, 'If you liked those you'll love this!' Holly read nothing but safe stories of settlers on prairies for the rest of her early teenage years, and still glares at me whenever Stephen King's name is mentioned.)

The second thing that fiction does is to build empathy. When you watch TV or see a film, you are looking at things happening to other people. Prose fiction is something you build up from twenty-six letters and a handful of punctuation marks, and you, and you alone, using your imagination, create a world, and people it and look out through other eyes. You get to feel things, visit places and worlds you would never otherwise know. You learn that everyone else out there is a me, as well. You're being someone else, and when you return to your own world, you're going to be slightly changed.

Empathy is a tool for building people into groups, for allowing us to function as more than self-obsessed individuals.

You're also finding out something as you read that will be vitally important for making your way in the world. And it's this:

THE WORLD DOESN'T HAVE TO BE LIKE THIS. THINGS CAN BE DIFFERENT.

Fiction can show you a different world. It can take you somewhere you've never been. Once you've visited other worlds, like those who ate fairy fruit, you can never be entirely content with the world that you grew up in. And discontent is a good thing:

people can modify and improve their worlds, leave them better, leave them different, if they're discontented.

And while we're on the subject, I'd like to say a few words about escapism. I hear the term bandied about as if it's a bad thing. As if 'escapist' fiction is a cheap opiate used by the muddled and the foolish and the deluded, and the only fiction that is worthy, for adults or for children, is mimetic fiction, mirroring the worst of the world the reader finds herself in.

If you were trapped in an impossible situation, in an unpleasant place, with people who meant you ill, and someone offered you a temporary escape, why wouldn't you take it? And escapist fiction is just that: fiction that opens a door, shows the sunlight outside, gives you a place to go where you are in control, are with people you want to be with (and books are real places, make no mistake about that); and more importantly, during your escape, books can also give you knowledge about the world and your predicament, give you weapons, give you armour: real things you can take back into your prison. Skills and knowledge and tools you can use to escape for real.

As C. S. Lewis reminded us, the only people who inveigh against escape are jailers.

Another way to destroy a child's love of reading, of course, is to make sure there are no books of any kind around. And to give them nowhere to read those books if there are.

I was lucky. I had an excellent local library growing up. I had the kind of parents who could be persuaded to drop me off in the library on their way to work in my summer holidays, and the kind of librarians who did not mind a small, unaccompanied boy heading back into the children's library every morning and working his way through the card catalogue, looking for books with ghosts or magic or rockets in them, looking for vampires or detectives or witches or wonders. And when I had finished reading the children's library I began on the adult books.

They were good librarians. They liked books and they liked the books being read. They taught me how to order books from other libraries on interlibrary loans. They had no snobbery about anything I read. They just seemed to like that there was this wide-eyed little boy who loved to read, and they would talk to me about the books I was reading, they would find me other books in a series, they would help. They treated me as another reader – nothing less, nothing more – which meant they treated me with respect. I was not used to being treated with respect as an eight-year-old.

Libraries are about Freedom. Freedom to read, freedom of ideas, freedom of communication. They are about education (which is not a process that finishes the day we leave school or university), about entertainment, about making safe spaces and about access to information.

I worry that here in the twenty-first century people misunderstand what libraries are and the purpose of them. If you perceive a library as a shelf of books, it may seem antiquated or outdated in a world in which most, but not all, books in print exist digitally. But to think that is to fundamentally miss the point.

I think it has to do with nature of information.

Information has value, and the right information has enormous value. For all of human history, we have lived in a time of information scarcity, and having the needed information was always important, and always worth something: when to plant crops, where to find things, maps and histories and stories – they were always good for a meal and company. Information was a valuable thing, and those who had it or could obtain it could charge for that service.

In the last few years, we've moved from an information-scarce economy to one driven by an information glut. According to Eric Schmidt of Google, every two days now the human race

creates as much information as we did from the dawn of civilisation until 2003. That's about five exabytes of data a day, for
those of you keeping score. The challenge becomes, not finding
that scarce plant growing in the desert, but finding a specific
plant growing in a jungle. We are going to need help navigating
that information to find the thing we actually need.

Libraries are places that people go for information. Books are
only the tip of the information iceberg: they are there, and libraries
can provide you freely and legally with books. More children
are borrowing books from libraries than ever before – books of
all kinds: paper and digital and audio. But libraries are also, for
example, a place that people, who may not have computers,
who may not have Internet connections, can go online without
paying anything: hugely important when the way you find out
about jobs, apply for jobs or apply for benefits is increasingly
migrating exclusively online. Librarians can help these people
navigate that world.

I do not believe that all books will or should migrate onto
screens: as Douglas Adams once pointed out to me, over twenty
years before the Kindle showed up, a physical book is like a
shark. Sharks are old: there were sharks in the ocean before
the dinosaurs. And the reason there are still sharks around is
that sharks are better at being sharks than anything else is.
Physical books are tough, hard to destroy, bath resistant, solar
operated, feel good in your hand: they are good at being books,
and there will always be a place for them. They belong in
libraries, just as libraries have already become places you can
go to get access to ebooks, and audiobooks and DVDs and Web
content.

A library is a place that is a repository of, and gives every
citizen equal access to, information. That includes health information. And mental health information. It's a community space.
It's a place of safety, a haven from the world. It's a place with

librarians in it. What the libraries of the future will be like is something we should be imagining now.

Literacy is more important than ever it was, in this world of text and e-mail, a world of written information. We need to read and write, we need global citizens who can read comfortably, comprehend what they are reading, understand nuance, and make themselves understood.

Libraries really are the gates to the future. So it is unfortunate that, round the world, we observe local authorities seizing the opportunity to close libraries as an easy way to save money, without realising that they are, quite literally, stealing from the future to pay for today. They are closing the gates that should be open.

According to a recent study by the Organisation for Economic Co-operation and Development, England is the 'only country where the oldest age group has higher proficiency in both literacy and numeracy than the youngest group, after other factors, such as gender, socio-economic backgrounds and type of occupations are taken into account'.

Or to put it another way, our children and our grandchildren are less literate and less numerate than we are. They are less able to navigate the world, to understand it to solve problems. They can be more easily lied to and misled, will be less able to change the world in which they find themselves, be less employable. All of these things. And as a country, England will fall behind other developed nations because it will lack a skilled workforce. And while politicians blame the other party for these results, the truth is, we need to teach our children to read and to enjoy reading.

We need libraries. We need books. We need literate citizens.

I do not care – I do not believe it matters – whether these books are paper or digital, whether you are reading on a scroll or scrolling on a screen. The content is the important thing.

But a book is also the content, and that's important.

Books are the way that the dead communicate with us. The way that we learn lessons from those who are no longer with us, the way that humanity has built on itself, progressed, made knowledge incremental rather than something that has to be relearned, over and over. There are tales that are older than most countries, tales that have long outlasted the cultures and the buildings in which they were first told.

I think we have responsibilities to the future. Responsibilities and obligations to children, to the adults those children will become, to the world they will find themselves inhabiting. All of us – as readers, as writers, as citizens: we have obligations. I thought I'd try and spell out some of these obligations here.

I believe we have an obligation to read for pleasure, in private and in public places. If we read for pleasure, if others see us reading, then we learn, we exercise our imaginations. We show others that reading is a good thing.

We have an obligation to support libraries. To use libraries, to encourage others to use libraries, to protest the closure of libraries. If you do not value libraries then you do not value information or culture or wisdom. You are silencing the voices of the past and you are damaging the future.

We have an obligation to read aloud to our children. To read them things they enjoy. To read to them stories we are already tired of. To do the voices, to make it interesting and not to stop reading to them just because they learn to read to themselves. We have an obligation to use reading-aloud time as bonding time, as time when no phones are being checked, when the distractions of the world are put aside.

We have an obligation to use the language. To push ourselves: to find out what words mean and how to deploy them, to communicate clearly, to say what we mean. We must not attempt to freeze language, or to pretend it is a dead thing that must be revered, but we should use it as a living thing, that flows, that borrows words, that allows meanings and pronunciations to change with time.

We writers – and especially writers for children, but all writers – have an obligation to our readers: it's the obligation to write true things, especially important when we are creating tales of people who do not exist in places that never were – to understand that truth is not in what happens but in what it tells us about who we are. Fiction is the lie that tells the truth, after all. We have an obligation not to bore our readers, but to make them need to turn the pages. One of the best cures for a reluctant reader, after all, is a tale they cannot stop themselves from reading. And while we must tell our readers true things and give them weapons and give them armour and pass on whatever wisdom we have gleaned from our short stay on this green world, we have an obligation not to preach, not to lecture, not to force predigested morals and messages down our readers' throats like adult birds feeding their babies premasticated maggots; and we have an obligation never, ever, under any circumstances, to write anything for children to read that we would not want to read ourselves.

We have an obligation to understand and to acknowledge that as writers for children we are doing important work, because if we mess it up and write dull books that turn children away from reading and from books, we've lessened our own future and diminished theirs.

We all – adults and children, writers and readers – have an obligation to daydream. We have an obligation to imagine. It is easy to pretend that nobody can change anything, that we are in a world in which society is huge and the individual is less than nothing: an atom in a wall, a grain of rice in a rice field. But the truth is, individuals change their world over and over, individuals make the future, and they do it by imagining that things can be different.

Look around you: I mean it. Pause, for a moment. Just look around this room that we're in. I'm going to point out something so obvious that it tends to be forgotten. It's this: that everything you can see, including the walls, was, at some point, imagined. Someone decided it might be easier to sit on a chair than on the ground and imagined the chair. Someone had to imagine a way that I could talk to you in London right now without us all getting rained on. This room and the things in it, and all the other things in this building, in this city, exist because, over and over and over, people imagined things. They daydreamed, they pondered, they made things that didn't quite work, they described things that didn't yet exist to people who laughed at them.

And then, in time, they succeeded. Political movements, personal movements, all begin with people imagining another way of existing.

We have an obligation to make things beautiful, to not leave the world uglier than we found it. An obligation not to empty the oceans, not to leave our problems for the next generation. We have an obligation to clean up after ourselves, and not to leave our children with a world we've shortsightedly messed up, short-changed and crippled.

We have an obligation to tell our politicians what we want, to vote against politicians of whatever party who do not understand the value of reading in creating worthwhile citizens, who do not want to act to preserve and protect knowledge and encourage literacy. This is not a matter of party politics. This is a matter of common humanity.

Albert Einstein was asked once how we could make our children intelligent. His reply was both simple and wise. 'If you want your children to be intelligent,' he said, 'read them fairy tales. If you want them to be more intelligent, read them more fairy tales.'

He understood the value of reading, and of imagining. I hope we can give our children a world in which they will read, and be read to, and imagine, and understand.

Thank you for listening.

I gave this lecture for the Reading Agency, a UK charity with a mission to help people become more confident readers, in 2013.

Telling Lies for a Living . . . and Why We Do It: The Newbery Medal Speech, 2009

I

In case you were wondering what I'm doing up here – and I think it's a safe bet that right now *I* am, so that makes at least two of us – I'm here because I wrote a book, called *The Graveyard Book*, that was awarded the 2009 Newbery Medal.

This means that I have impressed my daughters by having been awarded the Newbery Medal, and I impressed my son even more by defending the fact that I had won the Newbery Medal from the hilarious attacks of Stephen Colbert on *The Colbert Report*, so the Newbery Medal made me cool to my children. This is as good as it gets.

You are almost never cool to your children.

II

When I was a boy, from the ages of about eight to fourteen, during my school holidays I used to haunt my local library. It was a mile and a half from my house, so I would get my parents to drop me off there on their way to work, and when the library closed I would walk home. I was an awkward child, ill-fitting, uncertain, and I loved my local library with a passion. I loved the card catalogue, particularly the children's library card catalogue: it had subjects, not just titles and authors, which allowed me to pick subjects I thought were likely to give me books I liked – subjects like magic or ghosts or witches or space – and then I would find the books, and I would read.

But I read indiscriminately, delightedly, hungrily. Literally hungrily, although my father would sometimes remember to pack me sandwiches, which I would take reluctantly (you are never cool to your children, and I regarded his insistence that I should take sandwiches as an insidious plot to embarrass me), and when I got too hungry I would gulp my sandwiches as quickly as possible in the library car park before diving back into the world of books and shelves.

I read fine books in there by brilliant and smart authors – many of them now forgotten or unfashionable, like J. P. Martin and Margaret Storey and Nicholas Stuart Gray. I read Victorian authors and Edwardian authors. I discovered books that now I would reread with delight and devoured books that I would probably now find unreadable if I tried to return to them – *Alfred Hitchcock and the Three Investigators* and the like. I wanted books, and made no distinction between good books and bad, only between the ones I loved, the ones that spoke to my soul, and the ones I merely liked. I did not care how a story was written. There were no bad stories: every story was new and glorious. And I sat there, in my school holidays, and I read the children's library, and when I was done, and had read the children's library, I walked out into the dangerous vastness of the adult section.

The librarians responded to my enthusiasm. They found me books. They taught me about interlibrary loans and ordered books for me from all across southern England. They sighed and were implacable about collecting their fines once school started and my borrowed books were inevitably overdue.

I should mention here that librarians tell me never to tell this story, and especially never to paint myself as a feral child who was raised in libraries by patient librarians; they tell me they are worried that people will misinterpret my story and use it as an excuse to use their libraries as free day care for their children.

III

So. I wrote *The Graveyard Book,* starting in December 2005 and all through 2006 and 2007, and I finished it in February 2008.

And then it's January 2009, and I am in a hotel in Santa Monica. I am out there to promote the film of my book *Coraline.* I had spent two long days talking to journalists, and I was glad when that was done. At midnight I climbed into a bubble bath and started to read the *New Yorker.* I talked to a friend in a different time zone. I finished the *New Yorker.* It was three a.m. I set the alarm for eleven, hung up a 'DO NOT DISTURB' sign on the door. *For the next two days,* I told myself as I drifted off to sleep, *I will do nothing but catch up on my sleep and write.*

Two hours later I realized the phone was ringing. Actually, I realized, it had been ringing for some time. In fact, I thought as I surfaced, it had already rung and then stopped ringing several times, which meant someone was calling to tell me something. Either the hotel was burning down or someone had died. I picked up the phone. It was my assistant, Lorraine, sleeping over at my place with a convalescent dog.

'Your agent Merrilee called, and she thinks someone is trying to get hold of you,' she told me. I told her what time it was (*viz. and to wit,* five thirty in the bloody morning is she out of her mind some of us are trying to sleep here you know). She said she knew what time it was in LA, and that Merrilee, who is my literary agent and the wisest woman I know, sounded really definite that this was important.

I got out of bed. Checked voice mail. No, no one was trying to get hold of me. I called home, to tell Lorraine that it was all bosh. 'It's okay,' she said. 'They called here. They're on the other line right now. I'm giving them your cell phone number.'

I was not yet sure what was going on or who was trying to do what. It was five forty-five in the morning. No one had died, though, I was fairly certain of that. My cell phone rang.

'Hello. This is Rose Trevino. I'm chair of the ALA Newbery committee . . .' *Oh,* I thought, blearily. *Newbery. Right. Cool. I may be an honor book or something. That would be nice.* 'And I have the voting members of the Newbery committee here, and we want to tell you that your book . . .'

'THE GRAVEYARD BOOK,' said fourteen loud voices, and I thought, *I may be still asleep right now, but they probably don't do this, probably don't call people and sound so amazingly excited, for honor books . . .*

' . . . just won . . .'

'THE NEWBERY MEDAL,' they chorused. They sounded really happy. I checked the hotel room because it seemed very likely that I was still fast asleep. It all looked reassuringly solid.

You are on a speakerphone with at least fifteen teachers and librarians and suchlike great, wise and good people, I thought. *Do not start swearing like you did when you got the Hugo Award.* This was a wise thing to think because otherwise huge, mighty and four-letter swears were gathering. I mean, that's what they're for. I think I said, *You mean it's Monday?* And I fumfed and

mumbled and said something of a *thankyouthankyouthankyou-
okaythiswasworthbeingwokenupfor* nature.

And then the world went mad. Long before my bedside alarm
went off I was in a car on my way to the airport, being interviewed
by a succession of journalists. 'How does it feel to win the
Newbery?' they asked me.

Good, I told them. *It felt good.*

I had loved *A Wrinkle in Time* when I was a boy, even if they
had messed up the first sentence in the Puffin edition, and it
was a Newbery Medal winner, and even though I was English,
the medal had been important to me.

And then they asked if I was familiar with the controversy
about popular books and Newbery winners, and how did I think
I fitted into it? I admitted I was familiar with the discussion.

If you aren't, there had been some online brouhaha about what
kinds of books had been winning the Newbery Award recently,
and about what kind of book should win the Newbery in the
future, and whether awards like the Newbery were for children
or for adults. I admitted to one interviewer that *The Graveyard
Book*'s winning had been a surprise to me, that I had assumed
that awards like the Newbery tend to be used to shine a light onto
books that needed help, and that *The Graveyard Book* had not
needed help.

I had unwittingly placed myself on the side of populism, and
realized afterward that that was not what I had meant at all.

It was as if some people believed there was a divide between
the books that you were permitted to enjoy and the books that
were good for you, and I was expected to choose sides. We were
all expected to choose sides. And I didn't believe it, and I still
don't.

I was, and still am, on the side of books you love.

IV

I am writing this speech two months before I will deliver it. My father died about a month ago. It was a surprise. He was in good health, happy, fitter than I am, and his heart ruptured without warning. So, numb and heartsick, I crossed the Atlantic, gave my eulogies, was told by relations I had not seen in a decade just how much I resembled my father, and did what had to be done. And I never cried.

It was not that I did not want to cry. It was more that it seemed there was never any time in the maelstrom of events to just stop and touch the grief, to let whatever was inside me escape. That never happened.

Yesterday morning a friend sent me a script to read. It was the story of somebody's lifetime. A fictional person. Three-quarters of the way through the script, the fictional character's fictional wife died, and I sat on the sofa and cried like an adult, huge wrenching sobs, my face running with tears. All the unwept tears for my father came out, leaving me exhausted and, like the world after a storm, cleansed and ready to begin anew.

I'm telling you this because it's something that I forget and need to be reminded of . . . And this was a sharp and salutary reminder.

I've been writing now for a quarter of a century.

When people tell me that my stories helped them through the death of a loved one – a child, perhaps, or a parent – or helped them cope with a disease, or a personal tragedy; or when they tell me that my tales made them become readers, or gave them a career; when they show me images or words from my books tattooed on their skin as monuments or memorials to moments that were so important to them they needed to take them with them every-where . . . when these things have happened, as they have, over and over, my tendency is to be polite and grateful, but ultimately to dismiss them as irrelevant.

I did not write the stories to get people through the hard places and the difficult times. I didn't write them to make readers of non-readers. I wrote them because I was interested in the stories, because there was a maggot in my head, a small squirming idea I needed to pin to the paper and inspect, in order to find out what I thought and felt about it. I wrote them because I wanted to find out what happened next to people I had made up. I wrote them to feed my family.

So I felt almost dishonorable accepting people's thanks. I had forgotten what fiction was to me as a boy, forgotten what it was like in the library; fiction was an escape from the intolerable, a doorway into impossibly hospitable worlds where things had rules and could be understood; stories had been a way of learning about life without experiencing it, or perhaps of experiencing it as an eighteenth-century poisoner dealt with poisons, taking them in tiny doses, such that the poisoner could cope with ingesting things that would kill someone who was not inured to them. Sometimes fiction is a way of coping with the poison of the world in a way that lets us survive it.

And I remembered. I would not be the person I am without the authors who made me what I am — the special ones, the wise ones, sometimes just the ones who got there first.

It's not irrelevant, those moments of connection, those places where fiction saves your life. It's the most important thing there is.

V

So I wrote a book about the inhabitants of a graveyard. I was the kind of boy who loved graveyards as much as he feared them. The best thing – the very best, most wonderful possible thing

– about the graveyard in the Sussex town in which I grew up is that there was a witch buried in the graveyard, who had been burned in the High Street. My disappointment on reaching teen-agehood and realizing, on rereading the inscription, that the witch was nothing of the sort (it was the grave of three stake-burned Protestant martyrs, burned by order of a Catholic queen) stayed with me. It would become the starting place, along with a Kipling story about a jeweled elephant goad, for my story 'The Witch's Headstone'. Although it's chapter 4, it was the first chapter I wrote of *The Graveyard Book*, a book I had wanted to write for over twenty years.

The idea had been so simple, to tell the story of a boy raised in a graveyard, inspired by one image – my infant son, Michael, who was two, and is now twenty-five, the age I was then, and is now taller than I am – on his tricycle, pedaling through the graveyard across the road in the sunshine, past the grave I once thought had belonged to a witch.

I was, as I said, twenty-five years old, and I had an idea for a book and I knew it was a real one.

I tried writing it, and realized that it was a better idea than I was a writer. So I kept writing, but I wrote other things, learning my craft. I wrote for twenty years until I thought that I could write *The Graveyard Book* – or at least, that I was getting no better.

I wanted the book to be composed of short stories, because *The Jungle Book* was short stories. And I wanted it to be a novel, because it was a novel in my head. The tension between those two things was both a delight and a heartache as a writer.

I wrote it as best I could. That's the only way I know how to write something. It doesn't mean it's going to be any good. It just means you try. And, most of all, I wrote the story that I wanted to read.

It took me too long to begin, and it took me too long to finish. And then, one night in February, I was writing the last two pages.

In the first chapter I had written a doggerel poem and left the last two lines unfinished. Now it was time to finish it, to write the last two lines. So I did. The poem, I learned, ended:

> Face your life, its pain, its pleasure
> Leave no path untaken.

And my eyes stung, momentarily. It was then, and only then, that I saw clearly for the first time what I was writing. Although I had set out to write a book about a childhood – it was Bod's childhood, and it was in a graveyard, but still, it was a childhood like any other – I was now writing about being a parent, and the fundamental most comical tragedy of parenthood: that if you do your job properly, if you, as a parent, raise your children well, they won't need you any more. If you did it properly, they go away. And they have lives and they have families and they have futures.

I sat at the bottom of the garden, and I wrote the last page of my book, and I knew that I had written a book that was better than the one I had set out to write. Possibly a book better than I am.

You cannot plan for that. Sometimes you work as hard as you can on something, and still the cake does not rise. Sometimes the cake is better than you had ever dreamed

And then, whether the work was good or bad, whether it did what you hoped or it failed, as a writer you shrug, and you go on to the next thing, whatever the next thing is.

That's what we do.

VI

In a speech, you are meant to say what you are going to say, and then say it, and then sum up what you have said.

I don't know what I actually said tonight. I know what I meant to say, though:

Reading is important.

Books are important.

Librarians are important. (Also, libraries are not child-care facilities, but sometimes feral children raise themselves among the stacks.)

It is a glorious and unlikely thing to be cool to your children.

Children's fiction is the most important fiction of all.

There.

We who make stories know that we tell lies for a living. But they are good lies that say true things, and we owe it to our readers to build them as best we can. Because somewhere out there is someone who needs that story. Someone who will grow up with a different landscape, who without that story will be a different person. And who *with* that story may have hope, or wisdom, or kindness, or comfort.

And that is why we write.

This was my acceptance speech for the 2009 Newbery Medal, which was awarded to *The Graveyard Book.*

Four Bookshops

I

These are the bookshops that made me who I am. They are none of them there, not any longer.

The first, the best, the most wonderful, the most magical because it was the most insubstantial, was a traveling bookshop.

From the ages of nine to thirteen I attended a local boarding school, as a day boy. Like all such schools, it was a world in itself, which meant that it had its own 'tuck shop', its own weekly barbering facilities, and, once a term, it had its own bookshop. Up until then my book buying fortunes would rise or fall with what was for sale in my local W. H. Smith – the Puffin books and Armada paperbacks that I'd save up for, only from the children's shelves, as I had never thought to explore further. Nor had I the money to explore if I wanted to. School libraries were my friends, as was the local library. But at that age I was limited by my means and by what was on the shelves.

And then, when I was nine, the traveling bookshop came. It set up its shelves and stock in a large empty room in the old music school, and, this was the best bit, you didn't need any money. If you bought books, it went onto your school bill. It was like magic. I could buy four or five books a term, secure in the knowledge it would wind up in the miscellaneous bit of the school bill, down with the haircuts and the double bass lessons, and I'd never be discovered.

I bought Ray Bradbury's *The Silver Locusts* (a collection similar to, although not exactly the same as, *The Martian Chronicles*). I loved it, especially 'Usher II', Ray's tribute to Poe. I did not know who Poe was. I bought *The Screwtape Letters*, because anything the bloke that wrote Narnia did had to be good. I bought *Diamonds Are Forever* by Ian Fleming, the cover proclaiming that it was soon to be a major motion picture. And I bought *The Day of the Triffids*, and *I, Robot*. (The shop was very big on Wyndham and Bradbury and Asimov.)

There were few enough children's books there. That was the good thing, and the smart thing. The books they sold, when they came to town, were, in the main, rattling good reads – the kind of books that would be read. Nothing that would be controversial or confiscated (the first book of mine that was confiscated was a copy of *And to My Nephew Albert I Leave the Island What I Won off Fatty Hagan in a Poker Game*, because it had an artistically naked female body on the cover. I got it back from the headmaster by claiming that it was my father's book, which I'm pretty certain wasn't true). Horror was fine though – like most of my year I was a ten-year-old Dennis Wheatley addict, and loved (although rarely bought) the *Pan Books of Horror Stories*. More Bradbury – much more, in the wonderful Pan covers – and Asimov and Arthur C. Clarke.

It didn't last for long. A year or so, no more – perhaps too many parents read their school bills and complained. But I didn't mind. I had moved on.

II

In 1971, the United Kingdom went over to decimal currency. The familiar sixpences and shillings that I'd grown up with suddenly became new pence. An old shilling was now five new pence. And although we were assured it would make no real difference to the cost of things, it soon became obvious, even to a ten-going-on-eleven-year-old, that it had. Prices went up, and they went up fast. Books which had been two shillings and sixpence (er, twelve and a half new pence) were soon thirty new pence, or forty new pence.

I wanted books. But, on my pocket money, I could barely afford them. Still, there was a bookshop . . .

The Wilmington Bookshop was not a long walk from my house. They did not have the best selection of books, being also an art supply shop and even, for a while, a post office, but what they did have, I learned soon, were a lot of paperbacks that were waiting to sell. Not, in those days, the cavalier tearing-off of covers for easy returns. I'd simply browse the shelves looking for anything with the prices listed in both old and new money, and would stock up on cool books for 20p and 25p. Tom Disch's *Echo Round His Bones* was the first of these I found, which attracted the attention of the young bookseller. His name was John Banks, and he died a few months ago, in his fifties. His parents owned the shop. He had hippy-long hair and a beard, and was, I suspect, amused by a twelve-year-old buying a Tom Disch book. He'd steer me to things I might like, and we'd talk books, and SF.

The Golden Age of SF is when you are twelve, they say, and it was pretty damn golden, as golden ages go. It seemed like everything was available in quantity – Moorcock and Zelazny and Delany, Ellison and Le Guin and Lafferty. (I'd make people going to America find me R. A. Lafferty books, convinced that he must be a famous, bestselling author in America. What was strange in retrospect was, they would bring me back the books.) I found James Branch Cabell there, in the James Blish-introduced editions – and in fact, took my first book back (it was *Jurgen,* and the final signature was missing. I had to go to the library to find out how it ended).

When I was twenty and I told John Banks I was writing a book, he introduced me to the Penguin rep, who told me who to send it to at Kestrel. (The editor wrote back an encouraging no, and having reread the book recently, for the first time in twenty years, I'm terribly grateful that she did.)

There's a brotherhood of people who read and who care about books. The best thing about John Banks was that when I was eleven or twelve he noticed I was a member of the brotherhood, and would share his likes and dislikes, even solicit my opinion.

III

The man who owned Plus Books in Thornton Heath, on the other hand, was not of that brotherhood, or if he was, he never let on.

The shop was a long bus ride from the school I was at between the ages of fourteen and seventeen, so we didn't go there often. The man who ran it would glower at us when we went in, suspicious of us in case we were going to steal something (we weren't), and worried that we would upset his regular clientele which consisted of middle-aged gentlemen in raincoats nervously perusing the stacks of mild pornography (which, in retrospect, we probably did).

He would growl at us, like a dog, if we got too near the porn. We didn't, though. We headed for the back of the shop on a treasure hunt, thumbing through the books. Everything had a

PLUS BOOKS stamp on the cover or the inside, reminding us that we could bring it back for half the price. We bought stuff there, but we never brought it back.

Thinking about it now, I wonder where the books came from – why would a grubby little shop in what was barely South London have heaps of American paperbacks? I bought all I could afford: Edgar Rice Burroughs, with the Frazetta covers; a copy of Zelazny's *A Rose for Ecclesiastes* that smelled of scented talcum powder when I bought it and still does, a quarter of a century later. That was where I found *Dhalgren*, and *Nova*, and where I first discovered Jack Vance.

It was not a welcoming place. But of all the bookshops I've ever been in, that's the one I go back to in dreams, certain that in a pile of ragged comics I'll find *Action* #1, and that there with a stamp on the cover telling you that it can be returned for half price, and smelling of beer or of beeswax, is one of those books I've always wanted to read from the shelves of Lucien's library – Roger Zelazny's own Amber prequel, perhaps, or a Cabell book that had somehow escaped all the usual bibliographies. If I find them, I'll find them in there.

IV

Plus Books was not the furthest I went, after school. That was to London, on the last day of every term. (They taught us nothing on that day, after all, and our season tickets would take us all the way, and would die the day after.) It was to a shop that took its name from one of the Bradbury tales of the Silver Locusts: Dark They Were and Golden Eyed.

I'd heard about it from John Banks at the Wilmington Bookshop – I don't know if he'd been there or not, but either way he knew it was somewhere I had to go. So Dave Dickson and I trolled up to Berwick Street, in London's Soho, to find, on our first visit, that the shop had moved several streets away to a spacious building in St Anne's Court.

I had a term's worth of pocket money saved up. They had teetering piles of remaindered Dennis Dobson hardbacks – all the R. A. Lafferty and Jack Vance I could have dreamed of. They had the new American paperback Cabells. They had the new Zelazny (*Roadmarks*). They had shelf after shelf after shelf after shelf of all the SF and fantasy a boy could dream of. It was a match made in heaven.

It lasted several years. The staff were amused and unhelpful (I remember being soundly, loudly and publicly ridiculed for asking, timorously, if *The Last Dangerous Visions* was out yet) but I didn't care. It was where I went when I went to London. No matter what else I did, I'd go there.

One day I went to London and the windows in St Anne's Court were empty, and the shop was gone, its evolutionary niche supplanted by Forbidden Planet, which has survived for over twenty years, making it, in SF bookshop years, a shark: one of the survivors.

To this day, every time I walk through St Anne's Court I look and see what kind of shop is in the place that Dark They Were and Golden Eyed was, vaguely hoping that one day it'll be a bookshop. There have been all sorts of shops there, restaurants, even a dry cleaner's, but it's not a bookshop yet.

And writing this, all of those bookshops come back, the shelves, and the people. And most of all, the books, their covers bright, their pages filled with infinite possibilities. I wonder who I would have been, without those shelves, without those people and those places, without books.

I would have been lonely, I think, and empty, needing something for which I did not have the words.

V

And there is one more bookshop I haven't mentioned. It is old, and sprawling, with small rooms that twist to become doors and stairs and cupboards, all of them covered with shelves, and the shelves all books, all the books I've ever wanted to see, books that need homes. There are books in piles, and in dark corners. In my fancy I shall have a comfortable chair, near a fireplace, somewhere on the ground floor, a little way from the door, and I'll sit on the chair, and say little, browsing an old favorite book, or even a new one, and when the people come in I shall nod at them, perhaps even smile, and let them wander.

There will be a book for each of them there, somewhere, in a shadowy nook or in plain sight. It will be theirs if they can find it. Otherwise, they will be free to keep looking, until it gets too dark to read.

This was the preface to *Shelf Life: Fantastic Stories Celebrating Bookstores*, edited by Greg Ketter, 2002.

Three Authors. On Lewis, Tolkien and Chesterton: The MythCon 35 Guest of Honor Speech

I thought I'd talk about authors, and about three authors in particular, and the circumstances in which I met them.

There are authors with whom one has a personal relationship and authors with whom one does not. There are the ones who change your life and the ones who don't. That's just the way of it.

I was six years old when I saw an episode of *The Lion, the Witch and the Wardrobe* in black and white on television at my grandmother's house in Portsmouth. I remember the beavers, and the first appearance of Aslan, an actor in an unconvincing lion costume, standing on his hind legs, from which I deduce that this was probably episode two or three. I went home to Sussex and saved my meager pocket money until I was able to buy a copy of *The Lion, the Witch and the Wardrobe* of my own. I read it, and *The Voyage of the Dawn Treader*, the other book I could find, over and over, and when my seventh birthday arrived I had dropped enough hints that my birthday present was a boxed set of the complete Narnia books. And I remember what I did on my seventh birthday – I lay on my bed and I read the books all through, from the first to the last.

For the next four or five years I continued to read them. I

would read other books, of course, but in my heart I knew that I read them only because there wasn't an infinite number of Narnia books to read.

For good or ill the religious allegory, such as it was, went entirely over my head, and it was not until I was about twelve that I found myself realizing that there were Certain Parallels. Most people get it at the Stone Table; I got it when it suddenly occurred to me that the story of the events that occurred to Saint Paul on the road to Damascus was the dragoning of Eustace Scrubb all over again. I was personally offended: I felt that an author, whom I had trusted, had had a hidden agenda. I had nothing against religion, or religion in fiction – I had bought (in the school bookshop) and loved *The Screwtape Letters*, and was already dedicated to G. K. Chesterton. My upset was, I think, that it made less of Narnia for me, it made it less interesting a thing, less interesting a place. Still, the lessons of Narnia sank deep. Aslan telling the Tash worshippers that the prayers they had given to Tash were actually prayers to Him was something I believed then, and ultimately still believe.

The Pauline Baynes map of Narnia poster stayed up on my bedroom wall through my teenage years.

I didn't return to Narnia until I was a parent, first in 1988, then in 1999, each time reading all the books aloud to my children. I found that the things that I loved, I still loved – sometimes loved more – while the things that I had thought odd as a child (the awkwardness of the structure of *Prince Caspian,* and my dislike for most of *The Last Battle,* for example) had intensified; there were also some new things that made me really uncomfortable – for example the role of women in the Narnia books, culminating in the disposition of Susan. But what I found more interesting was how much of the Narnia books had crept inside me: as I would write there would be moment after moment of realizing that I'd borrowed phrases, rhythms, the way that words were put together; for example, that I had a hedgehog and a hare, in *The Books of Magic,* speaking and agreeing with each other much as the Dufflepuds do.

C. S. Lewis was the first person to make me want to be a writer. He made me aware of the writer, that there was someone standing behind the words, that there was someone telling the story. I fell in love with the way he used parentheses – the auctorial asides that were both wise and chatty – and I rejoiced in using such brackets in my own essays and compositions through the rest of my childhood.

I think, perhaps, the genius of Lewis was that he made a world that was more real to me than the one I lived in; and if authors got to write the tales of Narnia, then I wanted to be an author.

Now, if there is a wrong way to find Tolkien, I found Tolkien entirely the wrong way. Someone had left a copy of a paperback called *The Tolkien Reader* in my house. It contained an essay – 'Tolkien's Magic Ring' by Peter S. Beagle – some poetry, 'Leaf by Niggle' and *Farmer Giles of Ham*. In retrospect, I suspect I picked it up only because it was illustrated by Pauline Baynes. I would have been eight, maybe nine years old.

What was important to me, reading that book, was the poetry, and the promise of a story.

Now, when I was nine I changed schools, and I found, in the class library, a battered and extremely elderly copy of *The Hobbit*. I bought it from the school in a library sale for a penny, along with an ancient copy of W. S. Gilbert's *Original Plays,* and I still have it.

It would be another year or so before I was to discover the first two volumes of *The Lord of the Rings*, in the main school library. I read them. I read them over and over: I would finish *The Two Towers* and start again at the beginning of *The Fellowship of the Ring*. I never got to the end. This was not the hardship it may sound – I had already learned from the Peter S. Beagle essay in *The Tolkien Reader* that it would all come out more or less okay. Still, I really did want to read it for myself.

When I was twelve I won the school English Prize, and was allowed to choose a book. I chose *The Return of the King*. I still own it. I only read it once, however – thrilled to find out how the story ended – because around the same time I also bought the one-volume paperback edition. It was the most expensive thing I had bought with my own money, and it was that which I now read and reread.

I came to the conclusion that *The Lord of the Rings* was, most probably, the best book that ever could be written, which put me in something of a quandary. I wanted to be a writer when I grew up. (That's not true: I wanted to be a writer then.) And I wanted to write *The Lord of the Rings*. The problem was that it had already been written.

I gave the matter a great deal of thought, and eventually came to the conclusion that the best thing would be if, while holding a copy of *The Lord of the Rings*, I slipped into a parallel universe in which Professor Tolkien had not existed. And then I would get someone to retype the book – I knew that if I sent a publisher a book that had already been published, even in a parallel universe, they'd get suspicious, just as I knew my own twelve-year-old typing skills were not going to be up to the job of typing it. And once the book was published I would, in this parallel universe, be the author of *The Lord of the Rings*, than which there can be no better thing. And I read *The Lord of the Rings* until I no longer needed to read it, because it was inside me. Years later, I dropped Christopher Tolkien a letter, explaining something that he found himself unable to footnote, and was profoundly gratified to find myself thanked in the Tolkien book *The Return of the Shadow* (for something I had learned from reading James Branch Cabell, no less).

It was in the same school library that had the two volumes

of *The Lord of the Rings* that I discovered Chesterton. The library
was next door to the school matron's office, and I learned that,
when faced with lessons that I disliked from teachers who terrified me, I could always go up to the matron's office and plead
a headache. A bitter-tasting aspirin would be dissolved in a glass
of water; I would drink it down, trying not to make a face, and
then be sent to sit in the library while I waited for it to work.
The library was also where I went on wet afternoons, and whenever else I could.

The first Chesterton book I found there was *The Complete
Father Brown Stories*. There were hundreds of other authors I
encountered in that library for the first time – Edgar Wallace
and Baroness Orczy and Dennis Wheatley and the rest of them.
But Chesterton was important – as important to me in his way
as C. S. Lewis had been.

You see, while I loved Tolkien and while I wished to have
written his book, I had no desire at all to write like him. Tolkien's
words and sentences seemed like natural things, like rock formations or waterfalls, and wanting to write like Tolkien would have
been, for me, like wanting to blossom like a cherry tree or climb
a tree like a squirrel or rain like a thunderstorm. Chesterton was
the complete opposite. I was always aware, reading Chesterton,
that there was someone writing this who rejoiced in words, who
deployed them on the page as an artist deploys his paints upon
his palette. Behind every Chesterton sentence there was someone
painting with words, and it seemed to me that at the end of any
particularly good sentence or any perfectly-put paradox, you could
hear the author, somewhere behind the scenes, giggling with delight.

Father Brown, that prince of humanity and empathy, was a
gateway drug into the harder stuff, this being a one-volume
collection of three novels: *The Napoleon of Notting Hill* (my
favorite piece of predictive 1984 fiction, and one that hugely
informed my own novel *Neverwhere*), *The Man Who Was Thursday*

(the prototype of all twentieth-century spy stories, as well as being a Nightmare, and a theological delight), and lastly *The Flying Inn* (which had some excellent poetry in it, but which struck me, as an eleven-year-old, as being oddly small-minded. I suspected that Father Brown would have found it so as well). Then there were the poems and the essays and the art.

Chesterton and Tolkien and Lewis were, as I've said, not the only writers I read between the ages of six and thirteen, but they were the authors I read over and over again; each of them played a part in building me. Without them, I cannot imagine that I would have become a writer, and certainly not a writer of fantastic fiction. I would not have understood that the best way to show people true things is from a direction that they had not imagined the truth coming, nor that the majesty and the magic of belief and dreams could be a vital part of life and of writing.

And without those three writers, I would not be here today. And nor, of course, would any of you. I thank you.

This was the guest of honour speech I gave at MythCon 35, which was held at the University of Michigan, in 2004. This is the annual conference of the Mythopoeic Society. I also read them my just-finished short story 'The Problem with Susan', and nobody garotted me.

The Pornography of Genre, or the Genre of Pornography

This is a transcription of a talk I gave in Orlando to an audience mostly composed of academics. It's not the actual speech I wrote, because I departed so far from my notes in the giving of it.

Thank you so much. That was so moving. Oddly enough, I think in some ways my talk is about passionate unknowing. I've written a speech, because I'm nervous, but I've also made lots of little marks in green ink where I've told myself I'm allowed to go off and just sort of start talking if I want to. So I have no idea how long this is going to be. It depends on the green-ink bits. What is the official title?

[*From crowd: "'The Pornography of Genre, or the Genre of Pornography.'"*]

Yeah, or something like that. It's actually nothing at all about the genre of pornography. That was just put in to make it a catchy title. I make no apologies.

It is the job of the creator to explode. It is the task of the academic to walk around the bomb site, gathering up the shrapnel, to figure out what kind of an explosion it was, who was killed, how much damage it was meant to do and how close it came to actually achieving that.

As a writer I'm much more comfortable exploding than talking about explosions. I'm fascinated by academia, but it's a practical fascination. I want to know how I can make something work for me. I love learning about fiction, but the learning is only as interesting as it is something that I can use.

When I was a boy, we had a garden. Mr Weller was eighty-five, and he came in every Wednesday and did things in the garden, and the roses grew, and the vegetable garden put forth vegetables, as if by magic. In the garden shed every kind of strange hoe and spade and trowel and dibber hung, and Mr Weller alone knew what they were good for. They were his tools. I get fascinated by the tools.

The miracle of prose is this: it begins with the words. What we, as authors, give to the reader isn't the story. We don't give them the people or the places or the emotions. What we give the reader is a raw code, a rough pattern, loose architectural plans that they use to build the book themselves. No two readers can or will ever read the same book, because the reader builds the book in collaboration with the author. I don't know if any of you have ever had the experience of returning to a beloved childhood book. A book that you remember a scene from so vividly, something that was etched onto the back of your oyeballs when you read it, and you remember the rain whipping down, you remember the way the trees blew in the wind, you remember the whinnies and the stamps of the horses as they fled through the forest to the castle, and the jangle of the bits, and every noise. And you go back and you read that book as an adult and you discover a sentence that says something like, '"What a jolly awful night this would be,' he said as they rode their horses through the forest. "I hope we get there soon," and you realize you did it all. You built it. You made it.

Some of the tools that hang in the garden shed of a writer are tools that help us, as writers, to understand what the patterns

are. That teach us how to work with our collaborators – because
the reader is a collaborator.

We ask ourselves the big questions about fiction because they
are the only ones that matter: What's it for? What's fiction for?
What's the imagination for? Why do we do this? Does it matter?
Why does it matter?

Sometimes the answers can be practical. A few years ago, in
2007, I went to China for the first-ever, I believe, state-sponsored
science fiction convention, and at some point I remember talking
to a party official who was there and I said, 'Up until now I
have read in *Locus* that your lot disapprove of science fiction
and you disapprove of science fiction conventions and these
things have not been considerably encouraged. What's changed?
Why did you permit this thing? Why are we here?' And he said,
'Oh, you know for years we've been making wonderful things.
We make your iPods. We make phones. We make them better
than anybody else, but we don't come up with any of these
ideas. You bring us things and then we make them. So we went
on a tour of America talking to people at Microsoft, at Google,
at Apple, and we asked them a lot of questions about themselves,
just the people working there. And we discovered that they all
read science fiction when they were teenagers. So we think
maybe it's a good thing.'

I've spent the last thirty years writing stories. I'd been doing
this for a living for fifteen years before it occurred to me to
wonder what a story was, and to attempt to define it in a way
that was useful to me. It took me about a year of pondering,
and eventually I decided that a story was anything that I made
up that kept the reader turning the pages or watching, and did
not leave the reader or the viewer feeling cheated at the end.

As definitions go, it worked for me. And sometimes it helped
me figure out why a story wasn't working, and what I could do
to get it back onto the rails.

The other big thing that niggled at me was genre. I'm a genre writer, in the same way that this is a genre conference, and that only gets sticky or problematic in either case when one asks what the genre is, which leads us to a whole boatload of other questions.

My biggest question, first as a reader and then as a writer, was simply, what is genre fiction? What makes something genre fiction?

What is genre? Well, you could start out with a practical definition: it's something that tells you where to look in a bookstore or (if you can find one these days) a video store. It tells you where to go. It tells you where to look. That's nice and easy. Just recently Teresa Nielsen Hayden told me it wasn't actually telling you what to look at, where to go. It was telling you what aisles not to bother going down. Which I thought was astonishingly perceptive.

There are too many books out there. So you want to make it easier on the people shelving them and on the people looking for them by limiting the places they're going to go looking for books. You give them places not to look. That's the simplicity of book shelving in bookstores. It tells you what not to read.

The trouble is that Sturgeon's Law – which approximates to '90 percent of everything is crap' – applies to the fields I know something about (SF and fantasy and horror and children's books and mainstream fiction and non-fiction and biography) and I'm sure it applies equally as much to the places in the bookshops I don't go – from cookbooks to supernatural romances. And the corollary to Sturgeon's Law is that 10 percent of everything is going to be anywhere from good to excellent by any stretch of the imagination. It's true for all genre fiction.

And because genre fiction is relentlessly Darwinian – books come, books go, many have been unjustly forgotten, very few unjustly remembered – the turnover tends to remove the 90 percent of dross from the shelves, replacing it with another 90 percent of dross. But it also leaves you – as with children's literature – a core canon that tends to be remarkably solid.

Life does not obey genre rules. It lurches easily or uneasily from soap opera to farce, office romance to medical drama to police procedural or pornography, sometimes within minutes. On my way to a friend's funeral I saw an airline passenger stand up, bang his head on an overhead compartment, opening it and sending the contents over a hapless flight attendant in the most perfectly performed and timed piece of slapstick I've ever seen. It mixed genres appallingly.

Life lurches. Genre offers predictability within certain constraints, but then, you have to ask yourself, what's genre? It's not subject matter. It's not tone.

Genre, it had always seemed to me, was a set of assumptions, a loose contract between the creator and the audience.

An American film professor named Linda Williams wrote an excellent study of hard-core pornographic movies, back in the late eighties, called *Hard Core,* subtitled *Power, Pleasure and the 'Frenzy of the Visible',* which I read more or less by accident (I was a book reviewer and it landed on my desk to review) as a young man, and which made me rethink everything I thought I knew at the time about what made something genre.

I knew that some things were not like other things, but I didn't know why.

Professor Williams suggested in her book that pornographic films could best be understood by comparing them to musicals. In a musical you are going to have different kinds of song – solos, duets, trios, full choruses, songs sung by men to women and by women to men, slow songs, fast songs, happy songs, love songs – and in a porn film you have a number of different kinds of sexual scenarios that need to be gone through.

In a musical the plot exists to allow you to get from song to song and to stop all the songs from happening at once. So with a porn film.

And furthermore and most importantly, the songs in a musical are, well, they're not what you're there for, as you're there for the whole thing, story and all, but they are those things that if they were not there you as a member of the audience would feel cheated. If you've gone to a musical and there are no songs, you are going to walk out feeling that you did not get your musical money's worth. You are never going to walk out of *The Godfather* going, 'There weren't any songs.'

If you take them out – the songs from a musical, the sex acts from a porn film, the gunfights from a Western – then they no longer have the thing that the person came to see. The people who have come to that genre, looking for that thing, will feel cheated, feel they have not received their money's worth, feel that the thing they have read or experienced has broken, somehow, the rules.

And when I understood that, I understood so much more – it was as if a light had been turned on in my head, because it answered the fundamental question I'd been asking since I was a boy.

I knew there were spy novels and that there were novels with spies in them, cowboy books and books that took place among cowboys in the American West. But before that moment I didn't understand how to tell the difference and now I did. If the plot is a machine that allows you to get from set piece to set piece, and the set pieces are things without which the reader or the viewer would feel cheated, then, whatever it is, it's genre. If the plot exists to get you from the lone cowboy riding into town to the first gunfight to the cattle rustling to the showdown, then it's a Western. If those are simply things that happen on the way, and the plot encompasses them, can do without them, doesn't actually care if they are in there or not, then it's a novel set in the old West.

When every event is part of the plot, if the whole thing is important, if there aren't any scenes that exist to allow you to take your audience to the next moment that the reader or the viewer feels is the thing that he or she has paid for, then it's a story, and the genre is irrelevant.

Subject matter does not make genre.

Now, the advantage of genre as a creator is it gives you something to play to and to play against. It gives you a net and the shape of the game. Sometimes it gives you balls.

Another advantage of genre for me is that it privileges story.

Stories come in patterns that influence the stories that come after them.

In the eighties, as a young journalist, I was handed a thick pile of bestselling romances, books with one-word titles, like *Lace* and *Scruples,* and was told to write three thousand words about them. So I went off and read them, with initial puzzlement and then slow delight as I realized that the reason they seemed so familiar was that they were. They were retellings of fairy tales, old ones I'd known since I was a boy, retold in the here and now and spiced with sex and money. And although the genre in question was known in British publishing as shopping-and-fucking novels, the books were about neither shopping nor fucking, but mostly about what would happen next, in an utterly familiar and predictable structure.

I remember coldly and calculatingly plotting my own one of those. It concerned an extremely bright young woman, plunged into a coma by the machinations of her evil aunt, so she was unconscious through much of the book as a noble young scientist hero fought to bring her back to consciousness and save the family fortune, until he was forced to wake her with the shopping-and-fucking equivalent of a kiss. I plotted it, and I never wrote it. I wasn't cynical enough to write something I didn't believe, and if

I was going to rewrite 'Sleeping Beauty' I was sure I could find a better way to do it.

But story privileged is a good thing for me. I care about story. I'm always painfully certain that I'm not much good at story, always happy when a story feels right, or comes out properly. I love beautiful writing (although I'm never convinced that what the English think of as beautiful writing, which is writing that's as clean and straightforward as possible, is what the Americans think of as beautiful writing, and it's definitely not Indian beautiful writing nor Irish beautiful writing, which are other things entirely).

But I love the drive and the shape of story.

I spent much of the last four days with my ninety-five-year-old cousin Helen Fagin, who is a holocaust survivor and was professor of the holocaust at the University of Miami for some time, and a wonderful, remarkable woman, and she was telling me about when she was in the Radomsko ghetto in 1942. She had been at Kraków University until the war interrupted her studies, so she was assigned in the ghetto to teach younger kids (she would have been nineteen, maybe twenty), and in order to assert normality, these ten- or eleven-year-olds would come in the morning and she would teach them Latin and algebra and things that she was uncertain that they would have any use for, but she would teach them. And one night she was given a copy of the Polish translation of *Gone with the Wind*, and she explains this is significant in that books were banned. Books were banned by the Nazis in an incredibly efficient way, which was if they found you with a book they would put a gun against your head and shoot you. Books were very, very banned, and she was given a copy of *Gone with the Wind*. And each night she would draw the curtains and put the blackout in place and read, with a tiny light, two or three chapters, losing valuable sleep time, so that the next morning when the kids came in she could tell them the story of what she read, and that was all they wanted. And for an hour every day they got away. They got out of the Radomsko ghetto. Most of those kids went on to the camps. She says that she tracked them all later and discovered that four – out of the dozens of kids she taught – had survived. When she told me that it made me rethink what I do and made me rethink the nature of escapist fiction, because I thought actually it gave them an escape, just there, just then. And it was worth risking death for.

As I get older I'm more comfortable with genre. More comfortable deciding what points a reader would feel cheated without. But still, my main impulse in creating a story is to treat myself as my reader, as my audience, and tell myself a story that amazes or delights or thrills or saddens me, that takes me somewhere new.

But still, as Edgar Pangborn put it, I persist in wondering . . .

Do we transcend genre by doing amazing genre work or do we transcend it by stepping outside of it? Is there any merit in transcending genre?

For that matter, at what point does an author become a genre? I do not read Ray Bradbury for moments of genre gratification, I read him for moments of pure Ray Bradbury – the way the words are assembled.

I get told – most recently by a pedicab driver in Austin, Texas – that my writing is Gaimanesque, and I have no idea what that means, or if there's anything people are waiting for, anything they'd feel cheated if they didn't get. I hope all the stories are different. I hope the authorial voice changes with the stories. I hope I'm using the right tools from the potting shed at the bottom of the garden in my imagination to build the right tales.

And when I get stuck, sometimes, I'll think of porn films and I'll think about musicals: what's the thing that a lover of whatever it is I'm writing would want to see? And sometimes I'll do that. And on those days I'm probably writing genre. And on other days I'll do the opposite.

But I suspect I'm at my most successful and ambitious and foolish and wise as a writer when I have no idea what sort of thing it is that I'm writing. When I don't know what a lover of things like this would expect, because nobody's ever loved anything like this before: when for good or for evil, I'm out there on my own.

And at that point, when I only have myself as a first reader, then genre, or lack thereof, becomes immaterial. The only rule that can guide me as a writer is to keep going, and to carry on telling a story that will not leave me, as the first reader, feeling cheated or disappointed at the end.

This was the keynote speech I gave at the thirty-fifth International Conference on the Fantastic in the Arts, held in Orlando, Florida, in 2013.

Ghosts in the Machines:
Some Hallowe'en Thoughts

We are gathered here at the final end of what Bradbury called the October Country: a state of mind as much as it is a time. All the harvests are in, the frost is on the ground, there's mist in the crisp night air and it's time to tell ghost stories.

When I was growing up in England, Hallowe'en was no time for celebration. It was the night when, we were assured, the dead walked, when all the things of night were loosed and, sensibly, believing this, we children stayed at home, closed our windows, barred our doors, listened to the twigs rake and patter at the window glass, shivered and were content.

There were days that changed everything: birthdays and New Years and First Days of School, days that showed us that there was an order to all things, and the creatures of the night and the imagination understood this, just as we did. All Hallows' Eve was their party, the night all their birthdays came at once. They had license – all the boundaries set between the living and the dead were breached – and there were witches, too, I decided, for I had never managed to be scared of ghosts, but witches, I knew, waited in the shadows, and they ate small boys.

I did not believe in witches, not in the daylight. Not really even at midnight. But on Hallowe'en I believed in everything. I even believed that there was a country across the ocean where, on that night, people my age went from door to door in costumes, begging for sweets, threatening tricks.

Hallowe'en was a secret, back then, something private, and I would hug myself inside on Hallowe'en, as a boy, most gloriously afraid.

*

Now I write fictions, and sometimes those stories stray into the shadows, and then I find I have to explain myself to my loved ones and my friends.

Why do you write ghost stories? Is there any place for ghost stories in the twenty-first century?

As Alice said, there's plenty of room. Technology does nothing to dispel the shadows at the edge of things. The ghost-story world still hovers at the limits of vision, making things stranger, darker, more magical, just as it always has . . .

There's a blog I don't think anyone else reads. I ran across it searching for something else, and something about it, the tone of voice perhaps, so flat and bleak and hopeless, caught my attention. I bookmarked it.

If the girl who kept it knew that anyone was reading it, anybody cared, perhaps she would not have taken her own life. She even wrote about what she was going to do, the pills, the Nembutal and Seconal and the rest, that she had stolen a few at a time over the months from her stepfather's bathroom, the plastic bag, the loneliness, and wrote about it in a flat, pragmatic way, explaining that while she knew that suicide attempts were cries for help, this really wasn't, she just didn't want to live any longer.

She counted down to the big day, and I kept reading,

uncertain what to do, if anything. There was not enough iden-
tifying information on the Web page even to tell me which
continent she lived on. No e-mail address. No way to leave
comments. The last message said simply, 'Tonight.'

I wondered whom I should tell, if anyone, and then I shrugged,
and, best as I could, I swallowed the feeling that I had let the
world down.

And then she started to post again. She says she's cold and
she's lonely.

I think she knows I'm still reading . . .

*

I remember the first time I found myself in New York for
Hallowe'en. The parade went past, and went past and went past,
all witches and ghouls and demons and wicked queens and
glorious, and I was, for a moment, seven years old once more,
and profoundly shocked. *If you did this in England*, I found
myself thinking in the part of my head that makes stories, *things
would wake, all the things we burn our bonfires on Guy Fawkes
to keep away. Perhaps they can do it here, because the things
that watch are not English. Perhaps the dead do not walk here,
on Hallowe'en.*

Then, a few years later, I moved to America and bought a
house that looked as if it had been drawn by Charles Addams
on a day he was feeling particularly morbid. For Hallowe'en, I
learned to carve pumpkins, then I stocked up on candies and
waited for the first trick-or-treaters to arrive. Fourteen years later,
I'm still waiting. Perhaps my house looks just a little too unset-
tling; perhaps it's simply too far out of town.

* * *

And then there was the one who said, in her cell phone's voice mail message, sounding amused as she said it, that she was afraid she had been murdered, but to leave a message and she would get back to us.

It wasn't until we read the news, several days later, that we learned that she had indeed been murdered, apparently randomly and quite horribly.

But then she did get back to each of the people who had left her a message. By phone, at first, leaving cell phone messages that sounded like someone whispering in a gale, muffled wet sounds that never quite resolved into words.

Eventually, of course, she will return our calls in person.

*

And still they ask, why tell ghost stories? Why read them or listen to them? Why take such pleasure in tales that have no purpose but, comfortably, to scare?

I don't know. Not really. It goes way back. We have ghost stories from ancient Egypt, after all, ghost stories in the Bible, classical ghost stories from Rome (along with werewolves, cases of demonic possession and, of course, over and over, witches). We have been telling each other tales of otherness, of life beyond the grave, for a long time; stories that prickle the flesh and make the shadows deeper and, most important, remind us that we live, and that there is something special, something unique and remarkable about the state of being alive.

Fear is a wonderful thing, in small doses. You ride the ghost train into the darkness, knowing that eventually the doors will open and you will step out into the daylight once again. It's always reassuring to know that you're still here, still safe. That nothing strange has happened, not really. It's good to be a child again, for a little while, and to fear – not governments, not regulations, not infidelities or accountants or distant wars, but ghosts and such things that don't exist, and even if they do, can do nothing to hurt us.

And this time of year is best for a haunting, as even the most prosaic things cast the most disquieting shadows.

The things that haunt us can be tiny things: a Web page; a voice mail message; an article in a newspaper, perhaps, by an English writer, remembering Hallowe'ens long gone and skeletal trees and winding lanes and darkness. An article containing fragments of ghost stories, and which, nonsensical although the idea has to be, nobody ever remembers reading but you, and which simply isn't there the next time you go and look for it.

This was written for, and published in, the 31 October 2006 issue of the *New York Times*.

Some Reflections on Myth (with Several Digressions onto Gardening, Comics and Fairy Tales)

As a writer, and, more specifically, as a writer of fiction, I deal with myth a great deal. Always have. Probably always will.

It's not that I don't like, or respect, mimetic fiction; I do. But people who make things up for a living follow our interests and our obsessions into fiction, and mostly my interests have taken me, whether I wanted them to or not, into the realm of myth, which is not entirely the same as the realm of the imagination, although they share a common border.

I remember finding a copy, as a small boy, of a paperback *Tales of the Norsemen* and delighting in it as a treasure, reading it until the binding broke and the pages flew apart like leaves. I remember the sheer rightness of those stories. They felt right. They felt, to my seven-year-old mind, familiar.

'Bricks without straw are more easily made than imagination without memories,' said Lord Dunsany.

He was right, of course. Our imaginings (if they are ours) should be based in our own lives and experiences, all our memories. But all of our memories include the tales we were told as children, all the myths, all the fairy tales, all the stories.

Without our stories we are incomplete.

I

The process of composting fascinates me. I am English, and share with many of my countrymen an amateurish fondness for, frankly, messing around in gardens: it's not strictly gardening, rather it's the urge that, last year, meant I got to smile proudly at the arrival of half a dozen exotic pumpkins, each of which must have cost more than twenty dollars to grow and each of which was manifestly inferior to the locally grown produce. I like gardening, am proudly no good at it, and do not mind this at all.

In gardening, the process is most of the fun, the results are secondary (and, in my case, usually accidental).

And one learns a lot about compost: kitchen scraps and garden leftovers and refuse that rot down, over time, to a thick black clean nutritious dirt, teeming with life, perfect for growing things in.

Myths are compost.

They begin as religions, the most deeply held of beliefs, or as the stories that accrete to religions as they grow.

('If he is going to keep killing people,' says Joseph to Mary, speaking of the infant Jesus in the apocryphal Gospel of the Infancy, 'we are going to have to stop him going out of the house.')*

And then, as the religions fall into disuse, or the stories cease to be seen as the literal truth, they become myths. And the myths compost down to dirt, and become a fertile ground for other stories and tales which blossom like wildflowers. Cupid and Psyche is retold and half-forgotten and remembered again and becomes Beauty and the Beast.

* 'Then said Joseph to St Mary, Henceforth we will not allow Him to go out of the house; for everyone who displeases him is killed.' *The First Gospel of the Infancy of Jesus Christ*, chapter 20, verse 16.

Anansi the African Spider God becomes Br'er Rabbit, whaling away at the tar baby.

New flowers grow from the compost: bright blossoms, and alive.

II

Myths are obliging.

When I was writing *Sandman,* the story that, in many ways, made my name, I experimented with myth continually. It was the ink that the series was written in.

Sandman was, in many ways, an attempt to create a new mythology – or rather, to find what it was that I responded to in ancient pantheons and then to try and create a fictive structure in which I could believe as I wrote it. Something that felt *right,* in the way that myths feel right.

Dream, Death, Delirium and the rest of the Endless (unworshipped, for who would want to be worshipped in this day and age?) were a family, like all good pantheons; each representing a different aspect of life, each typifying a different personality.

I think, overall, the character that people responded to most was Death, whom I represented as a cheerful, sensible sixteen-year-old girl – someone attractive, and fundamentally *nice;* I remember my puzzlement the first time I encountered people who professed to believe in the characters I had created, and the feeling, half of guilt and half of relief, when I started to get letters from readers who had used my character Death to get through the death of a loved one, a wife, a boyfriend, a mother, a child.

(I'm still bewildered by the people who have never read the comics who have adopted the characters, particularly Death and Delirium, as part of their personal iconography.)

Creating a new pantheon was part of the experiment, but so was the exploration of all other myths. (If *Sandman* was about one thing, it was about the act of storytelling, and the, possibly, redemptive nature of stories. But then, it's hard for a two-thousand-page story to be about just one thing.)

I invented old African oral legends; I created cat myths, which cats tell each other in the night.

In *Sandman: Season of Mists* I decided to tackle myths head-on, to see both how they worked and how robust they were: at what point did suspension of disbelief roll over and die? How many myths could one, metaphorically, get into a phone booth, or get to dance on the head of a pin?

The story was inspired loosely by something the Abbé Mugnier had once said – that he believed that there was a Hell, because it was church doctrine that there was a hell. He was not required to believe that there was anyone in it. The vision of an empty Hell was one that fascinated me.

Very well; Hell would be empty, abandoned by Lucifer (whom I represented as a fallen angel, straight out of Milton), and as prime psychic real estate would be wanted by various factions: I culled some from the comics, took others from old myths – Egyptian, Norse, Japanese – added in angels and demons and, in a final moment of experiment, I even added in some fairies, and was astonished to find how robust the structure was; it should have been an inedible mess, and instead (to keep the cooking metaphor) seemed to be a pretty good gumbo. Disbelief continued to be suspended and my faith in myth as something fundamentally alive and workable was upheld.

The joy of writing *Sandman* was that the territory was wide open. I wrote it in the world of anything goes: history and geography, superheroes and dead kings, folktales, houses and dreams.

III

Mythologies have, as I said, always fascinated me. Why we have them. Why we need them. Whether they need us.

And comics have always dealt in myths: four-color fantasies, which include men in brightly colored costumes fighting endless soap opera battles with each other (pre-digested power fantasies for adolescent males); not to mention friendly ghosts, animal people, monsters, teenagers, aliens. Until a certain age the mythology can possess us completely, then we grow up and leave those particular dreams behind, for a little while or forever.

But new mythologies wait for us, here in the final moments of the twentieth century. They abound and proliferate: urban legends of men with hooks in lovers' lanes, hitchhikers with hairy hands and meat cleavers, beehive hairdos crawling with vermin, serial killers and barroom conversations; in the background our TV screens pour disjointed images into our living rooms, feeding us old movies, newsflashes, talk shows, adverts; we mythologize the way we dress and the things we say; iconic figures – rock stars and politicians, celebrities of every shape and size; the new mythologies of magic and science and numbers and fame.

They have their function, all the ways we try to make sense of the world we inhabit, a world in which there are few, if any, easy answers. Every day we attempt to understand it. And every night we close our eyes, and go to sleep, and, for a few hours, quietly and safely, we go stark staring mad.

The ten volumes of *Sandman* were my way of talking about that. They were my way of looking at the mythologies of the last decade of the twentieth century; a way of talking about sex and death, fear and belief and joy – all the things that make us dream.

We spend a third of our lives asleep, after all.

IV

Horror and fantasy (whether in comics form or otherwise) are
often seen simply as escapist literature. Sometimes they can be
– a simple, paradoxically unimaginative literature offering quick
catharsis, a plastic dream, an easy out. But they don't have to
be. When we are lucky the *fantastique* offers a roadmap – a
guide to the territory of the imagination, for it is the function
of imaginative literature to show us the world we know, but
from a different direction.

Too often myths are uninspected. We bring them out without
looking at what they represent, nor what they mean. Urban
legends and the *Weekly World News* present us with myths in
the simplest sense: a world in which events occur according to
story logic – not as they do happen, but as they should happen.

But retelling myths is important. The act of inspecting them
is important. It is not a matter of holding a myth up as a dead
thing, desiccated and empty ('Now, class, what have we learned
from the Death of Baldur?'), nor is it a matter of creating New
Age self-help tomes ('The Gods Inside You! Releasing Your Inner
Myth'). Instead we have to understand that even lost and forgotten
myths are compost, in which stories grow.

What is important is to tell the stories anew, and to retell the
old stories. They are our stories, and they should be told.

I do not even begrudge the myths and the fairy stories their
bowdlerization: the purist in me may be offended by the Disney
retellings of old tales, but I am, where stories are concerned,
cruelly Darwinist. The forms of the tales that work survive, the
others die and are forgotten. It may have suited Disney's dramatic
purposes to have Sleeping Beauty prick her finger, sleep and be
rescued, all in a day, but when the tale is retold it will always
be at least a hundred years until the spell is broken – even if
we have long since lost from the Perrault story the prince's

cannibal mother; and Red Riding Hood ends these days with a rescue, not with the child being eaten, because that is the form of the story that has survived.

Once upon a time, Orpheus brought Eurydice back alive from Hades. But that is not the version of the tale that has survived.

(Fairy tales, as G. K. Chesterton* once pointed out, are not true. They are more than true. Not because they tell us that dragons exist, but because they tell us that dragons can be defeated.)

V

Several months ago I found myself, somewhat to my own surprise, in a distant country attending a symposium on myths and fairy tales. I was a featured speaker, and was told that I would be addressing a group of academics from all over the world on the subject of fairy tales. Before this, I would listen to papers being delivered to the group, and address a roundtable discussion.

I made notes for the talk I would give, and then went along to the first presentation: I listened to academics talk wisely and intelligently about Snow White, and Hansel and Gretel and Little Red Riding Hood, and I found myself becoming increasingly irritated and dissatisfied, on a deep and profound level.

My difficulty was not with what was being said, but with the attitude that went along with it – an attitude that implied that these tales no longer had anything to do with us. That they were dead cold things, which would submit without resistance to dissection, that could be held up to the light and inspected from every angle, and would give up their secrets without resistance.

* Actually, it's me paraphrasing Chesterton.

Most of the people at the conference were more than willing to pay lip service to the theory of fairy tales as stories that had begun as entertainments that adults told adults, but became children's stories when they went out of fashion (much as, in Professor Tolkien's analogy, the unwanted and unfashionable furniture was moved into the nursery: it was not that it had been intended to be children's furniture, it was just that the adults did not want it any longer). 'Why do you write with myths and with fairy tales?' one of them asked me.

'Because they have power,' I explained, and watched the students and academics nod doubtfully. They were willing to allow that it might be true, as an academic exercise. They didn't believe it.

The next morning I was meant to make a formal address on the subject of myth and fairy tales. And when the time came, I threw away my notes, and, instead of lecturing them, I read them a story.

It was a retelling of the story of Snow White, from the point of view of the wicked queen. It asked questions like, 'What kind of a prince comes across the dead body of a girl in a glass coffin and announces that he is in love and will be taking the body back to his castle?' and for that matter, 'What kind of a girl has skin as white as snow, hair as black as coal, lips as red as blood, and can lie, as if dead, for a long time?' We realize, listening to the story, that the wicked queen was not wicked: she simply did not go far enough; and we also realize, as the queen is imprisoned inside a kiln, about to be roasted for the midwinter feast, that stories are told by survivors.*

It is one of the strongest pieces of fiction I've written. If you read it on your own, it can be disturbing. To have it read to you

---

* The story is called 'Snow, Glass, Apples.' You can find it in my collection of stories *Smoke and Mirrors*.

by an author on a podium, first thing in the morning, during a conference on fairy tales, must on reflection have been, for the listeners, a rather extreme experience, like taking a gulp of something they thought was coffee, and finding that someone had laced it with wasabi, or with blood.

At the end of a story that was, after all, just 'Snow White and the Seven Dwarfs', an audience of several dozen people looked pale and troubled, like people coming off a roller coaster or like sailors recently returned to land.

'As I said, these stories have power,' I told them as I finished. This time they seemed far more inclined to believe me.

VI

All too often I write to find out what I think about a subject, not because I already know.

My next novel will be, for me, a way of trying to pin down myths – modern myths, and the old myths, together, on the huge and puzzling canvas that is the North American continent.

It has a working title of *American Gods* (which is not what the book will be called, but what it is about).

It's about the gods that people brought with them as they came here from distant lands; it's about the new gods, of car crash and telephone and *People* magazine, of Internet and airplane, of freeway and mortuary; it's about the forgotten gods, who were here before Man, the gods of Buffalo and Passenger Pigeon, gods that sleep, forgotten.

All the myths I care about, or have cared about, will be in there, but there in order to try and make sense of the myths that make America.

I have lived here for six years, and I still do not understand it: a strange collection of homegrown myths and beliefs, the ways that America explains itself to itself.

Maybe I'll make an awful mess of it all, but I can't say that worries me as badly as I think it ought to. I look forward to putting my thoughts into some kind of order. I look forward to learning what I think.

VII

Ask me with a gun to my head if I believe in them, all the gods and myths that I write about, and I'd have to say no. Not literally. Not in the daylight, nor in well-lighted places, with people about. But I believe in the things they can tell us. I believe in the stories we can tell with them.

I believe in the reflections that they show us, when they are told.

And, forget it or ignore it at your peril, it remains true: these stories have power.

This was first published in *Columbia: A Journal of Literature and Art* #31, winter 1999, although I actually wrote it as a speech in 1998, which I delivered at the Chicago Humanities Festival.

How Dare You: On America, and Writing About It

Nobody's asked the question I've been dreading, so far, the question I have been hoping that no one would ask. So I'm going to ask it myself, and try to answer it myself.

And the question is this: *How dare you?*

Or, in its expanded form,

How dare you, an Englishman, try to write a book about America, about American myths and the American soul? How dare you try to write about what makes America special, as a country, as a nation, as an idea?

And, being English, my immediate impulse is to shrug my shoulders and promise it won't happen again.

But then, I did dare, in my novel *American Gods,* and it took an odd sort of hubris to write it.

As a young man, I began to write a comic book about dreams and stories called *Sandman.* I got a similar question all the time, back then: *'You live in England. How can you set so much of this story in America?'*

And I would point out that, in media terms, the UK was practically the fifty-first state. We get American films, watch American TV. 'I might not write a Seattle that would satisfy an inhabitant,' I used to say, 'but I'll write one as good as a New Yorker who's never been to Seattle.'

I was, of course, wrong. I didn't do that at all. What I did instead was, in retrospect, much more interesting: I created an America that was entirely imaginary, in which *Sandman* could take place. A delirious, unlikely place out beyond the edge of the real.

And that satisfied me until I came to live in America about eight years ago.

Slowly I realized both that the America I'd been writing was wholly fictional, and that the real America, the one underneath the what-you-see-is-what-you-get surface, was much stranger than the fictions.

The immigrant experience is, I suspect, a universal one (even if you're the kind of immigrant, like me, who holds on tightly, almost superstitiously, to his UK citizenship). On the one hand, there's you, and on the other hand, there's America. It's bigger than you are. So you try to make sense of it. You try to figure it out – something which it resists. It's big enough, and contains enough contradictions, that it is perfectly happy not to be figured out. As a writer, all I could do was to describe a small part of the whole.

And it was too big to see.

I didn't really know what kind of book I wanted to write until, in the summer of 1998, I found myself in Reykjavik, in Iceland. And it was then that fragments of plot, an unwieldy assortment of characters, and something faintly resembling a structure, came together in my head. Either way, the book came into focus. It would be a thriller, and a murder mystery, and a romance, and a road trip. It would be about the immigrant experience, about what people believed in when they came to America. And about what happened to the things that they believed.

I wanted to write about America as a mythic place.

And I decided that, although there were many things in the novel I knew already, there were more I could find by going on the road and seeing what I found. So I drove, until I found a place to write, and then, in one place after another, sometimes at home, sometimes not, for nearly two years, I put one word after another, until I had a book. The story of a man called Shadow and the job he is offered when he gets out of prison. It tells the story of a small Midwestern town and the disappearances that occur there every winter. I discovered, as I wrote it, why roadside attractions are the most sacred places in America. I discovered many other strange byways and moments, scary and delightful and just plain weird.

When it was almost done, when all that remained was to pull together all the diverse strands, I left the country again, holed up in a huge, cold, old house in Ireland, and typed all that was left to type, shivering, beside a peat fire.

And then the book was done, and I stopped. Looking back on it, it wasn't really that I'd dared, rather that I had had no choice.

This piece was originally published in June 2001 on the Borders.com website, when *American Gods* was released.

All Books Have Genders

ooks have sexes; or to be more precise, books have genders. They do in my head, anyway. Or at least, the ones that I write do. And these are genders that have something, but not everything, to do with the gender of the main character of the story.

When I wrote the ten volumes of *Sandman*, I tended to alternate between what I thought of as male storylines, such as the first story, collected under the title *Preludes and Nocturnes*, or the fourth book, *Season of Mists*; and more female stories, like *A Game of You*, or *Brief Lives*.

The novels are a slightly different matter. *Neverwhere* is a Boy's Own Adventure (Narnia on the Northern Line, as someone once described it), with an everyman hero, and the women in it tended to occupy equally stock roles, such as the Dreadful Fiancée, the Princess in Peril, the Kick-Ass Female Warrior, the Seductive Vamp. Each role is, I hope, taken and twisted 45 percent skew, but they are stock characters nonetheless.

Stardust, on the other hand, is a girl's book, even though it also has an everyman hero, young Tristran Thorne, not to mention seven Lords bent on assassinating each other. That may partly be because once Yvaine came onstage, she rapidly became the most interesting thing there, and it may also be because the relationships between the women – the Witch Queen, Yvaine, Victoria Forester, the Lady Una and even Ditchwater Sal – were so much more complex and shaded than the relationships (what there was of them) between the boys.

The Day I Swapped My Dad for Two Goldfish is a boy's book. *Coraline* (which will be released in May 2002) is a girl's book.

The first thing I knew when I started *American Gods* – knew even before I started it – was that I was finished with C. S. Lewis's dictum that to write about how odd things affect odd people was an oddity too much, and that *Gulliver's Travels* worked because Gulliver was normal, just as *Alice in Wonderland* would not have worked if Alice had been an extraordinary girl (which, now I come to think of it, is an odd thing to say, because if there's one strange character in literature, it's Alice). In *Sandman* I'd enjoyed writing about people who belonged in places on the other side of the looking glass, from the Dreamlord himself to such skewed luminaries as the emperor of the United States.

Not, I should say, that I had much say in what *American Gods* was going to be. It had its own opinions.

Novels accrete.

American Gods began long before I knew I was going to be writing a novel called *American Gods*. It began in May 1997, with an idea that I couldn't get out of my head. I'd find myself thinking about it at night in bed before I'd go to sleep, as if I were watching a movie clip in my head. Each night I'd see another couple of minutes of the story.

In June 1997, I wrote the following on my battered Atari palmtop:

A guy winds up as a bodyguard for a magician. The magician is an over-the-top type. He offers the guy the job meeting him on a plane – sitting next to him.

Chain of events to get there involving missed flights, cancellations, unexpected bounce up to first class, and the guy sitting next to him introduces himself and offers him a job.

His life has just fallen apart anyway. He says yes.

Which is pretty much the beginning of the book. And all I knew at the time was it was the beginning of *something*. I hadn't a clue what kind of something. Movie? TV series? Short story?

I don't know any creators of fictions who start writing with nothing but a blank page. (They may exist. I just haven't met any.) Mostly you have *something*. An image, or a character. And mostly you also have either a beginning, a middle or an end. Middles are good to have, because by the time you reach the middle you have a pretty good head of steam up; and ends are great. If you know how it ends, you can just start somewhere, aim, and begin to write (and, if you're lucky, it may even end where you were hoping to go). There may be writers who have beginnings, middles and ends before they sit down to write. I am rarely of their number.

So there I was, four years ago, with only a beginning. And you need more than a beginning if you're going to start a book. If all you have is a beginning, then once you've written that beginning, you have nowhere to go.

A year later, I had a story in my head about these people. I tried writing it: the character I'd thought of as a magician (although, I had already decided, he wasn't a magician at all) now seemed to be called Wednesday. I wasn't sure what the other guy's name was, the bodyguard, so I called him Ryder, but that wasn't quite right. I had a short story in mind about those two and some murders that occur in a small Midwestern town called Silverside. I wrote a page and gave up, mainly because they really didn't seem to come together.

There was a dream I woke up from, somewhere back then, sweating and confused, about a dead wife. It seemed to belong to the story, and I filed it away.

Some months later, in September 1998, I tried writing that story again, as a first-person narrative, sending the guy I'd called Ryder (who I tried calling Ben Kobold this time, but that sent out quite the wrong set of signals) to the town (which I'd called Shelby, because Silverside seemed too exotic) on his own. I covered about ten pages, and then stopped. I still wasn't comfortable with it.

By that point, I was coming to the conclusion that the story I wanted to tell in that particular little lakeside town . . . *Hmm, I thought somewhere in there, Lakeside, that's what it's called, a solid, generic name for a town* . . . was too much a part of the novel to be written in isolation from it. And I had a novel by then. I'd had it for several months.

Back in July 1998 I had gone to Iceland, on the way to Norway and Finland. It may have been the distance from America, or it may have been the lack of sleep involved in a trip to the land of the midnight sun, but suddenly, somewhere in Reykjavik the novel came into focus. Not the story of it – I still had nothing more than the meeting on the plane and a fragment of plot in a town by a lake – but for the first time I knew what it was about. I had a direction. I wrote a letter to my publisher telling them that my next book wouldn't be a historical fantasy set in restoration London after all, but a contemporary American phantasmagoria. Tentatively, I suggested *American Gods* as a working title for it.

I kept naming my protagonist: there's a magic to names, after all. I knew his name was descriptive. I tried calling him Lazy, but he didn't seem to like that, and I called him Jack and he didn't like that any better. I took to trying every name I ran into on him for size, and he looked back at me from somewhere in my head unimpressed every time. It was like trying to name Rumpelstiltskin.

He finally got his name from an Elvis Costello song (it's on *Bespoke Songs, Lost Dogs, Detours and Rendezvous*). It's performed by Was (Not Was) and is the story of two men named Shadow and Jimmy. I thought about it, tried it on for size . . . *and Shadow stretched uncomfortably on his prison cot, and glanced across at the Wild Birds of North America wall calendar, with the days he'd been inside crossed off, and he counted the days until he got out.*

And once I had a name, I was ready to begin.

I wrote chapter 1 around December 1998. I was still trying to write it in the first person, and it wasn't comfortable with that. Shadow was too damn private a person, and he didn't let much out, which is hard enough in a third-person narrative and really hard in a first-person narrative. I began chapter 2 in June 1999, on the train home from the San Diego comics convention. (It's a three-day train journey. You can get a lot of writing done there.) The book had begun. I wasn't sure what I was going to call it, but then the publishers started sending me mock-ups of the book's cover, and it said *American Gods* in big letters in the top, and I realized that my working title had become the title.

I kept writing, fascinated. I felt, on the good days, more like the first reader than the writer, something I'd rarely felt since *Sandman* days. Neither Shadow nor Wednesday was, in any way, an everyman figure. They were uniquely themselves, sometimes infuriatingly so. Odd people, perfectly suited for the odd events they would be encountering.

The book had a gender now, and it was most definitely male.

I wonder now, looking back, if the short stories in *American Gods* were a reaction to that. There are maybe half a dozen of them scattered through the book, and all (but one) of them are most definitely female in my head (even the one about the Omani trinket salesman and the taxi driver). That may have been it. I don't know. I do know that there were things about America and about its history that it seemed easier to say by showing rather than telling; so we follow several people to America, from a Siberian shaman sixteen thousand years ago, to a Cornish pickpocket two hundred years ago, and, from each of them, we learn things.

And after the short stories were done, I was still writing. And writing. And continuing to write. The book turned out to be twice as long as I had expected. The plot I thought I was writing twisted and snaked and I slowly realized it wasn't the plot at all. I wrote the book and wrote the book, putting one word after another, until there were close to two hundred thousand of them.

And one day I looked up, and it was January 2001, and I was sitting in an ancient and empty house in Ireland with a peat fire making no impression at all on the stark cold of the room. I saved the document on the computer, and I realized I'd finished writing a book.

I wondered what I'd learned, and found myself remembering something Gene Wolfe had told me, six months earlier. 'You never learn how to write a novel,' he said. 'You just learn how to write the novel that you're writing.'

This was originally published on Powells.com in 2001, to accompany the launch of *American Gods*.

The PEN Awards and *Charlie Hebdo*

Six writers had pulled out of hosting tables at the PEN literary gala in New York. To host a table, you sit with eight people who have bought expensive tickets to the shindig in the vague hope of mingling with real writers. Your task is to make pleasant writerly conversation and not to spill your wine. Also, not to show disappointment when you realise that the whole table has been block-booked by, say, Google, and the people next to you don't know who you are.

The six writer hosts who pulled out from the gala did so because among the awards that would be given that night was one for courage, going to the surviving staff of *Charlie Hebdo*. It was for having the courage to put out the magazine after the 2011 firebombing and after the 2015 murders – and the six writers did not want to be there when *Charlie Hebdo* got that award.

I was asked if I would host a table. I said of course. So did Art Spiegelman; so did the cartoonist Alison Bechdel.

I tell my wife. 'You are doing the right thing,' she says. Then, 'Will you wear a bulletproof vest?'

'No. I think the security in the natural history museum will be pretty tight.'

'Yes. But you should wear a bulletproof vest, anyway. Remember, I'm pregnant,' she points out, in case I have forgotten. 'And our child will need a father more than a martyr.'

My assistant Christine calls me regretfully on the afternoon of the gala. 'With a little more time,' she says, 'I could have got you a made-to-measure bulletproof vest, the kind the president wears under his shirt. But all I can find at this short notice is an oversized police flak jacket. You would have to wear it over your tuxedo . . .'

I weigh my options. On the one hand, possible death by gunfire. On the other, definite embarrassment. 'That's okay,' I tell her. 'I'll be fine.'

I wear a bow tie. Art Spiegelman wears his *Nancy* comic tie, to show that he is a cartoonist, and we travel uptown by subway. We reach the museum. There are police in the streets and on the steps and TV crews – mostly French TV crews. Nobody else is wearing a bulletproof vest. There is a metal detector, though, and we walk through it one by one, authors and officials and guests.

Hanging above us as we eat is a life-size fibreglass blue whale. If terrorist cells behaved like the ones in the movies, I think, they would already have packed the hollow inside of the blue whale with explosives, leading to an exciting third-act battle sequence on top of the blue whale between our hero and the people trying to set off the bomb. And if that whale explodes, I realise, even an oversized flak jacket worn over a dinner jacket could not protect me. I find this vaguely reassuring.

Tom Stoppard is given an award first. Then *Charlie Hebdo*'s award is given. Finally, they give an award to the arrested Azerbaijani journalist Khadija Ismayilova. I wonder why the idea of being in the room while *Charlie Hebdo* is honoured upset the six former table hosts enough that they had to not be there and why they couldn't have turned up for the bits they liked and supported and just sloped off to the toilets for the bit they felt uncomfortable with. But then, I don't get only supporting the freedom of the kind of speech you like. If speech needs defending, it's probably because it's upsetting someone.

I suspect that the reason why it seems so simple to me and to those of us from the world of comics is that we are used to having to defend our work against people who want it – and us – off the shelves.

The first comics work I was ever paid for was in the 1987 Knockabout Comics book *Outrageous Tales from the Old Testament*. I was one of a few writers and I retold several stories, mostly from the Book of Judges. One story immediately got us into trouble: an account of the attempted rape of a male traveller to a town, thwarted by a host who offers the rapists his virgin daughter and the traveller's concubine. A gang rape follows and the traveller takes his concubine's corpse home, cuts it up and sends a segment of it to each of the tribes of Israel. (It's Judges 19 if you want to go and look, and it's pretty noxious.)

I was twenty-six and soon after publication I found myself on the radio defending the book, as a Tory MP complained about the lack of prosecutions for criminal blasphemy and how both the book and those who made it should be locked up; I watched the *Sun* attempt to stir up popular anger against it; and then, a few years later, I watched the Swedish publisher of the book fight to stay out of prison for publishing it over there.

Outrageous Tales was, let us make no bones of it, an offensive comic (we weren't using the phrase 'graphic novel' much yet in 1987). Its purpose, at least as far as I was concerned, was to shock, to point out that the Bible contained material that was outrageously unpleasant and to bring that out into the open, to let it be talked about, seen, discussed. The book existed, in part, to shock and to offend, because it was a reaction to material in the Bible that we found shocking and offensive.

In retrospect, I am glad I was not sentenced to prison for blasphemous libel, like Denis Lemon a decade earlier; glad that Knockabout's Swedish publisher got off; and doubly glad that the fundamentalist Christian extremists back then mostly reserved their murders for doctors who performed abortions and did not, to the best of my knowledge, kill people who wrote or drew comics.

Comics and cartoons can viscerally upset and offend people. Cartoons and comics get banned and cartoonists get imprisoned and killed. Some comics are hard to defend, especially if you prefer prettier drawing styles, lack cultural context, or were hoping for subtlety. But that does not mean that they should not be defended.

Back beneath the fibreglass blue whale, Gérard Biard, the editor in chief of *Charlie Hebdo,* concludes his speech. 'Growing up to be a citizen,' he reminds us, 'is to learn that some ideas, some words, some images can be shocking. Being shocked is part of democratic debate. Being shot is not.'

Originally published in the 27 May 2015 issue of the *New Statesman,* 'Saying the Unsayable', which was guest-edited by me and by Amanda Palmer.

What the [Very Bad Swearword] Is a Children's Book, Anyway? The Zena Sutherland Lecture

I hope none of you are here for answers. Authors are notoriously bad at answers. No, that's not right. We're not bad at them. We come up with answers all the time, but our answers tend to be unreliable, personal, anecdotal and highly imaginative.

These things can be drawbacks, as far as answers go, if you're hoping to use our answers in your lives. But they are all good things, not drawbacks, when it comes to questions. Authors are good at posing questions, and our questions are often pretty solid. I don't write with answers in mind. I write to find out what I think about something. I wrote *American Gods* because I had lived in America for almost a decade and felt it was time that I learned what I thought about it.

I wrote *Coraline* because, when I was a child, I used to wonder what would happen if I went home and my parents had moved away without telling me.

(It could happen. Things sometimes slipped their minds. They were busy people. One night they forgot to pick me up from school, and it was only a wistful phone call from the school, at ten o'clock at night, asking if they were expected to keep me, that finally got me picked up. One morning my parents dropped me off at school without noticing that the half-term break had begun, and I wandered, confused, around a locked and empty school until I was eventually rescued by a gardener. So it was unlikely, but it was possible.)

And if my parents had moved away, what if other people moved in who looked just like them? How would I know? What would I do? And for that matter, what was behind the mysterious door at the far end of the oak-paneled drawing room, the one that opened to reveal only bricks?

I write stories to find out what I think about things.

I am writing this speech to find out what I think about something.

What I want to know is this: *what is a children's book?* Or more emphatically: *what the [very bad swearword] is a children's book?*

*

It was a tiny private school in the town in which I lived, and I only attended it for a year. I was eight. One day, one of the boys came in with a copy of a magazine with naked ladies in it, stolen from his father, and we looked at it, to discover what naked ladies looked like. I do not remember what these particular naked ladies looked like, although I remember the little biographies by the pictures: one of the ladies was a magician's assistant, which I thought very grand. We were, like all children, curious.

In the spring of that same year some kids that I used to encounter on my daily walk home from school told me a dirty joke. It had a swearword in it. In fact, I do not think it would be overstating matters to suggest that it had *the* swearword in it. It was not a particularly funny joke, but it was definitely sweary, and I told it to a couple of my school friends the following morning, thinking that they might find it funny, or failing that, think of me as sophisticated.

One of them repeated it to his mother that night. I never saw him again. His parents were to pull him out of that school, because of my joke, and he never even came back to say goodbye.

I was interrogated the next morning by the headmistress and the principal, who had just bought the school and was intent on maximizing every drop of profit from it before she sold it to property developers the following year.

I had forgotten about the joke. They kept asking me if I knew any 'four-letter words' and, while I had not run across that term before, I had an enormous vocabulary, and it was the kind of thing that teachers asked eight-year-olds, so I ran through every word made of four letters I could think of, until they told me to shut up, and asked me about rude jokes and where I had heard them, and to whom exactly I had repeated them.

That night, after school, my mother was summoned to a meeting with the headmistress and the principal. She came home and informed me that she had been told that I had said something so terrible, so awful, that the headmistress and the principal would not actually repeat it. What was it?

I was scared to answer, so I whispered it to her.

I had said *fuck*.

'You must never *ever* say that again,' said my mother. 'That is the worst thing that you can say.'

She informed me that she had been told that I would have been expelled – the ultimate punishment – from the little school that night, but, because the other boy had already been removed from that seething den of scatological iniquity by his parents, the principal had announced, with regret, that she was not prepared to lose two sets of school fees. And so I was spared.

I learned two very important lessons from this.

The first was that you must be extremely selective when it comes to your audience.

And the second is that words have power.

* * *

Children are a relatively powerless minority, and, like all oppressed people, they know more about their oppressors than their oppressors know about them. Information is currency, and information that will allow you to decode the language, motivations and behavior of the occupying forces, on whom you are uniquely dependent for food, for warmth, for happiness, is the most valuable information of all.

Children are extremely interested in adult behavior. They want to know about us.

Their interest in the precise mechanics of peculiarly adult behavior is limited. All too often it seems repellent, or dull. A drunk on the pavement is something you do not need to see, and part of a world you do not wish to be part of, so you look away.

Children are very good at looking away.

*

I do not think I liked being a child very much. It seemed like something one was intended to endure, not enjoy: a fifteen-year-long sentence to a world less interesting than the one that the other race inhabited.

I spent it learning what I could about adults. I was extremely interested in how they saw children and childhood. There was an acting copy of a play on my parents' bookshelf. The play was called *The Happiest Days of Your Life*. It was about a girls' school evacuated to a boys' school during the War, and hilarity ensued.

My father had played the school porter, in an amateur production. He told me that the phrase 'the happiest days of your life' referred to your school days.

This seemed nonsensical to me then, and I suspected it of being either adult propaganda or, more likely, confirmation of

my creeping suspicion that the majority of adults actually had
no memories of being children.

For the record, I don't think I ever disliked anything as long
or as well as I disliked school: the arbitrary violence, the lack
of power, the pointlessness of so much of it. It did not help that
I tended to exist in a world of my own, half-in-the-world, half-
out-of-it, forever missing the information that somehow everyone
else in the school managed to have obtained.

On the first day of term I felt sick and miserable, on the last
day, elated. To my mind, 'the happiest days of your life' was
just one of those things that adults said that not even they could
have believed; things like 'this isn't going to hurt' which were
simply never true.

*

My defense against the adult world was to read everything I
could. I read whatever was in front of me, whether I understood
it or not.

I was escaping. Of course I was – C. S. Lewis wisely pointed
out that the only people who inveigh against escape tend to be
jailers. But I was learning, I was looking out through other eyes,
I was experiencing points of view I did not have. I was devel-
oping empathy, realizing and understanding that all the different
incarnations of 'I' in stories, who were not me, were real, and
passing on their wisdom and experience, allowing me to learn
from their mistakes. And I knew then, as I know now, that things
need not have happened to be true.

I read everything I could find. If the cover looked interesting,
if the first few pages held my interest, I would read it, whatever
it was, whatever the intended audience.

This meant that sometimes I would read things I was not ready
for, things that bothered me, or that I wished I had not read.

Children tend to be really good at self-censorship. They have a pretty good sense of what they are ready for and what they are not, and they walk the line wisely. But walking the line still means you will go past it on occasion.

I still remember the stories that troubled me: a horror story by Charles Birkin about a couple who had lost a daughter visiting a carnival freak show a few years later and encountering a golden-eyed creature that was probably their daughter, stolen and deformed by an evil doctor; a short story probably called 'The Pace That Kills' about evil traffic wardens, in which I learned that women could be made to pee into bottles to have their alcohol levels checked; and a short story called 'Made in USA' by J. T. McIntosh, in which an android girl was forced at knifepoint to undress in front of a gang of boys, to show them that she had no belly button.

There was also a newspaper I read, aged nine or ten, while waiting for my parents, with nothing else to read, that turned out to be a factual sixteen-page description, with photographs, of Nazi concentration camp atrocities and horrors. I read it, and I wished that I had not, because my view of the world was so much darker afterwards. I had known about the millions of people who had been killed – I had lost almost all my European extended family, after all. I had not known about the medical tortures, the cold-blooded, efficient monstrousness that humans had inflicted on other, helpless, humans.

Helplessness upset me. The idea that I could be stolen from my family and turned into a monster and they would not know me. That people could be forced against their will to pee into bottles or forced at knifepoint to take their clothes off – both of which, for me, were about helplessness and embarrassment, that most crippling of English conditions. The stories upset me, and I did not have the engines to deal with them.

I don't remember ever being bothered by running into refer-

ences to sex, which, for the most part, I did not actually understand. Adult authors tended to write in something that seemed
like code, comprehensible only if you already knew what they
were saying.

(Years later, writing a long fairy tale called *Stardust*, I tried to
write a sex scene in the same coded way, and succeeded perhaps
too well, as kids seemed barely to notice it, while adults often
complained that it was embarrassingly explicit.)

There were things I read as a boy that troubled me, but nothing
that ever made me want to stop reading. I understood that we
discovered what our limits were by going beyond them, and
then nervously retreating to our places of comfort once more,
and growing, and changing, and becoming someone else.
Becoming, eventually, adult.

*

I read everything but Young Adult fiction. This was not because
I did not like it, merely that I do not remember coming across
any as a child or even as a young adult. There was always more
adult fiction around than there were children's books, and at
school from the age of about eleven the books that we read in
the quiet period after lunch, the books that we passed around,
that went from boy to boy as each of us was done with it, were
tales of James Bond and Modesty Blaise, *Pan Books of Horror
Stories,* the occult thrillers of Dennis Wheatley, books by authors
like Edgar Wallace and Chesterton and Conan Doyle, J. R. R.
Tolkien and Michael Moorcock, Ursula Le Guin and Ray Bradbury.

There were children's authors I still read and loved, but the
majority of them wrote books I never saw in bookshops, or on
any shelves other than my local library's: Margaret Storey, for
example, who wrote magical fantasies that fed my inner landscape
in a way that only matched the magic of C. S. Lewis and Alan

Garner, or J. P. Martin and his very peculiar books about an enormously rich elephant called Uncle, and Uncle's battles with Beaver Hateman and the Badfort gang. These were library books, to be read there, or to be borrowed and, reluctantly, returned.

My book-buying habits were driven by thrift. In England, the years immediately following decimalization were years of spiraling prices. I discovered that books priced in shillings would often be half the price of later printings, and so I would rummage my way through the shelves of bookshops checking the prices of books, looking for books priced in shillings, trying to get the most fiction for my limited pocket money. I read so many bad books just because they were cheap, and I discovered Tom Disch, who made up for all of them.

As a child, and as a young adult, I was reading adult fiction and children's fiction with the same eyes and the same head, and I was reading anything in the space I happened to be in, indiscriminately, which is, I am certain, the best way to read.

I worry when people ask me how to stop their children reading bad fiction. What a child takes from a book is never what an adult takes from it. Ideas that are hackneyed and dull for adults are fresh and new and world changing for children. And besides, you bring yourself to a book, and children are capable of imbuing words with magic that not even the author knew was there.

I had one book confiscated, when I was twelve, a cold war political farce by David Forrest called *And to My Nephew Albert I Leave the Island What I Won off Fatty Hagan in a Poker Game*, taken away because, if I remember it correctly, the cover showed two naked female breasts with American and Russian flags painted on them. I tried to get the book back from the teachers by explaining that the cover was misleading and, apart from a sunbathing young lady, there was pretty much no sex or nakedness in the book. This did not work. I eventually got it back from the teachers at the end of term by claiming, falsely, that it was my father's and I had taken it without his knowledge, and it was, reluctantly, returned.

I had learned not to read books in school with breasts on the cover, or, at least, to cover the covers with something else, if I did.

I was pleased that the Michael Moorcock Jerry Cornelius books I loved when I was twelve, with their surrealistic and extreme sex scenes, had such innocent, mostly breastless, covers.

And, of course, I learned the wrong lessons from this. Because I loved adult fiction as a child, when my daughter Holly developed a fondness for R. L. Stine's *Goosebumps* books at the age of eleven or twelve, I dashed down to my library and returned with a paperback copy of Stephen King's *Carrie*. 'If you like those, you'll love this,' I told her.

Holly spent the rest of her early teen years reading books in which cheerful young heroines traveled in covered wagons across the plains, and in which nothing conceivably nasty ever happened to anyone. And, even fifteen years later, sometimes, when Stephen King comes up in conversation, she glares at me.

*

American Gods contains scenes that I would not want a child to read, mostly because I would not want to explain those scenes to a child who had read them and demanded an explanation.

I do not worry about a ten-year-old picking it up and reading it, though. I think any young reader not ready for it would be bored by it. Kids censor their own reading, and dullness is the ultimate deterrent.

*

I've been a professional writer, earning my living through my words, for thirty years now. I have written books for adults and I have written books for children.

I have written several books for adults that were awarded the Alex Award by YALSA, the Young Adult Library Services Association, for being books for adults that younger readers enjoyed.

I have written books for children that were later republished in respectable editions which adults could buy and read in public without fear of being thought childish.

I have won awards for writing for adults, and awards for writing for children. I published my first book for children, *The Day I Swapped My Dad for Two Goldfish*, almost fifteen years ago now.

So it is embarrassing to admit that, as I write this, as I read it, and for most of the last five months, I have been trying to work out what a children's book is, and what an adult book is, and which one I was writing, and why.

I think that in general the key question of what is children's fiction is answered in the same way as pornography, on the 'I know it when I see it' principle. And that is true, up to a point.

But *Coraline* was only published as a children's book because Morgan DeFiore lied.

Her mother, Merrilee Heifetz, has been my literary agent for the last twenty-five years, and is the person whose opinion in all matters of books and publishing I trust the most. I sent her *Coraline*, and her opinion was that it wasn't a children's book. It was too scary for children.

'I will tell you what,' I told her. 'Why don't you read it to your girls? If they're scared by it, we'll send it to my adult editor.' Her girls were Emily, aged eight, and Morgan, aged six.

She read it to them, and they loved it, and they wanted to know what happened next. When she got to the end she called me and said, 'They weren't scared. I'm sending it to Harper Children's.'

Some years later I was sitting next to Morgan DeFiore, who was then about fifteen, at the off-Broadway opening night of a *Coraline* musical. I told my now-wife, Amanda, the story, and explained that it was because Morgan was not scared that *Coraline* was a children's book. And Morgan said, 'I was terrified. But I wasn't going to let on that I was scared, because then I wouldn't have found out how it ended.'

*

In the last year I've written three books.

I wrote a picture book called *Chu's Day* about a baby panda who sneezes. It may be the simplest book I've ever written. It's the only time I've ever imagined myself writing a book that I intended to be read to children who could not yet read.

It exists because none of my children's picture books have ever been published in mainland China. They have been published in Hong Kong and in Taiwan, but there has never been a Neil Gaiman-written picture book in China because, I was told, in my books the children do not respect their parents enough, and they do bad things without getting properly punished, and there is anarchy and destruction and insufficient respect for authority. So it became a goal of mine to create a picture book that would contain all of these things and also be published in mainland China.

I wrote it, and I drew pictures for it, to show an artist what happened, and I gave it to my publisher, who gave it to Adam Rex, who painted much better pictures for it, and I am still waiting to find out if it will be published in China.

Still, a baby panda who sneezes.

It's a children's book which I wrote, peculiarly, with an adult audience in mind. I wrote it because I wanted a picture book of mine to be read in China. I wrote it to make children imagine and dream and exult and pretend to be pandas and pretend to sneeze, so I wrote a book that I hoped adults would enjoy reading to children, and, more importantly, enjoy reading the tenth time that week or the third time that night.

It contains a simple world, in which a small child is not listened to, but should have been, with disastrous consequences for everyone except the child. The pictures are beautiful and filled with detail.

And as I made it, I looked at it with two sets of eyes: was I making a book I would have liked as a very small boy? Was I making a book that I would enjoy reading as a parent – soon, perhaps, as a grandparent, for life goes so quickly?

That was the first book.

I wrote another book, almost definitely for children. It was called *Fortunately, the Milk*. It was intended, when I began it, to be as short as *The Day I Swapped My Dad for Two Goldfish*, to which it was a thematic sequel. That was a book that contained a father physically present but so absent that children were able to swap him for other things, like a gorilla mask, or an electric guitar, or a white rabbit, or a goldfish, while he simply read the newspaper. I thought I should redress the balance. I would write about a father who would have incredibly exciting adventures, or at least, claim to have had them, while going to get milk for his children's breakfast cereal.

The book grew until it was entirely too long to be a children's picture book, then ran out of words before it was long enough to be a novel.

My editor's first, perfectly sensible question to me was, since this was a children's book, why was a father the hero? Shouldn't it, couldn't it, have been his son, our narrator, who had the amazing adventures? Which meant that I had to ponder whether an adult protagonist was right for this kind of children's book.

I had no rational response, mostly because the book had not

been written or composed or even conceived rationally. It was a book about a father who went out for milk and came back late and related his unbelievably exciting adventures to his disbelieving and unimpressed children. It was called *Fortunately, the Milk*. It was not created, rationally or otherwise: I had simply described it, as if I had stumbled across it and needed to record it for the world. I could not have changed it because that was what it was.

So the father remains the hero, and is the one who returns with the milk.

The third book I wrote is the one that inspired the title of this talk, and is the reason why I puzzle and I wonder.

It has a working title of *Lettie Hempstock's Ocean.** It is written, almost entirely, from the point of view of a seven-year-old boy. It has magic in it – three strange, science-fictional witches who live in an ancient farmhouse at the bottom of the protagonist's lane. It has some unusually black and white characters, including the most absolutely evil creature I've made since Coraline's Other Mother. It has Sense of Wonder in it, and strangeness. It's only fifty-four thousand words long, short for an adult book, but for years considered the perfect length of a juvenile. It has everything in it I would have loved as a boy . . .

And I don't think it's for kids. But I'm not sure.

It's a book about child helplessness. It's a book about the incomprehensibility of the adult world. It's a book in which bad things happen – a suicide sets the story in motion, after all. And I wrote it for me: I wrote it to try and conjure my childhood for my wife, to evoke a world that's been dead for over forty years. I set it in the house I grew up in and I made the protagonist almost me, the parents similar to my parents, the sister an analogue of my sister, and I even apologized to my baby sister because she could not exist in this fictional version of events.

* It would be published as *The Ocean at the End of the Lane*.

I would make notes for myself as I wrote it, on scraps of paper and in margins, to try to work out whether I was writing a book for children or for adults – which would not change the nature of the book, but would change what I did with it once it was done, who would initially publish it and how. They were notes that would say things like 'In adult fiction you can leave the boring bits in', and 'I don't think I can have the scene where his father nearly drowns him in the bath if it's a kids' book, can I?'

I reached the end of the book and realized that I was as clueless as when I began. Was it a children's book? An adult book? A young adult book? A crossover book? A . . . book?

I once wrote the English-language script for a beautiful and prestigious foreign animated film, and was asked by the film company, before I began, to try and include some swearwords in there somewhere, as they needed to be sure that the film had at least a PG-13 certificate. But I don't think it's swearing that makes fiction adult.

What makes a book an adult book is, sometimes, that it depicts a world that's only comprehensible if you are an adult yourself.

Often the adult book is not for you, not yet, or will only be for you when you're ready. But sometimes you will read it anyway, and you will take from it whatever you can. Then, perhaps, you will come back to it when you're older, and you will find the book has changed because you have changed as well, and the book is wiser, or more foolish, because you are wiser or more foolish than you were as a child.

I have told you all this in the hopes that the action of writing it all down and of talking to you would clarify things for me, that it would shine a perfect and illuminating light on that most vexing of questions, *what the fuck is a children's book anyway?*

And I have talked a lot tonight, but I suspect I have not answered the question. Not really.

But then, you do not come to authors for answers. You come to us for questions. We're really good at questions.

And I hope that, in the days, and weeks, and years to come, the question of where the dividing lines between adult and children's fiction really are, and why they blur so, and whether we truly need them – and who, ultimately, books are for – will rise up in your mind when you least expect it to, and vex you, as you also are unable, in an entirely satisfactory manner, to answer it.

And if that is the case, then our time together has been worthwhile. I thank you.

I gave this as the 2012 Zena Sutherland Lecture. It's given in Chicago every year in honour of the late Zena Sutherland, an internationally recognised scholar of young people's literature.

II

SOME PEOPLE I HAVE KNOWN

'Nothing much had changed, except everything.'

These Are Not Our Faces

These are not our faces. This is not what we look like.

You think Gene Wolfe looks like his photograph in this book? Or Jane Yolen? Or Peter Straub? Or Diana Wynne Jones? Not so. They are wearing play-faces to fool you. But the play-faces come off when the writing begins.

Frozen in black and silver for you now, these are simply masks. We who lie for a living are wearing our liar-faces, false faces made to deceive the unwary. We must be – for, if you believe these photographs, we look just like everyone else.

Protective coloration, that's all it is.

Read the books: sometimes you can catch sight of us in there. We look like gods and fools and bards and queens, singing worlds into existence, conjuring something from nothing, juggling words into all the patterns of night.

Read the books. That's when you see us properly: naked priest-esses and priests of forgotten religions, our skins glistening with scented oils, scarlet blood dripping down from our hands, bright birds flying out from our open mouths. Perfect, we are, and beautiful in the fire's golden light . . .

There was a story I was told as a child, about a little girl who peeked in through a writer's window one night, and saw him writing. He had taken his false face off to write and had hung it behind the door, for he wrote with his real face on. And she saw him; and he saw her. And, from that day to this, nobody has ever seen the little girl again.

Since then, writers have looked like other people even when they write (though sometimes their lips move, and sometimes they stare into space longer, and more intently, than anything that isn't a cat); but their words describe their real faces: the ones they wear underneath. This is why people who encounter writers of fantasy are rarely satisfied by the wholly inferior person that they meet.

'I thought you'd be taller, or older, or younger, or prettier, or wiser,' they tell us, in words or wordlessly.

'This is not what I look like,' I tell them. 'This is not my face.'

This was the text I wrote to accompany a photograph of me in Patti Perret's book of photographs of authors, *The Faces of Fantasy*, 1996.

Reflections:
On Diana Wynne Jones

It was easy, when you knew her, to forget what an astonishing intellect Diana Wynne Jones had, or how deeply and how well she understood her craft.

She would certainly strike you when you met her as being friendly and funny, easygoing and opinionated. She was a perceptive reader (I had the enormous pleasure of spending a week with her at Milford Writers' Workshop, hearing her opinions on story after story) but she rarely talked about stories technically. She would tell you what she loved, and she would tell you how much she loved it. She would tell you what she didn't like too, but rarely, and barely wasted breath or emotion on it. She was in conversation about stories, like a winemaker who would taste wine, and discuss the taste of the wine and how it made her feel, but rarely even mention the winemaking process. That does not mean she did not understand it, though, and understand every nuance of it.

The joy for me of reading these essays and thoughts, these reflections on a life spent writing, was watching her discuss both her life and the (metaphorical) winemaking process.

She does not describe herself in this book, so I shall describe her for you: she had a shock of curly, dark hair, and, much of the time, a smile, which ranged from easygoing and content to a broad whorl of delight, the smile of someone who was enjoying herself enormously. She laughed a lot, too, the easy laugh of someone who thought the world was funny and filled with interesting things, and she would laugh at her own anecdotes, in the way of someone who had simply not stopped finding what she was going to tell you funny. She smoked too much, but she smoked with enthusiasm and enjoyment until the end. She had a smoker's chuckle. She did not suffer fools of the self-important kind, but she loved and took pleasure in people, the foolish as well as the wise.

She was polite, unless she was being gloriously rude, and she was, I suppose, relatively normal, if you were able to ignore the swirls and eddies of improbability that crashed around her. And believe me, they did: Diana would talk about her 'travel jinx', and I thought she was exaggerating until we had to fly to America on the same plane. The plane we were meant to fly on was taken out of commission after the door fell off, and it took many hours to get another plane. Diana accepted this as a normal part of the business of travel. Doors fell off planes. Sunken islands rose up beneath you if you were in boats. Cars simply and inexplicably ceased to function. Trains with Diana on them went to places they had never been before and technically could not have gone.

She was witchy, yes, and in charge of a cauldron roiling with ideas and stories, but she always gave the impression that the stories, the ones she wrote and wrote so very well and so wisely, had actually happened, and that all she had done was to hold the pen. My favourite essay in this book describes her writing process, and shows the immense amount of craft and care that went into each book.

She made a family, and without her family she would not have written. She was well loved, and she was well worth loving.

This book shows us a master craftswoman reflecting on her

life, her trade and the building blocks she used to become a writer. We will meet, in these reflections, someone who has taken the elements of a most peculiar childhood (are there any non-peculiar childhoods? Perhaps not. They are all unique, all unlikely, but Diana's was unlikelier than most) and a formidable intellect, an understanding of language and of story, a keen grasp of politics (on so many levels – personal, familial, organisational and international), an education that was part autodidactic (but in which, as you will learn here, C. S. Lewis and J. R. R. Tolkien both lectured for her, even if she was never quite sure what Tolkien was actually saying), and then, armed with all these things, has become quite simply the best writer for children of her generation.

I am baffled that Diana did not receive the awards and medals that should have been hers: no Carnegie Medal, for a start (although she was twice a runner-up for it). There was a decade during which she published some of the most important pieces of children's fiction to come out of the UK: *Archer's Goon*, *Dogsbody*, *Fire and Hemlock*, the Chrestomanci books . . . these were books that should have been acknowledged as they came out as game-changers, and simply weren't. The readers knew. But they were, for the most part, young.

I suspect that there were three things against Diana and the medals:

Firstly, she made it look easy. Much too easy. Like the best jugglers or slack-rope walkers, it looked so natural that the reader couldn't see her working, and assumed that the writing process really was that simple, that natural, and that Diana's works were written without thought or effort, or were found objects, like beautiful rocks, uncrafted by human hand.

Secondly, she was unfashionable. You can learn from some of the essays in this volume just how unfashionable she was as she describes the prescriptive books that were fashionable, particularly with teachers and those who published and bought books for young readers, from the 1970s until the 1990s: books in which the circumstances of the protagonist were, as much as possible, the circumstances of the readers, in the kind of fiction that was considered Good For You. What the Victorians might have considered an 'improving novel'.

Diana's fiction was never improving, or if it was, it was in a way that neither the Victorians nor the 1980s editors would have recognised. Her books took things from unfamiliar angles. The dragons and demons that her heroes and heroines battle may not be the demons her readers are literally battling – but her books are unfailingly realistic in their examinations of what it's like to be, or to fail to be, part of a family, the ways we fail to fit in or deal with uncaring carers.

The third thing that Diana had working against her was this: her books are difficult. Which does not mean that they are not pleasurable. But she makes you work as a reader. As an adult reader coming to a Diana Wynne Jones book I expected to reread great chunks of a book as I reached the end, all puzzled and filled with brow-crinkling 'How did she do that?' and 'Now wait a minute, I thought . . .', and I would put it together, and then see what she had done. I challenged her on this, and she told me that children read more carefully than adults did, and rarely had that trouble – and indeed, when I came to read Diana's books aloud to Maddy, my daughter, I discovered that they weren't ever problematic or even hard. All the pieces were there for you. You just had to be paying attention to everything she wrote, and to understand that if there was a word on the paper, it was there for a reason.

I don't think she minded not having the medals. She knew how good she was, and she had generations of readers who had grown up reading and loving her work. She was read, and she was loved. As the years went on and the readers who had discovered her when young grew up and wrote about her, talked about her, wrote fiction influenced by her, as magical fiction for children became less unusual, as her books sold more with each year that passed, Diana knew that what she had written had worked, and found its readers, and that was all that, in the end, mattered.

I am a handful of years too old to have read Diana's books as a boy. I wish I had – she would have been one of those people who formed the way I saw the world, the way I thought about it and perceived it. Instead, reading her, it felt familiar, and when, in my twenties, I read all of Diana's books that I could find, it felt like I was coming home.

If, like me, you love Diana's fiction, and you wish to learn more about the person, who she was and how she thought, then this book will enlighten you. But it will give you more than that. Her writings assembled in one place tell us how she thought about literature and the reasons for literature, about the place of children's fiction in the world, about the circumstances that shaped her and her own understanding and vision of who she was and what she did. It is ferociously intelligent, astonishingly readable, and as with so much that Diana Wynne Jones did, she makes each thing she writes, each explanation for why the world is as it is, look so easy.

This is the foreword to *Reflections*, a book of essays and non-fiction by Diana Wynne Jones.

Terry Pratchett: An Appreciation

Right.

So it's February of 1985, and it's a Chinese restaurant in London, and it's the author's first interview. His publicist was pleasantly surprised that anyone would want to talk to him (the author has just written a funny fantasy book called *The Colour of Magic*), but she's set up this lunch with a young journalist anyway. The author, a former journalist, has a hat, but it's a small, black leathery cap, not a Proper Author Hat. Not yet. The journalist has a hat too. It's a grayish thing, sort of like the ones Humphrey Bogart wears in movies, only when the journalist wears it he doesn't look like Humphrey Bogart: he looks like someone wearing a grown-up's hat. The journalist is slowly discovering that, no matter how hard he tries, he cannot become a hat person: it's not just that it itches and blows off at inconvenient moments, it's that he forgets, and leaves it in restaurants, and is now getting very used to knocking on the doors of restaurants about eleven a.m. and asking if they found a hat. One day, very soon now, the journalist will stop bothering with hats, and decide to buy a black leather jacket instead.

So they have lunch, and the interview gets printed in *Space Voyager* magazine, along with a photo of the author browsing the shelves in Forbidden Planet, and most importantly, they make each other laugh, and like the way the other one thinks.

And the author is Terry Pratchett, and the journalist is me, and it's been two decades since I left a hat in a restaurant, and one and a half decades since Terry discovered his inner best-selling-author-with-a-Proper-Author-Hat.

We don't see each other much these days, what with living on different continents, and, when we're on each other's continents, spending all our time signing books for other people. The last time we ate together was at a sushi counter in Minneapolis, after a signing. It was an all-you-can-eat night, where they put your sushi on little boats and floated it over to you. After a while, obviously feeling we were taking unfair advantage of the whole all-you-can-eat thing, the sushi chef gave up on the putting sushi on little boats, produced something that looked like the Leaning Tower of Yellowtail, handed it to us, and announced that he was going home.

Nothing much had changed, except everything.

These are the things I realized back in 1985:

Terry knew a lot. He had the kind of head that people get when they're interested in things, and go and ask questions and listen and read. He knew genre, enough to know the territory, and he knew enough outside genre to be interesting.

He was ferociously intelligent.

He was having fun. Then again, Terry is that rarity, the kind of author who likes writing, not having written, or Being a Writer, but the actual sitting there and making things up in front of a screen. At the time we met, he was still working as a press officer for the Central Electricity Generating Board. He wrote four hundred words a night, every night: it was the only way for him to keep a real job and still write books. One night, a year later, he finished a novel, with a hundred words still to go, so he put a piece of paper into his typewriter, and wrote a hundred words of the next novel.

(The day he retired, to become a full-time writer, he phoned me up. 'It's only been half an hour since I retired, and already I hate those bastards,' he said cheerfully.)

This was something else that was obvious in 1985. Terry was a science fiction writer. It was the way his mind worked: the urge to take it all apart, and put it back together in different ways, to see how it all fit together. It was the engine that drove *Discworld*. Not a *what if . . .* or an *if only . . .* or even an *if this goes on . . .* ; it was the far more subtle and dangerous *If there was really a . . . , what would that mean? How would it work?*

In the Clute-Nicholls *Encyclopedia of Science Fiction* there was an ancient woodcut, of a man pushing his head through the back of the world, past the sky, and seeing the cogs and the wheels and the engines that drove the universe machine. That's what people do in Terry Pratchett books, even if the people doing it are sometimes rats and sometimes small girls. People learn things. They open their heads.

So we discovered we shared a similar sense of humor, and a similar set of cultural referents; we had read the same obscure books, took pleasure in pointing each other to weird Victorian reference books.

A few years after we met, in 1988, Terry and I wrote a book together. It began as a parody of Richmal Crompton's *William* books, which we called *William the Antichrist,* but rapidly outgrew that conceit and became about a number of other things instead, and we called it *Good Omens*. It was a funny novel about the end of the world and how we're all going to die. Working with Terry I felt like a journeyman working alongside a master craftsman in some medieval guild. He constructs novels like a guildmaster might build a cathedral arch. There is art, of course, but that's the result of building it well. What there is more of is the pleasure taken in constructing something that does what it's meant to do – to make people read the story, and laugh, and possibly even think.

(This is how we wrote a novel together. I'd write late at night. Terry wrote early in the morning. In the afternoon we'd have very long phone conversations where we'd read each other the best bits we'd written, and talk about stuff that could happen next. The main objective was to make the other one laugh. We posted floppy disks back and forth. There was one night when we tried using a modem to send some text across the country, at 300/75 speeds, directly from computer to computer, because if e-mail had been invented back then nobody had told us about it. We managed it too. But the post was faster.)

(No, we won't write a sequel.)

Terry has been writing professionally for a very long time, honing his craft, getting quietly better and better. The biggest problem he faces is the problem of excellence: he makes it look easy. The public doesn't know where the craft lies. It's wiser to make it look harder than it is, a lesson all jugglers learn.

In the early days the reviewers compared him to the late Douglas Adams, but then Terry went on to write books as enthusiastically as Douglas avoided writing them, and now, if there is any comparison to be made of anything from the formal rules of a Pratchett novel to the sheer prolific fecundity of the man, it might be to P. G. Wodehouse. But mostly newspapers, magazines and critics do not compare him to anyone. He exists in a blind spot, with two strikes against him: he writes funny books, in a world in which *funny* is synonymous with *trivial,* and they are fantasies – or more precisely, they are set on the Discworld, a flat world, which rests on the back of four elephants, who in turn stand on the back of a turtle, heading off through space. It's a location in which Terry Pratchett can write anything, from hard-bitten crime dramas to vampiric political parodies, to children's books. And those children's books have changed things. After all, Terry won the prestigious Carnegie Medal for his pied piper tale *The Amazing Maurice and His Educated Rodents,* awarded by the librarians of the UK, and the Carnegie is an award that even newspapers have to respect. (Even so, the newspapers had their revenge, cheerfully misunderstanding Terry's acceptance speech and accusing him of bashing J. K. Rowling and J. R. R. Tolkien and fantasy, in a speech about the real magic of fantastic fiction.)

The most recent books have shown Terry in a new mode – books like *Night Watch* and *Monstrous Regiment* are darker, deeper, more outraged at what people can do to people, while prouder of what people can do for each other. And yes, the books are still funny, but they no longer follow the jokes: now the books follow the story and the people. *Satire* is a word that is often used to mean that there aren't any people in the fiction, and for that reason I'm uncomfortable calling Terry a satirist. What he is, is A Writer, and there are few enough of those around. There are lots of people who call themselves writers, mind you. But it's not the same thing at all.

In person, Terry is genial, driven, funny. Practical. He likes writing, and he likes writing fiction. That he became a bestselling author is a good thing: it allows him to write as much as he wishes. He's guest of honor at the World SF Convention – in many ways the ultimate accolade that the world of speculative fiction can bestow on those who have given it much – and he'll still be writing, between panels, before breakfast, here and there. He'll probably write as much in a day at Worldcon as most other authors will manage on a quiet day when there aren't any DVDs that haven't been watched and the weather precludes spending time in the garden and the phone's out of order – and Terry will do this while doing his proper guest of honor share of panels and readings and socializing and drinking exotic drinks of an evening.

He wasn't joking about the banana daiquiris, although the last time I saw him we drank ice wine together in his hotel room while we set the world to rights.

I'm delighted that he's guest of honor at the Worldcon. He deserves it.

This was written to celebrate Terry Pratchett's role as Guest of Honour of the 2004 World Science Fiction Convention.

On Dave McKean

I was twenty-six when I first met Dave McKean. I was a working journalist who wanted to write comics. He was twenty-three, in his last year at art college, and he wanted to draw comics. We met in the offices of a telephone sales company, several members of which, we had been told, were going to bankroll an exciting new anthology comic. It was the kind of comic that was so cool that it was only going to employ untried new talent, and we certainly were that.

I liked Dave, who was quiet and bearded and quite obviously the most artistically talented person I had ever encountered.

That mysterious entity which Eddie Campbell calls 'the man at the crossroads', but everyone else knows as Paul Gravett, had been conned into running advertising in his magazine *Escape* for the Exciting New Comic. He came to take a look at it himself. He liked what Dave was drawing, liked what I was writing, asked if we'd like to work together.

We did. We wanted to work together very much.

Somewhere in there we figured out that the reason the Exciting New Comic was only employing untried talent was that no one else would work with the editor. And that he didn't have the money to publish it. And that it was part of history . . .

Still, we had our graphic novel to be getting on with for Paul Gravett. It was called *Violent Cases*.

We became friends, sharing enthusiasms, and taking pleasure

in bringing each other new things. (I gave him Stephen Sondheim, he gave me Jan Švankmajer. He gave me Conlon Nancarrow, I gave him John Cale. It continues.) I met his girlfriend, Clare, who played violin and was starting to think that, as she came up to graduation from university, she probably didn't want to be a chiropodist.

People from DC Comics came to England on a talent scouting expedition. Dave and I went up to their hotel room, and they scouted us. 'They don't really want us to do stuff for them,' said Dave, as we walked out of the hotel room. 'They were probably just being polite.'

But we did an outline for *Black Orchid* and gave them that and a number of paintings anyway, and they took them back to New York with them, politely.

That was fifteen years ago. Somewhere in there Dave and I did *Black Orchid* and *Signal to Noise,* and *Mr Punch* and *The Day I Swapped My Dad for Two Goldfish*. And Dave's done book covers and interior work for Jonathan Carroll and Iain Sinclair and John Cale and CD covers for a hundred bands.

This is how we talk on the phone: we talk, and we talk and we talk until we're all talked out, and we're ready to get off the phone. Then the one who called remembers why he called in the first place and we talk about that.

Dave McKean is still bearded. He plays badminton on Monday nights. He has two children, Yolanda and Liam, and he lives with them and with Clare (who teaches violin and runs Dave's life and never became a chiropodist) in a beautiful converted oast house in the Kent countryside.

When I'm in England I go and stay with them, and I sleep in a perfectly round room.

Dave is friendly and polite. He knows what he likes and what he doesn't like, and will tell you. He has a very gentle sense of humor. He likes Mexican food. He will not eat sushi, but has on several occasions humored me by sitting and drinking tea and nibbling chicken in Japanese restaurants.

You get to his studio by walking across an improvised log bridge over a pond filled with koi carp. I read an article once in the *Fortean Times* or possibly the *Weekly World News* about koi exploding, and I have warned him several times of the dangers, but he will not listen. Actually, he scoffs.

When I wrote *Sandman* Dave was my best and sharpest critic. He painted, built or constructed every *Sandman* cover, and his was the face *Sandman* presented to the world.

I never minded Dave being an astonishing artist and visual designer. That never bothered me. That he's a world-class keyboard player and composer bothers me only a little. That he drives amazing cars very fast down tiny Kentish back roads only bothers me if I'm a passenger after a full meal, and much of the time I keep my eyes shut anyway. That he's now becoming a world-class film and video director, that he can write comics as well as I can, if not better, that he subsidizes his art (still uncompromised after all these years) with highly paid advertising work which still manages, despite being advertising work, to be witty and heartfelt and beautiful . . . well, frankly, these things bother me. It seems somehow wrong for so much talent to be concentrated in one place, and I am fairly sure the only reason that no one has yet risen up and done something about it is because he's modest, sensible and nice. If it was me, I'd be dead by now.

He likes fine liqueurs. He also likes chocolate. One Christmas my wife and I gave Dave and Clare a hamper of chocolate. Chocolates, and things made of chocolate, and chocolate liqueur and even chocolate glasses to drink the liqueur from. There were chocolate truffles in that hamper and Belgian chocolates, and this was not a small hamper. I'm telling you, there was six months of chocolate in that hamper.

It was empty before New Year's Day.

He's in England, and I'm in America, have been for ten years, and I still miss him as much as I miss anyone. Whenever the opportunity to work with Dave comes up, I just say yes.

I was amused, when *Coraline* came out recently, to find people who only knew Dave for his computer-enhanced multi-media work were astonished at the simple elegance of his pen-and-ink drawings. They didn't know he could draw, or they'd forgotten.

Dave has created art styles. Some of what he does is recognizable enough as his that art directors will give young artists samples of Dave McKean work and tell them to do that – often a specific art style that Dave created to solve a specific problem, or a place he went as an artist for a little while, decided that it wasn't where he wanted to be and moved on.

(For example, I once suggested to him, remembering Arcimboldo and Josh Kirby's old Alfred Hitchcock paperback cover paintings, that the cover of *Sandman: Brief Lives* could be a face made up of faces. This was before Dave owned a computer, and he laboriously photographed and painted a head made of smaller faces. He's been asked to do similar covers many times since by art directors. And so have other artists. I wonder if they know where it came from.)

People ask me who my favorite artist is, to work with. I've worked with world-class artists, after all, heaps of them. World-class people. And when they ask me about my favorite, I say Dave McKean. And then people ask why. I say, because he surprises me.

He always does. He did it from the first thing we did together, and a couple of weeks ago I looked at the illustrations he's done for our new graphic novel for all ages, *The Wolves in the Walls*. He's combined paintings of people, amazing, funny-scary line drawings of wolves and photographs of objects (jam, tubas and so on) to create something that is once again not what I expected, nothing like what I had in my head, but better than anything I could have dreamed of, more beautiful and more powerful.

I don't think there's anything Dave McKean cannot do as an artist. (There are certainly things he doesn't want to do, but that's not the same thing at all.)

After sixteen years, some artists are content to rest on their laurels (and Dave has shelves full of laurels, including a World Fantasy Award for best artist). It's a rare artist who is as restless and as enthusiastic as he was when he was still almost a teenager, still questing for the right way to make art.

This was written for the World Fantasy Convention 2002 programme book. Dave was Artist Guest of Honour.

How to Read Gene Wolfe

Look at Gene: a genial smile (the one they named for him), pixie-twinkle in his eyes, a reassuring mustache. Listen to that chuckle. Do not be lulled. He holds all the cards: he has five aces in his hand, and several more up his sleeve.

I once read him an account of a baffling murder, committed ninety years ago. 'Oh,' he said, 'well, that's obvious,' and proceeded offhandedly to offer a simple and likely explanation for both the murder and the clues the police were at a loss to explain. He has an engineer's mind that takes things apart to see how they work and then puts them back together.

I have known Gene for almost twenty-five years. (I was, I just realized, with a certain amount of alarm, only twenty-two when I first met Gene and Rosemary in Birmingham, England; I am forty-six now.) Knowing Gene Wolfe has made the last twenty-five years better and richer and more interesting than they would have been otherwise.

Before I knew him, I thought of Gene Wolfe as a ferocious intellect, vast and cool and serious, who created books and stories that were of genre but never limited by it. An explorer, who set out for uncharted territory and brought back maps, and if he said, 'Here There Be Dragons,' by God, you knew that was where the dragons were.

And that is all true, of course. It may be more true than the embodied Wolfe I met twenty-five years ago, and have come to know with enormous pleasure ever since: a man of politeness and kindness and knowledge; a lover of fine conversation, erudite and informative, blessed with a puckish sense of humor and an infectious chuckle.

I cannot tell you how to meet Gene Wolfe. I can, however, suggest a few ways to read his work. These are useful tips, like suggesting you take a blanket, a flashlight and some candy when planning to drive a long way in the cold, and should not be taken lightly. I hope they are of some use to you. There are nine of them. Nine is a good number.

How to read Gene Wolfe:

1. Trust the text implicitly. The answers are in there.

2. Do not trust the text farther than you can throw it, if that far. It's tricksy and desperate stuff, and it may go off in your hand at any time.

3. Reread. It's better the second time. It will be even better the third time. And anyway, the books will subtly reshape themselves while you are away from them. *Peace* really was a gentle Midwestern memoir the first time I read it. It only became a horror novel on the second or the third reading.

4. There are wolves in there, prowling behind the words. Sometimes they come out in the pages. Sometimes they wait until you close the book. The musky wolf-smell can sometimes be masked by the aromatic scent of rosemary. Understand, these are not today-wolves, slinking grayly in packs through deserted places. These are the dire wolves of old, huge and solitary wolves that could stand their ground against grizzlies.

5. Reading Gene Wolfe is dangerous work. It's a knife-throwing act, and like all good knife-throwing acts, you may lose fingers,

toes, earlobes or eyes in the process. Gene doesn't mind. Gene is throwing the knives.

6. Make yourself comfortable. Pour a pot of tea. Hang up a DO NOT DISTURB sign. Start at page 1.

7. There are two kinds of clever writer. The ones that point out how clever they are, and the ones who see no need to point out how clever they are. Gene Wolfe is of the second kind, and the intelligence is less important than the tale. He is not smart to make you feel stupid. He is smart to make you smart as well.

8. He was there. He saw it happen. He knows whose reflection they saw in the mirror that night.

9. Be willing to learn.

This was written for the programme book of the World Horror Convention 2002, at which both Gene and I were guests of honour.

Remembering Douglas Adams

I met Douglas Adams towards the end of 1983. I had been asked to interview him for *Penthouse*. I was expecting someone sharp and smart and BBCish, someone who would sound like the voice of *The Hitchhiker's Guide to the Galaxy*. I was met at the door to his Islington flat by a very tall man, with a big smile and a big, slightly crooked, nose, all gawky and coltish, as if, despite his size, he was still growing. He had just returned to the UK from a miserable time in Hollywood, and he was happy to be back. He was kind, he was funny, and he talked. He showed me his things: he was very keen on computers, which barely existed at that point, and on guitars, and on giant inflatable crayons, which he had discovered in America, had shipped to England at enormous expense, before learning that they were, quite cheaply, available in Islington. He was clumsy: he would back into things, or trip over them, or sit down on them very suddenly and break them.

I learned that Douglas had died the morning after it happened, in May 2001, from the Internet (which had not existed in 1983). I was being interviewed on the phone by a journalist (the journalist was in Hong Kong), and something about Douglas Adams's dying went across the computer screen. I snorted, unimpressed by such nonsense (only a couple of days before, Lou Reed had gone onto *Saturday Night Live* to put to rest a round of Internet rumours about *his* death). Then I clicked on the link. I found myself staring at a BBC News screen, and saw that Douglas was, quite definitely, dead.

'Are you all right?' said the journalist in Hong Kong.

'Douglas Adams is dead,' I said, stunned.

'Oh yes,' he said. 'It's been on the news here all day. Did you know him?'

'Yes,' I said. We carried on with the interview, and I don't know what else was said. The journalist got back in touch several weeks later to say that there wasn't anything coherent or at least usable on the tape after I learned that Douglas died, and would I mind doing the interview again?

Douglas was an incredibly kind man, phenomenally articulate and amazingly helpful. In 1986 I found myself knocking around his life an awful lot while I was working on *Don't Panic*. I'd sit in corners of his office going through old filing cabinets, pulling out draft after draft of *Hitchhiker's* in its various incarnations, long-forgotten comedy sketches, *Doctor Who* scripts, press clippings. He was always willing to answer questions and to explain. He put me in touch with dozens of people I needed to find and interview, people like Geoffrey Perkins and John Lloyd. He liked the finished book, or he said he did, and that helped too.

(A memory from that period: sitting in Douglas's office, drinking tea and waiting for him to get off the phone, so I could interview him some more. He was enjoying the phone conversation, about a project he was doing for the *Comic Relief* book. When he got off he apologised, and then explained that he had to take that call because it was John Cleese, in a way that made it clear that this was a delighted name dropping: *John Cleese* had just phoned him, and they'd talked professionally like grown-ups. Douglas must have known Cleese for nine years at that point, but still, his day had been made, and he wanted me to know. Douglas always had heroes.)

Douglas was unique. Which is true of all of us, of course, but it's also true that people come in types and patterns, and there was only one Douglas Adams. No one else I've ever encountered could elevate Not Writing to an art form. No one else has seemed capable of being so cheerfully profoundly miserable. No one else has had that easy smile and crooked nose, nor the faint aura of embarrassment that seemed like a protective force field.

After he died, I was interviewed a lot, asked about Douglas. I said that I didn't think that he had ever been a novelist, not really, despite having been an internationally bestselling novelist who had written several books which are, a quarter of a century later, becoming seen as classics. Writing novels was a profession he had backed into, or stumbled over, or sat down on very suddenly and broken.

I think that perhaps what Douglas was was probably something we don't even have a word for yet. A Futurologist, or an Explainer, or something. That one day they'll realise that the most important job out there is for someone who can explain the world to itself in ways that the world won't forget; who can dramatise the plight of endangered species as easily (or at least, as astonishingly well, for nothing Douglas did was ever exactly easy) as he can explain to an analogue race what it means to find yourself going digital. Someone whose dreams and ideas, practical or impractical, are always the size of a planet, and who is going to keep going forward, and taking the rest of us with him.

This is a book filled with facts about someone who dealt in dreams.

My foreword to *Hitchhiker: A Biography of Douglas Adams*, by M. J. Simpson, 2005.

Harlan Ellison:
The Beast That Shouted Love at the Heart of the World

I 've been reading Harlan Ellison since I was a small boy. I have known him as long, although by no means as well, as his wife, Susan – we met in Glasgow in 1985 at the same convention at which he first met and wooed his better half.

I interviewed him then for *Space Voyager*, a magazine for which I had written for the previous two years, and which had, until that point, appeared perfectly healthy. The issue of the magazine that was to contain my interview with Harlan went to press . . . and the publishers pulled the plug on it, with the magazine half-printed, and fired the editor. I took the interview to an editor at another magazine. He paid me for it . . . and was fired the following day.

I decided at that point that it was unhealthy to write about Harlan, and retired the interview to a filing cabinet, in which it will sit until the end of the world. I cannot be responsible for the firing of any more editors, the closing of any more magazines.

There is no one in the world in any way like Harlan. This has been observed before, by wiser and abler people than me. This is true, and it is quite beside the point.

It has, from time to time, occurred to me that Harlan Ellison is engaged on a Gutzon Borglum-sized work of performance art

– something huge and enduring. It's called Harlan Ellison: a corpus of anecdotes and tales and adversaries and performances and friends and articles and opinions and rumors and explosions and treasures and echoes and downright lies. People talk about Harlan Ellison, and they write about Harlan, and some of them would burn him at the stake if they could do it without getting into too much trouble and some of them would probably worship at his feet if it weren't for the fact he'd say something that would make them feel very small and very stupid. People tell stories in Harlan's wake, and some of them are true and some of them aren't, and some of them are to his credit and some of them aren't . . .

And that is also quite beside the point.

When I was ten I had a lisp, and was sent to an elocution teacher called Miss Webster, who, for the next six years, taught me a great deal about drama and public speaking, and, incidentally, got rid of the lisp somewhere in year one. She must have had a first name, but I've forgotten it now. She was magnificent – a stumpy, white-haired old theatrical lesbian (or so her pupils assumed) who smoked black cigarillos and was surrounded at all times by a legion of amiable but rather stupid Scottie dogs. She had a huge bosom, which she would rest on the table while she watched me recite the tongue twisters and dramatic pieces I had been assigned. Miss Webster died about fifteen years ago, or so I was told by another ex-pupil of hers I met at a party some years back.

She is one of the very small number of people who have told me things for my own good that I've paid attention to. (There is, needless to say, a very large number of people – including, now I come to think of it, Harlan – who've told me perfectly sensible things for my own good that I've, for one reason or another, ignored completely.)

Anyway: I got to be fourteen years old, and, one day, after a particularly imaginative interpretation of a Caliban speech, Miss

Webster leaned back in her chair, lit a cigarillo with a flourish and said, 'Neil, dear. I think there's something you ought to know. Listen: to be eccentric, you must first know your circle.'

And I – for once – heard, and listened, and understood. You can fuck around with the rules as much as you want to – *after* you know what the rules are. You can be Picasso after you know how to paint. Do it *your* way, but know how to do it *their* way first.

I've had a personal relationship with Harlan Ellison for much longer than I've known him. Which is the scariest thing about being a writer, because you make up stories and write stuff down and that's what *you* do. But people read it and it affects them or it whiles away your train journey, whatever, and they wind up moved or changed or comforted by the author, whatever the strange process is, the one-way communication from the stuff they read. And it's not why the stories were written. But it is true and it happens.

I was eleven when my father gave me two of the Carr-Wollheim *Best SF* anthologies and I read 'I Have No Mouth and I Must Scream' and discovered Harlan. Over the next few years I bought everything of his I could find. I still have most of those books.

When I was twenty-one I had the worst day of my life (up to then, anyway. There have been two pretty bad days since. But this was worse than them.) And there was nothing in the airport to read but *Shatterday,* which I bought. I got onto the plane, and read it crossing the Atlantic. (How bad a day was it? It was so bad I was slightly disappointed when the plane touched down gently at Heathrow without bursting into flames. That's how bad it was.)

And on the plane I read *Shatterday,* which is a collection of mostly kick-ass stories – and introductions to stories – about the relationship between writers and stories. Harlan told me about wasting time (in 'Count the Clock That Tells the Time'), and I thought, fuck it, I *could* be a writer. And he told me that anything more than twelve minutes of personal pain was self-indulgence, which did more to jerk me out of the state of complete numbness I was in than anything else could have done. And when I got home I took all the pain and the fear and the grief, and all the conviction that maybe I *was* a writer, damn it, and I began to write. And I haven't stopped yet.

Shatterday, more or less, made me what I am today. Your fault, Ellison. And again, quite beside the point.

So: *The Beast That Shouted Love at the Heart of the World*, to which I bid you welcome.

My copy's the 1979 Pan (UK) edition: on the cover of this paperback, Blood's a purple thing that looks like a housecat; Vic, behind him, is apparently a boy in his forties, and is, I think, hopping about on one leg. Still, most of Harlan's British covers had spaceships on them, so I mustn't grumble. And the back cover calls Harlan 'the chief prophet of the New Wave in science fiction', attributing the opinion to the *New Yorker*.

Definition time, primarily for those of you born after 1970. *The New Wave:* a term almost as unproductive as *cyberpunk* would be fifteen years later on, used to describe a motley bunch of writers working in the latter half of the sixties, loosely orbiting but not exclusively confined to *New Worlds* magazine in the Moorcock era and the original *Dangerous Visions* anthology, edited by the author of this collection. (If you want more information than that, go and find a copy of the Clute-Nicholls *Encyclopedia of Science Fiction*, and check out the New Wave entry.)

Harlan may well have been a 'prophet of the New Wave', but his foremost prophecy seems to have consisted of pointing out, in the introduction to this volume, that there was no such thing, just a bunch of writers, some of whom were pushing the edge of the envelope.

I never noticed the New Wave as anything particularly distinct or separate, when it was happening. It was Stuff to Read. Good stuff to read, even if it sometimes skirted the edge of incomprehensibility. I read it as I read all adult fiction, as a window into a world I didn't entirely understand: found Spinrad's *Bug Jack Barron* a lot of fun, Moorcock's *A Cure for Cancer* addictive and curious. Ballard was distant and strange and made me think of stories told over the tannoy in far-off airports. Delany showed me that words could be beautiful, Zelazny made myths. And if they were the 'New Wave' I liked it. But I liked most things back then. ('Yeah, that's your trouble, Gaiman,' said Harlan, when I chided him recently for suggesting that someone I like should be sprinkled with sacred meal and then sacrificed. 'You like everyone.' It's true, mostly.)

I've digressed a little.

Fiction is a thing of its time, and as times change so does our take on the fiction. Consider the Reagan section of 'Santa Claus vs. S.P.I.D.E.R.'; consider Reagan's final smile 'like a man who has regained that innocence of childhood or nature that he had somehow lost'. Scary, in a way Harlan never intended, writing about the pompadoured governor of California. Yet in another few years Reagan and his smile will have begun to lose meaning. He'll lose significance, become a name in the past for the readers, an odd historical name (I'm *just* old enough to know why the Spiro Agnew gag was funny), just as the who and the what and the why of the SF New Wave fade into the black. In a couple of his books James Branch Cabell footnoted the famous of his time, something that was viewed as (and was perhaps partly) an ironic comment – after all, who, today, would bother with an explanatory footnote of John Grisham* or John Major† or

---

* Author of legal-based thrillers, popular in the early 1990s.

† British Conservative member of Parliament. Succeeded Margaret Thatcher as prime minister of England in 1991.

Howard Stern?* But Cabell's ironic footnotes are now useful
information. Time passes. We forget. The bestselling novel
in 1925 was (I am informed by Steve Brust) *Soundings* by
A. Hamilton Gibbs. Huh? And who? Still, 'Santa Claus . . .'
works, and will keep working as long as there are B-movie spy
plots to deconstruct; and as long as there is injustice.

It's true of the rest of the tales herein. They remain relevant;
the only thing in the anthology that feels dated is the introduction, as Harlan grooves to Jimi Hendrix and points to Piers
Anthony as an underground writer. But hell, no one reads introductions anyway. (Admit it. You're not reading this, are you?)

And along with Spiro Agnew and A. Hamilton Gibbs and
Howard Stern, the anecdotes and tales and the Legend in His
Own Lifetime stuff about Harlan (most of which is, more or less,
true-ish) and all the Gutzon Borglum stuff (and I ought to have
given Gutzon, who carved presidential faces into Mount
Rushmore, his own footnote), will also be forgotten.

But the stories last. The stories remain.

'To be eccentric,' says Miss Webster, dead for fifteen years, in
the back of my head, her voice dry, her elocution perfect, 'you
must first know your circle.' Know the rules before you break
them. Learn how to draw, then break the rules of drawing, learn
to craft a story and show people things they've seen before in
ways they've never seen.

That's what these stories are about. Some of them are quite
brilliant, and they sparkle and glitter and shine and wound and
howl, and some of them aren't; but in all of them you can see
Harlan experimenting, trying new things, new techniques, new
voices; craft and voices he'd later refine into the calm assurance
of *Deathbird Stories,* his examination of the myths we live by;
into the stories of *Shatterday,* in which he took apart, hard, the

---

* I'm not quite sure. I think he's something on the radio.

cannibalistic relationship between the writer and the story; or the bitter elegies of *Angry Candy*.

He knew his circle; and he dared to go outside it.

Being a preamble to Harlan is a strange and scary business. I take down the battered and thumbed and treasured paperbacks from the bookshelves and look at them and there's Harlan on the back cover, with a pipe or a typewriter, and I wonder at how young he looks (it would be foolish to remark that Harlan is the youngest a-whisker-away-from-sixty-year-old I've ever met – it's patronizing and implies that it's a wonder that he's still in full possession of his faculties and capable of telling the mah-jongg tiles apart; but he has a sense of wonder that's been beaten out of most people by the time they hit their twenties, and a certain cyclonic energy that puts me in mind of my eight-year-old daughter, Holly, or of a particularly fiendish explosive device with a ferocious sense of humor; and more than that, he still has convictions and the courage of them): and I then realize the company I'm in, and I reread Stephen King's introduction to *Stalking the Nightmare* and watch Steve making the same points I'm trying so haltingly to make, that it's not about the personality, or the tales about Harlan, or even about Harlan the person. It's not about the pleasure it gave me to hand Harlan the World Fantasy Award for Life Achievement, nor is it about the stunned expressions on the faces of the assembled banqueters, as they listened to his humble and gracious acceptance speech. (I lie through my teeth. Not humble. Not even gracious. Very funny, though. And they *were* stunned.)

Really, all it's about is a shelf of books, and a pile of stories, written as well as he could write them when he wrote them, which is not besides the point; which is, in fact, the whole point.

And Harlan continues to write well and passionately and fiercely. I commend to your attention his story 'The Man Who

Rowed Christopher Columbus Ashore' in the 1993 *Best American Short Stories* collection – every bit as experimental as anything produced in the wildest excesses of the New Wave and entirely successful. He knows his circle. He is willing to explore outside it.

So, twelve stories follow.

These are not stories that should be forgotten; and some of you are about to read them for the first time.

Prepare to leave the circle with a more-than-capable guide.

I envy you.

This was my foreword to the 1994 Borderlands Press edition of Harlan Ellison's *The Beast That Shouted Love at the Heart of the World*.

Banging the Drum for Harlan Ellison

Harlan Ellison, sir? Lor' bless you. Of course I remember Harlan Ellison. Why if it wasn't for Harlan Ellison, I doubt I'd even be in this line of work.

I first met Harlan Ellison in Paris in 1927. Gertrude Stein introduced us at one of her parties. 'You boys will get on,' she said. 'Harlan's a writer. Not a great writer, like I am. But I hear he makes up stories.'

Harlan looked her in the eye, and told her exactly what he thought of her writing. It took him fifteen minutes and he never repeated himself once. When he finished, the whole room applauded. Gertrude got Alice B. Toklas to throw us out into the rain, and we stumbled around Paris, clutching a couple of wet baguettes and a half a bottle of an indifferent Bordeaux.

'Where are the snows of yesteryear?' I asked Harlan.

He pulled out a map from an inside pocket, and showed me.

'I would never have guessed that was where they end up,' I told him.

'Nobody does,' he said.

Harlan knew all kinds of stuff like that. He was braver than lions, wiser than owls, and he taught me a trick with three cards which, he said, would prove an infallible method of making money if I was down on my luck.

The next time I saw Harlan Ellison was in London, in 1932. I was working in the music halls, which were still going fairly strong, though they weren't what they used to be. I had worked up a mentalist's act, in a small way. I wasn't exactly bottom of the bill – that was Señor Moon and his Amazing Performing Budgerigar – but I was down there. That was until Harlan came along. He found me at the Hackney Empire vainly trying to intuit the serial number on a temperance crusader's ten-shilling note. 'Give up this mentalism nonsense, and stick with me, kiddo,' he said. 'You've got a drummer's hands, and I'm a man needs a drummer. Together, we'll go places.'

We went to Goole and Stoke Poges and Accrington and Bournemouth. We went to Eastbourne and Southsea and Penzance and Torquay. We were doing literature: dramatic storytelling on the seafront to move and entertain the ice-cream-licking magnitudes, wooing them away from the baggy-trousered clowns and the can-can girls, the minstrel shows and the photographer's monkey.

We were the hit of the season wherever we went. I'd bang my drum to gather the people around, and Harlan would get up there and tell them one of his stories – there was one about a fellow who was the Paladin of the Lost Hour, another about a man who rowed Christopher Columbus ashore. Afterwards I would pass the hat around, or simply take the money from the hands of the stunned holidaymakers, who would tend simply to stand there when Harlan had finished, their mouths agape, until the arrival of the Punch and Judy man would send them fleeing to the whelk stall in confusion.

One evening, in a fish and chip shop in Blackpool, Harlan confided his plans to me. 'I'm going to go to America,' he told me. 'That's where they'll appreciate me.'

'But, Harlan,' I told him, 'we've got a great career here, performing on the seafronts. That new dramatic monologue of yours about the chappie who had no mouth but had to scream anyway – there was almost thirty bob in the hat after that!'

'America,' said Harlan. 'That's where it's at, Neil.'

'You'll have to find someone else to work the seafronts of America with, then,' I told him. 'I'm staying here. Anyway, what's America got you won't find in Skegness, or Margate, or Brighton? They're all in a hurry in America. They'll not stand still long enough for you to tell them one of your stories. That one about the mind-reading fellow in the prison, why it must have taken you almost two hours to tell.'

'That,' said Harlan, 'is the simplicity of my plan. Instead of going from town to town, I shall write down my stories, for people to read. All across America they'll be reading my stories. America first, and then the world.'

I must have looked a little dubious, for he picked up a battered saveloy from my plate and used it to draw a map of America with little arrows coming out of it on the table, using the vinegary tomato catsup as paint.

'Besides,' asked Harlan, 'where else am I going to find true love?'

'Glasgow?' I suggested bravely (for I 'died' once as a mentalist at the Glasgow Empire), but he was obviously no longer listening.

He ate my battered saveloy and we headed back to the streets of Blackpool. When we got to the seafront I banged my little drum until we had gathered together a small crowd, and Harlan proceeded to tell them a story about a week in the life of a man who accidentally telephoned his own house, and he answered the telephone.

There was almost fifty shillings in the hat at the end of that story. We split the proceeds, and Harlan caught the next train to Liverpool, where he said he thought he could work his passage on a steamer, telling stories to the people on board. There was one about a boy and his dog he thought would go over particularly well.

I hear he's doing all right in the New World. Well, here's to him. And as an occasional toiler in the fields of literature myself, I often have cause to remember, with pleasure, all the things I learned back then from Harlan Ellison.

I'm still using them now.

Anyway, sir. Three cards. Round and round and round they go, and where they stop, nobody knows. Are you feeling lucky today? D'you think you can find the lady?

I wrote this for the Readercon 11 programme book, 1999. It is not to be factually relied on.

On Stephen King,
for the *Sunday Times*

I began life as a journalist, interviewing authors. I don't do it any longer. But I'd never interviewed Stephen King. Cathy Galvin, then at the *Sunday Times*, called and asked if I would interview King for them. By perfect coincidence, I was in Florida writing a book, not far from where King was staying. I took a day off from my own book, and I drove west.

Preamble

The *Sunday Times* asked me to write something small and personal about King and me for the contributors' notes, and I wrote this:

I think the most important thing I learned from Stephen King I learned as a teenager, reading King's book of essays on horror and on writing, Danse Macabre. In there he points out that if you just write a page a day, just 300 words, at the end of a year you'd have a novel. It was immensely reassuring – suddenly something huge and impossible became strangely easy. As an adult, it's how I've written books I haven't had the time to write, like my children's novel Coraline.

Meeting Stephen King this time, the thing that struck me is how very comfortable he is with what he does. All the talk of retiring from writing, of quitting, the suggestions that maybe it's time to stop before he starts repeating himself, seems to be done. He likes writing, likes it more than anything else that he could be doing, and does not seem at all inclined to stop. Except perhaps at gunpoint.

The first time I met Stephen King was in Boston, in 1992. I sat in his hotel suite, met his wife, Tabitha, who is Tabby in conversation, and his then-teenage sons Joe and Owen, and we talked about writing and about authors, about fans and about fame.

'If I had my life over again,' said King, 'I'd've done everything the same. Even the bad bits. But I wouldn't have done the American Express "Do You Know Me?" TV ad. After that, everyone in America knew what I looked like.'

He was tall and dark haired, and Joe and Owen looked like much younger clones of their father, fresh out of the cloning vat.

The next time I met Stephen King, in 2002, he pulled me up onstage to play kazoo with the Rock Bottom Remainders, a ramshackle assemblage of authors who can play instruments and sing and, in the case of author Amy Tan, impersonate a dominatrix while singing Nancy Sinatra's 'These Boots Are Made for Walkin'.'

Afterwards we talked in the tiny toilet in the back of the theatre, the only place King could smoke a furtive cigarette. He seemed frail, then, and grey, only recently recovered after a long hospitalisation from being hit by an idiot in a van, and the hospital infections that had followed it. He grumbled about the pain of walking downstairs. I worried about him, then.

And now, another decade, and when King comes out of the parking bay in his Florida house to greet me, he's looking good.

He's no longer frail. He is sixty-four and he looks younger than he did a decade ago.

Stephen King's house in Bangor, Maine, is gothic and glorious. I know this although I have never been there. I have seen photographs on the Internet. It looks like the sort of place that somebody like Stephen King ought to live and work. There are wrought iron bats and gargoyles on the gates.

Stephen King's house on a key in Florida near Sarasota, a strand of land on the edge of the sea, lined with big houses ('that one was John Gotti's,' I learn as we pass one huge white high-walled building. 'We call it murder mansion'), is ugly. And not even endearingly ugly. It's a long block of concrete and glass, like an enormous shoe box. It was built, explains Tabby, by a man who built shopping malls, out of the materials of a shopping mall. It's like an Apple store's idea of a McMansion, and not pretty. But once you are inside the glass window-walls have a perfect view over the sand and the sea, and there's a gargantuan blue metal doorway that dissolves into nothingness and stars in one corner of the garden, and inside the building there are paintings and sculptures, and, most important, there's King's office. It has two desks in it. A nice desk, with a view, and an unimpressive desk with a computer on it, with a battered, much sat-upon chair facing away from the window.

That's the desk that King sits at every day, and it is where he writes. Right now he's writing a book called *Joyland*, about an amusement park serial killer. Below the window is a patch of well-fenced land, with an enormous African spurred tortoise nosing around in it, like a monstrous ambulatory rock.

My first encounter with Stephen King, long before I met him in the flesh, was on East Croydon station in about 1975. I was fourteen. I picked up a book with an all-black cover. It was called *'Salem's Lot*. It was King's second novel; I'd missed the first, a short book called *Carrie*, about a teenage girl with psychic powers. I stayed up late finishing *'Salem's Lot,* loving the Dickensian portrait of a small American town destroyed by the arrival of a vampire. Not a nice vampire, a proper vampire. *Dracula* meets *Peyton Place*. After that I bought everything King wrote as it came out. Some books were great, and some weren't. It was okay. I trusted him.

Carrie was the book that King started and abandoned, and which Tabby King pulled out of the wastepaper basket, read and encouraged him to finish. They were poor, and then King sold *Carrie*, and everything changed, and he kept writing.

Driving down to Florida I listened, for over thirty hours, to the audiobook of King's time travel novel, *11/22/63*. It's about a high school English teacher (as King was, when he wrote *Carrie*) who goes back from 2011 to 1958, via a wormhole in time located in the stockroom of an ancient diner, with a mission to save John F. Kennedy from Lee Harvey Oswald.

It is, as always with King, the kind of fiction that forces you to care what happens, page after page. It has elements of horror, but they exist almost as a condiment for something that's partly a tightly researched historical novel, partly a love story, and always a musing on the nature of time and the past.

Given the hugeness of King's career, it is difficult to describe anything he does as an anomaly. He exists on the border of popular fiction (and, on occasion, non-fiction). His career (writers do not have careers, most of us. We just write the next book) is peculiarly Teflon. He's a popular novelist, which used to be, perhaps still is, a description of the author of a certain type of book: one that will repay you for reading it in pleasure and in plot, like John D. MacDonald (to whom King tips his hat in *11/22/63*). But not just a popular novelist: it does not matter what he writes, it seems, he is always a horror writer. I wonder if that frustrates him.

'No. No it doesn't. I have got my family, and they are all okay.

We have enough money to buy food and have things. Yesterday, we had a meeting of the King Foundation [the private foundation King funds that gives to many charitable causes]. My sister-in-law, Stephanie, she organises it and we all sit down and give away money. That's frustrating. Every year we give away the same money to different people . . . it's like chucking money into a hole. That's frustrating.

'I never thought of myself as a horror writer. That's what other people think. And I never said jack shit about it. Tabby came from nothing, I came from nothing, we were terrified that they would take this thing away from us. So if the people wanted to say "You're this,' as long as the books sold, that was fine. I thought, *I am going to zip my lip and write what I wanted to write.* The first time that anything like what you're talking about happened, I did this book *Different Seasons,* they were stories that I had written like I write all of them, I get this idea, and I want to write this. There was a prison story, "Rita Hayworth and the Shawshank Redemption', and one based on my childhood called "The Body', and there is a story of this kid who finds a Nazi, "Apt Pupil'. I sent them to Viking, who was my publisher. My editor was Alan D. Williams – dead many long years – terrific editor – he always took the work dead level. He never wanted to pump it. I sent them *Different Seasons,* and he said, "Well, first of all you call it seasons, and you have just written three.' I wrote another one, "The Breathing Method', and that was the book. I got the best reviews in my life. And that was the first time that people thought, *Whoa, this isn't really a horror thing.*

'I was down here in the supermarket, and this old woman comes around the corner, this old woman – obviously one of the kind of women who says whatever is on her brain. She said, "I know who you are, you are the horror writer. I don't read anything that you do, but I respect your right to do it. I just like things more genuine, like that *Shawshank Redemption.*'

'And I said, "I wrote that.' And she said, "No you didn't.' And she walked off and went on her way.'

It happens, over and over. It happened when he published *Misery,* his chronicle of toxic fandom; it happened with *Bag of Bones,* his gothic ghost story about a novelist, with nods to du Maurier's *Rebecca;* it happened when he was awarded the National Book Foundation's Medal for Distinguished Contribution to American Letters.

We're not talking in the huge concrete shoe box house. We're sitting by the pool in a smaller house the Kings bought on the same street, as a guesthouse for their family. Joe King, who writes under the name of Joe Hill, is staying there. He still looks like his dad, although no longer a clonal teenage version, and now has a successful career of his own as a writer of books and graphic novels. He carries his iPad everywhere he goes. Joe and I are friends.

In *Bag of Bones,* Stephen King has an author who stops writing but keeps publishing stockpiled books. I wonder how long his publishers could keep his death a secret?

He grins. 'I got the idea for the writer in *Bag of Bones* having books because somebody told me years ago that every year Danielle Steel wrote three books and published two, and I knew Agatha Christie had squirreled a couple away, to put a final bow on her career. As of right now, if I died and everybody kept it a secret, it would go on until 2013. There's a new *Dark Tower* novel, *The Wind Through the Keyhole.* That comes out soon, and *Doctor Sleep* is done. So if I got hit by a taxicab, like Margaret Mitchell, what wouldn't be done, what would be done. *Joyland* wouldn't be done but Joe could finish it, in a breeze. His style is almost indistinguishable from mine. His ideas are better than mine. Being around Joe is like being next to a Catherine wheel throwing off sparks, all these ideas. I do want to slow down. My agent is dickering with the publishers about *Doctor Sleep*

– that's the sequel to *The Shining* – but I held off showing them the manuscript because I wanted time to breathe.'

Why would he write a sequel to *The Shining*? I do not tell him how much that book scared me when I was sixteen, nor how much I loved and at the same time was disappointed by the Kubrick movie.

'I did it because it was such a cheesed-off thing to do. To say you were going back to the book that was really popular and write the sequel. People think of that book, they read it as kids. Kids read it and say it was a really scary book, and then as adults they might read the sequel and think, *This isn't as good*. The challenge is, maybe it can be as good – or maybe it can be different. It gives you something to push up against. It's a challenge.

'I wanted to write *Doctor Sleep* because I wanted to see what would happen to Danny Torrance when he grew up. And I knew that he would be a drunk because his father was a drunk. One of the holes it seemed to me in *The Shining* is that Jack Torrance was this white-knuckle dry drunk who never tried one of the self-help groups, like Alcoholics Anonymous. I thought, okay, I'll start with Danny Torrance at age forty. He is going to be one of those people who says "I am never going to be like my father, I am never going to be abusive like my father was.' Then you wake up at thirty-seven or thirty-eight and you're a drunk. Then I thought, what kind of a life does that person like that have? He'll do a bunch of low-bottom jobs, he'll get canned, and now he works in a hospice as a janitor. I really want him to be a hospice worker because he has the shining and he can help people get across as they die. They call him Dr Sleep, and they know to call for him when the cat goes into their room and sits on their bed. This was writing about a guy who rides the bus, and he's eating in a McDonald's, or on a special night out maybe Red Lobster. We are not talking about a guy who goes to Sardi's.'

Stephen and Tabitha met in the stacks of the University of

Maine library in 1967, and they married in 1971. He couldn't get a teaching position when he graduated, so he worked in an industrial laundry and pumped gas, and worked as a janitor, supplementing his meagre income with occasional stories, mostly horror, sold to men's magazines with names like *Cavalier*. The couple were dirt poor. They lived in a trailer, and King wrote at a makeshift desk between the washer and the dryer. All that changed in 1974, with the paperback sale of *Carrie* for $200,000. I wonder how long it has been since King has stopped worrying about money.

He thinks for a moment. 'Nineteen eighty-five. For a long time Tabby understood that we didn't have to worry about these things. I didn't. I was convinced they would take all this away from me, and I was going to be living with three kids in a rental house again, that it was just too good to be true. Around about 1985 I started to relax and think, *This is good, this is going to be okay*.

'And even now this' – he gestures, taking in the swimming pool, the guesthouse, the Florida key and all the many McMansions – 'is all very strange to me, even though it's only three months of the year. Where we live in Maine is one of the poorest counties. A lot of the people we see and hang with cut wood for a living, drive trash, that sort of thing. I don't want to say I have the common touch, but I am just a common person, and I have this one talent that I use.

'Nothing bores me more than to be in New York and have a dinner in a big fancy restaurant, where you have to sit for three fucking hours, you know, and people will have drinks before, wine after, then three courses, then they want coffee and someone is going to ask for a fucking French press and all the rest of this crap. To me my idea of what's good is to drive here and go to Waffle House, get a couple of eggs and a waffle. When I see the first Waffle House, I know I'm in the South. That's good.

'They pay me absurd amounts of money,' he observes, 'for something that I would do for free.'

*

Stephen King's father went out for cigarettes when King was four, and he never came back, leaving King to be brought up by his mother. Steve and Tabby have three children: Naomi, a Unitarian minister with a digital ministry; Joe and Owen, both writers. Joe is finishing his third novel. Owen's first novel is coming out in 2013.

I wonder about distance and change. How easy is it to write about characters who are working blue-collar jobs in 2012?

'It is definitely harder. When I wrote *Carrie* and *'Salem's Lot*, I was one step away from manual labour. But it's like also true – Joe is going to find out this is true, that when you have small children of a certain age, it is easy to write about them because you observe them and you have them in your life all the time.

'But your kids grow up. It is harder for me to write about this little twelve-year-old girl in *Doctor Sleep* than it ever was for me to talk about five-year-old Danny Torrance because I had Joe as a model for Danny. I don't mean that Joe has the shining like Danny but I knew who he was, how he played, what he wanted to do and all that stuff. But look, here's the bottom line: if you can imagine all the fabulous stuff that happened in *American Gods*, and if I can imagine magic doors and everything, then surely I can still put my imagination to work and go: look, this is what I imagine it's like to work a ten-hour day in a blue-collar job.'

We're doing the writer thing, now: talking about craft, about how we do what we do, making things up for a living, and as a vocation. His next book, *The Wind Through the Keyhole*, is a *Dark Tower* novel, part of a sequence that King plotted and began when he was little more than a teenager himself. The sequence took him years to finish, and he only finished spurred on by his assistants, Marsha and Julie, who were tired of fielding fan letters asking when the story would be completed.

Now he's finished the story he is trying to decide how much he can rewrite it, if he views the sequence as one very long novel. Can he do a second draft? He hopes so. Currently, Stephen King is a character in the fifth and sixth *Dark Tower* books, and Stephen King the non-fictional author is wondering whether to take him out in the next draft.

I told him about the peculiarity of researching the story I was working on, that everything I needed, fictionally, was waiting for me when I went looking for it. He nods in agreement.

'Absolutely – you reach out and it's there. The time that it happened the clearest was when Ralph, my agent then, said to me, "This is a bit crazy, but do you have any kind of idea for something that could be a serialised novel like Dickens used to do?' and I had a story that was sort of struggling for air. That was *The Green Mile*. And I knew if I did this I had to lock myself into it. I started writing it and I stayed ahead of the publication schedule pretty comfortably. Because . . .' He hesitates, tries to explain in a way that doesn't sound foolish. ' . . . Every time I needed something that something was right there to hand. When John Coffey goes to jail – he was going to be executed for murdering the two girls. I knew that he didn't do it, but I didn't know that the guy who did do it was going to be there, didn't know anything about how it happened, but when I wrote it, it was all just there for me. You just take it. Everything just fits together like it existed before.

'I never think of stories as made things; I think of them as found things. As if you pull them out of the ground, and you just pick them up. Someone once told me that that was me low-balling my own creativity. That might or might not be the case. But still, on the story I am working on now, I do have an unresolved problem. It doesn't keep me awake at night. I feel like when it comes down, it will be there . . .'

King writes every day. If he doesn't write he's not happy. If he writes, the world is a good place. So he writes. It's that simple. 'I sit down maybe at quarter past eight in the morning and I work until quarter to twelve and for that period of time, everything is real. And then it just clicks off. I think I probably write about twelve hundred to fifteen hundred words. It's six pages. I want to get six pages into hard copy.'

*

I start to tell King my theory, that when people in the far future want to get an idea of how things felt between 1973 and today, they'll look to King. He's a master of reflecting the world that he sees, and recording it on the page. The rise and fall of the VCR, the arrival of Google and smartphones. It's all in there, behind the monsters and the night, making them more real.

King is sanguine. 'You know what, you can't tell what is going to last, what's not going to last. There's a Kurt Vonnegut quote about John D. MacDonald saying, "Two hundred years from now, when people want to know what the twentieth century was like they'll go to John D. MacDonald,' but I'm not sure that's true – it seems like he's almost been forgotten. But I try and reread a John D. MacDonald novel whenever I come down here.'

Authors populate the cracks in a conversation with Stephen King. And, I realise, all of them are, or were, popular authors, people whose work was read, and read with enjoyment, by millions.

'You know what's bizarre? I did the Savannah book fair last week . . . This is happening to me more and more. I walked out and I got a standing ovation from all these people, and it's like a creepy thing . . . either you've become a cultural icon, or they are applauding the fact that you are not dead yet.'

I tell him about the first time I ever saw a standing ovation in America. It was for Julie Andrews in Minneapolis on a tryout tour of *Victor/Victoria*. It was not very good, but she got a standing ovation for being Julie Andrews.

'That's so dangerous though, for us. I want people to like the work, not me.'

And the lifetime achievement awards?

'It makes them happy to give them to me. And they go out in the shed, but the people don't know that.'

Then Tabby King turns up to tell us that it is time for dinner, and she adds that back at the big house the gargantuan African spurred tortoise has just been discovered trying to rape a rock.

This interview originally ran in edited form in the *Sunday Times*, 8 April 2012.

Geoff Notkin: Meteorite Man

Some people change. Kids you knew at school become invest-ment bankers or bankruptcy specialists (failed). They fatten and they bald and somewhere you get the sense that they must have devoured the child they once were, eaten themselves bit by bit, mouthful by mouthful, until nothing is left of the smart, optimistic dreamer you knew when you were both young.

On a bad day, I worry that it's happening to me.

And then I see Geoff Notkin, and everything's all right.

True, sometimes, when he looks in the right direction, I see his father, Sam Notkin, a man so cool we used to talk obscure 1940s American science fiction authors together. But mostly I see Geoff, and he hasn't changed.

Geoffrey Notkin in 1976 was impetuous, brilliant, obsessed, really funny, easily angered but someone who would just as quickly forget that he'd ever been angry. We were both outsiders at school, Geoff because he was semi-American, me because I lived in books, and we bonded over music and comics. I took Geoff to a Lou Reed concert at the New Victoria, and we started a punk garage band, literally in his garage. Geoff was a terrific and passionate drummer.

We drew comics together, in the back of classes that bored us. Most classes bored us. We were smart kids who ignored most of school (we both liked the art rooms, I liked the school library) and taught ourselves, because that seemed like more fun. We liked being disliked by the teachers, and neither of us actually got around to graduating.

We were friends. We dated the same girls (although never at the same time). We read the same comics and listened to the same music (often at the same time) and even dyed our hair blond, or tried to. Geoff's parents did not mind that he had dyed his hair blond. My father minded that I had dyed my hair a straw orange, and made me dye it black, which was even stranger. We signed to a record label as young punks, and none of our music is around anywhere except possibly tapes somewhere in Geoff's storage lockers, and I like to think that as long as I get him this introduction on deadline any tapes will stay there. Geoff put me into the ambulance when I needed to get my face stitched up after a grumpy punter expressed his dislike of our band by throwing an (unopened) beer can at me . . .

I think it was after the beer can incident that I stopped dreaming of being a rock star.

I would see Geoff every few years, our lives strobing: the last time I saw his parents, introducing them to my infant daughter Holly, and found that I had been forgiven for the unfortunate events of the night of Geoff's party; the all-consuming envy of Geoff for inking Will Eisner at the School of Visual Arts, of knowing Will Eisner and Art Spiegelman and Harvey Kurtzman, people who were the gods and demigods of a twenty-four-year-old journalist in London who dreamed of one day doing comics; Geoff Notkin rocking-man-about-town as I started stumbling into New York as someone who made his living writing comics; and then the e-mails from Geoff, in which he was going off to Siberia to look for meteorites . . .

Truthfully, it had never occurred to me that anyone actually ever looked for meteorites. I assumed that you noticed them when they hit your house or your car, or landed, green and pulsing, in your meadow before they transformed you into something monstrous. I did not think that people went out and looked for them with rare-earth magnets and madness.

I watched *Meteorite Men* because Geoff was on it, and I was delighted to observe that Geoff is still, so obviously that it comes through the television screen, impetuous, brilliant, obsessed, truly funny, and capable of losing his temper really entertainingly whenever he's frustrated and of forgetting and forgiving almost instantly. But I kept watching it because I was hooked: Geoff has an autodidact's love of knowledge. He does not stop marveling at the universe, and, for Geoffrey Notkin, the quickest way to touch the rest of the universe is to find something that came from another part of it and landed here, like a meteorite.

He gave me a meteorite of my own for my fiftieth birthday. It has a hole in it.

And in my head, it's still 1977 somewhere, and Geoff Notkin and I have taken the afternoon off school to hit the secondhand book stores, and some record stores that have the real American punk imports that Geoff loved and the Velvet Underground bootlegs I dreamed about, and Geoff is standing on the side of the road shouting, 'We mean it, mannnnnnn,' at the cars going by, and we are kids in school uniforms and it's also now, thirty-five years later, and nothing's changed.

He still means it, every word.

This was my introduction to Geoff's memoir *Rock Star: Adventures of a Meteorite Man*, 2012.

About Kim Newman, with Notes on the Creation and Eventual Dissolution of the Peace and Love Corporation

I t was October 1983, I think, and I was twenty-two, and it was the room upstairs in the Royal Connaught pub in Holborn, and the British Fantasy Society was having one of its dos. It was the first of the dos I'd attended. BFS Social Nights are occasional events, where authors and fans and critics and people from the twilight worlds of publishing and movies get together and drink too much and talk a lot. There's no agenda, no speeches, nothing more organised than an occasional raffle.

Someone – probably editor and journalist Jo Fletcher – introduced me to a man wearing a white hat and a crisp black suit. He had a handlebar moustache and a pocket watch on an honest-to-goodness watch chain across his waistcoat. He was drinking a white wine spritzer and had total self-assurance. He was twenty-three, but came across somehow as much older. He looked like he should be carrying a swordstick, although, for reasons I was not to discover for some time, he wasn't.

Kim and I were both young and we were both quite full of ourselves – in hindsight we were probably insufferable. We compared credentials: he'd just had a story accepted by *Interzone* (it was, if memory serves, 'Patricia's Profession') and I'd just had a story rejected by *Interzone* and accepted by *Imagine* magazine. (And his story is in this collection, and is pretty damn good, and I just reread mine and decided not to include it in a collection of my short fiction because it was pretty terrible.) We were both young, although with me it showed, and with Kim it didn't, and we were both hungry.

And then the conversation lurched around to books we were going to write. Kim started telling me about a book he had planned called *The Set*. It was going to be about giant badgers going around England eating people. And I told Kim that I thought I'd quite like to do a book of science fiction quotations.

'That sounds like a good idea,' said Kim. 'You can do the books bit. I'll write the film section.' Kim was a film reviewer and critic, writing for *City Limits* and the *British Film Institute Journal*. He'd already written a book called *Nightmare Movies*, which had yet to be published by a soon-to-be-bankrupt and rather dodgy publisher (and which would eventually be revised and updated and become the definitive reference work on post-Hammer horror).

That's what I remember, anyway. That was how Kim entered my life. So we wrote an outline for our proposed book of quotations, and knowing Kim, and knowing me, he finished his half of the outline before I started to write mine. We sent the outline for *Ghastly Beyond Belief* out to a few publishers, and Arrow bought it, and my collaboration with Kim Newman had officially begun.

It lasted for about five years.

Kim was always the senior member of the partnership. He had a credit card and savoir faire. He had an electric typewriter. He was also the powerhouse – our work habits were very different: I have always tended to wait for deadlines, while Kim invariably does things way before deadlines, and then does something else in the time left over.

He got his half of the book finished a couple of months ahead of deadline. I got my half delivered the month after the deadline. It was pretty much the pattern of what was to come.

In the biographies at the beginning of *Ghastly Beyond Belief,* our editor, the lovely and talented Faith Brooker, described us both as 'aspiring novelists'. I don't think we were. We were young writers with the unshakable (and unshaken) confidence that amongst the things we'd probably wind up writing would be novels. But we were looking forward to writing everything.

The room Kim rented in a Muswell Hill flat was tiny. It was filled to bursting point with books and videos and magazines; stills from strange movies were Blu-Tacked to the walls. There was a bed, a small table with an electric typewriter (his typewriter had a name, but that's Kim's story, not mine), a chair, a television, a VCR.

Kim could watch, and not just watch but enjoy, the most awful movies. He had and doubtless still has a pretty photographic memory: plots and actors and trivia, high culture and low. He knows everything.

Kim was a great reviewer, and a fine critic. (Reviewers tell you whether or not a film's the kind of thing you'd like if you like that kind of thing. Critics, good ones anyway, tell you what you've seen.) He seemed to spend much of his life (when he wasn't writing, or watching old videos) in film screenings.

I started going to screenings too. I was very hungry, very young, and was amazed that if I wrote something about the films, or even meant to write something about them one day, I could see films without paying – and they gave you chicken legs and sausages and glasses of white wine. And because I was going to screenings with Kim, I wound up accumulating a couple of film columns.

All through the eighties we wrote together, mostly humour. Quite a lot of it was even funny. Once – and only once – we tried to write straight fiction together, three hundred words each on a turnabout basis. It was a story about a vampire girl picking someone up in a nightclub. It was terrible, and we never attempted it again.

Not like that, anyway.

Together, and later, as part of the somewhat amorphous entity known as the Peace and Love Corporation we wrote many hundreds of articles for dozens of publications. We told the world who Jack the Ripper really was. We blew the whistle on computer dating. We wrote what was perhaps the definitive guide to becoming a Mad Scientist (and Ruling the World).

It's more fun to look back on the things we didn't do: I remember plotting a computer game, the object of which was to find out who you were before your head exploded. We did it on spec, for a man who claimed to have invented the Swear Box. (It was a box that sat on your desk and said *fuck* or *shit* when you pressed a button.)

We plotted four cheap movies for a cheap movie director who wanted plots for cheap films. Kim later turned some of the plots into novels. They were probably better novels than they would have been low-budget movies.

Of course, by that time, we were part of the aforementioned Peace and Love Corporation.

The Peace and Love Corporation, which was never a corpo ration, although it was a bank account, and had nothing really to do with either Peace or Love, although I think on the whole we were pretty much in favour of both of them, was formed, more or less, during a party. We weren't at the party – it was being held in Kim's Crouch End flat by his landlord. But we – Kim, Stefan Jaworczyn, Eugene Byrne and myself – were on sleeping bags in Kim's room, listening to the party going on down the hall. Kim had the bed.

The party was long and loud and the partygoers (old hippies to a man) were playing old hippy music.

We started talking about hippies, lying in the darkness. And we began to rant about commune life and going to San Francisco and putting flour in our hair. It was a kind of free-form improvised stand-up routine, only we were lying on the floor.

The next day we wrote down what we could remember of the rant, added a plot of sorts, called it 'Peace and Love and All That Stuff' and sent it off to a magazine, and became the Peace and Love Corporation.

Clive Barker was fascinated by the Peace and Love Corporation. At one point he announced that he was going to write a story called 'Threshold', in which Kim, Stefan and I would be creatures from a far-future world beyond the boundaries of pleasure and pain, come to the here and now to hunt down a fugitive. When he finally wrote it it was called *The Hellbound Heart,* and was later filmed as *Hellraiser*. Which may mean that Kim Newman was the original inspiration for Pinhead. They are, after all, both snappy dressers.

Gradually Kim and I became successful. It was a slow, odd process. We'd paid our dues, I suppose, and it was our time. Kim wrote novels under his own name, and, emulating the American pulp writers he admires, he would write cheerfully subversive novels and short stories under his Jack Yeovil pseudonym, in a week or less.

We stopped collaborating. The markets that we'd been writing for had dried up, or died, and we were both too busy – Kim wrote more novels and short stories, reviewed movies on breakfast television, and became a star, and I was off mostly writing comic books. The eighties were over, and the Peace and Love Corporation bank account was formally closed.

It's a time I still don't feel I have a handle on: one cannot exactly peer through rose-coloured spectacles at those lost halcyon days of the mid-eighties. There is little nostalgia for that era, except in the most general terms, remembering the hustling, the fun of a time when we had little more than confidence, hubris and the terrifying certainty that we were destined for interesting things to keep us going.

Over ten years later Kim is still an advocate of cultural fusion and unself-conscious postmodernism – the references and correlations and nods between high and low culture in the stories in this book, and in the rest of Kim's oeuvre, aren't there to impress; they're there because that's how Kim is and what he's made of. He knows, as it were, his shit. His stories are a wild ride that will take you places you've never been. Sit back and enjoy yourself. It is to be assumed that you will miss some of the jokes, some of the references, some of the fleeting images in the collage of movie stills and videos and old books, of half-forgotten actors and almost wholly forgotten TV serials. Don't worry about it.

Of course you'll miss something. You're not Kim Newman.

Who is urbane, brilliant, unique, and once carried a swordstick.

Neil Gaiman. *Somewhere in America. Three months late.*

The introduction to *The Original Dr Shade and Other Stories* by Kim Newman, 1994.

Gumshoe: A Book Review

I never actually worked for the old regime. But I can't see them behaving like that; I mean, I've heard that nice Mister Coren on *Gardeners' Question Time,* or whatever that programme is ('Ah, this is the story about the lady in Luton with the ferrets down her knickers,' 'No, I'm afraid not.' 'Then it's Sir Geoffrey Howe?' 'Hoohoo, that's the one,'), and he always sounded very nice. Not a man who'd resort to cheap threats, at any rate.

Not like the current bunch.

One of them rings me up, says he wants a review. This week. Fair enough, I say, when this week? Tuesday, he says. That's tomorrow, I point out. He says yes, that's tomorrow. Tuesday.

What if I can't get it done in time? I ask, all innocent.

There's a pause at the other end of the line; you can hear him looking up at the Men in Black Suits in the *Punch* offices, and getting the nod.

Well, he says calmly, then we'd have a blank page. And we'd print your photograph on it. Possibly your address. And we'd tell the *Punch* readership exactly whose fault it was that they had a blank page this week.

I wouldn't be able to enter a dentist's waiting room ever again.

Right, I say. Tomorrow. Put down the phone and describe him out loud. One word. Rhymes with custard, almost.

Okay. Write a review.

Only trouble is, tidied the office last week. Know I had the book somewhere, been tripping over it for a month, called *Gumshoe,* by some American philosophy professor who gave it all up to become a private eye. Gold cover. Unique. Put it somewhere safe. Tidied it up. Very careful. Somewhere. Somewhere tidy and safe. Probably on a bookshelf. One of the bookshelves, anyway.

Only other trouble is, awful lot of books in here. No problem, just look for the gold cover. Up there on the top of top shelf, climb on the desk, reach up, nearly overbalance, pull it out: *Great Sex.*

Bugger.

Wonder briefly whether *Punch* would notice if review of *Great Sex* arrived tomorrow morning. Men in Black Suits in *Punch* offices. Suspicious bulges in jacket pockets. No sense of humour . . .

Forget *Great Sex.*

Review *Gumshoe.* Remember the title, anyway. Can't go too far wrong if you remember the title.

Don't have the book of course. Just *Great Sex,* funny there being two books with gold covers, flip it open, hope it'll be *Gumshoe* when I look at the pages. It isn't. 'She has a magnificent polished body, the globes of her buttocks round and smooth like summer fruit, her breasts high and proud.'

Wonder what *kind* of summer fruit. Raspberries? Gooseberries?

Go and check with encyclopedia.

Discover that the gooseberry may be white, yellow, green or red, and may have a prickly, hairy or smooth surface. Doesn't say a word about whether it's a summer fruit or not. Expect Alan Coren knows about that kind of thing, what with *Gardeners' Question Time* and everything . . .

Doesn't say a lot for her buttocks.

Give up.

Decide to write review from memory. Fake it convincingly. Right. No problem. This philosophy professor, wants to be a private eye, name of, name of, anyway, he's written all these books on Kierkegaard or possibly it was Wittgenstein, one of that mob, honest-to-goodness philosophy professor, earns good money, married with children, gives it all up, becomes a San Francisco private dick.

Was vaguely expecting something tacky, like this book I read once, forget the title, *My Life as a Private Eye Including Fifteen Surefire Ways to Cheat on Your Spouse Without Getting Caught*, something like that, or else maybe sub-Chandler stuff, 'Dame walks into my office, figure that'd get Descartes to come up with a new Proposition, sent my pulse rate over the speed limit, buttocks like thrusting gooseberries,' and was pleasantly surprised it's neither.

Not tacky.

Philosophy professor finds true happiness as penniless Sam Spade. Reads *The Maltese Falcon* a lot between cases. Good writer. Finds thirty thousand dollars of drug money under the floorboards of an attic. Gets kidnapped child out of India. Tries to save fitted-up Chinese-American from electric chair. Or gas chamber. One of those. Forget my own head next. Decides detection is Real Life. Never happier. Photo on the cover of the book: crinkly eyes, good man in a tough spot, copy of *The Maltese Falcon* open on his lap.

Wish I could remember his name. Begins with L, or S. Or P, maybe.

Best sections are long, boring bits, sitting in cars waiting for people who never show, pissing into Styrofoam cups. Convinced me I didn't want to be a private dick. Glad someone else is doing it, though.

Good private eye could find anything. Even copy of *Gumshoe* with gold cover. Probably look in most obvious place. Probably just sit down at desk, casual glance to the left, look over to stack of books writer's promised to review at some time or other . . .

Shit.

Gold cover.

Author's name Josiah Thompson. Book called *Gumshoe*, though; remembered that much. Says on the cover 'The best book ever written about the life of the private eye.'

I'd go along with that.

This is a true account of what happened when I was asked to review Josiah Thompson's *Gumshoe*, written for and first published in *Punch*, 1989.

SimCity

Cities are not people. But, like people, cities have their own personalities: in some cases one city has many different personalities – there are a dozen Londons, a crowd of different New Yorks.

A city is a collection of lives and buildings, and it has identity and personality. Cities exist in location, and in time.

There are good cities – the ones that welcome you, that seem to care about you, that seem pleased you're in them. There are indifferent cities – the ones that honestly don't care if you're there or not; cities with their own agendas, the ones that ignore people. There are cities gone bad, and there are places in otherwise healthy cities as rotten and maggoty as windfall apples. There are even cities that seem lost – some, lacking a centre, feel like they would be happier being elsewhere, somewhere smaller, somewhere easier to understand.

Some cities spread, like cancers or B-movie slime monsters, devouring all in their way, absorbing towns and villages, swallowing boroughs and hamlets, transmuting into boundless conurbations. Other cities shrink – once prosperous areas empty and fail: buildings empty, windows are boarded up, people leave, and sometimes they cannot even tell you why.

Occasionally I idle time away by wondering what cities would be like, were they people. Manhattan is, in my head, fast-talking, untrusting, well-dressed but unshaven. London is huge and confused. Paris is elegant and attractive, older than she looks. San Francisco is crazy, but harmless, and very friendly.

It's a foolish game: cities aren't people.

Cities exist in location, and they exist in time. Cities accumulate their personalities as time goes by. Manhattan remembers when it was unfashionable farmland. Athens remembers the days when there were those who considered themselves Athenians. There are cities that remember being villages. Other cities – currently bland, devoid of personality – are prepared to wait until they have history. Few cities are proud: they know that it's all too often a happy accident, a mere geographical fluke that they exist at all – a wide harbour, a mountain pass, the confluence of two rivers.

At present, cities stay where they are.

For now cities sleep.

But there are rumblings. Things change. And what if, tomorrow, cities woke, and went walking? If Tokyo engulfed your town? If Vienna came striding over the hill toward you? If the city you inhabit today just upped and left, and you woke tomorrow wrapped in a thin blanket on an empty plain, where Detroit once stood, or Sydney, or Moscow?

Don't ever take a city for granted.

After all, it is bigger than you are; it is older; and it has learned how to wait . . .

This was 'Easter Egg' text that popped up if you went to a library and clicked on RUMINATE while playing *SimCity 2000*, 1995.

Six to Six

I had recently retired from journalism, but Maria Lexton at *Time Out* asked me if I would like to stay out all night on the streets of London and write about whatever happened. It sounded exciting . . .

O h, don't do nightspots,' says My Editor, 'someone's already done them. Can you do somewhere else?'

I crumple up a carefully planned evening that takes in every London nightspot I've ever been to and a few I haven't. Fine. I'll just play it as it comes, then. Maybe hang around the West End streets. I tell her this.

She seems vaguely concerned. 'Be careful,' she warns. Warmed and heartened, pondering imaginary obituary notices, and adventures ahead, I stumble out into the late afternoon.

Six till six.

*

6:00 I'm seeing my bank manager. We're standing out in the hall, discussing the use of the word fucking in contemporary magazine articles. I tell him I can use fucking in *Time Out* whenever I want, at which point someone with a suit glides out of an office and stares at us. The tinkling laughter of his singular secretary, Maggie, follows me as I flee.

I try to get a cab at Baker Street, but the yellow 'TAXI' light, holy grail of London emergencies, proves usually elusive. I tube to Tottenham Court Road, where a queue of taxis lurk, yellow lights blazing.

Head down to the basement of My Publishers, make some phone calls, stumble over the road to the Café München in the shadow of Centre Point, where I drink with Temporary *Crisis* Editor James Robinson, awaiting the arrival of My Publisher.

My Publisher is late but I bump into huge rock star Fish (late of Marillion); we haven't seen each other for years, and catch up on recent events, interrupted only by a shady-looking fellow who's setting up 'the biggest charity in England' and wants Fish to lend support, and a prat who asks Fish to write out the lyrics to 'Kayleigh' on a napkin so he can win a £50 bet. Fish says he can't remember them and sends the guy away with an autograph. Still, somebody made £50 off of it.

My Publisher turns up, and we head off to grab something to eat (La Reach in Old Compton Street, great couscous), promising to meet Fish later in the new, moved Marquee. He'll put our names on the door.

11:15 We turn up at the Marquee to be met by 'Sorry, mate – we closed at eleven o'clock.' When I was a teenager the Marquee (possibly the cheapest sauna in the metropolis) scarcely opened before eleven. Dreams of a peculiar rock-'n'-rolloid night vanish. I still don't know what I'm going to be doing this evening.

My Publisher is heading down to Wimbledon to try to fix an antique laserdisc player he sold to an old friend. I go with him.

***

1:00 Laserdisc player still doesn't work, which means My Publisher is unable to view *Miami Spice* ('Those *Miami Spice* girls sure have a nose for torrid trouble . . . a porno pool party . . . our passionate policewomen are ready for the big bust . . .' Fnur fnur).

*

1:30 Driving back into town through empty Wimbledon we get pulled over by a police car – they've noticed the antique laser-disc player in the boot, and have leapt to the not unreasonable conclusion that My Publisher is in fact a burglar. Nervously, he hides *Miami Spice* under the seat, gets out of the car, hands the cop his mobile phone and tells him to phone people to prove his identity; the cop stares at it wistfully. 'They won't even give us one of those,' he sighs. He asks My Publisher about his (Barrow-in-Furness) accent and announces that he comes from Bridlington himself. Waves us on our way. My plans of an exciting night crusading against police brutality – or better yet, journalistically, spent in the cells – founder and crash.

*

1:45 Victoria Station. Something must be happening at Victoria . . . nope. A sterile expanse, full of fluorescent ads for things you can't buy at this time of night. (Prawn Waldorf sandwiches?) My Publisher explains that London pigeons have lost their toes through decades of inbreeding and pollution. Tell him this sounds unlikely.

*

2:10 Pass the Hard Rock Café. Nobody's queuing.

* * *

2:45 Soho. We walk past a street of empty wine bars and book-shops, and My Publisher tells me it used to be brothels once, a long time ago; then, *Miami Spice* and a functioning laserdisc player ahead of him, he tears off into the night.

I decide that I'm just going to wander aimlessly, resolve not to disappear into any seedy drinking clubs, even if I can find any (like Little Magic Shops, they have a tendency to vanish the next time you want them, replaced by brick walls or closed doors).

Under the tacky neon glare of Brewer Street a young woman holds a polystyrene head with a red wig on it. The Vintage Magazine Shop has the *OZ* 'schoolkids' issue in the window.

*

3:31 At an all-night food place – Mr Pumpernincks – on the corner of Piccadilly, I run into Ella. She's blonde, with smudged pink lipstick and red pumps, Day-Glo acidhouse wristbands. Looks fifteen, assures me she's really nearly nineteen and tells me not to eat the popcorn because it 'tastes like earwax'.

Turns out she's a nightclub hostess. I assume this is my first encounter tonight with the seamy side of London nightlife. She shakes her head. Her job, she explains, is to sell as much champagne as possible on commission, pour her glass on the floor when the customer 'goes to the loo', spill as much as she can. It's all a con, she sighs: £12 for a salmon sandwich, £12 for a packet of forty cigarettes, no one spends less than £100 a night, and last week she was offered £5,000 by five Swedish men to sleep with them.

She said no. She doesn't think she's hard enough for the business. Ella comes down to Mr Pumpernincks to drink the rotten coffee and sober up every night. She came up from Bath to the big city a month or so back; her ambition in life is to steal a Porsche 911 Turbo, and possibly even to get a driving licence.

* * *

4:30 I'm in Brewer Street again. Six pigeons on the road in front
of me; one of them doesn't have any toes. My Publisher was
right.

In Wardour Street a small heap of Goths huddle together,
walking warily. I can't figure out why: there's no one around to
menace them, but maybe they don't know that.

It's sort of boring; there's simply no one about. I start fanta-
sising a mugging to break up the monotony of empty chill streets;
I could probably claim it back on expenses.

Ella's gone the next time I pass Piccadilly.

In one of the back streets behind Shaftesbury Avenue, I walk
past some accordion doors with something written on them.
Walking towards them it reads OPRIG. Parallel it says NO PARKING.
Looking back over my shoulder it reads N AKN. I wonder briefly
if somebody is trying to tell me something, then conclude I'm
getting tired, or transcendently bored.

On the Charing Cross Road a little old Chinese lady
teeter-totters on the pavement, gesturing at taxis that ignore her.
She looks lost. Leicester Square is utterly deserted.

It's nearly five a.m. I stop a couple of cops I've seen across
the roads all evening. Ask them about the West End – is there
anything happening late at night? They say no, say the area's
still cruising on a reputation it hasn't deserved for over a decade.
They sigh, wistfully. 'You may get the odd rent boy hanging
round Piccadilly, but that's all they do: hang around.'

They'd seen three people in their last sweep through every
dangerous dead-end alley and mysterious Soho street. They're
almost as bored as I am; I'm probably the most interesting thing
that's happened to them all night. If I had a mobile phone I'd
let them play with it. Five thirty, they tell me, things hot up;
the cleaners begin to come round.

* * *

5:20 I pass a McDonald's. Already the McPeople who work there are in, McScrubbing the McCounters and unloading McMillions of McBuns from the McTruck.

*

5:40 Ponder the touching concern in My Editor's voice when I told her I'd wander the streets, her obvious worry that terrible things were going to happen to me. I should have been so lucky.

*

6:02 I'm in the taxi going home. I tell the driver about my abortive evening. 'Fing is,' he explains, 'everybody relates to Wardour Street, Brewer Street, Greek Street as where the action is. They fink people hang round the 'Dilly still, addicts waiting for their scrips. Fuck me, man, you're going back twenty years. Notting Hill, that's where it's all at these days. The action's always there. It just moves. And the West End's been cleaned up so hard it's dead.'

Conclusion (statistical breakdown):	
murders seen	0
car chases involved in	0
adventures had	0
foreign spies encountered	0
ladies of the night ditto	½ (Ella)
rock stars encountered (in Café München)	1
encounters with police	2

Originally published in *Time Out*, 1990.

III

INTRODUCTIONS AND MUSINGS: SCIENCE FICTION

'There are three phrases that make possible the world
of writing about the world of not-yet . . . and they are
simple phrases.
  'What if . . . ?
  'If only . . .
  'If this goes on . . .'

Fritz Leiber: The Short Stories

I met Fritz Leiber (it's pronounced Lie-ber, and not, as I had mispronounced it all my life until I met him, Lee-ber) shortly before his death. This was twenty years ago. We were sitting next to each other at a banquet at the World Fantasy Convention. He seemed so old: a tall, serious, distinguished man with white hair, who reminded me of a thinner, better-looking Boris Karloff. He said nothing, during the dinner, not that I can remember. Our mutual friend Harlan Ellison had sent him a copy of *Sandman* #18, *A Dream of a Thousand Cats*, which was my own small tribute to Leiber's cat stories, and I told him he had been an inspiration, and he said something more or less inaudible in return, and I was happy. We rarely get to thank those who shaped us.

My first Leiber short story. I was nine. The story, 'The White Flies', was in Judith Merril's huge anthology *SF12*. It was the most important book I read when I was nine, with the possible exception of Michael Moorcock's *Stormbringer*, for it was the place I discovered a host of authors who would become important to me, and dozens of stories I would read so often that I could have recited them: Chip Delany's 'The Star Pit', R. A. Lafferty's 'Primary Education of the Camiroi' and 'Narrow Valley' and William Burroughs's 'They Do Not Always Remember', J. G. Ballard's 'The Cloud-Sculptors of Coral D', not to mention Tuli Kupferberg's poems, Carol Emshwiller and Sonya Dorman and Kit Reed and the rest. It did not matter that I was much too

young for the stories: I knew that they were beyond me, and
was not even slightly troubled by this. The stories made sense
to me, a sense that was beyond what they literally meant. It was
in *SF12* I encountered concepts and people that did not exist
in the children's books I was familiar with, and it delighted me.

What did I make of 'The Winter Flies' then? The last time I
read it I saw it as semi-autobiographical fiction, about a man
who philanders and drinks when he is on the road, whose
marriage is breaking down and who interrupts a masturbatory
reverie to talk a child having a panic attack back to reality,
something that, for a moment, brings a family, fragmenting in
alcohol and lack of communication, together. When I read it as
a nine-year-old it was about a man beset by demons, talking his
son, lost among the stars, home again.

I knew I liked Fritz Leiber from that story on. He was someone
I read. When I was eleven I bought *Conjure Wife,* and learned
that all women were witches, and found out what a hand of
glory was (and yes, there is sexism and misogyny in the book
and in the concept, but there is, if you are a twelve-year-old
boy trying to make sense of something that might as well be an
alien species, also the kind of paranoid 'what if it's true?' that
makes reading books such a dangerous occupation at any age).
I read a 1972 issue of *Wonder Woman* written by Samuel
R. Delany, featuring Fafhrd and the Grey Mouser, and was disappointed that it felt nothing like a Chip Delany story, but had
now encountered our two adventurers, and, from the magic of
comics, knew what they looked like. I read *Sword of Sorcery,*
which was the Fafhrd and the Grey Mouser comic that DC comics
brought out in 1973, and finally found a copy of *The Swords of
Lankhmar* at the age of thirteen, in the cupboard at the back of
Mr Wright's English class, its cover (I would later discover) a
bad English copy of the Jeff Jones painting on the cover of the
US edition; and I read it, and I was content.

I couldn't enjoy Conan after that. Not really. I missed the wit.

Shortly after I found a copy of *The Big Time*, Leiber's novel of the Change War, being fought by two incomprehensible groups of antagonists using human beings as pawns, and read it, convinced it was a stage play cunningly disguised as a novella, and when I reread it twenty years on I enjoyed it almost as much (aspects of how Leiber treated the narrator bothered me) and was still just as convinced it was a stage play.

Leiber wrote some great books, and he wrote some stinkers: the majority of his SF novels in particular feel dated and throw-away. He wrote some great short stories in SF and fantasy and horror and there's scarcely a stinker among them.

He was one of the giants of genre literature and it is hard to imagine the world today being the same without him. And he was a giant partly because he vaulted over genre restrictions, sidled around them, took them in his stride. He created – in the sense that it barely existed before he wrote it – witty and intelligent sword and sorcery; he was the person who put down the foundations of what would become urban horror.

The best of Leiber has themes that recur, like an artist returning to his favorite subjects – Shakespeare and watches and cats, marriage and women and ghosts, the power of cities and bombs and the stage, dealing with the devil, Germany, mortality, never actually repeating, usually both smarter and deeper than it needed to be to sell, written with elegance and poetry and wit.

Good malt whisky tastes of one thing; a great malt whisky tastes of many things. It plays a chromatic scale of flavor in your mouth, leaving you with an odd sequence of aftertastes, and after the liquid has gone from your tongue you find yourself reminded of first honey, then woodsmoke, bitter chocolate and of the barren salt pastures at the edge of the sea. Fritz Leiber's short stories do the thing a fine whisky does. They leave aftertastes in memory, they leave an emotional residue and resonance that remains long after the final page has been turned. Like the stage manager in 'Four Ghosts in Hamlet', we feel that Leiber spent a lifetime observing, and he was adept at turning the straw of memory into the bricks of imagination and of story. He demanded a great deal of his readers – you need to pay attention, you need to care – and he gave a great deal in return, for those of us that did.

Twentieth-century genre SF produced some recognized giants – Ray Bradbury being the obvious example – but it also produced a handful of people who never gained the recognition that should have been their due. They were caviar (but then, so was Bradbury, and he was rapidly taken out of SF and seen as a national treasure). They might have been giants, but nobody noticed them; they were too odd, too misshapen, too smart. Avram Davidson was one. R. A. Lafferty another. Fritz Leiber was never quite one of the overlooked ones, not in that way: he won many awards; he was widely and rightly seen as one of our great writers. But he never crossed over into the popular conscious-ness: he was too baroque, perhaps; too intelligent. He is not on the roadmap that we draw that takes us from Stephen King and Ramsey Campbell back to H. P. Lovecraft in one direction, from every game of Dungeons and Dragons with a thief in it back to Robert E. Howard, in another.

He should be.

I hope this book reminds his admirers of why they love his work; but more than that, I trust it will find him new readers, and that the new readers will, in turn, find an author they can trust (as much as ever you can trust an author) and to love.

This was my introduction to *Selected Stories* by Fritz Leiber, 2010.

Hothouse

Annihilating all that's made
To a green thought in a green shade
– 'The Garden', Andrew Marvell

B rian Aldiss is now the preeminent English science fiction writer of his generation. He has now been writing for over fifty years with a restless energy and intellect that have taken him from the heart of genre science fiction to mainstream fiction and back again, with explorations of biography, fabulism and absurdism on the way. As an editor and as an anthologist he has done much to influence the kind of science fiction that people were reading through the sixties and seventies, and was responsible for shaping tastes of readers of science fiction in the UK. He has been a critic, and his examinations of the SF field, *Billion Year Spree* and its reinvention, *Trillion Year Spree*, were remarkable descriptions of the genre that Aldiss argued began with Mary Shelley's *Frankenstein* and defined as 'Hubris clobbered by Nemesis'. His career has been enormous: it has recapitulated British SF, always with a ferocious intelligence, always with poetry and oddness, always with passion; while his work outside the boundaries of science fiction, as a writer of mainstream fiction, gained respect and attention from the wider world.

Brian Aldiss is, as I write this, a living author, still working and still writing, and a living author who has restlessly crossed from genre to genre and broken genre lines whenever it suited him; as such he is difficult to put into context, problematic to pigeonhole.

As a young man in the army Brian Aldiss found himself serving in Burma and in Sumatra, encountering a jungle world unimaginable in grey England, and it is not too presumptuous to suggest that the inspiration for the world of *Hothouse* began with that exposure to the alien, in a novel that celebrates the joy of strange and savage vegetable growth.

He was demobbed in 1948, returned to England and worked in a bookshop while writing science fiction short stories. His first book was *The Brightfount Diaries,* a series of sketches about bookselling, and shortly thereafter he sold his first set of science fiction stories in book form – *Space, Time and Nathaniel* – began editing, became a critic and describer of SF as a medium.

Aldiss was part of the second generation of English science fiction writers; he had grown up reading American science fiction magazines, and he understood and spoke the language of 'Golden Age' science fiction, combining it with a very English literary point of view. He owed as much to early Robert Heinlein as to H. G. Wells. Still, he was a writer, and not, say, an engineer. The story was always more important to Aldiss than the science. (American writer and critic James Blish famously criticised *Hothouse* for its scientific implausibility; but *Hothouse* delights in its implausibilities, and its impossibilities – the oneiric image of the web-connected moon is a prime example – are its strengths, not weaknesses.)

Hothouse, Aldiss's next major work, like many novels of its time, was written and published serially, in magazine form, in America. It was written as a linked sequence of five novelettes, which were collectively given the Hugo Award (the science fiction field's Oscar) in 1962, for Best Short Fiction. (Robert A. Heinlein's *Stranger in a Strange Land* took the Hugo for Best Novel.)

There had been prominent English science fiction writers before Aldiss, writing for the American market – Arthur C. Clarke, for example, or Eric Frank Russell – but Aldiss came on the scene after the so-called Golden Age was over, began to write at a point where science fiction was beginning to introspect. Authors like Aldiss and his contemporaries, such as J. G. Ballard and John Brunner, were part of the sea change that would produce, in the second half of the sixties, coagulating around the Michael Moorcock-edited *New Worlds,* what would become known as the 'New Wave': science fiction that relied on the softer sciences, on style, on experimentation. And although *Hothouse* predates the New Wave, it can also be seen as one of the seminal works that created it, or that showed that the change had come.

Aldiss continued to experiment in form and content, experimenting with prose comedic, psychedelic and literary. His *Horatio Stubbs Saga,* published between 1971 and 1978, a sequence of three books which dealt with the youth, education and war experiences in Burma of a young man whose experiences parallel Aldiss's, were bestsellers, a first for Aldiss. In the early 1980s he returned to classical science fiction with the magisterial *Helliconia* sequence, which imagined a planet with immensely long seasons orbiting two suns, and examined the life-forms and biological cycles of the planet, and the effect on the planet's human observers, in an astonishing exercise in world-building.

Restlessly creative, relentlessly fecund, Brian Aldiss has created continually, and just as his hothouse Earth brings forth life of all shapes and kinds, unpredictable, delightful and dangerous, so has Aldiss. His characters and his worlds, whether in his mainstream fiction, his science fiction, or in the books that are harder to classify, such as the experimental, surreal *Report on Probability A,* are always engaged in, to use graphic novelist Eddie Campbell's phrase, the dance of Lifey Death.

Hothouse was Aldiss's second substantial SF novel. It is an uncompromising book, and it exists simultaneously in several science fictional traditions (for it is science fiction, even if the image at the heart of the story, of a moon and Earth that do not spin, bound together by huge spidery webs, is an image from fantasy).

It is a novel of a far-future Earth, set at the end of this planet's life, when all our current concerns are forgotten, our cities are long gone and abandoned. (The moments in the ruins of what I take to be Calcutta, as the Beauty chants long-forgotten political slogans from a time in our distant future, are a strange reminder of a world millions of years abandoned and irrelevant.)

It is an odyssey in which our male protagonist, Gren, takes a journey across a world, through unimagined dangers and impossible perils (while Lily-yo, our female protagonist, gets to journey *up*).

It is a tale of impossible wonders, part of a genre that, like *The Odyssey*, predates science fiction, its roots in the travellers' tales of Sir John Mandeville and before, tall tales of distant places filled with unlikely creatures, of headless men with their faces in their chests and men like dogs and of a strange form of lamb that is actually a vegetable.

But above and behind all else, *Hothouse* is a novel of conceptual breakthrough – as explained by John Clute and Peter Nicholls in their *Encyclopedia of Science Fiction*, the moment of conceptual breakthrough occurs as the protagonist puts his head through the edge of the world to see the cogs and gears and engines turning behind the skies, and the protagonist and the reader begin to understand the previously hidden nature of reality. In Aldiss's first science fiction novel, *Non-Stop*, the jungle is, as we will learn, inside a starship which has been travelling through space for many human generations – so long that the people on the ship have forgotten that they are on a ship. *Hothouse* is a novel of a different kind of conceptual breakthrough, for the various protagonists are more concerned with survival than they are with discovery, leaving the moments of 'Aha!' for the reader to discover: the life cycle of the fly-men, the role of fungus in human evolution, the nature of the world – all these things we learn, and they change the nature of the way we see things.

Hothouse is plotted by place and by event and, over and over, by wonder. It is not a novel of character: the characters exist at arm's length from us, and Aldiss intentionally and repeatedly alienates us from them – even Gren, the nearest thing we have to a sympathetic protagonist, gains knowledge from the morel and becomes estranged from us, forcing us from his point of view into his (for want of a better word) mate Yattmur's. We sympathise with the final humans in their jungle, but they are not us.

There are those who accuse science fiction of favouring idea over characters; Aldiss has proved himself over and over a writer who understands and creates fine and sympathetic characters, both in his genre and in his mainstream work, and yet I think it would be a fair accusation to make about *Hothouse*. Someone who made it would, of course, miss the point, much as someone accusing a Beatles song of being three minutes long and repeating itself in the choruses might have missed the point: *Hothouse* is a cavalcade of wonders and a meditation on the cycle of life, in which individual lives are unimportant, in which a nice distinction between animal and vegetable is unimportant, in which the solar system itself is unimportant, and in the end, all that truly matters is life, arriving here from space as fine particles, and now passing back on again, into the void.

It's the only science fiction novel I can think of that celebrates the process of composting. Things grow and die and rot and new things grow. Death is frequent and capricious and usually unmourned. Death and rebirth are constant. Life – and Wonder – remain.

The Sense of Wonder is an important part of what makes

science fiction work, and it is this Sense of Wonder that *Hothouse* delivers so effectively, and at a sustained level that Aldiss would not surpass until his trilogy of novels *Helliconia Spring, Helliconia Summer* and *Helliconia Winter*, almost thirty years later.

The world of *Hothouse* is our own planet, inconceivable gulfs of time from now. The Earth no longer spins. The moon is frozen in orbit, bound to the Earth by weblike strands. The day-side of the Earth is covered by the many trunks of a single banyan tree, in which many vegetable creatures live, and some insects, and Humankind. People have shrunk to monkey-size. They are few in number, as are the other remaining species from the animal kingdom (we will meet a few species, and we will converse with one mammal, Sodal Ye). But animals are irrelevant: the long afternoon of the Earth, as nightfall approaches, is the time of vegetable life, which occupies the niches that animals and birds occupy today, while also filling new niches – of which the traversers, the mile-long space-spanning vegetable spider-creatures, are, perhaps, the most remarkable.

The teeming life-forms – which, with their Lewis Carroll-like portmanteau names, feel as if they were named by clever children – fill the sun-side of the world. Gren, the nearest thing to a protagonist that Aldiss gives us, one letter away from the omnipresent green, begins as a child, and more animal than human. A smart animal, true, but still an animal – and he ages fast, as an animal might age.

His odyssey is a process of becoming human. He learns that there are things he does not know. Most of his suppositions are wrong, and in his world a mistake will probably kill you. Randomly, intelligently, fortunately, he survives and he learns, encountering a phantasmagoria of strange creatures on the way, including the lotus-eating tummy-bellies, a comic relief turn that gets increasingly dark as the book progresses.

At the heart of the book is Gren's encounter with the morel, the intelligent fungus who is at the same time both the snake in the Garden of Eden and the fruit of the tree of knowledge of good and evil, a creature of pure intellect in the same way that Gren and the humans are creatures of instinct.

Sodel Ye, the descendant of dolphins that Gren will encounter towards the end, and the morel are both intelligent, both know more about the world than the humans, and both are reliant on other creatures to move around and encounter the world, as parasites or symbiotes.

Looking back, one can see why *Hothouse* was unique, and why, almost fifty years ago, it won the Hugo and cemented Aldiss's reputation. Compare *Hothouse* with its most traditionally English equivalent, John Wyndham's disaster novel *The Day of the Triffids* (1951), a 'cosy catastrophe' (to use Aldiss-the-critic's phrase) in which blinded humans are victimised by huge, ambulatory, deadly plants, band together and learn how to keep themselves safe before, we assume, reestablishing humanity's dominion over the Earth. In the world of *Hothouse* there is nothing that makes us superior to plants, and the triffids would be unremarkable here, outclassed and outweirded by the doggerel monsters of the hothouse Earth, the crocksocks, hellyelms, killerwillows, wiltmilts and the rest.

Still, *Hothouse* remains British science fiction – its imperatives are very different to the American SF of the same period. In American SF from the early sixties, Gren would have gone on to explore the universe, to restore wisdom to the humans, to restore animal life on Earth, all endings that Aldiss is able to dangle before us before he rejects them, for *Hothouse* is not a book about the triumph of humanity, but about the nature of life, life on an enormous scale and life on a cellular level. The form of the life is unimportant: soon the sun will engulf the Earth, but the life that came to Earth, and stayed for a moment, will move on across the universe, finding new purchase in forms unimaginable.

Hothouse is a strange book, alienating and deeply, troublingly odd. Things will grow and die and rot and new things will grow, and survival depends upon this. All else is vanity, Brian Aldiss tells us, with Ecclesiastes, and even intelligence may be a burden of a kind, something parasitic and ultimately unimportant.

This was my introduction to the 2008 Penguin Modern Classics edition of *Hothouse*, by Brian Aldiss.

Ray Bradbury, *Fahrenheit 451* and What Science Fiction Is and Does

Sometimes writers write about a world that does not yet exist. We do it for a hundred reasons. (Because it's good to look forward, not back. Because we need to illuminate a path we hope or we fear humanity will take. Because the world of the future seems more enticing or more interesting than the world of today. Because we need to warn you. To encourage. To examine. To imagine.) The reasons for writing about the day after tomorrow, and all the tomorrows that follow it, are as many and as varied as the people writing.

This is a book of warning. It is a reminder that what we have is valuable, and that sometimes we take what we value for granted. There are three phrases that make possible the world of writing about the world of not-yet (you can call it science fiction or speculative fiction; you can call it anything you wish) and they are simple phrases:

What if . . . ?

If only . . .

If this goes on . . .

'What if . . . ?' gives us change, a departure from our lives. (What if aliens landed tomorrow and gave us everything we wanted, but at a price?)

'If only . . .' lets us explore the glories and dangers of tomorrow. (If only dogs could talk. If only I was invisible.)

'If this goes on . . .' is the most predictive of the three, although it doesn't try to predict an actual future with all its messy confusion. Instead, 'If this goes on . . .' fiction takes an element of life today, something clear and obvious and normally something troubling, and asks what would happen if that thing, that one thing, became bigger, became all-pervasive, changed the way we thought and behaved. (If this goes on, all communication everywhere will be through text messages or computers, and direct speech between two people, without a machine, will be outlawed.)

It's a cautionary question, and it lets us explore cautionary worlds.

People think, wrongly, that speculative fiction is about predicting the future, but it isn't – or if it is, it tends to do a rotten job of it. Futures are huge things that come with many elements and a billion variables, and the human race has a habit of listening to predictions for what the future will bring and then doing something quite different.

What speculative fiction is really good at is not the future, but the present. Taking an aspect of it that troubles or is dangerous, and extending and extrapolating that aspect into something that allows the people of that time to see what they are doing from a different angle and from a different place. It's cautionary. *Fahrenheit 451* is speculative fiction. It's an 'If this goes on . . .' story. Ray Bradbury was writing about his present, which is our past. He was warning us about things, and some of those things are obvious, and some of them, half a century later, are harder to see.

Listen.

If someone tells you what a story is about, they are probably right.

If they tell you that that is all the story is about, they are very definitely wrong.

Any story is about a host of things. It is about the author; it is about the world the author sees and deals with and lives in; it is about the words chosen and the way those words are deployed; it is about the story itself and what happens in the story; it is about the people in the story; it is polemic; it is opinion.

An author's opinions of what a story is about are always valid and are always true: the author was there, after all, when the book was written. She came up with each word and knows why she used that word instead of another. But an author is a creature of her time, and even she cannot see everything that her book is about.

More than half a century has passed since 1953. In America in 1953, the comparatively recent medium of radio was already severely on the wane – its reign had lasted about thirty years, but now the exciting new medium of television had come into ascendancy, and the dramas and comedies of radio were either ending for good or reinventing themselves with a visual track on the 'idiot box'.

The news channels in America warned of juvenile delinquents – teenagers in cars who drove dangerously and lived for kicks. The Cold War was going on – a war between Russia and its allies and America and its allies in which nobody dropped bombs or fired bullets because a dropped bomb could tip the world into a Third World War, a nuclear war from which it would never return. The senate was holding hearings to root out hidden Communists and taking steps to stamp out comic books. And whole families were gathering around the television in the evenings.

The joke in the 1950s went that in the old days you could tell who was home by seeing if the lights were on; now you knew who was home by seeing who had their lights off. The televisions were small and the pictures were in black and white and you needed to turn off the light to get a good picture.

'If this goes on . . .' thought Ray Bradbury, 'nobody will read books any more,' and the book began. He had written a short story once called 'The Pedestrian', about a man who is incarcerated by the police after he is stopped simply for walking. The story became part of the world he was building, and seventeen-year-old Clarisse McLellan becomes a pedestrian in a world where nobody walks.

'What if . . . firemen burned down houses instead of saving them?' Bradbury thought, and now he had his way in to the story. He had a fireman named Guy Montag, who saved a book from the flames instead of burning it.

'If only . . . books could be saved,' he thought. If you destroy all the physical books, how can you still save them?

Bradbury wrote a story called 'The Fireman'. The story demanded to be longer. The world he had created demanded more. He went to UCLA's Powell Library. In the basement were typewriters you could rent by the hour, by putting coins into a box on the side of the typewriter. Ray Bradbury put his money into the box and typed his story. When inspiration flagged, when he needed a boost, when he wanted to stretch his legs, he would walk through the library and look at the books.

And then his story was done.

He called the Los Angeles fire department and asked them at what temperature paper burned. *Fahrenheit 451*, somebody told him. He had his title. It didn't matter if it was true or not.

The book was published and acclaimed. People loved the book, and they argued about it. It was a novel about censorship, they said, about mind control, about humanity. About government control of our lives. About books.

It was filmed by Francois Truffaut, although the ending seems darker than Bradbury's, as if the remembering of books is perhaps not the safety net that Bradbury imagines, but is in itself another dead end.

I read *Fahrenheit 451* as a boy: I did not understand Guy Montag, did not understand why he did what he did, but I understood the love of books that drove him. Books were the most important things in my life. The huge wall-screen televisions were as futuristic and implausible as the idea that people on the television would talk to me, that I could take part, if I had a script. It was never a favorite book: it was too dark, too bleak for that. But when I read a story called 'Usher II' in *The Silver Locusts* (the UK title for *The Martian Chronicles*), I recognized the world of outlawed authors and imagination with a fierce sort of familiar joy.

When I reread it as a teenager, *Fahrenheit 451* had become a book about independence, about thinking for yourself. It was about treasuring books and the dissent inside the covers of books. It was about how we as humans begin by burning books and end by burning people.

Rereading it as an adult I find myself marveling at the book once more. It is all of those things, yes, but it is also a period piece. The four-wall television being described is the television of the 1950s: variety shows with symphony orchestras, and low-brow comedians and soap operas. The world of fast-driving, crazy teenagers out for kicks, of an endless cold war that sometimes goes hot, of wives who appear to have no jobs or identities save for their husbands', of bad men being chased by hounds (even mechanical hounds) is a world that feels like it has its roots firmly in the 1950s. A young reader, finding this book today, or the day after tomorrow, is going to have to imagine first a past, and then a future that belongs to that past.

But still, the heart of the book remains untouched, and the questions Bradbury raises remain as valid and important.

Why do we need the things in books? The poems, the essays, the stories? Authors disagree. Authors are human and fallible and foolish. Stories are lies after all, tales of people who never existed and the things that never actually happened to them. Why should we read them? Why should we care?

The teller and the tale are very different. We must not forget that.

Ideas, written ideas, are special. They are the way we transmit our stories and our ideas from one generation to the next. If we lose them, we lose our shared history. We lose much of what makes us human. And fiction gives us empathy: it puts us inside the minds of other people, gives us the gift of seeing the world through their eyes. Fiction is a lie that tells us true things, over and over.

I knew Ray Bradbury for the last thirty years of his life, and I was so lucky. He was funny and gentle and always (even at the end, when he was so old he was blind and wheelchair-bound, even then) enthusiastic. He cared, completely and utterly, about things. He cared about toys and childhood and films. He cared about books. He cared about stories.

This is a book about caring for things. It's a love letter to books, but I think, just as much, it's a love letter to people, and a love letter to the world of Waukegan, Illinois, in the 1920s, the world in which Ray Bradbury had grown up and which he immortalized as Green Town in his book of childhood, *Dandelion Wine.*

As I said when we began: if someone tells you what a story is about, they are probably right. If they tell you that that is all the story is about, they are probably wrong. So any of the things I have told you about *Fahrenheit 451*, Ray Bradbury's remarkable book of warning, will be incomplete. It is about these things, yes. But it is about more than that. It is about what you find between its pages. (As a final note, in these days when we worry and we argue about whether ebooks are real books, I love how broad Ray Bradbury's definition of a book is at the end, when he points out that we should not judge our books by their covers, and that some books exist between covers that are perfectly people-shaped.)

I was proud to be asked to write the introduction to the 2013 sixtieth-anniversary edition of Ray Bradbury's *Fahrenheit 451*.

Of Time, and Gully Foyle: Alfred Bester and *The Stars My Destination*

You can tell when a Hollywood historical film was made by looking at the eye makeup of the leading ladies, and you can tell the date of an old science fiction novel by every word on the page. Nothing dates harder and faster and more strangely than the future.

This was not always true, but somewhere in the last thirty years (somewhere between the beginning of the death of what John Clute and Peter Nicholls termed, in their *Encyclopedia of Science Fiction*, 'First SF' in 1957 when *Sputnik* brought space down to earth and 1984, the year that George Orwell ended and William Gibson started) we lurched into the futures we now try to inhabit, and all the old SF futures found themselves surplus to requirements, standing alone on the sidewalk, pensioned off and abandoned. Or were they?

SF is a difficult and transient literature at the best of times, ultimately problematic. It claims to treat of the future, all the what-ifs and if-this-goes-ons; but the what-ifs and if-this-goes-ons are always founded here and hard in today. Whatever *today* is.

To put it another way, nothing dates harder than historical fiction and science fiction. Sir Arthur Conan Doyle's historical fiction and his SF are of a piece – and both have dated in a way in which Sherlock Holmes, pinned to his time in the gaslit streets of Victorian London, has not.

Dated? Rather, they are of their time.

For there are always exceptions. There may, for instance, be nothing in Alfred Bester's *Tiger! Tiger!* (1956 UK; republished in the US under the original 1956 *Galaxy* magazine title, *The Stars My Destination*, in 1957) that radically transgresses the speculative notions SF writers then shared about the possible shape of a future solar system. But Gully Foyle, the obsessive protagonist who dominates every page of the tale, has not dated a moment. In a fashion which inescapably reminds us of the great grotesques of other literary traditions, of dark figures from Poe or Gogol or Dickens, Gully Foyle *controls* the world around him, so that the awkwardnesses of the 1956 future do not so much fade into the background as obey his obsessive dance. If he were not so intransigent, so utterly bloody-minded, so unborn, Gully Foyle could have become an icon like Sherlock Holmes. But he is; and even though Bester based him on a quote – he is a reworking of the Byronesque magus Edmond Dantès, whose revenge over his oppressors takes a thousand pages of Alexandre Dumas's *The Count of Monte Cristo* (1844) to accomplish – he cannot himself be quoted.

When I read this book – or one very similar; you can no more read the same book again than you can step into the same river – in the early 1970s, as a young teenager, I read it under the title *Tiger! Tiger!* It's a title I prefer to the rather more upbeat *The Stars My Destination*. It is a title of warning, of admiration. God, we are reminded in Blake's poem, created the tiger too. The God who made the lamb also made the carnivores that prey upon it. And Gully Foyle, our hero, is a predator. We meet him and are informed that he is everyman, a nonentity; then Bester lights the touchpaper, and we stand back and watch Foyle flare and burn and illuminate: almost illiterate, stupid, single-minded, amoral (not in the hip sense of being too cool for morality, but simply utterly, blindly selfish), he is a murderer – perhaps a multiple murderer – a rapist, a monster. A tiger.

(And because Bester began working on the book in England, naming his characters from an English telephone directory, Foyle shares a name with the largest and most irritating bookshop in London* – and with Lemuel Gulliver, who voyaged among strange peoples. Dagenham, Yeovil and Sheffield are all English places.)

We are entering a second-stage world of introductions to SF. It is not long since everyone knew everybody. I never met Alfred Bester: I did not travel to America as a young man, and by the time he was due to come to England, to the 1987 Brighton Worldcon, his health did not permit it, and he died shortly after the convention.

I can offer no personal encomia to Bester the man – author of many fine short stories, two remarkable SF novels in the first round of his career (*The Demolished Man* and the book you now hold in your hand); author of three somewhat less notable SF books in later life. (Also a fascinating psychological thriller called *The Rat Race*, about the world of New York television in the 1950s.)

He began his career as a writer in the SF pulps, moved from there to comics, writing Superman, Green Lantern (he created the 'Green Lantern Oath') and many other characters; he moved from there to radio, writing for *Charlie Chan* and *The Shadow*. 'The comic book days were over, but the splendid training I received in visualization, attack, dialogue and economy stayed with me forever,' he said in a memoir.

He was one of the only – perhaps the only – SF writers to be revered by the old-timers ('First SF'), by the radical 'New Wave' of the 1960s and early 1970s, and, in the 1980s, by the 'cyberpunks'. When he died in 1987, three years into the flowering of cyberpunk, it was apparent that the 1980s genre owed an enormous debt to Bester – and to this book in particular.

* 2016 note: Foyles is no longer irritating. It hasn't been for fifteen years.

The Stars My Destination is, after all, the perfect cyberpunk novel: it contains such cheerfully protocyber elements as multinational corporate intrigue; a dangerous, mysterious, hyperscientific McGuffin (PyrE); an amoral hero; a supercool thief-woman . . .

But what makes *The Stars My Destination* more interesting – and ten years on, less dated – than most cyberpunk, is watching Gully Foyle become a moral creature, during his sequence of transfigurations (keep all heroes going long enough, and they become gods). The tiger tattoos force him to learn control. His emotional state is no longer written in his face – it forces him to move beyond predation, beyond rage, back to the womb, as it were. (And what a sequence of wombs the book gives us: the coffin, the *Nomad,* the Gouffre Martel, St Pat's and finally the *Nomad* again.) It gives us more than that. It gives us:

Birth.

Symmetry.

Hate.

A word of warning: the vintage of the book demands more work from the reader than she or he may be used to. Were it written now, its author would have shown us the rape, not implied it, just as we would have been permitted to watch the sex on the grass in the night after the Gouffre Martel, before the sun came up, and she saw his face . . .

So assume it's 1956 again. You are about to meet Gully Foyle, and to learn how to jaunte. You are on the way to the future.

It was, or is, or will be, as Bester might have said, had someone not beaten him to it, the best of times. It will be the worst of times . . .

This is the introduction to the 1999 SF Masterworks edition of Alfred Bester's *The Stars My Destination.*

Samuel R. Delany and
The Einstein Intersection

Two misconceptions are widely held about that branch of
literature known as science fiction.

The initial misconception is that SF (at the time Delany
wrote *The Einstein Intersection* many editors and writers were
arguing that *speculative fiction* might be a better use of the
initials, but that battle was lost a long time back) is about the
future, that it is, fundamentally, a predictive literature. Thus
1984 is read as Orwell's attempt to predict the world of 1984,
as Heinlein's *Revolt in 2100* is seen as an attempted prediction
of life in 2100. But those who point to the rise of any version
of Big Brother, or to the many current incarnations of the Anti-Sex
League, or to the mushrooming power of Christian fundamen-
talism as evidence that Heinlein or Orwell was engaged in fore-
casting Things to Come are missing the point.

The second misconception, a kind of second-stage misconception, easy to make once one has traveled past the 'SF is about
predicting the future' conceit, is this: SF is about the vanished
present. Specifically SF is solely about the time when it was
written. Thus, Alfred Bester's *The Demolished Man* and *Tiger!
Tiger!* (vt. *The Stars My Destination*) are about the 1950s, just as
William Gibson's *Neuromancer* is about the 1984 we lived through
in reality. Now this is true, as far as it goes, but is no more true

for SF than for any other practice of writing: our tales are always the fruit of our times. SF, like all other art, is the product of its era, reflecting or reacting against or illuminating the prejudices, fears and assumptions of the period in which it was written. But there is more to SF than this: one does not only read Bester to decode and reconstruct the 1950s.

What is important in good SF, and what makes SF that lasts, is how it talks to us of our present. What does it tell us *now*? And, even more important, what will it always tell us? For the point where SF becomes a transcendent branch of literature is the point where it is about something bigger and more important than Zeitgeist, whether the author intended it to be or not.

The Einstein Intersection (a pulp title imposed on this book from without; Delany's original title for it was *A Fabulous, Formless Darkness*) is a novel that is set in a time after the people like us have left the Earth and *others* have moved into our world, like squatters into a furnished house, wearing our lives and myths and dreams uncomfortably but conscientiously. As the novel progresses, Delany weaves myth, consciously and unself-consciously: Lobey, our narrator, is Orpheus, or plays Orpheus, as other members of the cast will find themselves playing Jesus and Judas, Jean Harlow (out of Candy Darling) and Billy the Kid. They inhabit our legends awkwardly: they do not fit them.

The late Kathy Acker has discussed Orpheus at length, and Samuel R. Delany's role as an Orphic prophet, in her introduction to the Wesleyan Press edition of *Trouble on Triton*. All that she said there is true, and I commend it to the reader. Delany is an Orphic bard, and *The Einstein Intersection*, as will become immediately apparent, is Orphic fiction.

In the oldest versions we have of the story of Orpheus it appears to have been simply a myth of the seasons: Orpheus went into the Underworld to find his Eurydice, and he brought her safely out into the light of the sun again. We lost the happy ending a long time ago. Delany's Lobey, however, is not simply Orpheus.

The Einstein Intersection is a brilliant book, self-consciously suspicious of its own brilliance, framing its chapters with quotes from authors ranging from de Sade to Yeats (are these the owners of the house into which the squatters have moved?) and with extracts from the author's own notebooks kept while writing the book and wandering the Greek Islands. It was written by a young author in the milieu he has described in *The Motion of Light in Water* and *Heavenly Breakfast*, his two autobiographical works, and here he is writing about music and love, growing up and the value of stories as only a young man can.

One can see this book as a portrait of a generation that dreamed that new drugs and free sex would bring about a fresh dawn and the rise of *Homo superior*, wandering the world of the generation before them like magical children walking through an abandoned city – through the ruins of Rome, or Athens or New York: that the book is inhabiting and reinterpreting the myths of the people who came to be known as the hippies. But if that were all the book was, it would be a poor sort of tale, with little resonance for now. Instead, it continues to resonate.

So, having established what *The Einstein Intersection* is not, what is it?

I see it as an examination of myths, and of why we need them, and why we tell them, and what they do to us, whether we understand them or not. Each generation replaces the one that came before. Each generation newly discovers the tales and truths that came before, threshes them, discovering for itself what is wheat and what is chaff, never knowing or caring or even understanding that the generation who will come after them will discover that some of their new timeless truths were little more than the vagaries of fashion.

The Einstein Intersection is a young man's book, in every way:

it is the book of a young author, and it is the story of a young man going into the big city, learning a few home truths about love, growing up and deciding to go home (somewhat in the manner of Fritz Leiber's protagonist from 'Gonna Roll the Bones', who takes the long way home, around the world).

These were the things that I learned from the book the first time I read it, as a child: I learned that writing could, in and of itself, be beautiful. I learned that sometimes what you do not understand, what remains beyond your grasp in a book, is as magical as what you can take from it. I learned that we have the right, or the obligation, to tell old stories in our own ways, because they are our stories, and they must be told.

These were the things I learned from the book when I read it again, in my late teens: I learned that my favorite SF author was black, and understood now who the various characters were based upon, and, from the extracts from the author's notebooks, I learned that fiction was mutable: there was something dangerous and exciting about the idea that a black-haired character would gain red hair and pale skin in a second draft (I also learned there could be second drafts). I discovered that the idea of a book and the book itself were two different things. I also enjoyed and appreciated how much the author doesn't tell you: it's in the place that readers bring themselves to the book that the magic occurs.

I had by then begun to see *The Einstein Intersection* in context as part of Delany's body of work. It would be followed by *Nova* and *Dhalgren,* each book a quantum leap in tone and ambition beyond its predecessor, each an examination of mythic structures and the nature of writing. In *The Einstein Intersection* we encounter ideas that could break cover as SF in a way they were only beginning to do in the real world, particularly in the portrait of the nature of sex and sexuality that the book draws for us: we are given, very literally, a third, transitional sex, just as we are given a culture ambivalently obsessed with generation.

Rereading the book recently as an adult I found it still as beautiful, still as strange; I discovered passages – particularly toward the twisty end – that had once been opaque were now quite clear. Truth to tell, I now found Lo Lobey an unconvincing heterosexual: while the book is certainly a love story, I found myself reading it as the story of Lobey's courtship by Kid Death, and wondering about Lobey's relationships with various other members of the cast. He is an honest narrator, reliable to a point, but he has been to the city after all, and it has left its mark on the narrative. And I found myself grateful, once again, for the brilliance of Delany and the narrative urge that drove him to write. It is good SF, and even if, as some have maintained (including, particularly, Samuel R. Delany), literary values and SF values are not necessarily the same, and the criteria – the entire critical apparatus – we use to judge them are different, this is still fine literature, for it is the literature of dreams, and stories, and of myths. That it is good SF, whatever that is, is beyond question. That it is a beautiful book, uncannily written, prefiguring much fiction that followed, and too long neglected, will be apparent to the readers who are coming to it freshly with this new edition.

I remember, as a teen, encountering Brian Aldiss's remark on the fiction of Samuel R. Delany in his original critical history of SF, *Billion Year Spree:* quoting C. S. Lewis, Aldiss commented that Delany's telling of how odd things affected odd people was an oddity too much. And that puzzled me, then and now, because I found, and still find, nothing odd or strange about Delany's characters. They are fundamentally human; or, more to the point, they are, fundamentally, us.

And that is what fiction is for.

My foreword to the 1998 Wesleyan Press edition of Samuel R. Delany's *The Einstein Intersection*.

On the Fortieth Anniversary of the Nebula Awards: A Speech, 2005

Welcome to the Nebula Awards, on this, the fortieth anniversary of the founding of the SFWA.* That's the ruby anniversary, for anyone wondering what sort of gift to give. And forty years is a very short time in the life of a genre.

I suspect that if I had been given the opportunity to address a convocation of the most eminent writers of science fiction and fantasy when I was a young man – say around the age of twenty-three or twenty-four, when I was bumptious and self-assured and a monstrous clever fellow – I would have had a really impressive sort of speech prepared. It would have been impassioned and heartfelt. An attack on the bastions of science fiction, calling for the tearing down of a number of metaphorical walls and the building up of several more. It would have been a plea for quality in all ways – the finest of fine writing mixed with the reinvention of SF and fantasy as genres. All sorts of wise things would have been said.

And now I'm occupying the awkward zone that one finds oneself in between receiving one's first lifetime achievement award and death, and I realize that I have much less to say than I did when I was young.

* Science Fiction and Fantasy Writers of America.

Gene Wolfe pointed out to me, five years ago, when I proudly told him, at the end of the first draft of *American Gods,* that I thought I'd figured out how to write a novel, that you never learn how to write a novel. You merely learn how to write the novel you're on. He's right, of course. The paradox is that by the time you've figured out how to do it, you've done it. And the next one, if it's going to satisfy the urge to create something new, is probably going to be so different that you may as well be starting from scratch, with the alphabet.

At least in my case, it feels as I begin the next novel knowing less than I did the last time.

So. A ruby anniversary. Forty years ago, in 1965, the first Nebula Awards were handed out. I thought it might be interesting to remind you all of the books that were nominees for Best Novel in 1965 . . .

All Flesh Is Grass by Clifford D. Simak
The Clone by Theodore Thomas and Kate Wilhelm
Dr Bloodmoney by Philip K. Dick
Dune by Frank Herbert
The Escape Orbit by James White
The Genocides by Thomas M. Disch
Nova Express by William Burroughs
A Plague of Demons by Keith Laumer
Rogue Dragon by Avram Davidson
The Ship That Sailed the Time Stream by G. C. Edmondson
The Star Fox by Poul Anderson
The Three Stigmata of Palmer Eldritch by Philip K. Dick

I love that list. It has so much going on – SF and fantasy of all shapes and sizes, jostling side by side. Traditional and iconoclastic fictions, all up for the same Lucite block.

And if you're wondering, the 1965 Nebula winners were,

Novel: Dune by Frank Herbert

Novella: He Who Shapes by Roger Zelazny and *The Saliva Tree*
by Brian Aldiss (tie)

Novelette: 'The Doors of His Face, the Lamps of His Mouth' by
Roger Zelazny

Short Story: "'Repent, Harlequin!' Said the Ticktock-man' by
Harlan Ellison

. . . it was a good year.

Forty years on and we're now living in a world in which SF
has become a default mode. In which the tropes of SF have
spread into the world. Fantasy in its many forms has become a
staple of the media. And we, as the people who were here first,
who built this city on pulp and daydreams and four-color comics,
are coming to terms with a world in which we find several
things they didn't have to worry about in 1965.

For a start, today's contemporary fiction is yesterday's near-
future SF. Only slightly weirder and with no obligation to be in
any way convincing or consistent.

It used to be easy to recognize SF written by mainstream
authors. The authors always seemed convinced that this was
the first novel to tackle faster-than-light travel, or downloadable
intelligence, or time paradoxes or whatever. The books were
clunky and proud of themselves and they reinvented the wheel
and did it very badly, with no awareness of the body of SF that
preceded them.

That's no longer true. Nowadays things that were the most
outlandish topics of SF are simply building blocks for stories,
and they aren't necessarily ours. Our worlds have moved from
being part of the landscape of the imagination to being part of
the wallpaper.

There was a battle for the minds of the world, and we appear to have won it, and now we need to figure out what we're doing next.

I always liked the idea that *SF* stood for 'speculative fiction', mostly because it seemed to cover everything, and include the attitude that what we were doing involved speculation. SF was about thinking, about inquiring, about making things up.

The challenge now is to go forward and to keep going forward: to tell stories that have weight and meaning. It's saying things that mean things, and using the literature of the imagination to do it.

And that's something that each of us, and the writers who will come afterwards, are going to have to struggle with, to reinvent and make SF say what we need it to say.

Anyway.

Something that, after half a lifetime in this field and a lifetime as a reader, I think worth mentioning and reminding people of, is that we are a community.

More than any field in which I've been involved, the people in the worlds of SF have a willingness to help each other, to help those who are starting out.

When I was twenty-two, half a lifetime ago, I went to a Brian Aldiss signing at London's Forbidden Planet. After the signing, at the pub next door, I sat next to a dark, vaguely elfin gentleman named Colin Greenland who seemed to know a lot about the field and who, when I mentioned that I had written a handful of stories, asked to see them. I sent them to him, and he suggested a magazine that he'd done some work for that might publish one of them. I wrote to that magazine, cut the story down until it met their word-count requirements, and they published it.

That short story being published meant more to me at the time than anything had up to that point, and was more glorious than most of the things that have happened since. (And Colin and I have stayed friends. About ten years ago, he sent me, without the author's knowledge, a short story by someone he'd met at a workshop named Susanna Clarke . . . but that's another story.)

Six months later I was in the process of researching my first genre book. It was a book of SF and fantasy quotations, mostly the awful ones, called *Ghastly Beyond Belief*. [*And at this point in the speech I wandered off into an extempore bit of quoting from* Ghastly Beyond Belief, *by me and Kim Newman, mostly about giant crabs. And space crabs too. I'm not going to try and reproduce it here, sorry.*]

. . . and I found myself astonished and delighted by the response within the field. Fans and authors suggested choice works by authors they loved or didn't. I remember the joy of getting a postcard from Isaac Asimov telling me that he couldn't tell the good from the bad in his works, and giving me blanket permission to quote anything of his I wanted to.

I felt that I'd learned a real lesson back then, and it's one that continues to this day.

What I saw was that the people who make up SF, with all its feuds – the roots of most of which are, like all family feuds, literally, inexplicable – are still a family, and fundamentally supportive, and particularly supportive to the young and foolish.

We're here tonight because we love the field.

The Nebulas are a way of applauding our own. They matter because we say they matter, and they matter because we care.

They are something to which we can aspire. They are our way – the genre's way, the way of the community of writers – of thanking those who produced sterling work, those who have added to the body of SF, of fantasy, of speculative fiction.

The Nebulas are a tradition, but that's *not* why they're important.

The Nebula Awards are important because they allow the

people who dream, who speculate, who imagine, to take pride in the achievements of the family of SF. They're important because these Lucite blocks celebrate the ways that we, who create futures for a living, are creating our own future.

This speech was given in Chicago on 30 April 2005, in celebration of the fortieth anniversary of the Nebula Awards.

IV

FILMS AND MOVIES AND ME

'It's oneiric, a beautiful, formless sequence of silver nitrate shadows, and when it ends I wonder what happened.'

The Bride of Frankenstein

Films deliver their pleasures in different ways. Many films give you everything they have to offer the first time you see them, leaving you nothing for another viewing. Some deliver what they have grudgingly on first viewing, only to reveal their magic on subsequent occasions, when things become increasingly satisfying. Very few films are dreams, configuring and reconfiguring themselves in your mind on waking. These films, I think, you make yourself, afterwards, somewhere in the shadows in the back of your head. *The Bride of Frankenstein* is one of those dream-films. It exists in the culture as a unique thing, magical and odd: a lurching story sequence as ungainly and as beautiful as the monster itself, that culminates in a couple of minutes of film that have seared themselves onto the undermind of the world.

It's a lot of people's favourite horror film. Dammit, it's *my* favourite horror film. And yet . . .

My daughter Maddy loves the idea of *The Bride of Frankenstein*: she's ten. Last year, captivated by the little statue of Elsa Lanchester in frightwig that stands, facing a statue of Groucho Marx, on a window ledge halfway up the stairs, she decided to be the Monster's Bride for Hallowe'en. I had to find her imagery of Karloff and his bride-to-be, e-mail her photos of them. Several weeks ago, finding myself in sole charge of Maddy and her friend Gala Avary, I made them hot chocolate and we watched *The Bride of Frankenstein*.

They enjoyed it, wriggling and squealing in all the right places. But once it was done, the girls had an identical reaction. 'Is it over?' asked one. 'That was weird,' said the other, flatly. They were as unsatisfied as an audience could be.

I felt vaguely guilty – I knew they would have enjoyed *House* – or is it *Ghost*? – *of Frankenstein,* the one with Karloff as a mad scientist, and John Carradine's Dracula, not to mention a Lon Chaney Jr wolfman – so much more. It's a romp, after all. It may not be scary, but it feels like a horror film, and it would have delivered everything two ten-year-olds needed to be satisfying.

The Bride of Frankenstein doesn't romp. It's oneiric, a beautiful, formless sequence of silver nitrate shadows, and when it ends I wonder what happened, and then I begin to rebuild it in my head. I've seen it I do not know how many times since I was a boy, and I'm almost pleased to say that I still can't quite tell you the plot. Or rather, I can tell you the plot as it goes along. And then, when it's done, the film begins to scum over in my mind, to reconfigure like a dream does once you've wakened, and it all becomes much harder to explain.

The film begins with Mary Shelley, Elsa Lanchester, all sly smiles and period cleavage, talking to an intensely dull Byron and Shelley, introducing us to a sequel to the original Frankenstein story. And then it's moments after the first film, *Frankenstein,* and the story starts again. The monster survived. The status quo has been restored.

Henry Frankenstein (Colin Clive) is getting married to the wimpy Elizabeth (Valerie Hobson). (The wimpy Elizabeth is the real bride of Frankenstein, and is, I suspect, given the film's title, one of the main factors responsible for the confusion in the popular mind between the scientist and his monster.)

Ernest Thesiger's Dr Pretorius, a far madder scientist than our Henry, strides into Henry Frankenstein's life, like a man bringing a bottle of absinthe to a reformed addict. Dr Pretorius, waspish, camp, unforgettable, trolls in from a world much more dangerous than Henry's. He's sharp and funny, steals scenes and has a marvelous sequence with bottled homunculi – lovers, a king, a priest. This has something to do with his own alchemical researches into creating life, and, I find myself thinking whenever I watch it, nothing at all to do with the film at hand. It sits in the mind like a dream, inexplicable, a moment of movie magic. I find myself fancying director James Whale as Pretorius here, the homunculi his actors, ready to lust or lecture or die as he desires.

Henry Frankenstein himself is feverish, and strangely absent from the film that bears his name, emotionally and truly. The alcoholism (and perhaps the tuberculosis) that would soon enough carry off Colin Clive is already muting his vitality. All the monsters have more life in them than Henry Frankenstein does now, and watching the film I imagine that they will live longer, once the action is over.

Karloff plays the Monster. His face is part of the strange experience of the film: we have seen many people since Karloff who have portrayed Frankenstein's Monster, but none of them were the real thing: they looked too brutish, or too comical – Herman Munsters in waiting. Karloff is something else: sensitive, hurting, a former brute now learning language and longing and love. There is little in the monster to be frightened of.

Instead we pity him, sympathise with him, care about him.

(The sequence with the blind hermit is subject to slippage in my mind with its parody in *Young Frankenstein*. I worry, when I see the blind man in *Bride,* that he will pour hot soup on the monster, or set light to him, and am always relieved when they survive the meal unscathed. Instead, unable to see the monster, the hermit is the only one who is able to look at the monster without prejudice.)

James Whale, directing the film with elegance and panache, builds lovely catacombs. There is a terrible beauty in each perfectly composed shot, just as there is wit and poetry in William Hurlbut's script.

Of course, it's hard to care a twopenny fig for either Henry or Elizabeth, and I suspect that Whale knew that: from being the tragic focus of the first movie, Henry Frankenstein now becomes the film's Zeppo, a bland lover in a cast of shambling zanies. It's one reason why the film feels so subversive, and so deeply surreal. In *Bride of Frankenstein*, all is prelude to the unwrapping of Elsa Lanchester, the revelation of the true Bride, the one that the movie's really named after. She is revealed; she hisses, screeches, is terrified, is wonderful, and once we have seen her there is nothing left for us. As Karloff's monster realises that she, too, fears him, he slips from joyful hope to despair with a look, and moves over to pull the now traditional blow-up-the-lab switch.

But Elsa and Karloff are the perfect couple, too vivid, too alive to have died in the final explosion. Even as Henry and Elizabeth fade from the imagination, the monster and his mate live on forever, icons of the perverse, in our dreams.

This essay originally appeared in the collection *Cinema Macabre*, edited by Mark Morris, 2005.

MirrorMask: An Introduction

S omewhere in North London, as I type this, Dave McKean is
hard at work on *MirrorMask*. He's sighing and frowning and
working extremely long hours, just as he has for the last eighteen
months, compositing shots and solving problems. Dave designed
and directed and composed every shot in *MirrorMask*. The finished
film has to be delivered at the end of this month. If there's one
thing he doesn't have time for, it's writing introductions.

So this is the story of *MirrorMask* according to me.

It was the summer of 2001. The phone rang. It was Lisa
Henson, and she wanted to know whether I thought Dave McKean
would be interested in making a fantasy film for them – something in a similar vein to *Labyrinth*. Although, she said, *Labyrinth*
had cost the Jim Henson Company about forty million to make
twenty years earlier, and, while the funding for a new film
existed, there wasn't very much of it: only four million dollars,
which is a lot of money if you come across an abandoned suit-
case full of cash in a hollow tree somewhere, but won't get you
very far in the world of fantasy filmmaking. She had seen Dave's
small films and loved them. Did I think that Dave would be
interested? I said I didn't know.

Obviously, said Lisa, she couldn't afford to pay me for writing
a script. Maybe I could help a writer come up with the story
. . . ? I told her that if Dave said yes to directing it, I was writing
the script, and that was all there was to it.

Dave said yes.

I had half an idea, and I wrote it down and sent it to Dave. A girl from a traveling theater, who found herself kidnapped into some kind of fairyland by a fairy queen. An unreliable Puck-like guide. A girl forced to become or to pretend to become a fairy princess, while a real fairy princess was forced to try and pretend to be human.

Meanwhile, Dave had had a dream, and on waking decided it might be the basis for a good film: a mother in the real world who is extremely ill, a world of masks, a girl who had to wake the sleeping white queen, a white queen and a dark queen, a balance that was shifting and breaking. He sent me an e-mail, describing the dream, and his idea for a film, and several other ideas he had had for the feel of what he wanted to convey.

I wondered whether we could combine the two ideas.

In February of 2002, the Jim Henson Company sent me to England for two weeks. To save money, and because we both thought it an excellent idea, Dave and I stayed in the Henson family house in Hampstead. It hadn't been decorated since Jim Henson died, and everywhere we were surrounded by his world. In a cupboard in the lounge we found a video of an early edit of *Labyrinth*, over three hours long with the voices of the puppeteers doing their characters rather than the actors, and we watched it in the evening over a few nights, to help put us into the mood. Dave had a pile of art books with him, books on surrealism and sculpture, books filled with imagery that he thought might come into play in the story.

Dave McKean and I had worked together very happily for about sixteen years at that point. It had always been easy. This wasn't.

Mostly it wasn't, because Dave and I wrote, we discovered, in completely different ways. He plans it all out, and writes every idea down on little cards, needs it to all be done before the first word of script is written; whereas I'll talk about it to the point where I'm ready to start writing, and then I start writing and find out the rest of it as I go along. These methods of working are not entirely compatible. That was half of the problem. The other half of the problem was that Dave knew what he could and couldn't do, in order to make a film with the money that we had, and I didn't.

'I want to do a scene in Helena's school,' I'd say.

'Can't do it,' Dave would explain. 'Too expensive. We'd need the class, and a teacher and kids as extras,' and then, seeing my face fall, he'd add, 'but we can make the world crumple up like a piece of paper, if you want. That won't cost us anything.'

Still, Dave's certainties were reassuring. It's often easier to make art if you know what your boundaries are. In the case of *MirrorMask*, I wrote down in the basement kitchen, where it was warm (right now I'm writing this in the kitchen of a borrowed house, which goes to demonstrate consistency, I think), while Dave mostly worked several floors up, where there was light and a grand piano.

Our touchstone was something Terry Gilliam had once said about his wonderful film *Time Bandits*. He said he wanted to make a film intelligent enough for children, but with enough action in it for adults. And so did we.

I started writing.

Dave would suggest things that would, he hoped, be easy and relatively cheap to make in the world of computer animation – twining shadow-tentacles or formless black bird-shapes.

Several times during that week, Dave would go off and do a first draft of a scene on his own, to show me what he meant, and I'd fold that in – the first drafts of the Giants Orbiting sequence, the Monkeybirds and the scene looking for the dome in the Dreamlands were all Dave's, for example, as was the Librarian's Origin of the World speech, which Dave wrote long before we started writing the film. I'd tidy them up, and noodle with the dialogue. He for his part would look over my shoulder at the dialogue I was writing on the screen and point out whenever I was starting to sound like Terry Jones writing *Labyrinth,* and then I would try to make it sound a bit more like me writing *MirrorMask.*

Henson's had mentioned they thought there should be goblins in it somewhere, owing to their having already sold the film we were making to Sony under the working title of 'Curse of the Goblin Kingdom', so every now and again I would insert the word *goblin* in front of a character's name – 'Goblin Librarian' for example, while the character who doesn't have much of a name in the current script apart from 'Small Hairy' was called 'Dark Goblin' in that first draft. Dave took a jaundiced view of this practice. 'They'll want to see goblins,' he'd warn me. 'And there won't be any goblins. It'll lead to trouble.' I thought we'd probably be all right.

Neither of us was sure whether or not we were really making a film until the day Terry Gilliam came round to the house for a cup of tea. He looked at the sheet of paper we had covered with lines and scribbles to tell ourselves the shape of the film. *'That,'* he said, 'looks like a movie.'

Ah, we thought. Maybe it did, at that.

The unreliable juggler character was called 'Puck' in the first draft, and we knew we needed a better name for him. It was the second week in February, and we were surrounded by posters and signs telling us it was nearly Valentine's Day, so we called him Valentine. It was a slightly more flamboyant name, and he suddenly seemed, to both of us, a slightly more flamboyant character.

We sent the script off to Henson's, and we waited, nervously. They had comments, of course, extremely sensible ones – they wanted more ending and more beginning.

Dave sent us pictures of characters and moods and places, to try to show the kind of things that he meant: how the White City would feel, what Valentine would be like, all that.

The strange thing about looking at those pictures now, for me, is that they make complete sense. I can see exactly what Dave meant and why he sent them. At the time they came in I looked at them and wondered how they could possibly relate to the script we'd written.

Dave knew, though. Dave always knows.

Now, my theory about films is that it's probably safer to assume that they won't happen. That way, when, as you expected, they don't happen, you won't find yourself with six months' free time you have to fill. So while we did another draft of the script, and while Dave sat down and carefully storyboarded the entire film (the same storyboards you'll see in this book), and while Henson's seemed quite certain that it really was going to happen, it seemed easier to assume that at some point someone would wake up and see reason, and that it would never happen. Nobody ever saw reason.

What you're waiting for, in the world of filmmaking, is a 'Green Light'. It's like traffic lights – the Green Light means it's a go. Everything's happening. You're making your film.

'Do we have a Green Light on *MirrorMask*?' I'd ask. Nobody ever seemed quite sure.

And then it was May 2003, and I was in Paris, at the end of a European signing tour. Dave phoned and said, 'We're having a read-through of *MirrorMask*.' I got on the train to London and found myself sitting in a small room at Henson's London offices, where a bunch of actors sat around a table, and read. I was introduced to Gina McKee and Stephanie Leonidas. Brian Henson read many of the small odd creatures (I was particularly impressed with his reading of the Chicken). I scribbled on the script some more, cutting bits, adding lines and feeling pleased whenever something that I'd hoped was a joke actually got a laugh from the people around the table.

After the reading Dave and I asked Lisa Henson if we actually, finally, honestly and truly had a Green Light for the film. She tried to explain that this film wouldn't work like that, and no we didn't, but it would happen, so not to worry. We worried anyway.

And then, more or less to our surprise, Dave started shooting.

I wasn't there for most of it. I thought it wouldn't happen, and, by the time I realized it was actually happening, could only be there for a week.

A film crew is quickly bonded, through adversity and madness, into something between a family and a team of soldiers in a foxhole under fire. There's never enough time before the light goes, never enough time to retake that last shot, never enough money to throw at the problems and make them go away, the trumpet player in the circus band still hasn't arrived and tomorrow's shots in the hospital won't be what Dave's planning because the fish tank he's planning to shoot through will leak, and then the tiger barb fish will start eating the neon tetras . . .

Because I wasn't there, I will never understand why the cast and crew T-shirts that Dave made have 'Smell my lime' on them. Dave's explained it to me, but I think you really had to be there.

They shot the film in six weeks – two weeks on location, the rest of the time in front of a blue screen. They finished in July 2003. And then Dave started making the film. When he began there were fifteen animators, and Max. Now, fifteen months later, there's just Dave and Max.

I'm writing this in October 2004, and Dave says he's nearly finished, and I believe him. I've seen most of the film cut together, and am continually delighted by how far it is from what I'd imagined it was going to be, just as I'm delighted when actors who performed in front of a blue screen suddenly get to see what they were really doing all along.

I've now had eighteen years of being astonished by Dave, and you'd think I'd be used to it by now, but I'm not. I don't think I ever will be.

This was the introduction to *MirrorMask: The Illustrated Film Script of the Motion Picture*, and was written in 2004.

MirrorMask: A Sundance Diary

I 've never been to Sundance before, and I certainly didn't expect to be at Sundance with *MirrorMask*, but here I am anyway. It's not that *MirrorMask* isn't a good film, or even that it's not an independent film – it was made by hand by artist-director Dave McKean with a tiny amount of money and a handful of art-school graduates – but it's a film for kids of all ages (I'd call it a family film if that wasn't some kind of code that tells you it's not actually for families, just like adult film doesn't mean a film for adults). But we have distribution, through Sony, even if they don't seem quite clear what it is, or who would want to see it. Still, the Jim Henson Company submitted the film to Sundance, and Sundance accepted it. So we're here.

I get in on the Friday evening. My friend producer-director Matthew Vaughn is having a party on Main Street for his film *Layer Cake,* and I head down to Main Street. The street is a mad crush, thronged with people celebrity spotting, which makes me feel sort of useless, mostly because even if I was issued with a Handy Guide to Celebrities and a pair of binoculars, I'd still be celebrity-blind. It seems like there's a party behind every door – I get into three lines before I wind up in the *Layer Cake* party. I find myself part of a tiny entourage, and soon Matthew and I and a few managers and assistants are the only people in the VIP area of a party bar. 'What's this party for?' asks Matthew of a publicist, but nobody seems to know. His film premiered that afternoon. It's a party. I'm introduced to studio VIPs.

I decide that if this is Sundance, I don't like it.

I meet my director the following day on Main Street. I'm a bit worried. A few days before leaving, Dave showed the completed film to the cast and crew, and is now convinced that it's the worst film that anyone has ever made. If he had the money, he'd buy the film back, bury it and make a different film. One that he was happier with. Still, he seems pleased to see me. We're about to chat when a video crew calls my name, and in moments I find I'm being interviewed on the street about *MirrorMask*.

Sunday begins with a brunch from Adobe (I don't know why) and then a choice: I can go and see The Dresden Dolls play at the Music Café, or offer moral support to Dave McKean and *MirrorMask* producer Lisa Henson, on a panel on animation. They all tell me to go and see The Dresden Dolls, but duty (and a desire to see our trailer on a big screen) wins out. All the people on the panel except for us are from Big Movies – *The Lord of the Rings, A Series of Unfortunate Events, Shrek 2, The Polar Express* and so on, and I'm not quite sure how this relates to Sundance until Yair Landau from Sony points out that the software that makes hundred-million-dollar movies is the software that, a couple of years later, will be making low-budget movies, and I reflect that that's certainly true in our case.

People in red with clipboards stop me every few feet on Main Street, ask what movies I've seen that I liked. They are finding out what has *buzz*.

That evening we go and see the premiere of *The Jacket*. A man immediately behind us, narrating the events of the day into his cell phone, helpfully starts telling the friend what he can see: 'There's Adrien Brody . . . nice suit . . . and I can see Keira Knightley . . .' This is very useful, and makes me wish we'd brought some of our stars over with us. It's all very glam, and

The Jacket is a very slick film, with proper stars and a *Twilight Zone* plot.

I really don't like Sundance. And then it's midnight and Dave and Lisa Henson and I are standing in a chilly alley, waiting to get in to see David Slade's *Hard Candy,* and I notice that none of the people in the line are even slightly glamorous. The glamorous people are at parties. These are the festival rats, shivering at midnight to see a new movie. It helps that the film is sharp and small, essentially a grim and grueling two-hander. I start to realize that there are more Sundances than I had previously noticed.

Our film doesn't premiere until the end of the festival, but our first screening is in Salt Lake City for an audience of high school kids. We arrive for the last twenty minutes. Dave McKean is too worried to go in, but I do. I'm watching the magical imagery of *MirrorMask* on a big screen. Up until now I've only seen it in various stages of completion tiny on my laptop screen. This is something else.

The audience claps. The lights come up. A fifteen-year-old girl near me turns to her friend and says, 'That was soooo amaaaaaaaaazing,' and I breathe out. It's like I've been holding my breath for eighteen months. Our first review. Dave and I answer questions, then we sign things for the teens. One girl gets us to sign her arms: she has no idea who we are, but we made that film and it made her happy.

Dave appears to be cheering up.

We go and see a film that looked good from the Sundance program, and it's mediocre in most of the ways a film can be – poorly acted, badly shot and the plot again has been lifted from an old *Twilight Zone* episode. Oddly, this also cheers us up. Our film may not be perfect, but it was better than that. No teenage girls are asking the director to sign their limbs.

The interviews start. Some in person, some over the phone. Nobody's seen the film yet. We could tell them anything. I see

– and, to my surprise, love – *Kung Fu Hustle*. It's like a gift from Sundance. Utterly fun, and nothing Rod Serling would have found in any way familiar.

Wednesday morning, we go and see my friend Penn Jillette's film *The Aristocrats,* directed by Paul Provenza. I'm prepared to be polite about it, in the way you have to be when you know it's a film by a friend about a hundred comedians discussing one, not very funny, dirty joke. Instead Dave and I find ourselves transfixed and delighted. It's an incredibly funny, filthy and peculiarly cathartic film about art and why we make it. We tell the filmmakers how much we liked their film, and they tell us they want to come and see *MirrorMask*. We tell them that they probably don't want to, and that it doesn't have any swearing in it, but they insist. Penn has altitude sickness ('Pretty f——g ironic for a guy who's six foot seven,' says Paul Provenza) and will be going home early.

Wednesday afternoon we get the *Hollywood Reporter* review of *MirrorMask*. *'If "The Wizard of Oz' were reborn in the 21st century, it might look a lot like "MirrorMask,"* it begins, and after describing the film as *'endlessly inventive with creativity to burn'* continues in similar vein for several enthusiastic columns. That afternoon a reporter asks Dave if it was worth the eighteen months of toil and sweat, and he blinks and says, 'Well, up until now I didn't think it was. But yes, it was.'

We show *MirrorMask* to another enthusiastic audience of high school kids; to a couple of audiences of paying customers in Salt Lake City. I find myself getting into each screening, caring for nothing except the audience reactions: why does one audience laugh at one line and not at another? It's the same film each time, isn't it?

I go to a selection of short films. There are some duds, but the best of them, Brett Simon's *The Sailor's Girl,* is as good as anything I can remember. Everyone left takes the shuttle buses. I'm turning into a festival rat.

Back on Main Street, the festival's still going but the crowds have gone. All the frenzied buying has been done, the celebrity swag has been looted. Our film officially premieres on Friday. I stop and talk to a couple of the buzz-people in red with clipboards, and they tell me they leave on Thursday. Our film can then, by definition, not have buzz. I don't really mind. We got the *Hollywood Reporter*. We show *MirrorMask* to a packed premiere house and I have no idea whether anyone's enjoying it or not. The audience is almost too respectful. I wish we'd been able to bring some of our cast in, particularly Stephanie Leonidas, our star. I wish the sound had been remixed for simple stereo and not crushed down from Dolby 5.1, burying several lines of dialogue. I wish that there were more kids in the audience. The questions are limp ('Did you make this film under hallucinogenics?') and I find myself missing the high school audiences.

Afterwards, I drag my son to a sold-out midnight screening of *The Aristocrats,* on the basis that it's the sort of film you ought to take your son to, then Dave McKean and I give up our seats so that Steve Buscemi can get in. We don't mind. We go to the bar next door and start to discuss what our next film will be like.

The festival rats and the real people and the filmmakers are the only ones left at the tail end of Sundance.

Saturday afternoon's the final *MirrorMask* screening. There are people in the wait list line for five hours. Some of them were at the premiere the night before. Some were also at the Salt Lake City showings. This audience seems to love it, laughing at the jokes, cheering and clapping. The questions they ask at the end are appreciative and smart.

If this is Sundance, I think, as it ends, *I could get to like it.*

This was first published in 2005 in *Look Magazine*.

The Nature of the Infection: Some Thoughts on *Doctor Who*

I wrote this a few years before the brilliant Russell T. Davies and his cohorts brought the Doctor back onto our screens and into our lives.

T he years pass, and the arguments go back and forth over whether watched fiction actually has an effect on the reader or the viewer. Does violent fiction make a reader violent? Does frightening fiction create a watcher who is frightened, or desensitised to fear?

It's not a yes, or a no. It's a *yes but.*

The complaint about *Doctor Who* from adults was always, when I was small, that it was too frightening. This missed, I think, the much more dangerous effect of *Doctor Who:* that it was viral.

Of course it was frightening. More or less. I watched the good bits from behind the sofa, and was always angry and cheated and creeped out by the cliffhanger in the final moments. But that had, as far as I can tell, no effect on me at all, as I grew, the fear. The real complaint, the thing that the adults should have been afraid of and complaining about, was what it did to the inside of my head. How it painted my interior landscape. When I was three, making Daleks out of the little school milk bottles, with the rest of the kids at Mrs Pepper's Nursery School, I was in trouble and I didn't know it. The virus was already at work.

Yes, I was scared of the Daleks and the Zarbi and the rest. But I was taking other, stranger, more important lessons away from my Saturday tea-time serial.

For a start, I had become infected by the idea that there are an infinite number of worlds, only a footstep away. And another part of the meme was this: some things are bigger on the inside than they are on the outside. And, perhaps, some people are bigger on the inside than they are on the outside, as well.

And that was only the start of it. The books helped with the infection – the *Dalek World* one, and the various hardcovered *Doctor Who* annuals. They contained the first written SF stories I had encountered. They left me wondering if there was anything else like that out there . . .

But the greatest damage was still to come.

It's this: the shape of reality – the way I perceive the world – exists only because of *Doctor Who*. Specifically, from *The War Games* in 1969, the multipart series that was to be Patrick Troughton's swan song.

This is what remains to me of *The War Games* as I look back on it, over three decades after I saw it: the Doctor and his assistants find themselves in a place where armies fight: an interminable World War One battlefield, in which armies from the whole of time have been stolen from their original spatio-temporal location and made to fight each other. Strange mists divide the armies and the time zones. Travel between the time zones is possible, using a boxlike structure approximately the same size and shape as a smallish lift, or, even more prosaically, a public toilet: you get in in 1970, you come out in Troy or Mons or Waterloo. Only you don't come out in Waterloo, as you're really on an eternal plane, and behind it all or beyond it all is an evil genius who has taken the armies, placed them here, and is using the boxes to move guards and agents from place to place, through the mists of time.

The boxes were called SIDRATs. Even at the age of eight I figured that one out.

Finally, having no other option, and unable to resolve the story in any other way, the Doctor – who we learned now was a fugitive – summoned the Time Lords, his people, to sort the whole thing out. And was, himself, captured and punished.

It was a great ending for an eight-year old. There were ironies I relished. It would, I have no doubt at all, be a bad thing for me to try and go back and watch *The War Games* now. It's too late anyway; the damage has been done. It redefined reality. The virus was now solidly in place.

These days, as a middle-aged and respectable author, I still feel a sense of indeterminate but infinite possibility on entering a lift, particularly a small one with blank walls. That to date the doors that have opened have always done so in the same time, and world, and even the same building in which I started out seems merely fortuitous – evidence only of a lack of imagination on the part of the rest of the universe.

I do not confuse what has not happened with what cannot happen, and in my heart, Time and Space are endlessly malleable, permeable, frangible.

Let me make some more admissions.

In my head, William Hartnell was the Doctor, and so was Patrick Troughton. All the other Doctors were actors, although Jon Pertwee and Tom Baker were actors playing real Doctors. The rest of them, even Peter Cushing, were faking it.

In my head the Time Lords exist, and are unknowable – primal forces who cannot be named, only described: the Master, the Doctor and so on. All depictions of the home of the Time Lords are, in my head, utterly non-canonical. The place in which they exist cannot be depicted because it is beyond imagining: a cold place that only exists in black and white.

It's probably a good thing that I've never actually got my hands on the Doctor. I would have unhappened so much.

A final *Doctor Who* connection – again, from the baggy-trousered Troughton era, when some things were more than true for me – showed itself, in retrospect, in my BBC TV series, *Neverwhere*.

Not in the obvious places – the BBC decision that *Neverwhere* had to be shot on video, in episodes half an hour long, for example. Not even in the character of the Marquis de Carabas, whom I wrote – and Paterson Joseph performed – as if I were creating a Doctor from scratch, and wanted to make him someone as mysterious, as unreliable and as quirky as the William Hartnell incarnation. But in the idea that there are worlds under this one, and that London itself is magical, and dangerous, and that the underground tunnels are every bit as remote and mysterious and likely to contain Yeti as the distant Himalayas was something, author and critic Kim Newman pointed out to me, while *Neverwhere* was screening, that I probably took from a Troughton-era story called 'The Web of Fear'. And as he said it, I knew he was spot-on, remembering people with torches exploring the underground, beams breaking the darkness. The knowledge that there were worlds underneath . . . yes, that was where I got it, all right. Having caught the virus, I was now, I realised with horror, infecting others.

Which is, perhaps, one of the glories of *Doctor Who*. It doesn't die, no matter what. It's still serious, and it's still dangerous. The virus is out there, just hidden, and buried, like a plague pit.

You don't have to believe me. Not now. But I'll tell you this. The next time you get into a lift, in a shabby office building, and jerk up several floors, then, in that moment before the doors open, you'll wonder, even if only for a moment, if they're going to open on a Jurassic jungle, or the moons of Pluto, or a full-service pleasure dome at the galactic core . . .

That's when you'll discover that you're infected too.

And then the doors will open, with a grinding noise like a universe in pain, and you'll squint at the light of distant suns, and understand . . .

Taken from the introduction to Paul McCauley's 2003 Doctor Who novella, *Eye of the Tyger,* back when prose was pretty much the only way to get your *Doctor Who* fix.

On Comics and Films: 2006

I can still remember how excited everyone was, seventeen years ago, by the arrival of the *Batman* film. Frank Miller's story of an ageing Batman coming out of retirement, *The Dark Knight Returns*, had, along with Alan Moore and Dave Gibbons's *Watchmen* and Art Spiegelman's *Maus*, spearheaded the first, abortive, graphic novel explosion, and I believed that a good, serious Batman film was all that was needed to put it over the top, legitimise comics and change the world. Two decades later, we live in a world in which comics have spawned a generation of summer blockbusters. This summer it's a Marvel v. DC face-off, X-Men v. Superman, with Spider-Man waiting in the wings for 2007.

Comics and movies have always been a two-way street. Will Eisner's seminal *The Spirit*, back in the 1940s, took from Orson Welles and the films noirs as much as it borrowed from radio or Broadway, and there have been movies made from comics pretty much as long as either medium has existed. Last week an interviewer asked me whether I thought that the recent success of superhero movies meant that we might see a world in which comics that don't include the capes-and-tights brigade might also have a chance at making it onto the silver screen. 'You mean comics like *Road to Perdition, Ghost World, Men in Black, A History of Violence, Sin City, From Hell, American Splendor* . . . ?'

I started to suspect that there might be a cultural sea change occurring a few years ago, when *The League of Extraordinary Gentlemen* was released. It was not the first time that a bad film had been made from a good comic, not by a long shot, but it was the first time that the world at large seemed aware of this. Review after review pointed out that the film had none of the wit or brilliance, or even coherence, of the comic it was taken from.

Like many of my coworkers in the world of comics, I'm also involved in making films these days. This is seen, I realise from talking to acquaintances and journalists, as a step up, signalling that I've finally left the gutter. (Still, filmic legitimacy only goes so far. Opera seems to be the cultural front-runner, while books, with or without pictures, trail some way behind.) I like film. I am not very good at writing for film yet, which is what keeps me interested in it. Most of all I like the astonishing process – it's hard to get near a film set without remembering Orson Welles's description of a film studio as 'the biggest electric train set any boy could ever have'. When I first went to Hollywood, the only people who read comics were the most junior assistants, the kind who weren't allowed to speak, who just went and fetched the bottled water. But that was a while ago. Now those people are running studios.

There was a time when those of us who made comics would try and explain what advantages comics had over film. 'Comics have an infinite special-effects budget,' we'd say. But we missed the point, now that movies have, for all intents, an infinite special-effects budget. (I was writing a script for *Beowulf* last year, and, worried that a climactic airborne dragon battle was going a little over the top, I called the director, Robert Zemeckis, to warn him. 'Don't worry,' he said. 'There is nothing you could write that will cost me more than a million dollars a minute to film.')

Still, the 'unlimited special effects' nonsense hides a truth or two. Ink is cheaper than film. Film, especially big-budget film, often needs to compromise in order to be liked by the biggest possible number of people around the world. A comic tends to be a small enough, personal enough, medium that a creator can just make art, tell stories and see if anyone wants to read them. Not having to be liked is enormously liberating. The comic is, joyfully, a bastard medium that has borrowed its vocabulary and ideas from literature, science fiction, poetry, fine art, diaries, film and illustration. It would be nice to think that comics, and those of us who come from a comics background, bring something special to film. An insouciance, perhaps, or a willingness to do our learning and experimenting in public.

That was certainly how it was making *MirrorMask*, a film I wrote and which artist and director Dave McKean designed and directed recently for the Jim Henson Company. As long as we gave Sony something 'in the tradition of *Labyrinth*', Dave could make his film (it's my script, but in service of Dave's story and vision). It didn't have an unlimited special-effects budget, or any kind of unlimited budget at all, but Dave still managed to put things on-screen that hadn't been seen before – huge stone giants floating in the sky, a librarian made of books and voiced by Stephen Fry, a horde of Monkeybirds all called Bob (except for one, called Malcolm). We made *MirrorMask* on location in Brighton, and in a blue screen studio in London, then Dave took fifteen animators to an office in North London and worked for eighteen months telling the story of Helena and her peculiar dream.

Whether you're making comics or film, much of what you're doing is done for dollars and for US-based multinational corporations who sell back what you've done to the UK and to the world. *MirrorMask* was a very English film, albeit made with money from Sony. Alan Moore, tired of bad films made from good comics he had written, and of the accompanying Hollywood-associated irritants (including a legal suit over *The League of Extraordinary Gentlemen*), recently removed his name from the upcoming adaptation of his graphic novel *V for Vendetta*, disassociated himself from his previous films and, in the kind of definitive grand gesture that indicates that you really mean business, also declined his share of the money that came with them.

Even knowing that Alan's renounced it, I want to see *V for Vendetta*. *V* and I go back almost twenty-five years, to the first time I picked up a copy of *Warrior* magazine and saw those wonderful black-and-white David Lloyd-drawn people staring hopelessly back at me. (I find it hard enough to adjust to a world in which the *V* graphic novel is coloured; a colour *V for Vendetta* seems as pointless as colourising *Citizen Kane*.) Moore's story of one lone anarchist up against a fascist British state – in a world poised halfway between Tony Blair's dream and Eric Blair's warning – meant something important to me and to a handful of other comics readers, when it was first published, and the film trailer, composed primarily of images taken from *Warrior* covers, hooks into that.

Alan Moore himself is resigned, amused and wryly bitter about the process of turning comics into film. 'Comics are one step in the digestive process of Hollywood eating itself,' he told me. 'Are there any films made from the comics that are better than the original comics? Hollywood needs material to make into films as part of an economic process. It could be a Broadway play or a book, or a French film, or a good TV series from the 1960s that people want to see on the big screen, or a bad TV series from the 1960s that nobody cares about but still has a name, or a computer game or a theme park ride. I expect that the next subject of films will be breakfast-cereal mascots – a film that chronicles how Snap, Crackle and Pop met and explores their relationship. Or the Tony the Tiger movie.

'Films are no friend to comics,' he concluded. 'I think they actually impoverish the comic landscape. Turning it into a sort of pumpkin patch for movie studios to come picking.'

At my most cynical I also wonder whether the world of comics might simply become a cheap R & D lab for Hollywood. The San Diego comics convention, once a summer gathering of a few thousand comics readers and creators, has in recent years become a Sundance-style event with over one hundred thousand people in attendance and where the year's major SF, fantasy and horror movies are announced and previewed. I confess that I am always relieved when another year passes without anybody making a bad film based on *Sandman,* the comic on which most of my reputation within the medium rests.

But I remain optimistic. While Frank Miller's film of *Sin City* isn't as powerful as his comics, it was still his vision up there on the screen in the film he made with Robert Rodriguez, uncompromised by the change from one medium to another. *MirrorMask* is Dave McKean's film from first frame to last, visually and musically. Nearly twenty years after the first Batman film, I realise that film doesn't confer legitimacy on comics. But it's still an awful lot of fun.

This was originally published in the 3 March 2006 issue of the *Guardian*.

V

ON COMICS AND SOME OF THE
PEOPLE WHO MAKE THEM

'This is the magic trick upon which all good fiction depends: it's the angled mirror in the box behind which the doves are hidden, the hidden compartment beneath the table.'

Good Comics and Tulips: A Speech

I gave this speech at the Diamond Comics tenth annual retail seminar. It was April 1993, and the world of comics was at the height of an unprecedented commercial boom.

I want to talk about comics. I want to talk about good comics, and why you should do what you can to sell more of them. But first I want to talk about tulips.

I'm often asked – via letters to the editor and at signings – to suggest interesting books to the world, or assemble a reading list.

Well, one of my favorite old books is a remarkable volume called *Extraordinary Popular Delusions and the Madness of Crowds,* written almost a hundred and fifty years ago by a gentleman named Charles Mackay.

In it he details many of the pursuits, wise and otherwise, to which people have devoted their lives: he devotes chapters to such diverse subjects as, for example, alchemists, haunted houses, the slow poisoners, the great Louisiana land swindle and the popular street cries of Victorian London.

It's a book with a huge cast of characters within its pages that includes, for example, Matthew Hopkins, the self-proclaimed Witchfinder General, who wandered around England in the early 1640s, finding witches. He charged each village twenty shillings for the privilege of having him turn up and make them all feel uncomfortable, and another twenty shillings a head for each witch discovered and disposed of, and was turning a merry profit, finding witches and sending them to meet their maker, until one day he went to find witches in a little village in Suffolk, the elders of which, who were nobody's fools, pointed out to him that no man could find as many witches as he had unless he was getting his infernally accurate information straight from Beelzebub, and before Hopkins could come up with an adequate response for this, he was put to the test, and was a former Witchfinder General.

The moral of which, I suppose, is that it can be unwise to start witch hunts, and also . . .

But I didn't come here to tell you about witches, who after all have little enough to do with the vitally important business in front of us, which is that of comics and the retailing thereof.

No. As I said, I want to talk to you about something far more germane to the world we all share of the four-color funnies.

Tulips.

Picture the scene: seventeenth-century Holland. Imagine the screen going all wavy at this point, and a hasty montage of wooden clogs, windmills, dykes with fingers in them, and red-wax-wrapped cheeses that taste more or less like yellow rubber.

However, one thing is missing: tulips.

The first tulips in Western Europe arrived from the east in the late sixteenth century, and became very popular in Holland.

In 1634 the rage among the Dutch to possess them was so great that the ordinary industry of the country was neglected, and the population, even to the lowest dregs, embarked on the tulip trade. As the mania increased, prices augmented, until, in the year 1635 . . . it became necessary to sell them by their weight in perits, a small weight less than a grain.

One tulip bulb sold for twelve acres of prime building land in Haarlem. Another sold for 4,600 florins – about $10,000 in modern money – plus a new carriage, two gray horses and a complete set of harnesses for the horses.

A wealthy merchant once received a sailor, who came with news, and was rewarded with a gift of a smoked herring for his breakfast.

The sailor, who knew nothing of tulips, also took with him something he thought to be an onion, which, when he returned to his ship, he sliced and ate.

He had eaten a 3,000-florin tulip bulb, and spent some time in prison.

By 1636 there were tulip exchanges in every major town in Holland. These functioned as stock exchanges.

You had . . . but I'll quote from Mackay's book:

The tulip-jobbers speculated in the rise and fall of the tulip stocks, and made large profits by buying when prices fell, and selling out when they rose. Many individuals grew suddenly rich. A golden bait hung temptingly out before the people, and one after the other, they rushed to the tulip-marts, like flies around a honey-pot. Every one imagined that the passion for tulips would last for ever, and that the wealthy from every part of the world would send to Holland, and pay whatever prices were asked for them. The riches of Europe would be concentrated on the shores of the Zuyder Zee, and poverty banished from the favoured clime of Holland. Nobles, citizens, farmers, mechanics, sea-men, footmen, maid-servants, even chimney-sweeps and old clothes-women, dabbled in tulips. People of all grades converted their property into cash, and invested it in flowers. Houses and lands were offered for sale at ruinously low prices . . .

You had an entire country here, obsessed with getting rich, and convinced that it was impossible that tulips could ever be less than the ultimate, perfect investment object.

After all, when the rest of the world caught up with the Dutch, they'd have all the tulips and would be even richer than they were already.

And instead the rest of the world stared blankly at the Dutch for fussing foolishly after something that was, after all, only a tulip.

The entire economy of the country of Holland was destroyed. I wish I was exaggerating, but I'm not. There was a madness and a foolishness here that seems pretty apparent to an outside observer.

I am reminded of the time the South Sea Company infected all England with the joy of investing.

At the height of the craze, the so-called South Sea Bubble, share certificates traded hands down a London alley, going up in value as they went, until, one day . . . well, people were wiped out. Fortunes were lost, and a lot of people were made very miserable.

At least the Dutch could eat the tulip bulbs.

And if you think this has nothing to do with you, well, it does. Too many comic stores are trading in bubbles and tulips. I'm not here to play Cassandra. I don't have the figure or the legs. I merely point this out.

Personally I think any comic shop that sells multiple copies of the same comic to any child under, say, sixteen, because that child has somehow been given the impression that he or she has just been handed a license to print money, should, if nothing else, get the child to read a form explaining that comic values can go down as well as up, and require it to be signed by a parent or guardian.

I think any organization or store that pushes comics as investment items is at best shortsighted and foolish, and at worst, immoral and dumb.

You can sell lots of comics to the same person, especially if you tell them that they are investing money for high guaranteed returns.

But you're selling bubbles and tulips, and one day the bubble will burst, and the tulips will rot in the warehouses.

Which is why I want to talk about good comics.

I have a vested interest here: I write, or try to write, good comics. I don't write collectibles, nor do I write investment items. I write stories, the best I can: I write stories for people to read.

But before I wrote comics I was a journalist. Like writing comics, journalism is another profession that doesn't involve getting up in the morning. And I used to write, whenever people would let me, about comics.

A little digression, here: back in 1986 I was commissioned by the *Sunday Times Magazine*, in England, to do a feature article on comics. I interviewed a number of people for it – Alan Moore, Frank Miller, Dave Sim, Brian Bolland and many others. I worked incredibly hard on it – this was going to be the first major national article promoting comics as a medium in England.

I sent the article in to the gentleman who had commissioned it, and heard . . . nothing. Not a sausage.

So, after a couple of weeks, I rang him up. He sounded oddly subdued. 'How's the article?' I asked. He told me that he had a problem or two with it. I suggested that he tell me what the problem was. I could rewrite it, get it better.

'Well,' he said, 'it lacks balance.'

'In what way?'

'These comics.' He paused, then spat it out. 'You seem to think they're a *good* thing.'

He'd been hoping for something that Fredric Wertham would have been proud of, and that wasn't what he got.

Well, we agreed that I had no plans to rewrite it in order to give it the balance he felt it lacked, and he sent me a kill-fee for the article that was twice what I got for getting articles printed anywhere else. And I would rather have had the article printed. Because I *do* believe comics are a good thing.

If I didn't, I'd still be a journalist, or I'd be writing unproduced screenplays for mind-boggling sums in Hollywood, or growing tulips.

We're living in what the Chinese curse described as interesting times, and I like that.

The landscape is changing, erupting, exploding. New lines and titles and universes appear and vanish, some comics are selling in numbers undreamed-of in 1986, stores spring up like mushrooms after a heavy rain.

It's hard to tell what things will be like in five years' time. But I'll tell you this: stores that sell and push good comics will still be around. Because people who read will still be with us, and they'll still want comics.

Another flashback: Philadelphia, 1990, and I'm attending a small American convention. It was followed by a meeting of the CBRI, Comic Book Retailers International, and I was asked to stay on and be on a panel discussion.

The panel discussion consisted of marketing reps from all the major publishers of the time, someone from Diamond, someone from Capital, and, right down at the end, more than a little bemused, was me.

So first of all everyone talked about bar codes on comics, and I learned more than any human being would ever wish to know about bar-coding comics. And then they talked about other things, racking, and pricing and bar codes again – and I began to wonder just what I was doing there.

Steve Gursky, who was presiding over the shebang, might have thought the same thing. 'We have a creator here, remember,' he told the assembled retailers. 'Does anybody want to ask the creator anything?'

There was no sea of hands, no forest of waving arms. Just some puzzled faces. Eventually someone took pity on me, and asked a question.

'As a creator,' he asked, 'what's the difference between creating high-ticket items and low-ticket items?'

I suppose he wanted to be reassured that I was putting that extra three or four dollars' worth of verbs and adjectives into the high-ticket items. I don't know.

'There's no difference,' I said. 'What I try to do is write good comics.' There was a silence and, made bold by this, I added, 'And I wish that you people would do more to push good comics.'

Three hundred retailing eyes looked very puzzled indeed. Many of these are retailers who've since come up to me and told me proudly of the efforts they've made since then in that direction, and the success they've had.

Someone wisely asked me what I meant by the good stuff, and I told them, and someone else asked me what I meant by pushing it, and I told them as I will tell you.

What I mean by the good stuff is the comics you enjoy.

If you yourself have stopped reading comics, and sad to say, many retailers have – there's too much out there, or one day they found they no longer enjoyed *West Coast Avengers* and gave up on the whole field, disillusioned – then browse around. Ask friends, ask your staff, ask your customers.

But most of you have comics you like. And you should be pushing them.

How?

It doesn't involve much – for example, you can put a rack near the door of things you're proud of selling.

You can order just a few more copies of things you think are really good and try and sell them.

You could offer a money-back guarantee to anyone buying something you have faith in. It's not a hard thing to do.

Pick a comic of the week and push it.

Suggest to the customers who don't read what they buy that maybe they should read these things instead of just bagging them.

Try to familiarize yourself with what's out there, and let your tastes influence your customers.

If your customers are mostly adolescent boys who go away when they tire of childish things, well, make sure they know that there's life after Spider-Man. Put a little effort in and you have a customer for life.

This is a good thing.

We are living in a remarkable time for comics: there is more exciting material available now than ever before. I mean it: there's more excellent material currently in print and available, going all the way back to *Little Nemo*, than at any time.

This is also a good thing.

Do I want any of you to make less money? Of course not.

I want you all to have Jacuzzis in your Cadillacs, more stores than you can shake a stick at – or indeed, more sticks than you can shake a store at, if that's your idea of fun.

While we're at it, I'd like you to be happy, healthy and never again bothered by telephone salespeople. May your luggage always be first on the airport carousel, and may your pets never spontaneously combust. All these things I wish you.

But remember what it is that you're selling people.

When I go on tour I like to ask people how they started reading my stuff.

Mostly it's word of mouth. Friends tell friends. Friends force friends to sit and read it. And, in a lot of cases, store assistants tell customers they'd like it. Sometimes it's sexually transmitted.

In stores where the salespeople like *Sandman*, and push it

hard, we equal or outsell whatever's 'hot'. And the people who read *Sandman* buy a copy and lend it around. We get readers, and we get new readers.

And the new readers go back to the comic store and buy all the trade paperbacks, to catch up on the story so far, and then they buy an extra copy to give to their friends . . .

I have no desire to enforce my tastes on any of you. If I ran a comic store I'd be pushing *Bone* and *Cerebus* and *Love and Rockets*, *Sandman Mystery Theatre* and *Animal Man*, *Madman* and *Cages*, *Yummy Fur* and *Peepshow*, *Gregory* and *Groo* – to pick a very few examples from the stuff I happen to like.

I'm not telling you to push those titles, although I wouldn't mind if you did.

I want you to push the stuff you think is good. Push good children's comics to children, and good superhero comics to people who like them, and good grown-up comics to adults.

I'm really just asking you to think of comics as a reading material. Think of comics as an entertainment. Think of comics as stories.

You aren't selling investment items. You're selling dreams.

Never forget that.

Comics are for reading and enjoying, like tulips are for planting and blossoming and appreciating.

And the next time someone tells you about comics as the hot investment item of the nineties, do me a favor, and tell them about the tulips.

A speech I gave at Diamond Comic Distributors' tenth annual retailers seminar in April 1993. Delivered to a room filled with comics retailers at the statistical height of the bubble. It was barely applauded by a room filled with otherwise happy people, and I heard later that a lot of the retailers thought it was in bad taste. Which was a pity, because a year later the world of comics entered a recession it took almost a decade to get out of, and most of those people lost their livelihoods and their stores over the next few years. It gave me no pleasure to be right.

A Speech to Professionals Contemplating Alternative Employment, Given at ProCon, April 1997

T o begin with, a confession. I hate writing speeches. When I was asked to give this one, my immediate thought was that maybe I could give a speech I'd already written, and no one would notice. Unfortunately I've only ever written one speech before, which I gave in the spring of 1993, and which compared the 'investors boom' then going on with the seventeenth century Dutch tulip craze and warned an audience of assembled retailers that if this kept on there was going to be trouble. And while events unfortunately proved me right, I really didn't think that I'd get away with repeating that speech today.

When I was originally asked to come here and deliver the keynote address, I declined. I said I'd feel embarrassed and out of place. Right now – for the last fifteen months, in fact, since I finished writing *Sandman* – with the exception of a couple of short stories, I've stopped writing comics.

I told the person who phoned me that I'd feel like the kind of girl who dropped out of high school under dubious circumstances and was now returning, in a pink Cadillac, with big blond hair and far too much makeup, to give a graduating speech on the value of sticking to it and hard work.

The person on the phone – it was Larry Marder – said, 'Well, these are weird times. A lot of comics pros are looking at the world outside comics and wondering if that's where they'll be making their living in a year or so. You could at least tell them what's waiting for them out there.'

And I thought, *Well, he's got a point.*

And, after I put down the phone, I thought, *Well, it's also the prerogative of the elderly and the retired to share their knowledge, to drive from the backseat and to offer unsolicited advice.* 'And,' as a poet put it, 'being good for nothing else, be wise.' And there are certainly a number of things I learned in the decade I was actively working in comics.

So that's what we're going to talk about. Other media, and comics.

Many of you have done comics for longer than I have, and have experiences or knowledge that contradict mine. Many of you will have toiled in the vineyards beyond comics and may have had diametrically opposite experiences to mine.

So these thoughts are being offered as one set of opinions.

I began doing comics, continued doing comics, and finished doing comics for the wrong reason. It's a foolish reason, and a strange one.

I didn't do comics to have a career, nor to make money, nor to support my family. I certainly didn't do comics for awards or for notoriety.

I began doing comics because it fulfilled some kind of childhood dream and because it was truly the most exciting and delightful thing I could imagine anyone doing. I continued doing comics because it was fun, and because I discovered I loved the medium, and because I felt like I was getting to do things that were completely new, that, good or bad, no one had done before.

And I stopped doing comics because I wanted it to continue being fun, I wanted to continue to love and care for comics, and I wanted to leave while I was still in love.

When I began writing *Sandman*, it would take me a couple of weeks to write a script, leaving me with two weeks each month to do other things. As time went by I got slower and slower, until a script was taking me about six weeks a month to write. Which didn't leave much time for other things.

So there were a number of projects I wanted to do that I simply didn't get the chance to. Which meant that once *Sandman* was done I could throw myself into them headfirst.

My experiences with the world outside comics so far since finishing *Sandman* – I've written a bestselling novel and a children's book, written and cocreated a not-wholly-satisfactory six-part BBC TV series, and had lunch with an enormous number of people from Hollywood. I wrote the British Radio 3 adaptation of *Signal to Noise*, currently nominated for a Sony Award as best radio drama. I'm currently working on a bunch of stuff, including a couple of movies.

Bear in mind that these are not the opinions of someone who feels that any medium is more legitimate than any other, or that film or print somehow sanctifies or confers respectability on something otherwise grubby or unreal.

One of the delights of comics is that the price of ink and paper remains pretty constant, no matter what you're drawing. Film and television are expensive media. Cheap productions cost unimaginable amounts of money.

Comics, on the other hand, are cheap. If you have an idea for a comic, the odds are good that someone will publish it. And if they won't and you believe in it strongly, why, then publish it yourself. You may not get rich, but you will get read.

I have a friend who had an idea for a comic, and self-published it for a while, and certainly didn't lose any money, and had, at the end, a dozen or so issues of his comic, which he was fairly proud of. Then he decided to try the same tack with filmmaking, with a cast of enthusiastic amateurs, borrowed money and a willingness to max out his credit cards. At the point where the production crumbled, he had eleven minutes of film in the can and was forced to sell his house to stave off utter ruin.

Comics are unlikely to do that to you.

Film is expensive. This is why it's such a crazy medium.

I remember an afternoon in London several years ago. I was staying in a friend's flat, overlooking a canal. I was writing two different things that afternoon. One was a scene in which the Endless made a man out of clay, building him up from twigs and mud, and breathing life into him, before sending him to a hidden room in a monstrous underground necropolis. That was for *Sandman*. The other scene had an encounter, underneath a bridge in the fog, on a mud bank, between three travelers and some monks, during the course of which one of the travelers was pushed into the mud.

A few days later I had Michael Zulli's pencils of the comics sequence pinned up on the wall, and they were exactly what I'd imagined, and just what I'd hoped for and called for in the script.

A year later I found myself sitting in a freezing cellar, watching a dozen actors being frozen stiff, breathing thick smoke, while about fifty crew, including makeup people, lighting people, electricians and so on, stood around shivering watching the actors doing take after take of getting knocked down into the mud.

I didn't have my bridge. It wasn't really the scene I'd had in my head, and mostly I just felt guilty that real people were being put to so much trouble for something that had seemed like a good idea in a warm room a year before.

In comics you are unlikely to have to lose a character halfway through the comic because he broke his leg. You won't lose locations the night before you're meant to be shooting. You won't hand in a twenty-four-page script, and then be told that the artist drew it as a thirty-seven-page script, so thirteen pages have randomly been removed.

Most important, in comics there's one of you, or at most two or three people, with one vision. As a writer I think I'd been spoiled by the 'because I say so' factor. The point I realized that wasn't there in the TV show was the point I looked at the costume sketches and realized that they bore no relation to what was called for in the script.

I think one reason one becomes a writer may well be to have a certain amount of control over a vision, and unless you are working with a director whose vision parallels yours, then the odds are probably against you.

And bear in mind that the TV series is from a show that everyone was at least on the same page about. The *Sandman* film, which I am happily not involved with, has gone through eight script drafts, three writers and a director so far. And I heard the other day that they're about to hire a new writer with instructions to make it a romance.

After *Neverwhere* was done, I told my agent to pull out of another TV series I was creating for the UK, because I didn't want to do it unless I had more control than you get as a writer: in fantasy, the tone of voice, the look and feel, the way something is shot and edited, is vital, and I wanted to be able to be in charge of that.

I've agreed to work on the *Death* movie with the carrot being dangled in front of me that I could direct it. And we'll see if that happens, and if I'm a good director or not when the time comes.

So that's my wisdom on movies.

Books are a bit more straightforward.

A few years ago, when I still hung out on bulletin boards,

I was on CompuServe's comics forum, and I read a message by a writer of comics announcing petulantly that he was going to go and write real prose books because he wanted 'an audience'.

I told him his audience writing comics was much larger than he would have, barring some exceptional circumstances, for a first novel in prose. He took this as an attack on his as-yet-unproven abilities as a writer of prose, which it wasn't meant to be. It was simply a flat statement that in those days – and even in these dark days – any fairly healthy comic sells in numbers that most prose authors would be very happy to get.

For me, though, comics are much more interesting than prose, at least as a creator. One has greater control of how the information is received in comics than you do in prose – whether it's keeping control of the reader's eye to stop them skipping ahead, or simply making sure that they see the same character in their heads that you do in yours.

And comics have the joy that you never see in prose: the joy of being able to enjoy your own stuff. I can't enjoy a prose story I wrote, but I can enjoy what Dave McKean or Charles Vess or Jon Muth or P. Craig Russell does to one of my stories.

Prose has its advantages. You can give it to relatives without worrying about hearing 'Oh . . . I don't . . . *read* comics . . . dear.' You can buy it in airport bookstores. Book companies are more prone to advertise outside the comics world than comics publishers are. But for anyone who's doing this because they want to collaborate, comics are more fun.

Radio – I love radio drama. For a writer it's strangely close to comics: in one medium you're telling a story with pictures, in the other you're writing for everything but pictures. It's close to your vision, it's cheap, it's easy, there isn't any radio drama in America and the only way I could afford to do it regularly in England is by sending the children out to dance for pennies on the streets. It's also not a medium I particularly recommend for artists who don't write.

So those are my words of wisdom on the media outside comics. Now for my decades of wisdom on the world inside comics. So here, in no particular order, are the things I've learned.

1. *Big is not necessarily bad.* *Small is not necessarily good.*

Comics creators are an individualistic, unique and bolshy lot. A punch line of a comic I wrote once was 'Try getting a thousand cats to agree on anything at the same time,' and cats are pushovers compared to comics creators. They do not organize, do not trust organizations. It's a wonder as many of you are here, as are here. Certainly every shade of opinion, politics and belief is represented.

It used to be – it may still be – an item of belief in comics that all organizations are inherently dodgy. And that where companies are concerned, smaller is inherently better. Independence, however that's defined, is vital.

And if you're a Dave Sim or a Jeff Smith, your own publisher and a fine artist and writer, with complete control over your own destiny, then you have independence, or as much independence as the market will allow you.

Corporations are huge, slow, stupid lumbering things with brains in their tails. This may be true, but they do appear capable of learning, and changing.

You are no more likely to get screwed over by a huge company than you are by a small one. I'm not saying you won't get screwed over. I'm saying that there is no moral imperative towards smaller companies not screwing you.

This really is something it took me ages to learn. I kept doing projects or books for small, more independent companies because it seemed like the right thing to do, and because I was convinced that, in my case, DC Comics was a monolithic and ultimately evil organization that was just waiting for me to lower my guard before they screwed me like they screwed Siegel and Shuster.

It didn't happen. DC were easily the most amenable to reason, accessible and financially reliable of all the publishers I've dealt with. Which is not to say there was not and sometimes still isn't a great deal of frustration in dealing with some of the departments at DC. But it is to say that their royalty statements arrive on time, are comprehensible and, if one notices something bizarre, one is encouraged to phone the accounting department, who will either explain to you what they're doing, or apologize for having messed up and fix it.

For this, one can forgive many things.

In retrospect my one regret with Eclipse was that I didn't audit their accounts years before they went under. Their figures made no sense, and they would only send out royalties if threatened. On some level I knew that there had to be fraud of some kind going on, but Eclipse was only caught when Toren Smith moved his comics from Eclipse to Dark Horse, and his royalties shot up, despite the fact the deal was the same and the sales were constant.

I honestly do not believe there is any moral superiority to a large corporation or to one man working out of his kitchen. What matters is answerability, and honesty, and, above all, competence.

2. *Learn how to say no.*

This is still the one I have the hardest time with. I think it's part of the freelance mentality: we are so used to hustling, to going out and desperately peddling our skills, hoping that someone will be impressed enough by them or moved to raw pity enough by our plight to give us work, that we learn to say yes to everything.

I remember, as a starving freelance writer, in the early eighties, I would blithely proclaim competence in anything, if there was a check attached. Which meant I often found myself utterly out of my depth, interviewing the head of NASA or, for one very odd week, editing *Fitness* magazine – I don't remember, but I imagine that the phone call for that would have gone something along the lines of:

'Neil, can you edit a magazine?'

'Can I edit a magazine?'

'Silly question. Well, do you know anything about *Fitness*?'

'Do I know about *Fitness*?' (Sort of implication there that anything I didn't know about gyms and leotards and suchlike probably wasn't worth knowing. Note the way I didn't say, 'Well, I went into the gym a couple of times when I was at school. And I saw *Pumping Iron II: The Women*.' This was because I was a hungry freelance writer, and I said yes a lot.)

As a comics professional, it's too easy to say yes.

Most of the things I've done that in retrospect were astonishingly stupid ideas (as, often, my friends were ready to point out immediately) I did because someone asked me to do something, and, hell, it seemed like a good idea at the time.

Next thing you know there are unreadable, even offensive comics with your name on them that you never wrote in the world. Or whatever.

I learned early on that most of the people at the top of their professions – and I'm not talking about comics here, I'm talking about everything – were the nicest people, easy to deal with and with little side to them. And I also learned that the people who were most insistent on having VIP status, on making a loud noise about everything – the kind of people who would actually say things like 'Do you know who I am?' – were the second-division talents, the ones who hadn't made it, the ones who never would.

It took me longer to learn that you can say no. And it's an easy thing to say. It helps define your boundaries.

3. *Get it in writing. Or put it in writing.*

This is important. And those few times I haven't put something in writing, I've regretted it. Right now I'm locked in a fairly heated and as yet unresolved situation with one publisher about payments for characters, for toys, spin-off comics and other uses of a bunch of characters I made up for this publisher. And part of our dispute is over verbal agreements made on the phone four years ago. If we'd put it in writing then – I'm not even talking about contracts, I'm talking about my writing down what was said and faxing him a copy with a 'just to confirm this was what we said' – life would be easier now.

4. *Everything is negotiable.*

If someone sends you a contract, whether you are dealing with it yourself or getting someone else – an attorney or agent or someone – to vet your contracts, remember that absolutely everything is negotiable. In the early days I used to think that contracts were a take-it-or-leave-it proposition. And they aren't.

And, by the same token, contracts are renegotiable, something that I first discovered after the first year of *Sandman*. I wanted a creator credit and a creator share of the character, which, according to DC's original 'take it or leave it' contract, was entirely theirs. And I wrote a long, sensible, perfectly friendly letter to Paul Levitz explaining why this was a good idea, demonstrating that the Sandman character that I'd created was no more the Simon and Kirby Sandman than it was the Lee and Ditko Sandman. And, after some to-ing and fro-ing, a new contract was issued, giving me a share of the character.

One reason I did it this way was that I'd observed over the previous few years that when people gave DC Comics ultimata, whether DC were right or wrong, they would become inflexible. Corporate history perhaps: Siegel and Shuster wanted the rights to Superman back, and were shafted, and left with only the rights to Superboy. They went back for another legal go-around, and lost even that. Meanwhile Bob Kane was 'taken care of'.

Do not be afraid to negotiate. And if you have people whose job it is to negotiate on your behalf, don't be afraid to use them. Nor to accept input. You are not looking a gift horse in the mouth, nor is the contract going to go away because you got someone to look it over.

This is speaking as someone who has been, from time to time, screwed over by overlooked clauses in otherwise pretty good contracts, and who has, from time to time, been astonished by what, in a contract, the other party let slide.

5. *Trust your obsessions.*

I remember Alan Moore in the late 1980s telling me about a documentary he'd seen on TV about Jack the Ripper. And then, over the course of the next few months, telling me about Jack the Ripper books he'd read. By the point where he was asking

me to go and find rare and forgotten biographies of possible
Ripper suspects at the British Museum, I thought it quite possible
that a Jack the Ripper comic would be in the offing. *From Hell*
didn't start with Alan going, 'I wonder what I'll write about
today.' It started as an obsession.

Trust your obsessions. This is one I learned more or less
accidentally.

People sometimes ask whether the research or the idea for
the story comes first for me. And I tell them, normally the first
thing that turns up is the obsession: for example, all of a sudden
I notice that I'm reading nothing but English seventeenth-century
metaphysical verse. And I know it'll show up somewhere –
whether I'll name a character after one of those poets, or use
that time period, or use the poetry, I have no idea. But I know
one day it'll be there waiting for me.

You don't always use your obsessions. Sometimes you stick
them onto the compost heap in the back of your head, where
they rot down, and attach to other things, and get half-forgotten,
and will, one day, turn into something completely usable.

Go where your obsessions take you. Write the things you must.
Draw the things you must.

Your obsessions may not always take you to commercial places,
or apparently commercial places. But trust them.

A footnote to this, for writers:

When I was working with new artists on *Sandman* the first
question I would ask was 'What kind of stuff do you want to
draw?' The second was often 'What don't you like to draw?' I
found both of these pieces of information astonishingly useful,
and often very surprising.

Play to an artist's strengths; it makes you look good. Play to
your own strengths if you're an artist – but don't relax into shtick
or into the dozen things that you do.

6. *Don't stop learning.*

It's too easy to achieve a level of competence in your field, whatever it is, and to stop there.

Competence is one thing, but writers and artists are like sharks: when we stop moving we die. (I got that piece of information from reading *Jaws* at a young age. I have no idea whether it's true that sharks die when they stop, or go into reverse, but I now believe it utterly, just as I know that double-bass music signals a shark attack.)

I tend to think of *technique* as the kind of gardening tools one keeps in the potting shed (an English expression that has no equivalent that I know of) at the bottom of the garden, grabbing a garden fork, or a hoe, or one of those metal things you find hanging from a hook that the previous owner left behind and no one ever quite knows what to do with.

At Will Eisner's eightieth-birthday bash several months ago, in Florida, I was most impressed by some lithographs Will had done recently, because these were the first lithographs he'd done since art college, over sixty years earlier, and he thought it was a technique he should master.

You never know what tool you'll need. Every now and then I'll set myself writing exercises – types of formal verse, or styles from other times and other places. Sometimes I surprise myself, and wind up with something wonderful. Sometimes I wind up with something that leaves me hoping I don't die before I get a chance to clean out that directory, because if it were published posthumously, it'd kill me. But either way I have, literally, learned something.

As an artist, study other artists to see what they do, then look at life and see how it does something.

As a writer, read other writers, good writers, even writers who don't write the kind of stuff you like, and see how they do what they do. And then forget about fiction, and forget about comics, and read everything else. Learn.

7. *Be you. Don't try to be someone else more commercial. Don't try to be that other guy.*

This is about art. It may be about commerce too, but for all our description of ourselves as an industry, we're also an art form. We may have come into the field because of talent, but we're also here because we're artists. We are creators. When we begin, separately or together, there's a blank piece of paper. When we are done, we are giving people dreams and magic and journeys into minds and lives that they have never lived. And we must not forget that.

I don't want to sound like an inspirational speaker here. 'Be you. Be the best you that you can be.' But this is really important. It's something that we mostly lose track of when we start, because when we start in comics we're kids, and we have no idea who we are or what our voices are, as artists or as writers.

Young artists want to be Rob Liefeld, or Bernie Wrightson, or Frank Miller, just as young writers want to be Alan Moore, or Chris Claremont, or, well, Frank Miller. You've seen their portfolios. You've read the scripts.

We all swipe when we start. We trace, we copy, we emulate. But the most important thing is to get to the place where you're telling your own stories, painting your own pictures, doing the stuff that no one else could have done but you.

Dave McKean, when he was much younger, as a recent art school graduate, took his portfolio to New York, and showed it to the head of an advertising agency. The guy looked at one of Dave's paintings – 'That's a really good Bob Peak,' he said. 'But why would I want to hire you? If I have something I want done like that, I phone Bob Peak.'

You may be able to draw kind of like Rob Liefeld, but the day may come, may have already come, when no one wants a bargain-basement Rob Liefeld clone any more. Learn to draw like you.

And, as a writer, or as a storyteller, try to tell the stories that only you can tell. Try to tell the stories that you cannot help telling, the stories you would be telling yourself if you had no audience to listen. The ones that reveal a little too much about you to the world.

It's the point I think of in writing as walking naked down the street: it has nothing to do with style, or with genre, it has to do with honesty. Honesty to yourself and to whatever you're doing.

Don't worry about trying to develop a style. Style is what you can't help doing. If you write enough, or draw enough, you'll have a style, whether you want it or not.

Don't worry about whether you're 'commercial'. Tell your own stories, draw your own pictures. Let other people follow you.

As a corollary to that, let me say something else.

In this strange, small market we're in, no one knows anything. All bets are off. The kind of comics which were sure-fire commercial certainties five years ago are as likely to tank as they are to succeed, while the kind of oddball cult comics which, five years ago, would never have registered on anyone's radar are now solid commercial successes, or as solid as anything is these strange days.

If you believe in it, do it. If there's a comic or a project you've always wanted to do, go out there and give it a try. If you fail, you'll have given it a shot. If you succeed, then you succeeded with what you wanted to do.

8. *And last of all, know when to leave the stage.*

I thank you.

This speech was given in April 1997 at ProCon, a comics professionals convention, in Oakland, California.

'But What Has That to Do with Bacchus?' Eddie Campbell and *Deadface*

I want to talk about Eddie Campbell.

Our word *tragedy* comes from the Greek *tragos-oide:* 'the song of the goat'. Anybody who has ever heard a goat attempt to sing will know why.

A man called Thespis is credited as being 'the Father of Tragedy'. He was an itinerant player, who traveled from Greek town to Greek town, in a cart, about 535 BC. The cart was both a form of transportation and a stage, and in each town he would recite his poetry, and his actors – a novelty in themselves – their faces 'daubed with the lees of wine' (the earliest stage makeup), would entertain the crowd.

As the story goes, until then all songs and performances had been about Bacchus, the god of wine. Thespis first tried to experiment by sticking into the songs little recitations he had written about Bacchus – a remarkable innovation which the people bore nobly, up to a point. Then he decided to experiment further, and began to speak and recite about other things.

This failed miserably.

'What has that to do with Bacchus?' they would ask him, and chastened, he would return to the subject of the god of the vine.

As far as they were concerned, *real* songs, and poems and stories, were about Bacchus.

They would have liked *Deadface* too.

So who was Bacchus?

Like most gods, he accumulated to himself a number of names – amongst them, *Dionysus* ('the God from Nyssa'), *Bimater* ('twice mothered'), *Omadios* ('Eater of Raw Flesh'), *Bromios* ('the noisy'), *Bacchus* ('the Rowdy'), and of course *Enorches*, 'the betesticled'.

He was the son of Zeus and Semele, god of wine and drama, who taught mankind how to cultivate the earth, the use of the vine, the collecting of honey. The fir, the fig, the ivy and the vine were sacred to him, as were all goats (whether they could sing or not). He was the most beautiful of all gods (despite often being represented as having horns), and many of the stories of his life and miracles have remarkable parallels to those of both Jesus Christ (whose biographers may have pinched them) and Osiris (from whose legends they were probably nicked in the first place).

Probably the best and strangest of Euripides's plays is *The Bacchae*, the story of Bacchus's revenge on Pentheus, king of Thebes, who refused to acknowledge the divinity of this new god. Pentheus gets – literally – torn to pieces by his mother and his two aunts.

Really shitty things happen to people who piss off Bacchus. It's a tragedy, really.

But what has that to do with Eddie Campbell?

I don't suppose anyone much (except maybe me, and I'm weird about that stuff), cares that mythologically speaking (and any other way of speaking lacks something important) *Deadface* is correct and on the money in every detail, but it is anyway. It's joyful and funny and magical and wise.

It is also a tragedy – quite literally. (I was kidding about the goats singing. Actually the singer of the best tragic song got a goat as a prize. I think.) Tragedy tells us of the hero with one tragic flaw, of *hubris* (something between pride and arrogance) being clobbered by Nemesis. For Joe Theseus it's a tragedy. For Bacchus, of course, it's a comedy.

Most things go back to Bacchus.

Within these pages you'll find the old mythology and new. The Eyeball Kid and the Stygian Leech rub shoulders with older gods and heroes. *Deadface* mixes air hijacks and ancient gods, gangland drama and legends, police procedural and mythic fantasy, swimming pool cleaners and the classics. It shouldn't work, of course, and it works like a charm.

But what has that to do with Eddie Campbell?

Well, Eddie Campbell is the unsung king of comic books. While the rest of us toil away on what we imagine, certainly mistakenly, to be Olympus, Eddie is traveling from island to island, thyrsus in one hand, scritchy pen and Letratone in the other, surrounded by short men with hairy ears and women who suckle panthers and eat human flesh, and all of them are drinking far too much wine and having much too much fun. (The Silenus for this tale is Ed Hillyer, who wanders in, in the second half of the book, and inks over Eddie's pencils.)

I hope that this book, along with Eclipse's collection of Eddie's *Alec* stories (which don't have all the fun killing and flying and running about that this one has, but are, in my opinion, probably about as good as comics ever get) and *From Hell* (in Spiderbaby Grafix's *Taboo*, which Eddie's drawing. It's being written by a talented Englishman called Alan Moore – definitely someone to watch if you ask me), will raise his reputation to the heights where it ought to be. The man's a genius, and that's an end to it.

If you're one of the lucky ones who read this series when it first came out, you'll need no further recommendation or praise from me: you know how good it is. If you're discovering *Deadface* for the first time, I envy you: you have a treat in store.

But what has this to do with Bacchus? Or Eddie? Or the
Eyeball Kid?

Keep reading.

You'll find out.

This was the introduction to Eddie Campbell's *Deadface*, volume 1:
Immortality Isn't Forever, 1990.

Confessions: On *Astro City* and Kurt Busiek

L isten, now. Read this carefully, because I am going to tell you something important. More than that: I am about to tell you one of the secrets of the trade. I mean it. This is the magic trick upon which all good fiction depends: it's the angled mirror in the box behind which the doves are hidden, the hidden compartment beneath the table.

It's this:

There is room for things to mean more than they literally mean.
That was it.

Doesn't seem that important to you? Not impressed? Convinced you could get deeper, sager advice about writing from a fortune cookie? Trust me. I just told you something important. We'll come back to it.

There are, in my opinion, two major ways in which super-heroes are used in popular fiction. In the first way superheroes mean, purely and simply, what they mean on the surface. In the second kind of fiction, they mean what they mean on the surface, true, but they also mean more than that – they mean pop culture on the one hand, and hopes and dreams, or the converse of hopes and dreams, a falling away of innocence, on the other.

The lineage of superheroes goes way back: it starts, obviously, in the 1930s, and then goes back into the depths of the newspaper strip, and then into literature, co-opting Sherlock Holmes, Beowulf and various heroes and gods along the way.

Robert Mayer's novel *Superfolks* used superheroes as a metaphor for all that America had become in the 1970s: the loss of the American dream meant the loss of American dreams, and vice versa.

Joseph Torchia took the iconography of Superman and wrote *The Kryptonite Kid*, a powerful and beautiful epistolary novel about a kid who believes, literally, in Superman, and who, in a book constructed as a series of letters to Superman, has to come to terms with his life and his heart.

In the 1980s, for the first time writers began writing superhero comics in which the characters were as much commentary upon superheroes as they were superheroes: Alan Moore led the way in this, as did Frank Miller.

One of the elements that fused back into comics at that time was the treatment of some comics themes in prose fiction: *Superfolks* and *The Kryptonite Kid*, short stories such as Norman Spinrad's 'It's a Bird! It's a Plane!,' essays like Larry Niven's (literally) seminal 'Man of Steel, Woman of Kleenex'.

The resurgence that hit comics at this time also surfaced in prose fiction – the early volumes of the George R. R. Martin-edited *Wild Cards* anthologies did a fine job of reinvoking the joy of superheroes in a prose context.

The problem with the mid-eighties revival of interesting superheroes was that the wrong riffs were the easiest to steal. *Watchmen* and *The Dark Knight Returns* spawned too many bad comics: humorless, gray, violent and dull. When the *Wild Cards* anthologies were turned into comics what made them interesting as commentaries upon comics evaporated, too.

So after the first Moore, Miller and Martin-led flush of superheroes (they weren't deconstructed. Just, briefly, respected), things returned, more or less, to status quo, and a pendulum swing gave us, in the early nineties, superhero comics which were practically contentless: poorly written, and utterly literal. There was even one publisher who trumpeted four issues of good writers as the ultimate marketing gimmick – every bit as good as foil-embossed covers.

There is room to move beyond the literal. Things can mean more than they mean. It's why *Catch-22* isn't just about fighter pilots in the Second World War. It's why 'I Have No Mouth, and I Must Scream' is about more than a bunch of people trapped inside a supercomputer. It's why *Moby-Dick* is about (believe fifty thousand despairing college professors or not, but it's still true) a lot more than whaling.

And I'm not talking about allegory, here, or metaphor, or even the Message. I'm talking about what the story is about, and then I'm talking about what it's about.

Things can mean more than they literally mean. And that's the dividing line between art and everything that isn't art. Or one of the lines, anyway.

Currently, superhero fictions seem to break into two kinds: there are the workaday, more or less pulp fictions which are turned out by the yard by people who are trying their hardest, or not. And then there are the other kind, and there are precious few of them.

There are two obvious current exceptions – Alan Moore's *Supreme*, an exercise in rewriting fifty years of Superman into something that means something.

And then – and some of you might have thought that I might have forgotten it, given how far we've got into this introduction without its being mentioned, there is *Astro City*. Which traces its lineage back in two directions – into the world of classic superhero archetypes, but equally into the world of *The Kryptonite Kid,* a world in which all this stuff, this dumb wonderful four-color stuff, has real emotional weight and depth, and it means more than it literally means.

And that is the genius and the joy of *Astro City*.

Me? I'm jaded, where superheroes are concerned. Jaded and tired and fairly burned out, if truth be told. Not utterly burned out, though. I thought I was, until, a couple of years ago, I found myself in a car with Kurt Busiek, and his delightful wife, Ann. (We were driving to see Scott McCloud and his wife, Ivy, and their little girl Sky, and it was a very memorable and eventful evening, ending as it did in the unexpected birth of Scott and Ivy's daughter Winter.) And in the car, on the way, we started talking about Batman.

Pretty soon Kurt and I were co-plotting a complete Batman story; and not just a Batman story, but the coolest, strangest Batman story you can imagine, in which every relationship in the world of Batman was turned inside out and upside down, and, in the finest comic book tradition, everything you thought you knew turned out to be a lie.

We were doing this for fun. I doubt that either of us will ever do anything with the story. We were just enjoying ourselves.

But, for several hours, I found myself caring utterly and deeply about Batman. Which is, I suspect, part of Kurt Busiek's special talent. If I were writing a different kind of introduction, I might call it a superpower.

Astro City is what would have happened if those old comics, with their fine simplicities and their primal, four-color characters, had been about something. Or rather, it assumes they were about something, and tells you the tales that, on the whole, slipped through the cracks.

It's a place inspired by the worlds and worldviews of Stan Lee and Jack Kirby, of Gardner Fox and John Broome, of Jerry Siegel and Bob Finger and the rest of them: a city where anything can happen. In the story that follows we have (and I'm trying hard not to give too much away) a crime-fighter bar, serial killing, an alien invasion, a crackdown on costumed heroes, a hero's mysterious secret . . . all of them the happy pulp elements of a thousand comics-by-the-yard.

Except that, here, as in the rest of *Astro City*, Kurt Busiek manages to take all of these elements and let them mean more than they literally mean.

(Again, I am not talking about allegory here. I'm talking story, and what makes some stories magic while others just sit there, lifeless and dull.)

Astro City: Confession is a coming-of-age story, in which a young man learns a lesson. (Robert A. Heinlein claimed in an essay in the 1940s, published in Lloyd Arthur Eshbach's collection of SF writer essays *Of Worlds Beyond*, that there are only three stories, which we tell over and over again. He said he had thought there were only two, 'Boy Meets Girl' and 'The Little Tailor', until L. Ron Hubbard pointed out to him that there was also 'A Man Learns a Lesson'. And, Heinlein maintained, if you add in their opposites – someone fails to learn a lesson, two people don't fall in love, and so on – you may have all the stories there are. But then, we can move beyond the literal.) It's a growing-up story, set in the city in Kurt's mind.

One of the things I like about *Astro City* is that Kurt Busiek lists all of his collaborators on the front cover. He knows how important each of them is to the final outcome. Each element does what it is meant to, and each of them gives of their best and a little more: Alex Ross's covers ground each issue in a photo-real sort of hyper-reality; Brent Anderson's pencils and Will Blyberg's inks are perfectly crafted, always wisely at the service of the story, never obtrusive, always convincing. The coloring by Alex Sinclair and the Comicraft lettering by John Roshell are both slick, and, in the best sense of the word, inconspicuous.

Astro City, in the hands of Kurt Busiek and his collaborators, is art, and it is good art. It recognizes the strengths of the four-color heroes, and it creates something – a place, perhaps, or a medium, or just a tone of voice – in which good stories are told. There is room for things to mean more than they literally mean, and this is certainly true in *Astro City*.

I look forward to being able to visit it for a very long time to come.

This was written as the introduction to Kurt Busiek's *Astro City: Confession*, 1999. The Batman story idea I talk about, that we came up with in the car, wound up being one of my favourite sequences in 'Whatever Happened to the Caped Crusader?', a Batman story I would write a decade later.

Batman: Cover to Cover

I 've almost never written Batman, but he's what drew me into comics. I was six years old and my father mentioned that, in America, there was a Batman TV series. I asked what this was, and was told it was a series about a man who fought crime while dressed as a bat. My only experience of bats at this point was cricket bats, and I wondered how someone could convincingly dress as one of those. A year later the series began to be shown on English TV, and I was caught, as firmly and as effectively as if someone had put a hook through my cheek.

I bought – with my own pocket money – the paperback reprints of old Batman comics: two black and white panels to a page drawn by Lew Sayre Schwartz and Dick Sprang, Batman fighting the Joker, the Riddler, the Penguin and Catwoman (who had to share a book). I made my father buy me *Smash!,* a weekly British comic that reprinted what I now suspect must have been an American Batman daily newspaper strip as its cover feature. I was once thrown out of our local newsagents – literally picked up by the proprietor and deposited on the sidewalk – for spending too much time examining each and every one of the pile of fifty American comics, in order to decide which Batman product would receive the benison of my shilling. ('No, wait!' I said, as they dragged me out. 'I've decided!' But it was already too late.)

What got me every time was the covers. DC's editors were masters of the art of creating covers which proposed questions about mysteries that appeared to be insoluble. Why was Batman imprisoned in a giant red metal bat, from which not even Green Lantern could save him? Would Robin die at dawn? Was Superman really faster than the Flash? The stories tended to be disappointments, in their way – the question's sizzle was always tastier than the answer's steak.

You never forget your first time. In my case, the first Batman cover artist was Carmine Infantino, whose graceful lines, filled with a sly wit and ease, were a comfortable stepping-off point for a child besotted by the TV series. Text-heavy covers, all about relationships – Batman being tugged between two people: look at the first appearance of Poison Ivy (will she ruin Batman and Robin's exclusive friendship? Of course not. Why did I even worry about such trifles?), looking here as if she's just escaped from the label of a tin of sweetcorn. Batman thinks she's cute. Robin's not impressed. That was what I needed as a kid from a Batman cover. Bright colors. Reassurance.

While humans tend to be conservative, sticking with what they like, children are *utterly* conservative: they want things as they were last week, which is the way the world has always been. The first time I saw Neal Adams's art was in *The Brave and the Bold* (I think it was a story called ' . . . But Bork Can Hurt You'). I read it, but was unsure of whether or not I liked it: panels at odd angles, nighttime colors in strange shades of blue, and a Batman who wasn't quite the Batman I knew. He was thinner and odder and wrong.

Still, when I saw Adams's cover for 'The Demon of Gothos Mansion' (*Batman* 227), I knew that this was something special, and something *right*, and that the world had changed forever. Gothic literature tends to feature heroines, often in their night-dresses, running away from big old houses which always have, for reasons never adequately explained, one solitary light on in a top-floor room. Often the ladies run while holding candelabras.

Here we have instead a dodgy-looking evil squire running after our heroine, between what look suspiciously like two wolves. The spectral, Robin-less, Batman is not swinging from anything. Instead he is a gray presence, hovering over the image: this tale is indeed a gothic, it tells us, and Batman is a gothic hero, or at least a gothic creature. I may only have been ten, but I could tell gothic at a glance. (Although I wouldn't have known that the cover that Adams was intentionally echoing, *Detective Comics* 31, was also part of the gothic tradition – an evil villain called the Monk reminds the reader of Matthew 'Monk' Lewis's novel *The Monk,* and, as I learned a couple of years later, when the story was reprinted in a 100 Page Super Spectacular, the Monk from this story was a vampiric master of werewolves. Or possibly vice versa, it's been a long time since I read it. I do remember that Batman opened the Monk's coffin at the end, and, using his gun – the only time I remember Batman using a gun – shot the becoffined Monk with a silver bullet, thus permanently confusing me as to the Monk's werewolfish or vampiric nature.)

By the time I was twelve Len Wein and Berni Wrightson's *Swamp Thing* was my favorite comic; it was, I think, the comic that made me want to write comics when I grew up. *Swamp Thing* 7, 'Night of the Bat', was the comic that sealed Batman in my mind as a gothic figure. The cover only implies what's inside, as Batman, his cloak enormous behind him, swings towards the muck-encrusted swamp monster, inexplicably hanging from the side of a skyscraper. The feeling that this was something happening at night, artificially lit, in the city, was there, almost tangible. But the things that made me remember this cover fondly are really inside – Bernie drew Batman with no pretense of realism. It was as far as one could get from Adam West: behind Batman an unwearably long cloak blew out: was it fifteen feet long? Twenty feet long? Fifty? And the ears, stabbing upward like devil horns, were even longer than Bob Kane's

Batman ears on the cover of *Detective* 31. Wrightson's Batman was not a man – obviously: a man would have tripped over that cloak when he walked, the ears would have poked holes in ceilings – he was part of the night. An abstract concept. Gothic.

One of the greatest joys to the concept of Batman is that he isn't one thing, that he contains all the Batmans that have walked the streets of Gotham City in the last sixty-five years, Infantino's elegant Batman, Sprang and Schwartz's big gray Boy Scout, Frank Miller's Dark Knight. None of them more real, more valid, more true than any other. But in my heart, he is a spectral presence, a creature straight out of the gothic romances, and that, for me, is how he will always remain.

This was written for *Batman: Cover to Cover*, 2005. It's a book of covers of comics with Batman on them, with occasional essays. A web search will show you the covers I talk about here.

Bone: An Introduction, and Some Subsequent Thoughts

I An Introduction

I was reading *Bone* from almost the beginning, handed the first two comics by Mark Askwith after a signing in Toronto. 'You'll like these,' he said. I bought *Bone* until I met Jeff Smith and he started sending them to me, and I stopped buying it, but, month in and month out, I read it as the years went by, until at last it was done.

I even wrote an introduction to the second volume of *Bone*, *The Great Cow Race*. (Which, because the edition with the introduction in it has been out of print for over a decade now, you probably haven't read it, and if you have you've forgotten it, I shall now proceed to reprint here.)

Readers tend to have two reactions to Herman Melville's remarkable novel *Moby-Dick; or, The Whale*.

Either they respond to the seafaring adventure yarn, with its huge, gaping, obsessive travelogue, but they hurry through Melville's chapters with titles like 'The Sperm Whale's Head – Contrasted View'; or they find themselves becoming obsessed with Melville's retelling of the minutiae of whaling and the physiognomy of whales, and with all the strange, experimental layers of creaking, wind-lashed, bloody-handed life aboard the *Pequod,* but becoming almost impatient with the tale of Ahab and Moby Dick (and why *Moby-Dick* is hyphenated when it's the title of the book and not when it's the name of the whale is a mystery that passeth all understanding).

The first time I read *Moby-Dick,* as a boy of ten, I read it for the exciting bits (and finished it convinced that it would make a terrific comic; then again, I recall, at about the same age, finishing *King Solomon's Mines* utterly certain that it would make a brilliant musical. I must, in retrospect, have been an odd child). More recently, as an elderly gentleman of three-and-thirty, sent back to *Moby-Dick* by the urgings of Jeff Smith and a long plane flight or two, I discovered that I was enjoying the thing as a whole: a great, misshapen humpbacked whole, with the broken spars of previous drafts sticking out of its side.

Which is analogous in some ways to the experience of reading *Bone.* When I first read the stories here assembled, the parts I prized were the glittering set-pieces: the stupid, stupid rat-creatures, the honey hunt, the Great Cow Race, Fone Bone's heartbreakingly heartfelt love poems. That stuff's the accessible level of *Bone,* the stuff one latches on to immediately. It took a second reading – significantly, it took reading the whole six issues in one go – for me to appreciate the subtler backstory, the delicate, dreamlike hints about Thorn's childhood, the sensation of huge forces massing on innocents.

The first long slurp of *Bone* has a certain aroma of Walt Kelly, and a bracing tang of Chuck Jones. It's the second sip that lingers, though. That's when you realize that there's more than that, a little Tolkien, a touch of Mallory, even a smidgen of the Brothers Grimm . . .

I was introduced to *Bone* by Mark Askwith, who (and I place my life upon the line here for revealing one of the Big Secrets to the reading public) is one of the Secret People Behind

Everything. He gave me the first few *Bones* when I was in Toronto being interviewed on the television show Mark produced, the late, lamented *Prisoners of Gravity*. I read them in an airport waiting room, and I laughed and winced and admired as I read. Since then my admiration for its creator and publisher has only increased.

Jeff Smith can pace a joke better than almost anyone in comics (the only person who gives him a run for his money here is the brilliant Dave Sim); his dialogue is delightful, and I am in love with all his people, not to mention his animals, his villains and even his bugs. This collection, the second, contains a number of individual moments you will enjoy (I say this without knowing you, perhaps presuming on our relationship a little, foreword-writer to potential reader, but I daresay I'm right nonetheless), and, I repeat, it bears rereading.

The locale of *Bone* is that of the imagination. 'It is not down on any map,' as Melville said of the island of Kokovoko. 'True places never are.'

The world of *Bone* is a true place. And the map is only another part of the puzzle . . .

And with that, I pass you over to Jeff Smith. You are in capable hands. There is no one else I would trust to orchestrate a cow race; except, perhaps, Herman Melville, and his wouldn't have been anywhere near as funny.

Neil Gaiman, 1995

II Some Subsequent Thoughts

There. That was what I thought when I wrote that, fourteen years ago. I'm happy to say that there's nothing in there that, with the benefit of hindsight, I'd want to retract or amend.

Still, as the comic went on I began to miss the earlier issues
– in Woody Allen's phrase, 'the early funny stuff'. I missed the
shtick, the perfectly paced jokes. The cow race. The slapstick. I
wasn't convinced that the adventure comic that *Bone* seemed to
have transmuted into was enough of a replacement.

Rereading *Bone* now that it's all over and collected and in
one place, I am struck chiefly by how wrong I was while I was
reading it, and how very right Jeff Smith was, and how it was
always, unquestionably, one thing, albeit one thing with tension
– and a tension that, I suspect, helped make *Bone* what it was.

The economic model of making long comics stories is one
that is based upon the theory that the creator will need to eat
while writing and drawing a page (perhaps) a day. So the food
and roof are provided either by a healthy advance from a publisher
(for longer works), or, more often, in a regular paycheck, by
publishing a story in installments. So the normal model – the
one on which *Bone* was built – is to publish a comic of around
twenty pages every month or so. These comics are then collected
together and published in book-length collections every year or
thereabouts, and thus food happens, and a roof, and, in the case
of successful comics, even clothing and shoes.

Thus the challenge for a writer or a writer-artist is to create
something that works in installments, and also works as part of
a whole. In a monthly-more-or-less story you need to recap
information about a character last seen four years back, or about
the sweep of a grand plot, or just to remind your readers what
was going on in the story they read a month ago. (A lot can
happen in your reader's life in a month.) You need to give your
audience moments and sequences complete in themselves, reso-
lutions that pay off and, most of all, you need to make it a
sensible thing for the readers to have spent their dollars and
cents on an installment of serial literature.

Dickens had similar problems.

But what you create as a monthly installment will eventually be read as a whole. A recap at the beginning of one episode might throw the timing of what you are doing off completely. The rhythms of the entire story – in the case of *Bone*, a story covering more than a thousand pages – and the rhythms of the collected part of the story, and the rhythms of a monthly comic have different demands and different needs.

This is most obvious in the collected *Bone* in the first couple of chapters, when the Walt Kelly influence is at its height, and when Jeff Smith most needed to make the work accessible and bring people on board and occasionally the pacing feels more like a newspaper Sunday page than an ongoing comic. The story is, or seems to be, in second place.

As a periodical reader, reading the book an installment at a time, when the story darkened I missed the tone of the first few years. I missed the Jeff Smith who could 'pace a joke better than almost anyone', because the jokes were getting fewer and further between. I suspected that the nature of the comic had changed and I worried that the lurch from Walt Kelly and Carl Barks to something closer to Tolkien had unbalanced the whole thing.

As I now, I was wrong, and deep down I knew it, but it was not until I reread the whole of *Bone* that I understood how wrong I had been.

The Bones themselves are an anomaly. They stumble into the story much as Uncle Scrooge, Donald and his three nephews might have crossed a mountain range and found themselves in a fantastic world. They are anachronistic, apparently irrelevant to the world they have found themselves in – twentieth-century creatures in a medieval world of the fantastic. And it's here, I suspect, that the narrative tension is created. In formal Carl Barks-style storytelling, creatures like the Bone family inhabit a world like ours and wander from our world into another, more primitive world – a desert crossing, a mist-shrouded valley, an almost impassible mountain range, these are the things that keep us from Oz or the Lost World. They adventure, change things for the better, then cross the barrier to return to their own world.

Here, though, the world they enter is more complex than they – or we – initially perceive it to be. Characters who seem to be introduced for simple comedic effect have huge backstories, until the whole of the *Bone* tale begins to feel like the tip of an iceberg, or the end of something huge. The joy of *Bone* is that Jeff Smith knows more than we do. The events of *Bone* are driven by what has gone before. Lucius the amusing elderly innkeeper has a history with Granma Ben. Granma Ben is also Queen Rose. The Hooded One is her sister Briar. The love triangle between Briar and Lucius and Rose is one of the engines of plot. Still, even their plot seems like a postscript to the tale of the Locust spirit and the Dragons, as if the plot is a sequence of Russian nesting dolls, each of which is paradoxically larger than the one in which it was hidden. Each of the human characters changes hugely, both in our perception of them and in the way that they come to terms with their past and complete their already-begun stories.

The Bone cousins barely change, no more than Barks's ducks are changed by their experiences. Phoney is a creature of greed whose plans will backfire, Smiley always simple, good-hearted, easily led. Fone Bone undergoes tribulations including a broken heart, and takes a fragment of the Locust into his soul, but even he leaves the story more or less as he entered. Deepened, but still. Lessons learned are easily forgotten. Were Jeff Smith to take the Bone boys and send them into another adventure, it would be perfectly legitimate under the genre rules to which they are subscribed, although it might have the effect of lessening the impact of the first story, of Bone and the Harvestars. The Bones are cartoon characters (something that we are reminded of in the color editions of *Bone* – they work best with flat color, as if they are extra-real. The shading that works so well on everything else seems to lessen them by forcing us to consider characters who are looping brushstrokes are actually realistically drawn, in the same way that, say, Lucius is.)

The Bones have served as a bridge between the ongoing comic and the huge overstory that fills the complete *Bone*. They acted as comedic relief, as subplots, as 'bits', providing instant accessibility for readers who may not realize the significance of something set up, literally, years before. But most of all, they gave us narrative tension. They set the plot in motion (after all, without Phoney's balloon none of it might ever have happened) and they made us care about it and learn about it, incrementally, in a way that we could never have done if Jeff Smith had simply told us the story of Thorn. They solve the problem of the big story, and the problem of the issue-by-issue story.

I had always known, panel to panel, issue to issue, how good Jeff Smith was. There is a special delight, however, in realizing that over the long haul he proves himself a master.

This is an essay written for *Bone and Beyond*, the catalogue for the Wexner Center's 2008 exhibition on Jeff Smith and *Bone*, and includes the original introduction for *The Great Cow Race*, 1996.

Jack Kirby: King of Comics

I never met Jack Kirby, which makes me less qualified than a thousand other people to write this introduction.

I saw Jack, the man, once, across a hotel lobby, talking to my publisher. I wanted to go over and to be introduced, but I was late for a plane and, I thought, there would always be a next time.

There was no next time, and I did not get to meet Jack Kirby.

I had known his work, though, for about as long as I had been able to read, seen it on imported American comics or on the two-color British reprints that I grew up on. With Stan Lee, he created the original X-Men, the Fantastic Four (and all that we got from that, the Inhumans and the Silver Surfer and the rest), the Mighty Thor (where my own obsession with myth probably began).

And then, when I was eleven or twelve, Kirby entered my consciousness as more than the other half of Smilin' Stan and Jolly Jack. There were house ads in the DC Comics titles I was reading, that told me that Kirby Was Coming. And that he was coming to . . . *Jimmy Olsen*. It seemed the least likely title Kirby could possibly turn up on. But turn up on *Jimmy Olsen* he did, and I was soon floundering delightedly in a whirl of unlikely concepts that were to prove a gateway into a whole new universe.

Kirby's Fourth World turned my head inside out. It was a space opera of gargantuan scale played out mostly on Earth with comics that featured (amongst other things) a gang of cosmic hippies, a super escape artist, and an entire head-turning pantheon of powerful

New Gods. Nineteen seventy-three was a good year to read comics.

And it's the Iggy Pop and the Stooges title from 1973 that I think of when I think of Jack Kirby. The album was called *Raw Power*, and that was what Jack had, and had in a way that nobody had before or since. Power, pure and unadulterated, like sticking knitting needles into an electrical socket. Like the power that Jack conjured up with black dots and wavy lines that translated into energy or flame or cosmic crackle, often imitated (as with everything that Jack did), never entirely successfully.

Jack Kirby created part of the language of comics and much of the language of superhero comics. He took vaudeville and made it opera. He took a static medium and gave it motion. In a Kirby comic the people were in motion, everything was in motion. Jack Kirby made comics move, he made them buzz and crash and explode. And he *created* . . .

He would take ideas and notions and he would build on them. He would reinvent, reimagine, create. And more and more he built things from whole cloth that nobody had seen before. Characters and worlds and universes, giant alien machines and civilizations. Even when he was given someone else's idea he would build it into something unbelievable and new, like a man who was asked to repair a vacuum cleaner, but instead built it into a functioning jet-pack.

(The readers loved this. Posterity loved this. At the time, I think, the publishers simply pined for their vacuum cleaners.)

Page after page, idea after idea. The most important thing was the work, and the work never stopped.

I loved the Fourth World work, just as I loved what followed it – Jack's magical horror title, *The Demon;* his reimagining of *Planet of the Apes* (a film he hadn't seen) as *Kamandi: The Last Boy on Earth;* and I even loved, to my surprise (because I didn't read war comics, but I would follow Jack Kirby anywhere), a World War Two comic called *The Losers*. I loved *Omac: One Man Army Corps*.

I even liked *The Sandman* – a Joe Simon-written children's story that Jack drew the first issue of, and which would wind up having a perhaps disproportionate influence on the rest of my life.

Kirby's imagination was as illimitable as it was inimitable. He drew people and machines and cities and worlds beyond imagining – beyond my imagining anyway. It was grand and huge and magnificent. But what drew me in, in retrospect, was always the storytelling, and, in contrast to the hugeness of the imagery and the impossible worlds, it was the small, human moments that Kirby loved to depict. Moments of tenderness, mostly. Moments of people being good to each other, helping or reaching out to each other. Every Kirby fan, it seems to me, has at least one story of his they remember not because it awed them, but because it touched them.

I did not meet Jack Kirby. Not in the flesh. And I wish I had walked across that room and shaken his hand and, most importantly, said thank you. But Kirby's influence on me, just like Kirby's influence on comics, was already set in stone, written across the stars in crackling bolts of black energy dots and raw power, and honestly that's all that matters.

Neil Gaiman
September 2007, London

P.S.: In a perfect universe you would walk around a huge Kirby museum and stare at Kirby originals and also at the printed and colored versions of Kirby's art, and Mark Evanier would stroll along beside you, telling you about what you were looking at, what it is, when and how Jack did it and why, because Mark is wise and funny and the best-informed guide you could have. He knows stuff. This is not a perfect world and that museum does not exist, not yet, so you will have to settle for Mark Evanier on the page.

The introduction to Mark Evanier's *Kirby: King of Comics*, 2008.

The Simon and Kirby Superheroes

I've written about Jack Kirby in the past, about the power and the energy of his art and his storytelling. He was one of the people who made comics what they are today. He was the most dynamic, most innovative, most creative (if we were only talking quantity, not quality, given the list of important comics characters Jack co-created, he'd still be a giant) artist in twentieth-century comics.

Take that as read. It's true. In this book you'll see beautiful Simon and Kirby work: you'll watch Jack's art move from the fluid and powerful work he was doing in the 1940s to something much closer to his later 'Kirbyesque' style: jaws get craggier, anatomy and ways of representing things become more personal. You'll see some art assists by others, as well: the Ditko work in particular is a delight (and I am sure I can see some Ditko pencils in there with Jack's in the jungle *Stuntman* story).

There is praise aplenty out there for Jack Kirby. That's not why I wanted to write this introduction. This is my chance to write about Joe Simon. I've never met Joe Simon, but he's been a part of my life for over forty years. I wonder sometimes who I would be today, if not for Joe Simon.

After all, Joe Simon wrote *Sandman*. First he and Jack reinvented the mysterious night avenger with the gasmask (it was not they who put him into a yellow and purple skintight costume and gave him a kid sidekick, but they were the ones who made it work). And then, thirty years later, Joe Simon brought back the Sandman. He teamed up with Jack Kirby for the first time in many years for a one-shot, the Dream Stream incarnation of the Sandman, who had nothing in common with his predecessor except the name; an 'eternal being, outside time' who, with the nightmares Brute and Glob in tow, rescued a boy named Jed from bad dreams and the things that were causing them. I bought my copy of *Sandman* #1 from a comics dealer in South London, put it into a bag, and began to wonder who this strange figure in his red and yellow costume was. The things that Joe didn't explain were as powerful for me as the things that he did.

Nearly twenty years later, I would write *Sandman*.

Joe Simon (who created Captain America and so much else) was doing more, always, than just writing comics, but Joe Simon is a remarkable writer of comics. In his 1940s heyday he wrote comics that were always powerful, always filled with energy and madness, stories that simply never stopped moving. They were filled with larger-than-life characters, with strange caricature-villains. They were pure story, filled with Joe Simon's own energy, which was unlike anyone else's. And, very often, even if lop-sidedly, they were funny.

He did little work for DC Comics in the sixties and seventies: He wrote *Brother Power the Geek*, the story of a dressmaker's dummy who comes to life as a hippy, and is fired off into space, and *Prez*, a comic about the first teenage president of the USA. They were drawn by Jerry Grandenetti. In the only issue of *Swamp Thing* I ever wrote, I brought Brother Power the Geek back down to Earth. Later, with artist Michael Allred, I would retell the story of Prez, from *Prez* #1, as if it were a synoptic gospel. I love playing with Joe Simon's toys. One of the first projects I pitched to DC Comics was a revival of *Boy Commandos*, 1987 style, another great Simon and Kirby comic from the 1940s.

But none of those were the things that would change my life. *Sandman* was. And it started with the Simon/Kirby Sandman from the 1970s – wondering what would happen if you took him a little more seriously, wondering why he dressed like that, what the sand was for, whether he looked different if he was in someone else's dream.

I talked about my ideas to DC Comics' former president Jenette Kahn and editor Karen Berger when they were in England, and some months later wound up being invited to write a monthly *Sandman* comic, but to use my ideas about Joe's work as a jumping-off point and do something else (since writer Roy Thomas would be writing his own stories using the Simon/Kirby Sandman). It changed my life, and I owe it to Joe Simon.

And I think what attracted me to Simon's stories was how unlike anyone else's they were, how full of life. He created strange villains part cartoon, part caricature, part embodiment of whatever he wished to talk about. While the trends in comics were towards realism in writing, Joe Simon marched in the opposite direction, creating his own reality. One of my favorite early-twentieth-century American authors is Harry Stephen Koolor, a mystery writer who wrote stories that were, in terms of plot, dialogue and geography, nothing like anyone else's. He was derided for it at the time, but is now collected and remembered while many of his contemporaries are forgotten. He was an odd writer. Joe Simon plotted more efficiently than Keeler, but, like Keeler, he wrote stories that no one else could have written, and they linger in the memory and in the heart.

The oddness of Joe Simon's work is where it gets its power.

Joe Simon stories – and the Simon and Kirby stories you'll read in this book – make no pretense of being anyone else's art or stories. They are in motion all the way, or almost: they begin with something happening, they pile on the event, and only end, when they end, at the final panel, or the penultimate, leaving a final panel of exposition and explanation and plot wrap almost as an afterthought: they hurtle until they stop.

Here you'll see that pattern over and over. And you'll see stories and characters that shouldn't work, or rather, that under anyone else's hand wouldn't work, that work like a dream.

Jack Kirby was inimitable, and the Simon–Kirby team was inimitable.

These are things that people who love comics know.

But you know something else? There's never been another Joe Simon.

The introduction to *The Simon and Kirby Superheroes*, 2010.

The Spirit of Seventy-Five

The first *Spirit* comic I bought was the Harvey *Spirit* #2. I bought it from Alan Austin's shop, which was not a shop but a basement with occasional opening hours, in those antediluvian days of 1975 when there were no comic shops, somewhere in South London.

It was the last day of school. And instead of doing all the things we were meant to do on the last day of school, I snuck out of school and got on a bus with my friend Dave Dickson, and went off to South London. Dave was a lot smaller than me, and had hurt his foot recently. (I have not told anyone this story for fifteen years. But back when I did tell it, if Dave was around he would leap in early and tell people he had hurt his foot, at the beginning of the story. So they knew.) On the way to the shop we were mugged, very badly. *Badly* is probably not quite the word I want to use. *Ineptly* might be closer to the truth. The mugger was only a little older than we were, skinny and extremely nervous. He was trailing along behind us.

'Eh,' he shouted. We carried on walking.

'Eh,' he said again. We were getting further away from him.

He ran alongside us and shouted, 'Hey! I've got a knife in my pocket. Give me your money.'

I looked him up and I looked him down and, with the arrogance and refusal to be impressed of a fourteen-year-old boy, I told him, 'You have not got a knife in your pocket.'

'Yes, I do.'

'You don't.'

'Do.'

'You have not got a knife in your pocket.' I mean, he didn't have a knife. I was almost certain that he didn't have a knife.

'I do.'

'No, you don't. Show it to me. If you've got a knife, let's see it.'

I started to suspect that I was going to win this particular argument. At any rate, he said, 'Look, whether or not I've got a knife in my pocket, give me your money.'

'No.'

'Why not?'

'Because,' I said flatly, 'it's my money. Not yours. Now go away.'

And he seemed ready to leave, when Dave Dickson, who was quite terrified (and who had, remember, hurt his foot), stammered out the first thing he had said during the whole mugging. He said, 'How much do you want?'

And our mugger turned back to me and said, 'How much have you got?'

I thought about this. I had forty English pounds on me: money I had saved up over the whole term, saved for this end-of-term comics-buying blowout. More money than I had ever had on me at one time in my whole fourteen-year-old life. (It would probably have been equivalent to about a hundred 1975 dollars.)

'I've got twenty pence on me,' I told him, grudgingly. 'But I need ten pence for the bus home.'

'Give me ten pence then,' said the mugger.

So I did, and he went away. 'You weren't a lot of help,' I told Dave.

'I hurt my leg,' he said. 'So I couldn't run away. It was all right for you. You could have run away.'

When we got to the basement comic shop, it was closed. We knocked on the door until it was opened.

'Go away,' said Alan Austin. 'We're closed.'

'But,' I said, 'We came all the way here from Croydon, and we got mugged and I've got all my money for the whole term with me!'

I think it was the mugging that impressed them, more than the money. Anyway, they let us in. I bought lots of old comics, but all I remember now is *Sandman #1*, *Creepy #1*, and *The Spirit* #2.We read them on the bus, on the way home. I thought The Spirit was the coolest thing in the whole world.

'I'm Plaster of Paris, the toast of Montmartre, I stick to my man until death us do part!' That was one of the stories in there. I had no idea that the stories I was reading were over-thirty-year-old reprints: they were as up-to-date and immediate as anything I had ever read.

I had always wanted to be a writer of comics: now I decided I was also going to be a comic artist when I grew up, and to celebrate this decision, I drew a picture of the Spirit with his shirt ripped and everything. I sent it to *Comics Unlimited,* a British fanzine edited by the same Alan Austin who owned the basement comic shop. The drawing came back with a letter from Alan, telling me that they had recently improved the standard of their fan art, and now they had people like Joan-Daniel Brèque drawing for them, and they were sorry they couldn't print it. I decided that I wouldn't be a comics artist when I grew up after all.

By the time I was seventeen I had stopped buying comics. There was nothing I wanted to read that I could find in comics any more; I became quite grumpy about the medium. Except for the Spirit. I kept reading and buying *Spirit* reprints – the older Warren ones and the current Kitchen Sink ones. The stories never palled and the joy of reading them never faded. (A couple of years later, as a young journalist, I was very jealous of my school friend Geoff Notkin, who was studying at the School of Visual Arts in New York, under Will Eisner himself. This seemed almost unfair somehow, like getting God in to run your Bible studies group.)

And then time went on, and all of a sudden, I was writing comics.

Since being a comics-writing person, I have met Will on many occasions, all over the world: in Germany and San Diego and Dallas and Spain.

I remember watching Will receive an award for life achievement in Germany, the thrill of seeing a thousand people on their feet and clapping until their hands hurt and then we still clapped, and Will looked modestly embarrassed, and Ann Eisner beamed like a lighthouse.

The last time we met was on the north coast of Spain, where the world fades out into a kind of warm autumnal haze. We spent almost a week together, Will and Ann, and Jaime and Koko Hernandez, and me, a tight-knit fraternity of people who spoke no Spanish. One day Ann and Will and I walked down along the edge of the sea. We walked for a couple of miles, talking about comics, and the medium, and the history of the medium, and the future of comics, and the Spirit, and the people Will had known. It was like a guided tour of the medium we loved. I found myself hoping that when I got to be Will's age I could be that sharp, that wise, that funny.

I told Will, when we were walking, that even when I stopped reading comics I read *The Spirit*, and I told him that it was his Spirit stories that had left me wanting to write comics, and that the Sandman, like the Spirit, was conceived as a machine for telling stories.

But I didn't tell him that a drawing of the Spirit began and ended my career as a fan artist. Nor did I ever tell him just how badly I was mugged, on my way to buy my first *Spirit*.

I wrote this for the Chicago Comics Convention 'ashcan' tribute to Will Eisner in 1996.

The Best of the Spirit

It isn't yet easy or comfortable for me to write about Will Eisner. He was too important, and making notes for this introduction reminded me how much I miss Will Eisner my friend, and rereading the stories in here reminded me that I miss Will Eisner the storyteller, the craftsman, the dreamer, the artist. Which is probably the wrong place to start something that is an unabashed celebration of part of Will Eisner's work, but it's nonetheless true.

When Will Eisner died he was as respected and as revered around the world as he would let us respect and revere him. He was a teacher and an innovator. He started out so far ahead of the game that it took the rest of the world literally sixty years to catch up.

Will's life is, in miniature, a history of American comics. He was one of the very first people to run a studio making commercial comic books, but while his contemporaries dreamed of getting out of the comics ghetto and into more lucrative and respectable places – advertising, perhaps, or illustration, or even fine art – Will had no desire to escape. He was trying to create an art form.

There are arguments today about whether or not Will was actually the first person to coin the term 'graphic novel' for his book of short stories *A Contract with God,* the book that kicked off the third act of Will's creative life. There are far fewer arguments about what Will actually did in the 1940s with the Spirit stories, or about the influence Will had on the world of comics all through his creative life – and that his stories had too.

I'll step forward here: I bought my first copy of *The Spirit* in 1975, in a basement comics shop in South London. I saw it hanging on a wall, and I knew that, whatever it was, I wanted it. I would have been about fourteen. It was the second (and final) issue of Harvey Comics' *Spirit* reprints, and reading it on the train home I had no idea that the stories I was reading were thirty years old at the time. They were fresher and smarter than anything I'd seen in comics – seven-page stories that somehow managed to leave out everything that wasn't the story, while telling wonderful tales of beautiful women and unfortunate men, of human fallibility and of occasional redemption, stories through which the Spirit would wander, bemused and often beaten up, a McGuffin in a mask and hat.

I loved *The Spirit* then. I loved the choices that Will made, the confidence, the way the art and the story meshed. I read those stories and I wanted to write comics too.

Two or three years later I stopped reading comics, disappointed and disillusioned by the medium as only a sixteen-year-old can be, but even then I kept reading *The Spirit* – I would go to London and bring back copies of the Kitchen Sink reprints, and the Warren reprints, and read them with unalloyed pleasure, such that when, as a twenty-five-year-old, I decided it was time to learn how to write comics, I went out and bought Will Eisner's *Comics and Sequential Art*, and pored over it like a rabbinical student studying his Torah.

As a respectable adult, twenty years later, Will Eisner's work on *The Spirit* makes me remember why I wanted to write comics in the first place.

The joy of *The Spirit*, as soon as it had become what it was going to be, which was more or less once Eisner came back from the war in 1945 and reassumed control of the comic (published

as a Sunday supplement in newspapers at the time, an avenue
that allowed Eisner, who was always a wise businessman, the
creative control and ownership he could never have had at that
time on the newsstands), was not in the words, nor in the pictures,
but in the smoothness and the brilliance and the willingness to
experiment of the storytelling. In seven pages – normally less
than sixty panels – Eisner could build a short story worthy of
O. Henry, funny or tragic, sentimental or hard-bitten, or simply
odd. The work was uniquely comics, existing neither in the
words nor in the pictures but in the place where the words and
the pictures come together, commenting on each other, reinforcing
each other. Eisner's stories were influenced by film, by theater,
by radio, but were ultimately their own medium, created by a
man who thought that comics was an art form, and who was
proved right – but who might not have been quite so right if he
had not built such a solid body of work, both in *The Spirit* and
in the work he did from 1976 until his death, if he had not
taught and inspired along the way.

A lot of the delight in *The Spirit* is in watching Eisner invent
and discover new ways of telling stories – the use of white space
and panels to represent freedom and captivity in one story, the
echoing, reflecting dual panels in another, the use of the murder
er's point of view in a third. The stories in this book are, in
addition to being astoundingly entertaining, a lesson in how to
tell stories in comics form. 'ACTION MYSTERY ADVENTURE'
the panel on the top right of each *Spirit* splash page tells us –
and to those three things one could add humor, craft, pathos,
wisdom and the most beautiful (and dangerous) women in
comics.

In a world in which the idea of graphic novels – big, thick
collections of comics that have heft and value – is becoming
widespread and accepted, bookshops, librarians and individuals
want to know what the important books are, to know which

books are vital to have on their shelves. There are a few books that no self-respecting collection of graphic novels should be without, after all – *Maus,* for example, or *Watchmen,* or *Jimmy Corrigan,* or *Bone.* I'd like to suggest that this book, as an example of what the young Will Eisner could do, should be added to that set and guaranteed a place on those shelves. The postwar *Spirit* was a masterpiece, in the strict sense of the word – a piece of work that demonstrates that a young journeyman has now become a master of his craft.

If you enjoy these tales there are more where they came from – many more, I'm happy to say. DC Comics has been publishing *The Spirit Archives* for several years now, and the material in the book you are holding is a selection from those volumes: a few early stories to give you context, and some stories, as good as, as interesting as, as exciting as, other Eisner Spirit stories. Which, if you're looking for ACTION MYSTERY ADVENTURE, not to mention the rest, is pretty much as good as it gets.

My introduction to *The Best of the Spirit*, by Will Eisner, 2005.

Will Eisner: New York Stories

Rereading the four original graphic novels that make up this book, I was prepared for sentiment, and was surprised at how brutal so many of these stories are. They are tales as brutal, as uncaring, as a city. Two garment workers and a baby die in a fire; a hydrant that is an immigrant's only source of water is sealed off; an old woman is robbed in front of witnesses who do nothing but jeer; a man's life is destroyed by a newspaper typo. There's sentiment in here, true, for sentiment is part of being human, and it would be a foolish observer of humanity who would leave it out (certainly Dickens didn't), and Will Eisner was indeed a remarkable observer, but there is little sentimentality.

Eisner himself is visible in the stories of the City People Notebook, drawing, observing, moving through the city. You learn little about the man, his face hidden, so I shall pull a few scraps from my own mental notebook, by way of introduction.

When I first met Will he was well past the age at which most people have retired, yet there was nothing old about him – not about the way he moved (purposefully, easily), about the way he thought, the way he smiled or the way he treated others. One was only reminded that Will had been in comics since the very beginning, back since Genesis, when discussing some new wrinkle with him, some idea that would change the way that the world of comics would operate forevermore. 'When we tried that in 1942 . . .' he'd say, and tell us whether or not it had worked back then, and why it had fallen out of use.

The working life of Will Eisner could be a three-act play. In the first act, as chronicled by Will's semi-autobiographical roman à clef 'The Dreamer', he was a man who believed in comics as a medium, a man who wrote and drew excellent comics, particularly *The Spirit*, perhaps the finest and most consistently ambitious creation of its kind, a man who created business models in which he kept the ownership of his work and his creations; in the second act Will Eisner left comics at a time when the future for comics looked bleak, and the Spirit newspaper supplement was in the decline, and comics for adults were seen as an impossibility, so Will went off to take his knowledge of comics to create *PS* magazine for the US Army, a maintenance magazine – chiefly of educational comics for adults – that he drew for the first twenty years of its existence. And the third act consisted of an entire career, begun – at an age when most people are planning their retirement – with the short stories that made up *A Contract with God*. Eisner's was a remarkable body of work, produced over a period of more than sixty years, clear-eyed and consistent.

Will Eisner was amiable, gentle, friendly, approachable, encouraging, yet with steel beneath. He had a practicality, an awareness of human frailty and fallibility, an enormous generosity of spirit. In the work of his third career, Eisner demonstrated himself an American storyteller, like Ray Bradbury, like O. Henry, unashamedly populist while creating stories for a populace who were not there to read them, not yet.

It would be easy and dishonest to view the stories in this book as valentines to the Big City, to New York. And yet, if they are, these are peculiar valentines – a concatenation of unconsummated desires, unmet loves, fates avoided and unavoidable, people – damaged and bruised, hopefully or hopelessly on their way to the grave, with or without each other.

The Big City is a series of vignettes, of tiny plays, some silent, some not; some are stories and some merely moments. While Eisner was producing most of the drawings in this book, he was teaching at the School of Visual Arts in New York, and there is a teacher's eye in the way many of these stories and especially the short-shorts are told. Eisner's mastery of silent storytelling is apparent. Dialogue, when he uses it, tends to be drawn with a broad brush, a cartoon of speech with never a word wasted, but his ear for the rhythms of the ways New Yorkers talk is remarkable. On occasion, rereading these, I was reminded that Jules Feiffer was Eisner's assistant, over half a century ago: 'Go to work, Charlie,' repeats the wife in 'Trash', who has thrown out Charlie's cap and with it all his hopes and dreams and youth. Charlie says, 'I don't feel so good. I'm tired, my feet hurt . . . Maybe I shouldn't carry so many samples. That bag gets heavier every day.' And he carries the heavy bag past the garbagemen who are disposing of his past.

All his life, Eisner was, as I have remarked, an observer of people. The tales and fragments in *City People Notebook* are, as the title suggests, observations – notebook pages, and stories built up from notebook pages, ranging from sketches all the way to complete short stories, stories about Space and Time, neither of which is quite the same in a city.

'The Building' is a ghost story, although the four ghosts in it are, we learn, as much ghosts while they are alive as they ever are when dead. Mensh, who could not save children; Gilda Greene, who did not marry a poet; Tonatti, the street violinist who died as the building died; and Hammond the developer, a driven man. The optimistic ending of 'The Building', though, contrasts painfully with the last three short stories, *Invisible People*. The protagonists of 'Sanctum', of 'Mortal Combat' of 'The Power' could be characters from *The Spirit*, forty years earlier, but the fundamental hospitality and (occasionally ironic) justice of the world of *The Spirit* has been replaced by a place as bleak and unwelcoming as Kafka's. There is no justice here: there is no place for you in the world, magic will not help you, and nor will love. The last three stories are cold things, as unsentimental as three stories could be.

Will died a year ago today, and I still miss him. He was modest and wise and, above all, *interested*.

'What keeps you working?' I asked Will Eisner in 2001 at the Chicago Humanities Festival, where he, and I, and Art Spiegelman and Scott McCloud were guests – something unthinkable in the 1930s, when Will began to draw comics. I was interviewing him. I wanted to know why he kept going, why he kept making comics when his contemporaries (and his contemporaries were people like Bob Kane – *before* he did Batman, remember) had long ago retired and stopped making art and telling stories, and are gone.

He told me about a film he had seen once, in which a jazz musician kept playing because he was still in search of the Note. That it was out there somewhere, and he kept going to reach it. And that was why Will kept going: in the hopes that he'd one day do something that satisfied him. He was still looking for the Note . . .

My introduction to *Will Eisner's New York: Life in the Big City*, 2006.

The Keynote Speech for the 2003 Eisner Awards

Being the Eisner keynote speaker is a huge honor. Not just because they're the Eisner Awards, our industry and our art form's Oscars and Pulitzers and Tonys, but because it's a rare opportunity to speak, without being interrupted, to thousands of people who actually create comics, who sell comics, who care about comics – and because it's still early in the evening, and the awards have not yet been handed over, people have to pretend to listen to what I say.

I thought I'd talk about awards, and why they matter, and comics and why they matter and making art and why it matters.

I don't have anything huge and controversial to say. The last time I had anything controversial to say was ten years ago, when I told retailers not to get caught up in a speculator bubble that would, I predicted, soon pop like the Dutch Tulip Bubble. Creators, publishers and retailers were bathing, Uncle Scrooge-like, in money, and I got up and told them that there were bad times just around the corner, and what mattered was selling stories that people cared about and wanted to read.

And most of my predictions, bizarrely, came true.

Ten years on, I think it's a good time to take stock of where we are. A state of the comics nation, if you will . . .

And we aren't doing badly at all.

I started working professionally in comics about seventeen
years ago. I was writing about comics as a journalist, whenever
anyone would let me, for two or three years before that.

In my dreams, back then, I would think about a comics utopia.
A future golden age.

So let's look back and remember what that comics utopia
would be.

First and foremost, I wanted comics to be taken seriously.

That didn't mean that I wanted all comics to be serious. I
wanted all kinds of comics. And I wanted them to be able to
stand beside theater, cinema, books, TV, grand opera, as a valid
and unique way of telling stories. A fairly young medium, perhaps,
in which a lot of great work was still to come, but a medium
that shouldn't be sneered at for simply existing: a medium whose
name can be used as a put-down has a long way to go.

When I was a journalist, as once upon a time I was, I would
ask editors to be allowed to write about comics. Normally I'd
be reprimanded, and told that I couldn't write about *Watchmen,*
or *Maus,* or *Dark Knight,* or *Love and Rockets,* because something
had already been written about comics within the last year – it
had recently been English comics character Desperate Dan's
fortieth birthday, and simply mentioning this had soaked up all
the available newspaper column inches. I tried to explain that
the action of acknowledging the existence of a book or a film
didn't preclude interviewing authors or directors in the future,
and sometimes they'd let me write something about comics just
to shut me up, and if they ran it it would run under the heading
'Wham! Bam! Pow! Comics Are Growing Up!', a headline that
every editor around the globe was convinced was original and
smart.

So in my utopia, if a journalist wanted to write about comics
or comics creators, his or her editor would say, 'Of course.'

I wanted to explain why people should know who Alan Moore

and Art Spiegelman were, and who the Hernandez brothers and Frank Miller were and why people should care.

I wanted people to know who Will Eisner was.

I wanted to live in an alternate universe, in which the cool comics stories from the past, the ones I'd read about in the fanzines but would never have a hope of actually reading, stories by Jack Cole and Bernie Krigstein and Winsor McCay and George Herriman, in which those stories were in print, and available. A world in which lots of good, long comics stories were collected. A world in which libraries stocked graphic novels. A world in which girls read comics, and in which girls and women made comics.

I wanted a world in which collections of comics existed and were routinely sold in places that other things were sold. Like bookshops.

I wanted a world in which superheroes existed, and did just fine, but in which there was also room for any other kind of comic one could imagine.

And, frankly, we're getting there. We may not have reached that glorious shining comic book utopia yet, but we're getting there. Things are different. A world in which Chris Ware's *Jimmy Corrigan* can take the *Guardian* best first novel award is the kind of future I wanted. It's an alternate universe . . .

I read reviews of a recent movie in which the complaint in most of the media seemed to be that the filmmakers had dumbed down a witty and intelligent comic. Now, this has happened scores of times over the years, and it is not unique. What was unique is that people had noticed – that the journalists writing the reviews knew. That's the kind of future I wanted, when I started out.

We are, for good or ill, where we always wanted to be: just another medium. The bastard child of Art and Commerce has become, if not respectable, then at least no less respectable than any other.

So. Now is the time we learn that we should have been careful of what wished for . . .

On the one hand, we are, right now, this minute, in a golden age. There are, quite simply, more good comics available to be read than there ever have been before. More classic books, more good books of recent vintage.

Last summer, at the American Library Association, a number of comics people were invited to talk to librarians. I was one of them. I went along, expecting to be talking to the two hundred fifty comics fans who had grown up to be librarians. I couldn't have been more wrong: the librarians were getting pressure from their readers. The librarians knew that graphic novels – whatever they are – were popular, and they wanted to know what they were. So they got me, and Jeff Smith, and Colleen Doran, and Art Spiegelman, and several other people in to tell them what we thought they should know. And the libraries have started ordering the books.

There's a potential downside, of course. Comics as an industry seems particularly prone to a peculiar sort of boom and bust. It's the place where commerce takes over from art, and we suddenly find ourselves staring at yard after yard of shelving containing lots more things kind of like what the people were buying last month, only not as good. Bad comics, bad graphic novels, drive out the good. And then, in six months, or two years, we find ourselves staring at empty shops and empty shelves.

Let's try not to let that happen again.

One way we can help avoid the next implosion is by trying to do good work. Do your best work, and then try to get better for the one after that.

The Eisner Awards, like all awards, are flawed. But they reflect something very important, which is a striving toward excellence.

Fifty, sixty years ago, Will Eisner was an oddity and a weirdo.

In a world of people who were writing or drawing comics until they could find more respectable work, who lied to their friends about what they did, people who couldn't wait to get out and make real money, make real art, Will was one of the few people convinced that this nascent mixture of words and pictures really was an art form. Other people believed it was about the quick buck. Will was certain, against much of the available evidence, that there could be well-written comics, well-drawn comics, and that the strange magic of comics that comes from combining sequential pictures and words into a story was really something powerful and unique and true.

It was true then, and it's no less true today. This is an art form in which you can make magic. Magic for kids, magic for adults. And that is what these awards are about, and notwithstanding those who like to think of comics as a cheap feeder unit for Hollywood, that's what this convention is about.

The awards that bear Will's name are about that. They're about more than patting ourselves on the back. They are more than marketing tools, more than pretty things to hang on a wall and be proud of, if you've got one, or to envy or disdain if you haven't.

They represent striving for excellence. Doing it as well as you can, and doing it better.

They're about improving the medium. If you want an Eisner Award, strive for excellence. If you want one, do it better. If you feel it went to the wrong man or woman, and it should have been yours, then do it better next year, whatever it is that you do. Strive toward excellence. If the judges don't put you on the Eisner list, then fuck 'em, and let posterity be your judge. If you feel that great work by other people is going unrecognized and unrewarded, then make a noise about it. Tell everyone you know. Word of mouth is still one of the best sales tools there is.

Nobody wants a world of identikit comics. Do the comics

only you can do. Tell the stories only you can tell. Do not lose
sight of the fact that this is an industry that can create real art.
And in the meanwhile, do it better. And love what you do.

I gave this as the keynote speech before the handing out of the 2003
Eisner Awards, given for creative achievement in American comic books.

2004 Harvey Awards Speech

The Harvey Awards, named after writer-artist-editor Harvey Kurtzman, and the Eisner Awards are, I suppose, the Oscars and the Golden Globes of the comics world. Both are prestigious. The Harveys tend to be voted on by comics professionals, rather than by everyone. This was the speech I gave at the Harveys in 2004, having given one at the 2003 Eisners, and I decided I wanted to address the creators in the audience. This also was the original prototype for the Make Good Art speech I would give eight years later.

I'm in the middle of writing a novel currently, and unlike the pleasant social world of comics, where, if you're me, you talk on a daily basis to editors and artists, to letterers or colorists or cover artists, writing a novel is something that's done solo. It's just me and a lot of pieces of paper. Even my family leaves me alone to write.

This means that when finally offered the opportunity to speak, I'm liable to begin with apologizing for being so out of practice, and then to start blithering unstoppably.

Forgive me if I blither.

Harvey Kurtzman was a genius. And that was not what made his work special. We've had a number of geniuses in comics, and we have a number of them still. Some brilliant work is cold. There are some things one admires, but one cannot love.

Kurtzman was someone who was doing what he wanted to do, enjoying himself. Happy to rewrite the rules because there were no rules, as long as you were creating art.

Most of us are happy to have created just one world-class, life-changing work. Harvey did it a number of times. He is one of the people who created the world in which we exist.

He endured Senate hearings, commercial exploitation, watching some of his most treasured creations fail. Along the way he created art that will remain forever, and inspired a list of people longer than your arm, all of whom watched Harvey strive toward excellence, break new ground, tell new stories. Some of them went on to become cartoonists or writers or filmmakers – people like R. Crumb or Terry Gilliam. Others simply discovered that the worlds and visions that Harvey Kurtzman gave them changed their world, in the way that real art does. It gave them new eyes. Perhaps a more cynical view of the world, certainly a more pragmatic one. Harvey's worlds were, at least in their EC incarnations, never fair. You got what you needed, and what you deserved, and you normally got it in the neck.

I was fortunate enough to have met Harvey Kurtzman, in 1990, at the Dallas Fantasy Fair. He told me how much he appreciated what I was doing, which I took, not as any indication that he had read anything I had written, but as him expressing his pride in a younger generation of comics writers and artists. That there were bright young creators out there who cared about comics as an art form mattered to Harvey Kurtzman. He'd invested his life in the crazy belief that comics were art, and not anything to apologize for, and that investment reaped its dividends in the lives it influenced, in those of us who believed it too, and acted accordingly.

* * *

When, as a young man, my dream of getting to make comics started to become a reality, I started to meet comics people. These were the people whom I had looked up to in my teens, in my twenties, as gods upon the earth. These were the names that I conjured with. I would read everything I could about them when I was growing up, in a time when there was precious little about them to read, and even less of what they had done still in print.

And now I was to meet them.

And I discovered, to my surprise, that quite a lot of them were cranky old Jews. Or wannabe cranky old Jews – they seemed to be enjoying themselves too much to be properly cranky, and not all of them were actually Jewish.

And now, approaching my mid-forties, eighteen years after writing my first comic, I find myself heading down the conveyor belt towards cranky old Jewhood. I'm at the age where they start to give you lifetime achievement awards, and you rather wish they wouldn't, because it may be some kind of a hint that it's time for you to sit down and shut up.

It is the prerogative, however, of those who are one day to be cranky old Jews to give advice to the generations that will follow them. And while some of you are my contemporaries, and others are my seniors, I shall advise anyway. My first piece of advice is this:

Ignore all advice.

In my experience, most interesting art gets made by people who don't know the rules, and have no idea that certain things simply aren't done: so they do them. Transgress. Break things. Have too much fun.

Two: Read outside of comics. Learn from places that aren't comics. Don't do what anyone else is doing. Steal from places where people aren't looking. Go outside. Many years ago, when it was almost unheard of for foreigners to write American comics, people used to ask why British writers were different.

I had no idea. I did notice that when I spoke socially to people like Alan Moore, or to Grant Morrison, we mostly weren't talking about comics. We were talking about avant-garde forms of poetry, about nonfiction writers, about weird things we'd found. Grant Morrison discovered a long-forgotten Victorian children's author named Lucy Clifford, who wound up influencing both his *Doom Patrol* and, much later, my *Coraline*. We loved comics, but they weren't all we knew. There's a whole cool world out there. Use it.

Three: Read all the comics you can. Know your comics.

The history of comics is not a long one, and it's not unknowable. We can argue about whether or not hieroglyphics were the earliest comics, or the Bayeux Tapestry or what. At the end of the day, we don't have a long history. You can learn it. You can, these days more easily than you ever could before, study it. And the high points of the last century in comics are quite astonishing. There are things that Winsor McCay did in *Little Nemo* that are still unsurpassed. Things in Herriman's *Krazy Kat* that are jaw-dropping. There are things, as a writer and as a storyteller, that Harvey Kurtzman did, that Will Eisner did, that Robert Crumb did that you should familiarize yourself with and learn from.

There's more classic and important material in print now in affordable editions than there has ever been. Let it inspire you. See how high people have taken the medium in the past, and resolve to take it further.

Isaac Newton, even as he created the foundations of huge swatches of science, said that if he had seen a little further than most men, it was because he was standing on the shoulders of giants. We've inherited an art form from giants, some of whom were cranky old Jews, and some of whom weren't Jews, and some of whom weren't even cranky.

Another piece of advice:

I've learned over the years that everything is more or less the same amount of work, so you may as well set your sights high and try and do something really cool.

There are other people around who can do the mediocre, meat-and-potatoes work that anybody can do. So let them do that. You make the art that only you can make. You tell the stories only you can tell.

As a solution to various problems you may encounter upon the way, let me suggest this:

Make Good Art.

It's very simple. But it seems to work. Life fallen apart? Make good art. True love ran off with the milkman? Make good art. Bank foreclosing? Make good art.

Keep moving, learn new skills. Enjoy yourself.

Most of the work I've done that's been highly regarded has happened in places where, when I was working on it, I tended to suspect that it would go one of two ways – either I was doing something cool that, if I was lucky, people would talk about for some time, or I was doing something that people would have a particularly good laugh about, in the places where they gather to discuss the embarrassing mistakes of those who went before them.

Be proud of your mistakes Well, *proud* may not be exactly the right word, but respect them, treasure them, be kind to them, learn from them.

And, more than that, and more important than that, make them.

Make mistakes. Make great mistakes, make wonderful mistakes, make glorious mistakes. Better to make a hundred mistakes than to stare at a blank piece of paper too scared to do anything wrong, too scared to do anything.

Critics will grumble. Of course they will. That's one of the functions of critics. As an artist it's your job to give them ulcers, and perhaps even something to get apoplectic about.

Most of the things I've got right over the years, I got right because I'd got them wrong first. It's how we make art.

As a keynote speaker last year for the Eisners I said that compared to where I dreamed that comics could be, as a young journalist in 1986, we're in a Golden Age.

And I was taken to task in certain circles for this, as if I'd said that this was as good as things could get, or that there was nothing at all wrong with the world of comics. Obviously neither statement is true.

We're in 2004, the year that Dave Sim and Gerhard finished the three hundred issues of *Cerebus*, the year that Jeff Smith completed *Bone*, both monumental tasks, both unique. *Cerebus* cannot be compared with anything anyone else has done. It's unparalleled in its evolving portrait of its subject and its subject's creator. *Bone* is, beginning to end, the best fantasy tale anyone's told in comics. That in itself gives me hope for the future.

It's the year that my daughter Maddy discovered *Betty and Veronica*, and that gives me another kind of hope. Any world in which a nine-year-old girl can become, off her own bat, a mad keen comics collector because she cares about the stories, is a good one.

I think the Internet is changing things.

Twice in the last eighteen months the Internet has been used as a way of rallying around publishers who needed help. Good publishers who had cash flow problems, and who put out appeals for assistance, let people know that now was the time to buy. And people did. The Internet meant that information was given to the people who needed it.

Last week, a Web cartoonist with a large readership told his readership that he would really like to quit his day job and devote the time to the comic, if they could raise the same money he made in his day job. His readers dipped into their pockets, five dollars here and ten dollars there, and delivered the annual wages from his day job.

The Internet gives your comics cheap access to the world,

without printing bills. It still hasn't worked out a reliable way to pay people for their work, but Randy Milholland quit his job yesterday to do *Something Positive* full-time, and Top Shelf and Fantagraphics are both still here.

Despite the grumblers, I think the Internet is a blessing, not a curse.

And if I have a prediction it's simply this: the often-predicted Death of Comics won't happen. There will be more booms and there will be more busts. Fads and fashions turn up in comics, as with all things, and, as fads and fashions always do, they will end, normally in tears.

But comics is a medium, not a fad. It's an art form, not a fashion. The novel was once so called because it was indeed something novel, but it's lasted, and I think, after a few shake-downs, the graphic novel, in whatever form, will do likewise.

Already some things are changing:

When I started writing about comics, before I ever began to write comics, I wanted a world in which comics would simply be regarded as a medium like any other, and in which we were accorded the same respect that any other medium was given. The amount of respect that novels and films and great works of art got. I wanted us to get literary awards. I wanted comics to turn up on the shelves of bookshops, and to sit next to books on the bestseller lists. Maybe one day a comic could come out and be on the *NYT* bestseller list.

We've got all that. And I don't think it's important after all.

Right now I actually believe that the best thing about comics may well be that it is a gutter medium. We do not know which fork to use, and we eat with our fingers. We are creators of a medium, we create art in an art form, which is still alive, which is powerful, which can do things no other medium can do.

I don't believe that a fraction of the things that can be done with comics have yet been done.

For now, I think we've barely scratched the surface.

And I think that's exciting. I don't know where comics as a medium will go in the future. But I want to be amazed, and I'm pretty sure that I shall be.

And I trust that one day when you, whatever age, race, gender or ethnicity you may lay claim to, are in your turn a cranky old Jew up here giving a speech, that will always remain true.

Keynote speech for the 2004 Harvey Awards.

The Best American Comics 2010

Page 1 panel 1

Space. The infinite vastness of everything. Seeing that's a bit hard to fit into one panel, you'll probably have to suggest it. I mean, if you can fit the whole universe in, then go for it. Otherwise, a galaxy.

NO DIALOGUE

Page 1 panel 2

The Earth, as seen from space. I think this would best be representational, rather than hyperrealistic. (Would we even recognize a realistic Earth, as seen from space?) North should be up, and North America should be easy to find.

NO DIALOGUE

Page 1 panel 3

A bigger panel. It's America, the country, as seen from space, with bits of Canada at the top and Mexico at the bottom. All of it. Feel free to add labels to it. Amber waves of grain can be labeled 'amber waves of grain'. Purple mountains majesty ditto. Also skyscrapers of Manhattan, alligators of Florida, the cable cars of San Francisco, and ever-so-slightly to the right of Minneapolis is the end of a tip of an arrow. It is labeled.

ARROW LABEL: Your Editor.

Page 1 panel 4

> And this, from above, looking up at the world, is the
> editor of this volume. He is nearly fifty. He needs a
> haircut, has bags under the eyes, is wearing a black
> T-shirt and jeans. He has the little potbelly of a man
> who has spent too much of his life behind a desk and
> the haunted expression of a man one missed deadline
> away from disaster. His hands are in his jacket pockets,
> looking up toward our virtual camera, that has been
> zooming in on him. He's talking to us:

EDITOR: It's just wrong!

And about this point I decide that it's probably kinder on the
reader if I don't write the rest of this introduction as a script to
an undrawn comic, because comics really are a visual medium
and a written description of what you would be seeing if I'd
written this whole introduction as a comic is not the easiest
way to assimilate information.

Comics, of course, *are* the easiest way to assimilate information,
at least according to a study done by the CIA back in the 1980s.
But a comics script is a strange hybrid beastie, part blueprint, part
correspondence, part theoretical yogurt-starter. Let's go to prose.

Imagine me telling you this. I would be outside in the garden
of an old *Addams Family*-style house an hour's drive from
Minneapolis.

It's just wrong.

It's just wrong and I am a participant, dammit. I am a collaborator in this madness.

I have drawn you in by lending my name and my endorsement
and my time. I have done my best to give you the impression
that the volume you hold contains the Year's Best American

Comics. That by purchasing it, you will become au fait with the cutting edge. It says so on the cover, after all.

Buy it, read it, and know that you know what's happening in comics . . .

Well, yes. Up to a point.

Take *The Year's*. In this case, the year runs August to August. The biggest, the most important and, to my mind, the most fascinating comic of 2009, Robert Crumb's retelling of the Book of Genesis, makes it into this book because an advance extract was run in the *New Yorker*.

Some of this material was published for the first time in 2008/2009. Some was simply collected in that time frame. Things I loved were excluded, and previous editors had not chosen them and nor would upcoming editors pick them. Oh, the injustice.

Best. It's a weird sort of a word. I didn't read every comic published in America over the time span of this book. I wish I had: it would have been fun. Jessica Abel and Matt Madden did not read everything published in America either. Twenty years ago, it might have been barely possible: today it's a pipe dream.

(I remember arguing with Scott McCloud about his book *Reinventing Comics*, published in 2000, taking issue with his hypothesis that comics would find an easy outlet on the web. I mocked him, pointed out how long it took comics to load, explained that paper would always be first port of call for young cartoonists, and was wrong about everything I could have been, except about the problems with getting people paid for their work. Sorry, Scott. You were right.)

We did our best. Still, I lay awake some nights wondering about the choices I made, suspecting that on another day I might have chosen a completely different set of pages.

American? A slippery term at the best of times, and here it slips through your fingers like mercury. *American* is, as a term, in this case, strangely parochial, fundamentally irrelevant and extremely difficult to define. The comics community is global. There are comics published in America by people who are not American that qualify as American and there are comics that don't. (I loved a small strip in an American-published magazine that turned out to be by a Swede and is thus not here. Eddie Campbell is not represented in *The Best American Comics* purely because he is a Scot living in Brisbane, Australia.) (Your editor is English. He lives in America, and most of the comics he has written, during a career of writing stuff, have been published in America. Were they more or less American before I moved here? I do not know. Matt and Jessica are editing this book from Paris, the French one. I know that, left to myself, I would have declared all comics writers and cartoonists honorary Americans and made the issue moot.)

And finally, and most frustratingly, maddeningly, that peculiar and elusive term *Comics*, which started as strips and as Sunday pages over a hundred years ago, then became eight page sequences in longer periodicals, then grew to become twenty-plus pages of monthly story, and then mutated to become books, to become webcomics (often closer in spirit to the strips and Sundays than anything else), to become graphic novels, whatever exactly they are (and they are, I suspect, anything you want them to be).

Now, so many comics are being created and intended as books, as longer stories. Which on the one hand is a very good thing, as excellent art is being made. It also has its downside: books are long things, filled with reverses and characters, plot and event. They are mad marathons in which the reader and the creators collaborate. Any extract from a longer work, no matter how well chosen, is simply that: an extract from a longer work: and the real art is the longer work, with a beginning and a middle and an end, often in that order.

In this collection I've tried to find sequences that worked on their own, that gave a flavor of a book, that would interest, intrigue or irritate you enough that they would perhaps send you out to buy the whole thing, while always aware that what you are seeing is incomplete.

(Insert a silent panel here. The editor is looking out at us. He looks out of sorts, yet, having ranted and raged and grumbled for several pages, is nowhere near as grumbly as one would imagine.)

But having said all that . . .

The power of comics is simply this: that it is a democracy; the most level of playing fields.

One of my favorite comics of 2009, which is not reprinted here for reasons of utter redundancy and avoidance of infinite self-reference, was Lynda Barry's introduction to the previous volume but one in this series. It touched on what comics are and what they do so well. And it revealed the biggest secret in comics: that anyone can do them.

You just need something to draw with and something to draw on. A pen, some paper. A computer program. You do not need to know anything. You just need to do it. To make it. And then you send it out into the world.

It can be about anything: an account of Hurricane Katrina and its aftermath, a small-town punk-rock adventure, an imaginary story of the life and loves of a failed architect on the run from his life, the story of two robots arguing about gnomes and a retelling of the first book of the Bible, all of these are comics: small colored glass squares in the mosaic that forms a picture of what was happening in comics this year, all wonderful, essential parts of a medium that is so often mistaken for a genre.

And if this book impels one person to dig deeper into the world of comics out there, or if one teenager picks it up in a library and sees a way to get something out of her head and into someone else's and begins to draw her own comics, then its purpose is fulfilled.

Page 4 panel 4

And now, another silent panel. The editor appears to have cheered up enormously. His hair has also cheered up, and is now sticking up all over the place, as if he has been running his hands through it while talking, as a necessary aide to communication. Which is in fact the case.

NO DIALOGUE

Page 4 panel 5

Penultimate panel. An idea has struck him. It's getting late. He's raised a finger, and is making a suggestion.

EDITOR: Y'know, if you just pretend that the real title for this book is A Sampler: Some Really Good Comics, Including Extracts from Longer Stories We Thought Could Stand on Their Own, you could ignore everything I've said so far.

Page 4 panel 6

Last panel. We've pulled back a way. The stars are coming out. We are still looking at our editor. Now he's got all that off his chest the editor looks both relieved and pleased with himself. He's sort of smiling, a bit nervously, perhaps pushed both hands deep into his pockets. And being English, he allows himself the highest possible form of praise for the book he's introducing.

EDITOR: It's not bad, actually.

This was my introduction to *The Best American Comics 2010.*

VI

INTRODUCTIONS AND CONTRADICTIONS

'Having a place the story starts and a place it's going: that's important.

Telling your story, as honestly as you can, and leaving out the things you don't need, that's vital.'

Some Strangeness in the Proportion: The Exquisite Beauties of Edgar Allan Poe

We are gathered here together so that I may tell you, and myself, several matters concerning Edgar A. Poe, 'Edgar, a poet to a T,' as he once described himself, and the strange tales and poems by him that are here assembled.

I met Poe first in an anthology with a title like *Fifty Stories for Boys*. I was eleven, and the story was 'Hop-Frog', that remarkable tale of terrible revenge, which sat incongruously beside the tales of boys having adventures of desert islands or discovering secret plans hidden inside hollowed-out vegetables. As the king and his seven courtiers, tarred and chained, were hauled upwards, as the jester they had called Hop-Frog clambered up the chain, holding his burning torch, I found myself astonished and elated by the appropriateness of his monstrous revenge. I do not believe there were any other murders in *Fifty Stories for Boys* and certainly none with such a colorful and satisfactory cast, nor such terrible and appropriate cruelty.

Suddenly it seemed like Poe was everywhere. I discovered the Sherlock Holmes stories, and in the first tale, 'A Study in Scarlet', Holmes is found decrying Poe's detective Auguste Dupin – but decrying him in a way that made it very obvious that Dupin was Holmes's literary progenitor. Ray Bradbury's story 'Usher II' solidified my fascination; it's a short story (a hybrid, from Bradbury's *Fahrenheit 451* future set on the Mars of *The Martian Chronicles*) in which a set of bloodless critics and reformers of fiction, of fantasy, of horror, are walked around a house filled with tableaus of Poe's stories, and watch themselves murdered – by Pit and Pendulum, by murderous robotic orangutan, and so on.

And so, for my thirteenth birthday, I asked for and received a copy of *Complete Stories and Poems of Edgar Allan Poe*. I have no idea whether Poe is an author appropriate for thirteen-year-old boys. But I still remember the deliciousness of the final bodily death of M. Valdemar, as he came out of his trance; I remember the thrill I took the first time I read 'The Masque of the Red Death', and Prospero's doomed attempt to continue the party, and that final, perfect sentence; I remember the tingle of delighted horror that prickled the back of my neck when I encountered the first words of 'The Tell-Tale Heart', as the narrator assures us that he is not mad, and I knew that he was lying; I remember wondering – as I still wonder – what insult Fortunato gave to Montresor that demanded that damp journey through the catacombs, in search of a cask of amontillado . . . That was thirty years ago.

Even today I return, time and again, to Poe: an audiobook of Poe's stories and poems read by Vincent Price and Basil Rathbone recently kept me company on a long drive from the Midwest to Florida. I found myself experiencing them in a way I never had before, treasuring the experience of driving through the darkness listening to the narratives of people suffering from morbid acutenesses of the senses, or the groaning of people 'neither brute nor human, they are ghouls' and the throbbing of the bells they were tolling . . . 'I cannot, for my soul, remember how, when, or even precisely where I first became acquainted with the lady Ligeia,' said the velvet voice of the late Vincent Price, as I drove into Tennessee mountain country at midnight, and I worried immediately for the sanity of our narrator, obsessed by a dead wife who was almost his mother, and who would return in the shroud-wrapped corpse of his second wife and in so doing cause me to miss my highway turnoff . . .

Edgar Allan Poe wrote poems, stories, criticism, journalism. He was a working writer who kept himself alive with his words, for much of his life supporting, as best he could, his wife, who was his cousin Virginia (he married her when she was thirteen; she died aged twenty-five, having spent much of her time with him dying), and her mother, Muddy. He was vain, envious, good-hearted, morbid, troubled and a dreamer. He invented the form we now see as the detective story. He wrote tales of horror and of dread which even the critics admit were art. He had trouble with money and with drink for much of his life. He died in poverty and in hospital, in 1849, after a final week in which we have no knowledge of his movements – in all probability a lonely drunken week.

While he lived he was America's finest writer, a poet and a craftsman whose work made him very little money, even as his poems, such as 'The Raven', were widely quoted, adored, parodied and reviled, while writers he envied, such as Longfellow, were far more successful, commercially. Still, Poe, for all his short life and unfulfilled potential, remains read today, his finest stories as successful, as readable, as contemporary as anyone could desire. Fashions in dead authors come and go, but Poe is, I would wager, beyond fashion.

He wrote about death. He wrote about many things, but death, and the return from death, and the voices and remembrances of the dead pervade Poe's work – like dramatist John Webster in Eliot's poem, Poe 'was much obsessed with death. He saw the skull beneath the skin.' Unlike Webster, though, Poe also saw the skull, and could not forget the skin that had once covered it.

('The death of a beautiful woman,' Poe wrote in an essay on the writing of 'The Raven', 'is, unquestionably, the most poetical topic in the world.')

People today still examine Poe's life, trying to use his life to illuminate his work: his actor parents – his father vanished, his mother dead by the time he was three; his strained relationship with John Allan, his foster father; Poe's child bride and her tuberculosis; his troubles with the bottle; his mysterious and early death (he was forty). The life, short, tangled, strange, becomes a frame for the work, giving it context, and supplying both unanswerable mysteries and a shape in which the stories and the poems wait for each new generation of readers to discover them.

And discover them we do.

The best of Poe doesn't date. 'The Cask of Amontillado' is as perfect a tale of vengeance as ever was crafted. 'The Tell-Tale Heart' is a clear-eyed look through the eyes of madness. 'The Masque of the Red Death' seems more relevant with every year that passes. The stories still delight. I suspect they always will.

Poe isn't for everyone. He's too heady a draught for that. He may not be for you. But there are secrets to appreciating Poe, and I shall let you in on one of the most important ones: read him aloud.

Read the poems aloud. Read the stories aloud. Feel the way the words work in your mouth, the way the syllables bounce and roll and drive and repeat, or almost repeat. Poe's poems would be beautiful if you spoke no English (indeed, a poem like 'Ulalume' remains opaque even if you do understand English – it implies a host of meanings, but does not provide any solutions). Lines which, when read on paper, seem overwrought or needlessly repetitive or even mawkish, when spoken aloud reshape and reconfigure.

(You may feel peculiar, or embarrassed, reading aloud; if you would rather read aloud in solitude I suggest you find a secret place; or if you would like an audience, find someone who likes to be read to, and read to him or to her.)

For a long time, one of my favorite books-as-an-object has been a copy of *Tales of Mystery and Imagination,* illustrated by the Irish stained-glass artist Harry Clarke, with a passion and a madness and an intense sense of shadows and of the wrongnesses of angle and form that seem perfectly suited to Poe's nightmarish tales.

But then, Poe's stories will always cry out to be illustrated. They contain central and primary images, blasts of color, and maddening visual shapes (imagine: a black raven on the pale bust of Pallas Athene; the rooms of all colors but one in Prospero's doomed palace; the bottles and the bones in Montresor's cata-combs; a single black cat in a wall, on the head of a dead woman; a heart beating beneath the floorboards – a tell-tale heart . . .). Pictures come unbidden as you read the tales; you craft them in your head.

Poe's stories – even his humorous tales, even his detective stories – are populated by amnesiacs and obsessives, by people doomed to remember what they desire only to forget, and are told by madmen and liars and lovers and ghosts. They are powered by what remains untold as much as by what Poe tells us, each of them split and shivered by a crack as deep and as dangerous as the fissure that runs from top to bottom of the gloomy house inhabited by Roderick and Madeline Usher.

For some of you this will be the first encounter with Poe, while others of you will be here because you already appreciate Poe's work, or because you treasure beautiful books, and beautiful poems. And still, and still, *'There is no exquisite beauty,'* as Poe reminds us, in 'Ligeia', *'without some strangeness in the proportion . . .'*

From the introduction to the 2004 Barnes & Noble Deluxe Edition of *Selected Poems and Tales* by Edgar Allan Poe, illustrated by Mark Summers.

On *The New Annotated Dracula*

A few days ago there was an article in the English newspapers which purported to show how badly history was being taught these days, or perhaps display the state of ignorance of history in Britain. In it we learned that many British teenagers believe that Winston Churchill and Richard the Lionheart were mythical or fictional, while over half of them were sure that Sherlock Holmes was a real person, just as they believe in King Arthur. Nothing was said in the article about Dracula, however – perhaps because he was not British, although the adventure that brought him to public consciousness was certainly British, even though the chronicler was an Irishman.

I wonder what people would have said if they had been asked, how many of them would have believed that there really was a Dracula. (Not the historical Dracula, mind, Vlad Dracula, the son of the Dragon, the impaler. He existed all right, although whether he shares anything more than a name with the real, as opposed to the historical, Dracula is debatable.)

I think they would have believed in him.

I do.

I first read Bram Stoker's book *Dracula* when I was about seven, having found it on a friend's father's bookshelf, although my encounter with Dracula at that point consisted of reading the first part of the story, Jonathan Harker's unfortunate visit to Castle Dracula, and then immediately turning to the end of the book, where I read enough of it to be certain that Dracula died and could not get out of the book to harm me. Having established this, I put it back on the shelf, and did not pick up another copy of the book until I was a teenager, impelled by Stephen King's vampire novel *'Salem's Lot* and by *Danse Macabre*, King's examination of the horror genre.

(I watched the film *Son of Dracula* as an eight-year-old, though, wondering whether young Quincey Harker had, as I expected, grown up to be a vampire, and was disappointed to discover that the son was only Dracula himself, in the bayou, calling himself 'Count Alucard', a name that seemed fairly transparent even then. But I digress.)

Every so often, other books would send me back to reread *Dracula:* Fred Saberhagen's *The Dracula Tape;* Kim Newman's *Anno Dracula*. Books which would, by reimagining the events or the results of the novel, cast enough light on it to make me want to revisit the castle, the madhouse, the graveyard for myself, to lose myself in the letters and the newspaper clippings, the diary entries, and to wonder once more about Dracula's actions and his motives. To wonder about the things in the book that are, ultimately, unknowable. The characters do not know them, so neither do we.

Dracula the novel spawned Dracula the cultural meme – all the various Nosferati, the movie Draculas, Bela Lugosi and the fanged throngs who followed him. Over 160 films, according to Wikipedia, feature Dracula in a major role ('Second only to Sherlock Holmes'), while the number of novels that feature Dracula himself, or Dracula-inspired characters, is impossible to guess at. And then there are novels that lead into or lead out of Dracula. Even poor, mad, bug-devouring Renfield has two prose novels named after him, by two different authors, not to mention a graphic novel, all telling the story from his point of view.

In the twenty-first century any encounter with vampire literature or vampire tales is like hearing a million variations on a musical theme, and the theme began, not with *Varney the Vampire,* nor even with *Carmilla,* but with Bram Stoker and with *Dracula.*

Even so, I suspect that the reasons why *Dracula* lives on, why it succeeds as art, why it lends itself to annotation and to elaboration, is, paradoxically, because of its weaknesses as a novel.

Dracula is a Victorian high-tech thriller, at the cutting edge of science, filled with concepts like dictation to phonographic cylinders, blood transfusions, shorthand and trepanning. It features a cast of stout heroes and beautiful, doomed women. And it is told entirely in letters, telegrams, press cuttings and the like. None of the people who are telling us the story knows the entirety of what is actually going on. This means that *Dracula* is a book that forces the reader to fill in the blanks, to hypothesize, to imagine, to presume. We know only what the characters know, and the characters neither write down all they know, nor know the significance of what they do tell.

So it's up to the reader to decide what's happening in Whitby; to connect Renfield's rants and behavior in the asylum with the events that happen in the house next door; to decide what Dracula's true motives are. It's also up to the reader to decide whether Van Helsing knows anything about medicine, whether Dracula crumbles to dust at the end, or even, given the combination of *kukri* knife and bowie knife that, unconvincingly, finishes the vampire off, whether he simply transmutes into fog and vanishes . . .

The story is built up in broad strokes, allowing us to build up our picture of what's happening. The story spiderwebs, and we begin to wonder what occurs in the interstices. Personally, I have my doubts about Quincey Morris's motives. (The possibility that he is Dracula's stooge – or even Dracula himself – cannot, I am convinced, entirely be discounted. I would write a novel to prove it, but that way lies madness.)

Dracula is a book that cries out for annotation. The world it describes is no longer our world. The geography it describes is often not of our world. It is a book that it's good to traverse with someone informed and informative by your side.

Les Klinger is both of those things. I first met Les Klinger, who is, in his daily life, a lawyer, at the annual dinner of the Baker Street Irregulars, a group of people who, like 58 percent of British teenagers, are pleased to believe that Sherlock Holmes was indeed a real person. Mr Klinger is best known for his work annotating the Sherlock Holmes stories: his knowledge of Victoriana, of crime, of travel, is remarkable. His enthusiasm is delightful and contagious; his convictions and discoveries are, of course, uniquely his own.

One of the remarkable things about Mr Klinger's annotations is that they are illuminating whether or not you subscribe to the theories you will encounter here, of whether or not Dracula actually exists or existed, of whether Bram Stoker compiled and edited this book or whether he wrote it. Whatever you choose to believe, you will learn about Carpathian geography and Victorian medical theories. You will learn about the differences between the hardback and paperback editions of *Dracula*. You will be alerted to the wandering location of Shooter's Hill.

One of the drawbacks to reading editions of *Dracula* is they come, like this one, with introductions, and the introductions tell you how *Dracula* should be read. They tell you what it is about. Or rather, what it is 'about'. It is 'about' Victorian sexuality. It is 'about' Stoker's presumed repressed homosexuality, or his relationship with Henry Irving, or his rivalry with Oscar Wilde for the hand of Florence Balcombe. Such introductions will comment ironically on Stoker's writing against pornographic books when there is so much that is sexual seething in *Dracula*, barely under the surface, text, not subtext.

This introduction does not presume to tell you what *Dracula*

is about. (It is about Dracula, of course, but we see so little of
him, less than we would like. He does not wear out his welcome.
It is not about Van Helsing and we would happily see so much
less of him. It might be about lust or desire or fear or death. It
might be about a lot of things.)

Instead of telling you what the book you are holding is about,
this introduction merely cautions you: *Beware. Dracula* can be
a flypaper-trap. First you read it, casually, and then, once you've
put it away, you might find yourself, almost against your will,
wondering about things in the crevices of the novel, things hinted
at, things implied. And once you begin to wonder it is only a
matter of time before you will find yourself waking in the moon-
light unable to resist the urge to begin writing novels or stories
about the minor characters and offstage events – or worse, like
mad Renfield forever classifying and sorting his spiders and his
flies, before, finally, consuming them, you might even find yourself annotating it . . .

My introduction to *The New Annotated Dracula*, annotated by Leslie
S. Klinger, 2008.

Rudyard Kipling's
Tales of Horror and Fantasy

Years ago, back when I was just starting to write *Sandman*, I was interviewed by some long-defunct magazine, and in the interview I was asked to name some of my favorite authors. I listed happily and with enthusiasm. Several months later, when the interview had been printed, a fan letter arrived at DC Comics for me, and was forwarded to me. It was from three young men who wanted to know how I could possibly have listed Kipling as a favorite author, given that I was a trendy and enlightened young man and Kipling was, I was informed, a fascist and a racist and a generally evil person.

It was obvious from the letter that they had never actually read any Kipling. More to the point, they had been told not to.

I doubt I am the only person who writes replies to letters in his head he never sends. In my head I wrote many pages in reply, and then I never wrote it down or sent it.

In truth, Kipling's politics are not mine. But then, it would be a poor sort of world if one were only able to read authors who expressed points of view that one agreed with entirely. It would be a bland sort of world if we could not spend time with people who thought differently, and who saw the world from a different place. Kipling was many things that I am not, and I like that in my authors. And besides, Kipling is an astonishing writer, and was arguably at his best in the short story form.

I wanted to explain to my correspondents why 'The Gardener' had affected me so deeply, as a reader and as a writer – it's a story I read once, believing every word, all the way to the end, where I understood the encounter the woman had had, then started again at the beginning, understanding now the tone of voice and what I was being told. It was a tour de force. It's a story about loss, and lies, and what it means to be human and to have secrets, and it can and does and should break your heart.

I learned from Kipling. At least two stories of mine (and a children's book I am currently writing) would not exist had he not written.

Kipling wrote about people, and his people feel very real. His tales of the fantastic are chilling, or illuminating or remarkable or sad, because his people breathe and dream. They were alive before the story started, and many of them live on once the last line has been read. His stories provoke emotion and reaction – at least one of the stories in this volume revolts me on a hundred levels, and has given me nightmares, and I would not have missed reading it for worlds. Besides, I would have told my correspondents, Kipling was a poet, as much a poet of the dispossessed as he was a poet of the empire.

I said none of those things back then, and I wished that I had. I've said them now, to you. *Trust the tale, not the teller*, as Stephen King reminded us. The best of Rudyard Kipling's tales are, simply, in the first rank of stories written in the English language. Enjoy them.

This is the introduction to *Rudyard Kipling's Tales of Horror and Fantasy*, edited by Stephen Jones, 2008.

From the Days of Future Past: *The Country of the Blind and Other Stories* by H. G. Wells

H. G. Wells, Bertie to his parents and H. G. to his friends, was, with Jules Verne, the person who gave us the scientific romance – the forerunner of that branch of literature we now know as science fiction. His short stories, and his proto-science fiction novels, have lasted and are still read today, while many of the mainstream novels he considered more important and significant are gone and, for the most part, forgotten, perhaps because the novels were very much of their time, and swallowed by the change in time, while some of the science fiction and fantasy novels and tales are, for all their late Victorian or Edwardian settings, quite timeless.

Wells's novels set a pattern. The madman on his island making people out of animals, the journey through time or into space, all have been imitated, consciously or unconsciously, ever since, taken as templates for stories by hundreds, perhaps thousands of other authors: the arrival in a small Sussex village of an Invisible Man – his self-imposed confinement to his room, the brilliant but forgettable hero barely introduced until we are past the hundredth page, the revelation and explanation of poor, mad albino Griffin, is not just the story of *The Invisible Man*, but it is the shape, the recipe for a thousand other stories in which there are Some Things Mankind Was Not Meant to Know, in which the borders between science and madness are frayed. Wells's science fiction books are novels of ideas as much as they are novels of people; while arguably they are also all novels of class, either metaphorically (as Dr Moreau creates an underclass of beast-men in *The Island of Dr Moreau;* or *The Time Machine*'s Traveller encounters in the distant future an effete upper class and a monstrous lower class) or literally – crazy Griffin is a lower-middle-class creature out of his depth.

The short stories, for the most part, tend to be something else. Something unique to Wells.

It has been said that the Golden Age of science fiction is when you were twelve years old, and it could certainly be argued that Wells wrote his short stories for twelve-year-olds, or for the twelve-year-olds inside adults. His fabulism tends to be asexual, unproblematic, straightforward. (A personal admission: I read most of these stories first as an eleven-year-old boy. I found a thick, red-covered collection of *The Science Fiction Short Stories of H. G. Wells* on a shelf in a schoolroom and read it several times over the next two years, fascinated and transported. The tales were old, undoubtedly, but they did not feel dusty or anachronistic or even outdated. The flowering of the strange orchid disturbed me and unsatisfactory nature of the Magic Shop left me wondering. It was good.)

These are tales of obsession and revelation and discovery. Some of them swash, sometimes, buckle and adventure. Mostly, however, they remind us that they are, in some sense, eyewitness reports, with all the limitations and power of such. We are told repeatedly what was seen, and only a little more, and left to draw our own inferences. We are left to wonder. Was a man translated through the fourth dimension, and did he see hungry spirit-creatures there? Was that what he truly saw? Did man-eating cephalopods come ashore on stolid British beaches, to feast on human flesh? What was seen worshipping in the depths of the ocean abyss? How did the crystal egg arrive in the shop, and where is it now? We know only what was seen, and that, in its way, is convincing.

There is an old saw that in a short story one thing happens. Wells's short stories exemplify this. His writing is effective: as good as it needs to be, with little in the way of grace notes. Still, the best of them are haunting in their implications.

All too often they are tales of failed revelation. In Wells's world the fruit of the tree of knowledge is not eaten – not because of fear or difficulty, but because of embarrassment – and over and again knowledge or something equally as magical (the secret of making diamonds, an egg that shows us life on Mars, the formula for invisibility) is lost to the world. At the end of many of these stories the world is unchanged, and yet it *could* have been changed utterly and irrevocably. If one of the social functions of science fiction is to prepare us for change, Wells's stories began that process. Darwin adumbrated change. Wells was a scientist or at least, when young, a science teacher and science writer, taught by a disciple of Darwin's, and he was not scared by ideas or by the practicalities of science. Wells used his fiction to illuminate change, celebrating it as he warned of what change could mean.

The most successful Wells short stories are not what we today would view as stories, not really. They are anecdotes and journalism: carnivorous squid arrive in a tale that feels like an article from a turn-of-the-century scientific paper, while the ants, armed with poison, conclude their tale fifty years away from arriving in Europe (in those slow, comfortable days before container ship and jet plane). It's not a weakness – indeed, it's where these stories derive a significant amount of their power and effect from, and it's one of the places that these stories can be seen as early branches on the science fiction family tree: part of SF is the literature of ideas, and several of these stories are almost

pure idea, uncluttered by plot or narrative. Still, by today's
standards (and those of the time Wells was writing) this was
not on. They were not proper short stories – a criticism that
Wells took to heart in his 1911 introduction to *The Country of
the Blind and Other Stories*, when he says,

> We suffered then, as now, from the à priori critic. Just as nowa-
> days he goes about declaring that the work of such-and-such a
> dramatist is all very amusing and delightful, but 'it isn't a Play,'
> so we had a great deal of talk about the short story, and found
> ourselves measured by all kinds of arbitrary standards. There
> was a tendency to treat the short story as though it was as defin-
> able a form as the sonnet, instead of being just exactly what
> anyone of courage and imagination can get told in twenty minutes'
> reading or so. It was either Mr Edward Garnett or Mr George
> Moore in a violently anti-Kipling mood who invented the distinc-
> tion between the short story and the anecdote. The short story
> was Maupassant; the anecdote was damnable.
>
> It was a quite infernal comment in its way, because it permitted
> no defence. Fools caught it up and used it freely. Nothing is so
> destructive in a field of artistic effort as a stock term of abuse.
> Anyone could say of any short story, 'A mere anecdote' just as
> anyone can say 'Incoherent!' of any novel or of any sonata that
> isn't studiously monotonous. The recession of enthusiasm for this
> compact, amusing form is closely associated in my mind with
> that discouraging imputation. One felt hopelessly open to a para-
> lysing and unanswerable charge, and one's ease and happiness
> in the garden of one's fancies was more and more marred by the
> dread of it. It crept into one's mind, a distress as vague and
> inexpugnable as a sea fog on a spring morning, and presently
> one shivered and wanted to go indoors . . . It is the absurd fate
> of the imaginative writer that he should be thus sensitive to
> atmospheric conditions.

Wells seems painfully aware here that many of his most effective short stories were not explorations of character and event, and was uncomfortable with this. He need not have been. The truth is that they work because they lack, sometimes, plot, often, character. What they have instead is brevity and conviction. Arthur Conan Doyle's eleven-thousand-word story 'When the World Screamed' (1928) in Wells's hands would have been a journalistic report of half the length, devoid of people. It would have been only about the event. The world of the finest of Wells's short stories is one of possibilities, of breakthrough in science or society or of the Unknown which changes the world.

The stories, particularly the more fantastic of them, are most easily read as if they were postcards from an alternate future that is already past. Many of these stories are about futures and changes that have long since been carried away by time and memory: it is hard to remain on the cutting edge well over a century after the stories were written.

Wells described the art of the short story as 'the jolly art of making something very bright and moving; it may be horrible or pathetic or funny or beautiful or profoundly illuminating, having only this essential, that it should take from fifteen to fifty minutes to read aloud. All the rest is just whatever invention and imagination and the mood can give – a vision of buttered slides on a busy day or of unprecedented worlds. In that spirit of miscellaneous expectation these stories should be received.'

And that suggestion holds as true now as when he wrote it.

(THE READER IS ADVISED THAT SOME PLOT DETAILS ARE GIVEN AWAY IN THIS SECTION.)

'The Lord of the Dynamos' – Here we meet the New Theology, in a tale of 'a blackleg, and Azuma-zi, who was a mere black'. Azuma-zi, come to England from the East, sees the Dynamo as 'greater and calmer even than the Buddhas he had seen at Rangoon'. A reminder of attitudes and language we would no longer view as reasonable, and a story that presaged one of the themes of science fiction; that our machines, if we permit them, can become our gods.

'The Remarkable Case of Davidson's Eyes' – An example of Wells's technique of presenting the reader with an impossibility and then buttressing it with just enough detail to convince.

'The Moth' – Science fiction in that it is a fiction about scientists, but it takes on the mantle of a ghost story and then, in its view of the descent into madness, shades gently into the weird tale. As our scientist accepts that only he can see the moth he embraces his madness, and that is true horror.

'A Catastrophe' – A heartbreakingly biographical story, but one that gives a happy ending to a world that in Wells's own life ended in disaster. A what-if story. In reality Wells's father lost his shop, his mother went into service. Here is fiction as time-travel, a way to fix the unfixable.

'The Cone' – A small, tragic, eternal triangle (a cone is a triangle in three dimensions). Reminiscent of the tales of horror and revenge told in the American EC Comics line in the 1950s, in which a metaphor is taken literally and lethally: blood boils in the veins of both the artist and the cuckolded husband, and in the case of one of them it is not merely a figure of speech. With its machinery dominating the landscape, the story reminds us of 'The Lord of the Dynamos', and the end can be seen as a similar act of sacrifice.

'The Argonauts of the Air' – A small piece of science fiction, now consigned forever to an alternate past. A fascinating little story in which Wells's every guess and instinct was wrong, save for his understanding that mankind would be travelling by air, and sooner than most people believed. Despite the death at the end of the story, this is not shaped as a tragedy. This could be a space flight story, a little too early. While Wells was wrong about the early days of heavier-than-air flight – it wasn't a million-aire's game, but a relatively cheap playing field – he would have been right about space travel, which is a billionaire's game of the kind where one can imagine the gilding of aluminium.

'Under the Knife' – A death that crosses the universe, in a story that is predicated upon changes in scale, as we gaze upon the handiwork, and the hand (although not the face), of God.

'A Slip Under the Microscope' – SF in the sense that it is a fiction with scientists in it; a fiction that reminds us of Wells's own early failure to graduate. Again, in every sense, a tale of class. Again, a tale of rivalry, here played out as a morality play in which success and failure mean two very different things to two very different people.

'The Plattner Story' – again, an anecdote, in which we find ourselves convinced of its truth by the initial shock of the reversal of right-and-left-handedness of things, as if Plattner has been mapped through another dimension and returned to us in mirror-form (the branch of chemistry known as *chirality*). We see ghosts and a nine days' wonder (there are many nine days' wonders in Wells's tales – *Here*, we are told in one way or another, several times, as the stories begin, *is something remarkable – something that has already been replaced in the imagination of the populace, and now I shall tell you something about it you did not know*.)

'The Story of the late Mr Elvesham' – A body swap tale, as poor Eden is subsumed into the mysterious Mr Elvesham. It's proto-SF that shades into pure horror.

'In the Abyss' – Again, a fragmentary, almost anecdotal piece, in which we gain a glimpse of a world deep beneath our own, and lose it once more.

'The Sea Raiders' – A tale I last read when I was twelve or thirteen. I remember the fear I felt then at the incursion of some-thing deeply alien and dangerous in places I knew and was familiar with. Another battle in the War of the Worlds, although the threat comes from below, not from Mars. The style is journalistic, the intent purely to convince. The inconclusive nature of the ending adds to the feeling that this happened, or could have happened, just as Wells describes.

'The Crystal Egg' – The nature of seeing is a theme that echoes through many of Wells's short stories and here (as in 'The Remarkable Case of Davidson's Eyes') we encounter seeing at a distance. Once more a revelation that is only partially revealed, wrapped in a series of mysteries and, eventually, lost due to human fallibility, not malevolence. The glimpse of another world the tale (and the Egg) gives us is otherworldly and haunting, and poor Cave, the small businessman on the edge, sustained by his visions of another world, is a perfectly Wellsian character, giving an odd humanity to what would otherwise be an anecdote about an interplanetary television before its time.

'A Story of the Stone Age' – Now an almost forgotten story, it feels like an aborted novel, one that should have continued. Wells is an early explorer of a genre that others have returned to over the years – that of conceptual breakthrough in Stone Age man, in a time when all ideas are new. The hero becomes the first man to ride a horse, and he creates an early doomsday weapon, a club inset with lion's teeth. While the story he gives us is satisfying, it still reads like something Wells meant to go back to and complete, a book that would have been the *Clan of the Cave Bear* of its day.

'The Star' – Wells enjoys changing scale, the slow pull back from the personal to the cosmic, and employs the technique here to great effect.

'The Man Who Could Work Miracles' – Justly famous, often dramatised – this story has been a film, and adapted many times for television and radio. Like many of Wells's fantasies, it loops back to where it began.

'A Dream of Armageddon' – Wells built a 'future history' – a consistent history of the future, in which he set several stories. This tale of a dream of events that have not yet happened, of future war and political and personal disaster, and of death, fits vividly into that history.

'The New Accelerator' – A remarkably joyful story of super speed and mischief. A playful story – for once in a Wells tale the Accelerator is neither lost nor destroyed, nor does it result in madness and death. Instead we end in possibility.

'The Truth About Pyecraft' – In the main, the narrator is indistinguishable from Wells. This is not true of the narrator of 'Pyecraft', who is a thin man, of Indian descent. Pyecraft himself, who thinks he wants to lose weight but actually wants not to be fat, is a real character, in a Bunterish sort of way, a marvellous and memorable 'great, fat self-indulgent man'. It's a genuinely funny fantasy story which leaves us – almost – where it began.

'The Country of the Blind' – For me, one of the most interesting of Wells's stories, partly because of his need to rewrite the story decades later, or rather, his need to give it a new ending. It's an unusual story in many ways: in its easy reversal of the common saw that in the Country of the Blind, the one-eyed man is king; in the inability of the protagonist to communicate; in the way that entire concepts become meaningless when the sensory information they carry becomes redundant.

The first iteration of the story (1904, given here) follows the classic Wells short-story pattern of an encounter with the impossible, and an unsatisfactory resolution, the story convincing us by its own awkwardness.

The later version (1939, missing the last three hundred words and with an additional two thousand words) is both more and less satisfactory – the convincing anecdote now becomes a real short story. The pattern is more familiar. Now the sighted man does more than simply escape – his vision gives him the power to return and warn the villagers, Cassandra-like, of their impending doom; the ending contains real love between a man and a woman, and the thrust of the story has changed from reportage to art. Each version of the story is perfectly satisfying, but the immediacy and conviction of the first ending is exchanged for something that demonstrates that, had Wells had the spirit for it, he might in later life have produced some remarkably moving short stories of the fantastic. (It was not that he was not asked, nor that he did not have a market. More that the fecundity of ideas went away, and that his mind and attention went elsewhere. As Wells explained, in apology, 'I find it a little difficult to disentangle the causes that have restricted the flow of these inventions. It has happened, I remark, to others as well as to myself, and in spite of the kindliest encouragement to continue from editors and readers. There was a time when life bubbled with short stories; they were always coming to the surface of my mind, and it is no deliberate change of will that has thus restricted my production.')

'Empire of the Ants' – A story of eco-disaster. An idea that would be seen now as a bouncing-off point, here is the whole story. Which makes sense, of course: the idea was original, and Wells is a remarkable tale-teller. The story ends with the worrying suggestion by the narrator, Wells, that the second act of this disaster story will occur in Europe in 1950 or 1960.

'The Door in the Wall' – One of my favourite stories, by anyone. Haunting, magical and sad, and none the less satisfying for being so perfectly predictable. Like a silent comedy, the delight is not in what happens, but in how each event in the chain happens at the perfect moment for it to happen.

'The Wild Asses of the Devil' – A little brimstone, a little political commentary. What more could anyone wish for?

*

There are few enough writers in any field whose short stories will be read a hundred years after they were written. Science fiction in particular has a short enough sell-by date, one that only the finest writers surpass. Ray Bradbury's Martian short stories transcend our knowledge that there are no canals on Mars and no atmosphere; too many near-future tales from too many fine authors were overtaken by events or by breakthroughs in scientific knowledge and became, simply, redundant. H. G. Wells's stories are, as this collection demonstrates, still astonishingly readable, and, ultimately, the joy of a volume like this is that the stories can and will be read, not as curiosities from the past, but as living things. Wells himself said of his short stories, 'I make no claims for them and no apology; they will be read as long as people read them. Things written either live or die . . .' And of all the things one can say about these stories, to my mind unquestionably the best is this: long after they were written, they live.

My introduction to the Penguin Modern Classics edition of *The Country of the Blind and Other Stories* by H. G. Wells, 2007. All Wells quotations are from his introduction to *The Country of the Blind and Other Stories*, 1911.

Business as Usual, During Alterations: *Information Doesn't Want to Be Free* by Cory Doctorow

George shook his head slowly. 'You're wrong, John. Not back to where we were. This morning, we had an economy of scarcity. Tonight, we have an economy of abundance. This morning, we had a money economy – it was a money economy, even if credit was important. Tonight, it's a credit economy, one hundred percent. This morning, you and the lieutenant were selling standardization. Tonight, it's diversity.

'The whole framework of our society is flipped upside down.' He frowned uncertainly.

'And yet, you're right too, it doesn't seem to make much difference, it is still the same old rat race. I don't understand it.'

–'Business as Usual, During Alterations' by Ralph Williams (Astounding Science Fiction, *1958)*

I bought a box of SF pulps when I was in my late teens from one of my father's friends, who kept them in the garage. English editions of *Astounding Science Fiction*, for the most part. Stories written by authors whose names I barely recognized, despite being a science fiction reader from about as soon as I could read.

I paid more than I could afford for them.

I suspect that one story paid for all of them, though.

It's a thought experiment. I'd forgotten the opening of the story (aliens decide to Mess with Us) but remembered what happened after that.

We're in a department store. And someone drops off two matter duplicators. They have pans. You put something in pan one, press a button, its exact duplicate appears in pan two.

We spend a day in the department store as they sell everything they have as cheaply as possible, duplicating things with the matter duplicator, making what they can on each sale, and using checks and credit cards, not cash (you can now perfectly duplicate cash – which obviously is no longer legal tender). Towards the end they stop and take stock of the new world waiting for them and realize that all the rules have changed, but craftsmen and engineers are more necessary than ever. That companies won't be manufacturing millions of identical things, but they'll need to make hundreds, perhaps thousands, of slightly different things, that their stores will be showrooms for things, that stockrooms will be history. That there will now be fundamental changes including, in 1950s-style retailing, in a phrase that turned up well after 1958, a long tail.

Being *Astounding Science Fiction,* the story contains the moral of 95 percent of *Astounding Science Fiction* stories, which could perhaps be reduced to: People are smart. We'll cope.

When my friends who were musicians first started complaining sadly about people stealing their music on Napster, back in the 1990s, I told them about the story of the duplicator machines. (I could not remember the name of the story or the author. It was not until I agreed to write this introduction I asked a friend, via e-mail, and found myself, a Google later, rereading it for the first time in decades.)

It seemed to me that copying music was not stealing. It was something else. It was the duplicator machine story: you were pressing a button and an object appeared in the pan. Which meant, I suspected, that music-as-object (CD, vinyl, cassette tape) was going to lose value, and that other things – mostly things that could not be reproduced, things like live shows and personal contact – would increase in value.

I remembered what Charles Dickens did, a hundred and fifty years before, when copyright laws meant that his copyrights were worth nothing in the US: he was widely read, but he was not making any money from it. So he took the piracy as advertising, and toured the US in theaters, reading from his books. He made money, and he saw America.

So I started doing *Evenings with Neil Gaiman* as fund-raisers for the Comic Book Legal Defense Fund, and learning how to do that; to make an evening interesting for an audience, with just me and a stage and things I'd written, partly because it seemed to me that one day it might not be as easy to make money from selling stories in the traditional way, but that business might still continue more or less as usual, during the alterations, if there were other things I could do.

And as the nature of music-selling changed utterly and fundamentally, I just stood and watched and nodded. Now the nature of book publishing is changing, and the only people who claim to know what the landscape of publishing will look like a decade from now are fools or deluding themselves. Some people think the sky is falling, and I do not entirely blame them.

I never worried that the world was ending, because as a teen I'd read a thought experiment in an SF pulp published two years before I was born. It stretched my head.

I know that the view is going to be very different in the future, that authors are going to get their money from different places. I am certain that not all authors can be Charles Dickens, and many of us became authors in order to avoid getting up on stages in the first place, and that it's not a solution for everybody or even for most of us.

Fortunately, Cory Doctorow has written this book. It's filled with wisdom and with thought experiments and with things that will mess with your mind. Cory once came up with an analogy while we argued that explained the world that we were heading into in terms of mammals versus dandelions to me, and I've never seen anything quite the same way since.

Mammals, he said, and I paraphrase here and do not put it as well as Cory did, invest a great deal of time and energy in their young, in the pregnancy, in raising them. Dandelions just let their seeds go to the wind, and do not mourn the seeds that do not make it. Until recently, creating intellectual content for payment has been a mammalian idea. Now it's time for creators to accept that we are becoming dandelions.

The world is not ending. Not if, as *Astounding Science Fiction* used to suggest, humans are bright enough to think our way out of the problems we think ourselves into.

I suspect that the next generation to come along will puzzle over our agonies, much as I puzzled over the death of the Victorian music halls as a child, and much as I felt sorry for the performers who had only needed thirteen minutes of material in their whole life, and who did their thirteen minutes in town after town until the day that television came along and killed it all.

In the meanwhile, it's business as usual, during alterations.

This is one of two introductions to Cory Doctorow's *Information Doesn't Want to Be Free: Laws for the Internet Age*, 2014.

The Mystery of G. K. Chesterton's Father Brown

It is not that the Father Brown stories lack color. Chesterton was, after all, an artist, and begins almost every story by painting in light. 'The evening daylight in the streets was large and luminous, opalescent and empty' ('The Man in the Passage'); 'It was one of those chilly and empty afternoons in the early winter, when the daylight is silver rather than gold, and pewter rather than silver' ('The God of the Gongs'); 'The sky was as Prussian a blue as Potsdam could require, but it was yet more like that lavish and glowing use of the color which a child extracts from a shilling paint box' ('The Fairy Tale of Father Brown') – three examples picked at random from *The Wisdom of Father Brown*, each occurring in the first paragraph.

We first meet him in 'The Blue Cross', a bumbling Essex curate, laden down with brown paper parcels and an umbrella. Chesterton borrowed the parcels, the umbrella, and perhaps the central character from his friend Father John O'Connor – once he had discovered, with surprise, that a priest (whom society assumes to be unworldly) must by profession be on close terms with the World and its sins. 'The Blue Cross' illustrates this principle: Flambeau, the master thief, is out-thought every step of the way by the little priest, because the priest understands theft.

He had black clerical garb and a flat hat, sandy hair, and gray eyes as 'empty as the North Sea'. He was Father Brown (possible initial J, possible first name Paul), one of the greatest colorless figures of detective fiction, who continued through another sixty-odd short stories; less concerned with hounding down criminals, relentlessly bringing them to justice, or with solving crimes, than with offering the offender a chance at forgiveness, or merely being the commonsense vehicle that illuminates a Chestertonian paradox. Other great fictional detectives receive biographies, as aficionados backfill details of their lives and exploits (where *was* Watson's wound?); but Father Brown defies attempts to round out the details of his life outside of the canon. He had no home life, no early years, no last bow. He lacked color.

It was Chesterton himself who pointed out that his subtitle to the novel *The Man Who Was Thursday, A Nightmare,* tended to be overlooked. Perhaps that explains something else about the Father Brown stories: their logic is dream logic. The characters from a Father Brown story have little existence before the story starts, none after it has finished: each cast of innocents and malefactors is assembled to make the story work, and for no other reason. The tales are not exercises in deduction, for rarely is the reader presented with a set of clues and logical problems to work through. Instead they are the inspired magic tricks of a master showman, or *tromp l'oeil* paintings in which the application of a little brown suddenly turns an Eastern swami into a private secretary, or a suicide into a murder and back again.

The Father Brown stories are a game of masks – it is rare that an unmasking of some kind does not occur. The denouement tends less to be a summation of misdirected clues, than a revelation of who, in the story one has read, was really whom.

It has been said that Chesterton was not proud of Father Brown; it is true that he wrote the stories, especially in the latter days, to fund *GK's Weekly,* the mouthpiece for his theories of

Distributionism (a sort of bucolic socialism, in which every right-thinking Englishman would own his own cow, and a plot of land to graze it on). It is also true that many of the Father Brown stories are repetitive; there are only so many masks, so many times a man can disguise himself as himself. But even the worst of the stories contains something magical and rare: a sunset, perhaps, or a fabulous last line.

Chesterton himself was colorful, larger than life: one would imagine that in the creation of a detective he would have opted for the flamboyant – his hero would be a Flambeau, or a Sunday. Father Brown, on the other hand, seems created less as a detective than as a reaction to detectives, in a milieu in which, as GKC complained, 'the front of the cover shows somebody shot / And the back of the cover will tell you the plot' ('Commercial Candour').

You cannot celebrate Father Brown, for he doesn't exist. In the Chestertonian game of masks, the detective is the McGuffin, significant by his very insignificance. A plain little goblin of a man, less disorganized and flustered the more the tales go on, but still colorless to the extreme as he walks among the mirrors and the ever-changing lights.

'One of the wise and awful truths which this brown-paper art reveals is this,' said Chesterton, discussing his fondness for drawing with chalks on brown paper, 'that white is also a colour.' And it is also a wise and awful truth that the most colorless of all detectives was employed to reveal the most colorful of all detective stories.

An essay from *100 Great Detectives*, 1991.

Concerning Dreams and Nightmares: The Dream Stories of H. P. Lovecraft

I f literature is the world, then fantasy and horror are twin
cities, divided by a river of black water. The Horror place is
a rather more dangerous place, or it should be: you can walk
around Fantasy alone.

And if Horror and Fantasy are cities, then H. P. Lovecraft is
the kind of long street that runs from the outskirts of one city
to the end of the other. It began life as a minor thoroughfare,
and is now a six-lane highway, built up on every side.

That's H. P. Lovecraft, the phenomenon. H. P. Lovecraft, the
man, died at the age of forty-seven, over fifty years ago.

*

The man: thin, ascetic, an anachronism in his own time.

There's a World Fantasy Award sitting on my stairs; I pat its
head as I walk past: a Gahan Wilson sculpture of Howard Phillips
Lovecraft (1890–1937). It's a portrait of a thin-lipped man, with
a high forehead, a long chin and wide eyes. He looks vaguely
uncomfortable, vaguely alien, an Easter Island statue of a man.

He was a solitary individual, an inhabitant of Providence,

Rhode Island. He communicated with the outside world through letters, some of them the length of short novels.

He wrote for the pulps: fiction for disposable publications like *Weird Tales*, its covers showing vaguely arty lesbian bondage scenes. He ghostwrote a Houdini story, rewrote the work of aspiring writers; he sold two tales – 'At the Mountains of Madness' and 'The Shadow Out of Time'– to *Astounding Stories*.

He was a believer in unpleasant doctrines of racial superiority, and an Anglophile. He was a student of horror. There is an abundance of conjectures as to the circumstances of his life and death, the roots of his fiction, but they remain theories.

In his lifetime, he wasn't a major writer. He wasn't even a minor writer. He was a minor pulp writer, as forgettable as any of his time (quick! can you name five other writers for *Weird Tales* in the twenties and thirties?). But there was something there which, like Lovecraft's own Cthulhu, did not die.

(Poor Robert E. Howard, creator of Conan and of King Kull, is one of the other *Weird Tales* authors who's still remembered, when Seabury Quinn and many of the rest of them have blown away into the footnotes. Howard killed himself at the age of thirty, in 1936, when he heard of his mother's impending death. Then there's Robert Bloch, who, at the age of eighteen, published his first professional short story in *Weird Tales*, and went on to a long and distinguished career.)

Some of the influence of Lovecraft was immediate. His correspondents and fellow writers, including Bloch, Fritz Leiber, Manly Wade Wellman and others, played with the mythos he created: a world in which we exist in a tiny fragment of space-time, in which space, inner and outer, is vast, and inhabited by things that mean us harm, and by other things to which we matter less than cosmic dust. Much of Lovecraft's influence on fiction, however, would not really be felt for fifty years after his death.

His fiction was not collected while he lived. August Derleth,

Wisconsin author, cofounded with Donald Wandrei the small-press publisher Arkham House, in order to publish Lovecraft's fiction: and Derleth first collected Lovecraft's prose in *The Outsider and Others*, two years after Lovecraft's death. Since then Lovecraft's stories have been collected and re-collected internationally, in many anthologies, in many permutations.

This anthology is about dreams.

*

Dreams are strange things, dangerous and odd.

Last night I dreamed I was on the run from the government, somewhere in middle Europe – the last holdout of a decayed communist regime. I was kidnapped by the secret police, thrown in the back of a van. I knew that the secret police were vampires, and that they were scared of cats (for all vampires were scared of cats, in my dream). And I remember escaping from the van at a traffic light, running from them through the city, trying to call several unresponsive city cats to me: gray and sleek and skittish, they were, unaware that they could save my life . . .

It is possible to go mad, looking for symbolism in dreams, looking for questions, correspondences with life. But the cats are Lovecraft's. And the vampiric secret police, in their own way, are his too.

*

Lovecraft got better as he went on.

That's a polite way of putting it.

He was pretty dreadful when he started out: he seemed to have no ear for the music of words, no real sense of what he was trying to do with stories. There's no feeling in the earliest material of someone putting their life, or even the inside of their head, down on paper; instead, we watch Lovecraft in the beginning, copying, pastiching awkwardly – here's a dash of Poe, there's a little Robert W. Chambers – and over and above all the other voices of Lovecraft's early days, the awkward Anglophilic imitation of the voice of Lord Dunsany, the Irish lord and fantasist, whom Lovecraft admired more, perhaps, than was good for his fiction.

Dunsany was one of the great originals. His prose voice resonated like an oriental retelling of the King James Bible. He told stories of strange little gods of faraway lands, of visits to dreamlands, of people with odd, but perfectly apt names: always with a slight amused detachment. Many of the stories you'll find in this anthology, like 'Hypnos', or 'The Quest of Iranon', are vaguely Dunsanyish in tone.

Somewhere in there, however, as time passed, Lovecraft's own voice began to emerge. The writing became assured. The landscape slowly becomes the inside of Lovecraft's head.

*

It was September 1983, at the New Imperial Hotel in Birmingham, in the English Midlands: I had come to Birmingham for the British Fantasy Convention, to interview authors Gene Wolfe and Robert Silverberg for English magazines.

It was my first convention of any kind. I went to as many panels as I could, although I remember only one panel. The panelists were, if memory serves, authors Brian Lumley, Ramsey Campbell and the late Karl Edward Wagner, and Irish illustrator Dave Carson.

They talked about the influence of Lovecraft on each of them: Campbell's hallucinatory tales of urban menace, Lumley's muscular horror, Wagner's dark sword and sorcery and modern, slick tales: they talked about the psychology of Lovecraft, the nightmarish visions, how each of them had found something in Lovecraft to which he responded, something that had inspired him:

three very different authors, with three very different approaches.

A thin, elderly gentleman in the audience stood up and asked the panel whether they had given much thought to his own theory: that the Great Old Ones, the many-consonanted Lovecraftian beasties, had simply used poor Howard Phillips Lovecraft to talk to the world, to foster belief in themselves, prior to their ultimate return.

I don't remember what the panel's response was to that. I don't recall them agreeing with it, though.

Then they were asked why they liked Lovecraft. They talked of the huge vistas of his imagination, of the way his fiction was a metaphor for everything we didn't know and feared, from sex to foreigners. They talked about all that deep stuff.

Then Dave Carson, the artist, was handed the mike. 'F—— all that,' he said happily, having drunk a great deal of alcohol, dismissing all the erudite psychological theories about Lovecraft and cutting to the chase: 'I love H. P. Lovecraft because I just like drawing monsters.'

Which got a laugh from the audience, and a bigger laugh when Dave's head gently touched down on the table a few seconds later, and then Karl Edward Wagner took the microphone from Dave's fingers, and asked for the next question. (And, now, a decade later, Dave Carson's still with us, last heard of fishing off the pier at Eastbourne, probably fishing up strange Lovecraftian beasties he draws so well from the depths of the English Channel, but the bottle carried away poor Karl.)

It's true, though. Lovecraft's influenced people as diverse as Stephen King and Colin Wilson, Umberto Eco and John Carpenter. He's all over the cultural landscape: references to Lovecraft, and Lovecraftian ideas, abound in film, television, comics, role-playing games, computer games, virtual reality . . .

Lovecraft is a resonating wave. He's rock and roll.

I'm introducing a collection here that takes us through the

dream-fiction of H. P. Lovecraft, weaving it into a huge tapestry that drives from Fantasy to Horror and back again. Here's the tale of 'Pickman's Model' – pure horror, and vintage Lovecraft – and then there's Richard Upton Pickman, creeping through 'The Dream Quest of Unknown Kadath' . . . The chronological arrangement of stories forms odd patterns. Dreams and nightmares, too. Vampires and cats.

*

There's something about Lovecraft's fiction, about his worlds, that is oddly alluring for a writer of fantasy or horror. I've written three Lovecraftian stories: one obliquely, in *Sandman* – a quiet, dreamlike story (it's the first story in the *Worlds' End* collection. You can tell it's Lovecraftian, because I use the word *cyclopian* in it); one a hard-boiled 'Maltese Falcon' variant with a werewolf as hero (in Steve Jones's fine anthology *Shadows over Innsmouth*), and a third, when I was much younger, that was an awkward attempt at humor, an extract from Cthulhu's autobiography. If I go back to Lovecraft again (and I'm sure I shall, before I die) it will probably be for something else entirely.

So what is it about Lovecraft that keeps me coming back? That keeps any of us coming back? I don't know. Maybe it's just that we like the way he gives us monsters to draw with our minds.

If this is your first excursion into H. P. Lovecraft's world, you may find the way a little bumpy at first. But keep going.

You'll soon find yourself driving down a road that will take you through the twin cities, and off into the darkness beyond.

If literature's the world.

And it is.

This was my introduction to *The Dream Cycle of H. P. Lovecraft: Dreams of Terror and Death*, 1995.

On *The 13 Clocks* by James Thurber

*Something very much like nothing anyone had ever seen before
came trotting down the stairs and crossed the room.*

'What is that?' the Duke asked, palely.

*'I don't know what it is,' said Hark, 'but it's the only one there
ever was.'*

This book, the one you are holding, *The 13 Clocks* by James
Thurber, is probably the best book in the world.

And if it's not the best book, then it's still very much
like nothing anyone has ever seen before, and, to the best of my
knowledge, no one's ever really seen anything like it since.

I had a friend call me one evening in tears. She was fighting
with her boyfriend and her family, her dog was sick and her
life was a shambles. Furthermore anything I said – *everything* I
said – only served to make matters worse. So I picked up a copy
of *The 13 Clocks* and began to read it aloud. And soon enough
my friend was laughing, baffled and delighted, her problems
forgotten. I had, finally, said the right thing.

It's that sort of book. It's unique. It makes people happier,
like ice cream.

James Thurber, who wrote it, was a famed humorist (most of
his stories and articles were for adults) and a cartoonist with a
unique style of drawing (lumpy men and women who looked
like they were made out of cloth, all puzzled and henpecked

and aggrieved). He did not illustrate this book because his eyesight had got too bad. He got his friend Marc Simont to illustrate it instead. In England, it was illustrated by cartoonist Ronald Searle, and that was the version I read when I was about eight. I was fairly certain it was the best book I had ever read. It was funny in strange ways. It was filled with words. And while all books are filled with words, this one was different. It was filled with magical, wonderful, tasty words. It slipped into poetry and out of it again, in a way that made you want to read it aloud, just to see how it sounded. I read it to my little sister. When I was old enough, I read it to my children.

The 13 Clocks isn't really a fairy tale, just as it isn't really a ghost story. But it feels like a fairy tale, and it takes place in a fairy-tale world. It is short – not too short, just perfectly short. Short enough. When I was a young writer, I liked to imagine that I was paying someone for every word I wrote, rather than being paid for it; it was a fine way to discipline myself only to use those words I needed. I watch Thurber wrap his story tightly in words, while at the same time juggling fabulous words that glitter and gleam, tossing them out like a happy madman, all the time explaining and revealing and baffling with words. It is a miracle. I think you could learn everything you need to know about telling stories from this book.

Listen: it has a prince in it, and a princess. It has the evilest duke ever written. It has Hush and Whisper (and Listen). Happily, it has Hagga, who weeps jewels. Terrifyingly, it has a Todal. And best and most marvelously and improbably of all, it has a Golux, with an indescribable hat, who warns our hero,

'Half the places I have been to, never were. I make things up.
Half the things I say are there cannot be found. When I was
young I told a tale of buried gold, and men from leagues around
dug in the woods. I dug myself.'

'But why?'

'I thought the tale of treasure might be true.'

'You said you made it up.'

'I know I did, but then I didn't know I had. I forget things, too.'

Every tale needs a Golux. Luckily for all of us, this book has one.

There are stories out there where it helps to have an introduction, where you need someone to explain things for you before you begin. An introduction to set the scene, where the introducer shines light into dark places and lets the story shine more brightly, just as a precious stone polished and placed in a fine setting looks better than it might in a dusty corner or glued to a duke's grimy glove.

The 13 Clocks is not one of those stories. It doesn't need an introduction. It doesn't need me. It is like one of Hagga's jewels of laughter, and likely to dissolve if it is examined too long or too closely.

It's not a fairy tale. It's not a poem, it's not a parable or a fable or a novel or joke. Truly, I don't know what *The 13 Clocks* is, but whatever it is, as someone else said of something else at the top of this introduction, it's the only one there ever was.

This introduction was originally written for the 2008 New York Review of Books edition of James Thurber's *The 13 Clocks*.

Votan and Other Novels
by John James

T he hardest part of being a writer, particularly being someone who writes fiction for a living, is that it makes it harder to reread a book you loved. The more you know about the mechanics of fiction, the craft of writing, the way a story is put together, the way words work in sequence to create effects, the harder it is to go back to books that changed you when you were younger. You can see the joins, the rough edges, the clumsy sentences, the paper-thin people. The more you know, the harder it is to appreciate the things that once gave you joy.

But sometimes it's nothing like that at all. Sometimes you return to a book and find that it's better than you remembered, better than you had hoped: all the things that you had loved were still there, but you find that it's even more packed with things that you appreciate. It's deeper, cleaner, wiser. The book got better because you know more, have experienced more, encountered more. And when you meet one of those books, it's a cause, as they used to say on the back of the book jackets, for celebration.

So. Let's talk about *Votan*.

I'm really late in getting this introduction in, mostly because I've been trying to work out how to introduce *Votan* without giving it all away. One does not want to explain the jokes, nor does one feel the need to assign homework before one gives someone a book to read. But it will not hurt if you are familiar with your Norse myths. They will make *Votan* a deeper book, a game of mirrors and reflections and twice-told tales. It might be a good thing to read *The Mabinogion*, and the Irish *Táin*. They will make you smile wider and shake your head in wonder when you read *Not for All the Gold in Ireland*.

So. First of all, you should feel free to skip this introduction and go and read the book. You are holding a beautiful book here, written by a remarkable writer: it contains three novels. Two novels about a Greek trader called Photinus, who is at least the equal of, and, dare I say it, a finer rogue and tale-spinner than George MacDonald Fraser's Flashman; and a darker retelling, or re-creation, of a Welsh epic poem.

I read them as a young man – they were republished as fantasy novels in the early eighties, having been published in the sixties as historical novels. They are not fantasy novels, nor are they strictly historical novels: instead they are novels, set in historical periods, which people who read fantasy might also appreciate. The Photinus novels (there are only two, with a third novel implied but, alas, never written) are based on mythic and magical stories. (*Men Went to Cattraeth* is bleaker, and based on an old Welsh poem, the *Y Gododdin*.)

Photinus's mind and his point of view, his voice if you will, is not ours. It is this voice that lingers longest for me. His attitudes and his world are those of the past. Occasionally he commits atrocities. He does not have a twenty-first-century head. Many characters in historical novels are us, with our point of view, wearing fancy dress. Votan's dress is rarely fancy. The conceit that all protagonists in historical novels should share our values, our prejudices and our desires is a fine one (I've used it myself), and it is much more difficult and much more of an adventure to create characters who are not us, do not believe what we believe, but see things in a way that is alien to us and to our time.

My own novel *American Gods* has a sequence where the hero, Shadow, spends nine nights on the tree, like Odin, a sacrifice to himself: I did not dare to reread *Votan* in the years running up to writing *American Gods*, then once my book was written, it was the first thing I read for pleasure, like a chocolate I had put away as a boy until the perfect time. I was nervous, and should not have been. Instead I discovered a whole world inside a book I already knew. (And yes, I am sure that Shadow's tree-hanging owed a huge debt to *Votan*'s.)

So. Here are the things I will tell you, that might make reading this book more pleasant for you.

Votan is the story of a man called Photinus – a young man, a Greek trader, a magician, heartless and in it for profit – who seeks amber, and finds wealth and companionship and also finds himself Odin Allfather, the Norse god. The sagas and the tales and the poems that tell us about the Aesir, about Odin and Thor (Donar is Donner is Thunder), all reconfigure here, as if seen through a dark mirror: bleak tales they are, and dark.

It is not that James demythologises the stories, strips off all the beauty and the magic. It is more that he gives us reflection. At their best, these books are like holding a conversation with somebody from two thousand years ago. Occasionally, James can be too knowing or too wry (it is worth observing how many of Photinus's observations are common sense and utterly wrong – where amber comes from, for example, or the commercial possibilities of coal) but these moments are swept away into the next glorious story.

And the more you know, the more there is to find. I do not want to give away anything that James hid so well in his text, but here, I shall give you a couple of early ones for free: Loki is of the Aser, but not of them, trading on their behalf from his base in Outgard, not Asgard. In one of the most famous Norse legends, we visit, with Thor, Utgard, where the giants live, and meet the crafty trickster who is also King of the Giants, Utgardloki. (Loki is half giant, half Aesir.) In the Norse sagas, Fenrir (from old Norse, meaning 'fen dweller') is a monstrous wolf, the offspring of Loki, who bites off the hand of Tyr: here, our own Tyr tells the story of his own encounter with Fenris.

The stories of the Norse gods are dark stories, and they do not end well: there is always Ragnarok waiting, the end of all things, the destruction of Asgard and the Aesir and all they hold dear. While Photinus/Votan becomes a god, he is doing it as a servant of another god, in this case an aspect of Apollo, who desires chaos, and who is laying, in his own way, the steps that will bring about the end of the world, in fire. We meet the gods in this book, in a way that reminds me of Gene Wolfe's Latro tales.

Remember, when reading these books, Google is your friend. Wikipedia is your friend. If you are curious, look it up. Were there really Celts in Galatea – modern Turkey – that the British would have recognised as cousins, speaking a similar tongue? (Why yes, there were. Wikipedia tells me that three Gaulish tribes travelled southeast, the '*Trocmi, Tolistobogii* and *Tectosages*. They were eventually defeated by the Seleucid king Antiochus I, in a battle where the Seleucid war elephants shocked the Celts.') Were there really *vomitoria*, where Romans went to vomit? (No, there weren't. It's a common misconception. A *vomitorium* was actually a kind of hallway. But this is a rare slip.)

Not for All the Gold in Ireland brings us an older Photinus. I'm not sure that he's wiser, but he's softer, less monstrous. And he's funnier (both books are funny, although the humour of *Votan* is gallows humour). He's off to get back a document, and on the way he's going to wander a long way into a number of stories. He'll become Manawydan, son of Llyr, the hero of several branches of the great Welsh prose work known as *The Mabinogion* (as are many of the people we will meet on the way – Pryderi, for example, and Rhiannon. Taliesin turns up too, centuries before we would expect the legendary Taliesin, but it is a title, we learn, not a name, handed down from bard to bard).

And there's a strange and glorious achievement here: for the people are human, yes. But they are also mythical, larger than life. Not always in the way that we expect culture heroes and gods to be, but in a new way: they are avatars of gods, avatars of heroes: are these the Odin and the Loki and the Thor of legend, or do they echo them? Do the gods and heroes have a separate existence from Photinus and his crew, and are our protagonist and his friends being pushed through tales that will need to exist?

As the tale goes on, we meet other heroes (is Photinus a hero? He is the hero of his own story) and when we encounter Setanta, the given name of the Irish hero known as Cú Chulainn, we can predict that we will slip, as we do, from *The Mabinogion* into the *Táin*. And *Not for All the Gold in Ireland* concludes itself in a manner that is both a valid conclusion to the book we have been reading and a cliffhanger, and perhaps also a setup for another book, one in which, I suspect, Photinus would have found himself Quetzalcoatl of the Aztecs and Kukulkan of the Mayans.

That book was never written. John James did not return to Photinus: he wrote other novels, fine and powerful, and different. These are books that have been brought back into print by people who love them, and would not let them be forgotten. If you are willing to walk and ride with Photinus, who was called Votan and Manannan and many other names, and who only wanted to increase his family's wealth, and to bed the willing wives of absent officers, then he will repay you, not with amber, or mammoth ivory, or Irish gold, but with stories, which are the finest gift of all.

This is the introduction to the Fantasy Masterworks edition of *Votan and Other Novels*, 2014.

On *Viriconium:* Some Notes Toward an Introduction

People are always pupating their own disillusion, decay, age.
How is it they never suspect what they are going to become, when
their faces already contain the faces they will have twenty years
from now?

– A Young Man's Journey to Viriconium

And I look at the *Viriconium* cycle of M. John Harrison and
wonder whether *The Pastel City* knew it was pupating *In*
Viriconium or the heartbreak of 'A Young Man's Journey
to Viriconium' inside its pages, whether it knew what it was
going to become.

Some weeks ago and halfway around the world, I found myself
in the center of Bologna, that sunset-colored medieval towered
city which waits in the center of a modern Italian city of the
same name, in a small used bookshop, where I was given a copy
of the *Codex Seraphinianus* to inspect. The book, created by the
artist Luigi Serafini, is, in all probability, an art object: there is
text, but the alphabet resembles an alien code, and the illustrations (which cover such aspects of life as gardening, anatomy,
mathematics and geometry, card games, flying contraptions and
labyrinths) bear only a passing resemblance to those we know
in this world at this time: in one picture a couple making love

becomes a crocodile, which crawls away; while the animals, plants and ideas are strange enough that one can fancy the book something that has come to us from a long time from now, or from an extremely long way away. It is, lacking another explanation, art. And leaving that small shop, walking out into the colonnaded shaded streets of Bologna, holding my book of impossibilities, I fancied myself in Viriconium. And this was odd, only because until then I had explicitly equated Viriconium with England.

Viriconium, M. John Harrison's creation, the Pastel City in the Afternoon of the world; two cities in one, in which nothing is consistent, tale to tale, save a scattering of place-names, although I am never certain that the names describe the same place from story to story. Is the Bistro Californium a constant? Is Henrietta Street?

M. John Harrison, who is Mike to his friends, is a puckish person of medium height, given to enthusiasms and intensity. He is, at first glance, slightly built, although a second glance suggests he has been constructed from whips and springs and good, tough leather, and it comes as no surprise to find that Mike is a rock climber, for one can without difficulty imagine him clinging to a rock face on a cold, wet day, finding purchase in almost invisible nooks and pulling himself continually up, man against stone. I have known Mike for over twenty years: in the time I have known him his hair has lightened to a magisterial silver, and he seems to have grown somehow continually younger. I have always liked him, just as I have always been more than just a little intimidated by his writing. When he talks about writing he moves from puckish to possessed. I remember Mike in conversation at the Institute for Contemporary Art trying to explain the nature of fantastic fiction to an audience: he described someone standing in a windy lane, looking at the reflection of the world in the window of a shop, and seeing, sudden and unexplained, a shower of sparks in the glass. It is an image that raised the hairs on the back of my neck, that has remained with me, and which I would find impossible to explain. It would be like trying to explain Harrison's fiction, something I am attempting to do in this introduction, and at which I am, in all probability, failing.

There are writers' writers, of course, and M. John Harrison is one of those. He moves elegantly, passionately, from genre to genre, his prose lucent and wise, his stories published as SF or as fantasy, as horror or as mainstream fiction. In each playing field, he wins awards, and makes it look so easy. His prose is deceptively simple, each word considered and placed where it can sink deepest and do the most damage.

The Viriconium stories, which inherit a set of names and a sense of unease from a long-forgotten English Roman city (*English antiquaries have preferred Uriconium, foreign scholars Viroconium or Viriconium, and Vriconium has also been suggested. The evidence of our ancient sources is somewhat confused,* a historical website informs us), are fantasies, three novels and a handful of stories which examine the nature of art and magic, language and power.

There is, as I have already mentioned, and as you will discover, no consistency to Viriconium. Each time we return to it, it has changed, or we have. The nature of reality shifts and changes. The Viriconium stories are palimpsests, and other stories and other cities can be seen beneath the surface. Stories adumbrate other stories. Themes and characters reappear, like tarot cards being shuffled and redealt.

The Pastel City states Harrison's themes simply, in comparison to the tales that follow, like a complex musical theme first heard played by a marching brass band: it's far-future SF at the point where SF transmutes into fantasy, and the tale reads like the script of a magnificent movie, complete with betrayals and battles, all the pulp ingredients carefully deployed. (It reminds me on rereading a little of Michael Moorcock and, in its end-of-time ambience and weariness, of Jack Vance and Cordwainer Smith.) Lord tegeus-Cromis (who fancied himself a better poet than swordsman) reassembles what remains of the legendary Methven to protect Viriconium and its girl-queen from invaders to the north. Here we have a dwarf and a hero, a princess, an inventor and a city under threat. Still, there is a bittersweetness to the story that one would not normally expect from such a novel.

A Storm of Wings takes a phrase from the first book as its title and is both a sequel to the first novel and a bridge to the stories and novel that follow and surround it: the voice of this book is, I suspect, less accessible than the first book, the prose rich and baroque. It reminds me at times of Mervyn Peake, but it also feels like it is the novel of someone who is stretching and testing what he can do with words, with sentences, with story.

And then, no longer baroque, M. John Harrison's prose becomes transparent, but it is a treacherous transparency. Like its predecessors, *In Viriconium* is a novel about a hero attempting to rescue his princess, a tale of a dwarf, an inventor and a threatened city, but now the huge canvas of the first book has become a small and personal tale of heartbreak and of secrets and of memory. The gods of the novel are loutish and unknowable, our hero barely understands the nature of the story he finds himself in. It feels like it has come closer to home than the previous stories – the disillusion and decay that was pupating in the earlier stories has now emerged in full, like a butterfly, or a metal bird, freed from its chrysalis.

The short stories which weave around the three novels are stories about escapes, normally failed escapes. They are about power and politics, about language and the underlying structure of reality, and they are about art. They are as hard to hold as water, as evanescent as a shower of sparks, as permanent and as natural as rock formations.

The Viriconium stories and novels cover such aspects of life as gardening, anatomy, mathematics and geometry, card games, flying contraptions and labyrinths. Also, they talk about art.

Harrison has gone on to create several masterpieces, in and out of genre, since leaving Viriconium: *Climbers*, his amazing novel of rock climbers and escapism, takes the themes of 'A Young Man's Journey to Viriconium' into mainstream fiction; *The Course of the Heart* takes them into fantasy, perhaps even horror; *Light*, his transcendent twining SF novel, is another novel about failed escapes – from ourselves, from our worlds, from our limitations.

For me, the first experience of reading *Viriconium Nights* and *In Viriconium* was a revelation. I was a young man when I first encountered them, half a lifetime ago, and I remember the first experience of Harrison's prose, as clear as mountain-water and as cold. The stories tangle in my head with the time that I first read them – the Thatcher Years in England seem already to be retreating into myth. They were larger-than-life times when we were living them, and there's more than a tang of the London I remember informing the city in these tales, and something of the decaying brassiness of Thatcher herself in the rotting malevolence of Mammy Vooley (indeed, when Harrison retold the story of 'The Luck in the Head' in graphic novel form, illustrated by Ian Miller, Mammy Vooley was explicitly drawn as an avatar of Margaret Thatcher).

Now, on rereading, I find the clarity of Harrison's prose just as admirable, but find myself appreciating his people more than ever I did before – flawed and hurt and always searching for ways to connect with each other, continually betrayed by language and tradition and themselves. And it seems to me that each city I visit now is an aspect of Viriconium, that there is an upper and a lower city in Tokyo and in Melbourne, in Manila and in Singapore, in Glasgow and in London, and that the Bistro

Californium is where you find it, or where you need it, or simply what you need.

M. John Harrison, in his writing, clings to sheer rock faces, and finds invisible handholds and purchases that should not be there; he pulls you up with him through the story, pulls you through to the other side of the mirror, where the world looks almost the same, except for the shower of sparks . . .

This is the introduction to M. John Harrison's *Viriconium*, 2005.

So Long, and Thanks for All the Fish: An Introduction

N*ote to the reader from the Introducer:* If you have not read this book before, and have come here having just read the previous three books, you should skip this introduction and go straight to the beginning of the book. I give stuff away here. There are spoilers ahead. Just read the book.

I'll be here when you get back.

No, I mean it.

I'll put down some asterisks. I'll see you after them, when you've read the book.

ʌ ʌ ʌ

Douglas Adams was tall. He was brilliant: I've met a handful of geniuses, and I'd count him as one of them. He was a frustrated performer, a remarkable explainer and communicator, an enthusiast. He was an astonishing comic writer: he could craft sentences that changed the way a reader viewed the world, and sum up complex and difficult issues in aptly chosen metaphors. He combined the trappings of science fiction with profound social commentary and a healthy sense of humour to create fresh worlds. He loved computers, was an astonishingly fine public speaker. He was a bestselling author. He was a competent guitarist, a world traveller, an environmentalist, a man who held remarkably wonderful parties, a gourmand.

What he was not, and this may seem somewhat odd, especially when you consider how many of them he wrote and sold, and how famously well he wrote them, was a novelist. And this, I suspect unarguably, is the oddest of his novels.

So Long, and Thanks for All the Fish was Douglas's first attempt to write a novel from scratch.

In many ways it could be seen as an experiment. A transitional novel between the galaxy-spanning romps of the first three *Hitchhiker's* books and the more Earthbound adventures of Dirk Gently. It was, after all, the first of the three of Douglas's books not to have originated in the extraordinary period of creativity that took him from the creation of the *Hitchhiker's* radio series to the end of his time as script editor of *Doctor Who*. His first two books, *The Hitchhiker's Guide to the Galaxy* and *The Restaurant at the End of the Universe,* had strong foundations: they were built on the backs of the scripts that Douglas, and (for the second series) Douglas and John Lloyd, had crafted for the original *Hitchhiker's Guide to the Galaxy* BBC Radio 4 series. The third book, *Life, the Universe and Everything* was adapted from an unused outline Douglas had written for a *Doctor Who* film, *Doctor Who and the Krikketmen*. His next book, the remarkable *Dirk Gently's Holistic Detective Agency,* was adapted from Douglas's unfilmed *Doctor Who* story *Shada* (with a sprinkling of ideas from the filmed *Doctor Who* story *City of Death*).

The first *Hitchhiker's* books had been written by Douglas as a young man for a world that expected nothing, and were published as paperback originals. Now Douglas was, for the first time, being published in hardback. He was a bestselling novelist, who had not yet written a book he was proud of. This may partly have been because he was not a novelist.

Now he needed to write a book he had been paid a lot of

money to write. His accountant had embezzled most of the money and then killed himself. Douglas Adams had gone to Hollywood on his first, abortive, quest to get *The Hitchhiker's Guide to the Galaxy* made into a film. He had lived there for over a year, doing drafts of the film, did not have a good time there, and, surprised and a little battered, he had returned home to a little converted stable house off Upper Street in Islington, and, eventually, and under pressure, put off actually writing *So Long, and Thanks for All the Fish*.

His publisher, Pan, found themselves, early in 1984, soliciting a book that was, for the most part, unwritten and for that matter mostly unplotted. The lenticular image on the original cover showed a walrus that became a dinosaur, because Douglas had mentioned that there would be a walrus in the book.

There would be no walrus in the book.

It became part of the story of the book that, as the publishing date of the book got closer and the book got no closer to being written, publisher Sonny Mehta had taken a hotel suite and essentially locked Douglas in to write it, editing the pages as they came through. It was a strange way for a book to be written, and something Douglas used as an excuse for any problems that the book had.

But it was a book he was still particularly proud of when it came out. I remember that.

Douglas Adams had returned from America to Islington, and *So Long, and Thanks for All the Fish* occurs in the space that Southern California isn't. Which is to say that both Douglas's Outer Space and his Southern California are extremely Californian: the hotel in which rock stars read *Language, Truth and Logic* by the pool and the bar in which Ford Prefect attempts to pay his bill with an American Express card are not a galaxy apart, and the hooker who has a special service for rich people could exist as easily in one world as another.

Arthur Dent, in previous stories a flat character who existed mostly to boggle at the improbabilities, often infinite, he was confronted with, became someone significantly more like Douglas. Douglas's return from America was echoed in Arthur Dent's return from hitchhiking across all of time and space to an Earth that the readers believed to have been destroyed, and his explanation to the world that he had been in America.

It might be seen as a problem for a writer who was considered a social satirist to have, a few pages into the first book in a bestselling series, destroyed the Earth. On the good side it sets you free to explore the vastness of the infinite. On the downside, it rather limits you as an observational humorist, when it comes to specifics, and while Douglas may not have been a novelist, he was definitely an observational humorist.

Still, I think there's another reason for the restoration of the Earth at the beginning of this book.

Like it or not, and when it came out some people did and some people didn't, *So Long, and Thanks for All the Fish* is a love story, and the novel puts an Earth back for there to be a love story on. Underneath all the glitter, Arthur and Fenchurch, and the unlikely circumstances of their meeting, their love and the travails thereof, is the true subject of the book.

And as we grow older our reading of books changes. As a young man, writing a book about Douglas Adams and *The Hitchhiker's Guide to the Galaxy*, I remember picking up on the awkwardness of chapter 25, and Douglas's rhetorical question as to whether or not Arthur Dent has . . .

' . . . *spirit? Has he no passion? Does he not, to put it in a nutshell, fuck?'*

Those who wish to know should read on. Others may wish to skip on to the last chapter, which is a good bit and has Marvin in it.

I took it, at the time, as Douglas's contempt for and discomfort with his audience, and was uncomfortable with it. Rereading it a quarter of a century later, I found myself reading those paragraphs as worried bluster, as if Douglas was scared that he was out of his depth, and was trying to respond to critics or to friends ahead of time. I still suspect that, had there been time to rewrite, to rethink, to revise, that strange breaking of the fourth wall and the author-reader compact might never have happened.

I do not think it would have been a better book for not having been finished in a hotel bedroom, while Sonny Mehta watched videos in the room next door. After all, it is part of its charm that *So Long, and Thanks for All the Fish* reads as if it has been not so much plotted as stumbled upon or backed into. It is surrealist in the way that only a book extracted from the author without pause for inspection, for second thoughts or thousandth thoughts, can be. Characters appear and fade, dreamlike. Reality is frangible. The novel circles one event: a couple making love naked in the clouds, in perfect flying magical dream-sex, an event that is practically a poem.

So Long, and Thanks for All the Fish has, beneath the elegant veneer, the simplest, easiest, most traditional of plots: boy meets girl, boy loses girl, boy finds girl, makes love to her in the clouds, and sets off with her to find God's Final Message to His Creation. And does. After all, for a book suffused from start to finish with gloom and melancholia, a book in which the universe itself is fundamentally perverse, when it is not actually malicious, *So Long, and Thanks for All the Fish* is often peculiarly upbeat: chapter 18, for example, gives us, triumphantly, something unseen in the *Hitchhiker's* universe until now: transient and barely recognisable, but it's there: joy.

He hadn't realised that life speaks with a voice to you, a voice that brings you answers to the questions you continually ask of it, had never consciously detected it or recognised its tones till it now said something it had never said to him before, which was 'Yes.'

This was my introduction to Pan Books' 2009 reissue of *So Long, and Thanks for All the Fish*.

Dogsbody by Diana Wynne Jones

D on't read this introduction.

Read the book first.

I'm going to talk, in general terms, about the end of this book, and I'm going to talk about Diana Wynne Jones, and they intertwine (one made the other, after all), and it'll be better for all of us if you've read the book before you read my introduction. It's out of order and jumbled up, but that can't be helped.

If you need an introduction before you start reading, here's one: this is the story of the Dog Star, Sirius, who is punished for a crime by being incarnated as a real dog, here on Earth. It's a detective story, and an adventure; it's a fantasy, and sometimes it's science fiction, and then it breaks all the rules by twining myth into the mix as well, and does it so well that you realize that really, there aren't any rules. It's an animal story for anyone who has ever had, or wanted, a pet – or a human story for any animal that has ever wanted a person. It's funny, and it's exciting and honest, and it has some sad bits too.

If you read it, you'll like it.

Trust me. Come back when you've read the book.

* * *

Welcome back.

Diana Wynne Jones wrote some of the best children's books

that have ever been written. She started writing them with *Wilkins' Tooth* (a.k.a. *Witch's Business*) in 1973, and she continued writing them until she died in March 2011. She wrote about people, and she wrote about magic, and she wrote both of them with perception and imagination, with humor and clearness of vision.

We met in 1985, at a British Fantasy Convention, and we met before the convention started because we had both got there early, so I introduced myself, and I told her that I loved her books, and we were friends that quickly and that easily, and we stayed friends for over a quarter of a century. She was a very easy person to stay friends with, smart and funny and wise and always sensible and honest.

At her best, Diana's stories feel *real*. The people, with their follies and their dreams, feel as real as the magic does. In this book, she takes you inside the head of someone learning to be a dog, and it is real, because the people are real, and the cats are real, and the voice of the sunlight feels real as well.

Her books are not easy. They don't give everything up on first reading. If I am reading a novel by Diana Wynne Jones to myself, I expect to have to go back and reread bits to figure everything out. She expects you to be bright: she has given you all the pieces, and it is up to you to put them together.

Dogsbody isn't easy. (It's not hard, either. But it's not easy.) It begins in the middle, at the end of a trial. Sirius, the Dog Star, is being tried in a court of his peers. It's five pages of science fiction, and just as we're getting used to it we are thrust, like Sirius, into the mind, what there is of it, of a newborn puppy, and we are in a dog's-eye-view look at the world.

The magic of *Dogsbody* is that it's a book about being a dog. And it's a book about being a star. It's a love story, and Diana Wynne Jones wrote very few love stories, and normally in those she wrote, the love was flawed and imperfect. But the love of this dog for this girl, and of this girl for her dog, is a perfect and unconditional thing, and we know this is true as soon as we meet Kathleen. We learn about her life – the politics of the family she's in, and the greater politics that put her there.

Had Diana simply written a story about Kathleen and her dog from the dog's point of view, one that felt as right as this one does, that would have been an achievement, but she does so much more than that: she creates a whole cosmology of effulgences – creatures who inhabit stars, or, perhaps, who are stars. There is something called a Zoi that must be found before Sirius runs out of time. Then she adds the Wild Hunt, the hounds of Annwn, the Celtic underworld, to the tale, while never losing sight of the humanity at the heart of it.

I remember reading *Dogsbody* to my youngest daughter, almost ten years ago.

When I finished it, she didn't say very much. Then she looked at me and put her head on one side and said, 'Daddy? Was that a happy end? Or a sad one?'

'Both,' I told her.

'Yes,' she said. 'That was what I thought. I was really happy, but it made me want to cry.'

'Yeah,' I admitted. 'Me too.'

It also made me try to figure out *why* and *how* Diana had made the ending work so well, triumphant and heartbreaking at the same time. I wanted to be able to do that.

Three weeks ago, I was in England, in Bristol, in a hospice, which is a place that provides care for people who are going to die. I sat beside Diana Wynne Jones's bed.

I felt very alone, and very helpless. Watching someone you care for die is hard.

And then I thought of this introduction. I had been looking forward to writing it, looking forward to talking to Diana about the book, and now it would never happen. I thought, *If Diana was a star, I wonder which star she would be,* and I imagined her shining in the night sky, and I was comforted.

Once, long ago, people thought that heroes were placed in the night sky, as stars or as constellations, after their death. Diana Wynne Jones was my hero: a brilliant writer who wrote satisfying book after satisfying book for generations of readers; the kind of writer whose work will be remembered and loved forever, and who was as funny and smart and honest and wise in person as she was on the page. She will shine for a long time to come.

(My friend Peter Nicholls, who was Diana's friend too, told me that he thought she could be Bellatrix, the Female Warrior, who is the star in the constellation Orion's left shoulder, and I think that is a fine suggestion. Diana was a warrior, even if her weapon was not a sword.)

This is one of her best books, although many of her books are good, and all of them are different in their own respective ways. I hope it made you happy and sad.

This is the introduction to *Dogsbody*, by Diana Wynne Jones, and was written in 2011.

Voice of the Fire by Alan Moore

*O*ne measures a circle starting anywhere, said Alan Moore quoting Charles Fort, at the beginning of his exploration of Victorian society, *From Hell*. The circle here is temporal, and the circle is geographical. It is a circle made of black dogs and November fires, of dead feet and severed heads, of longing and loss and lust. It is a circle that will take you several miles and six thousand years.

I am sitting in a room in the Netherlands, in an anachronistic Victorian castle, writing an introduction to a book called *Voice of the Fire*, by Alan Moore. It is not the best introduction to this book, of course. The best introduction is the final chapter of the book, written in a smoky room in November 1995 by Alan Moore in the voice of Alan Moore, dry and funny and much, much too smart for our own good, written in a room piled with the books he has used as research, written as a final act of magic and faith.

One measures a circle starting anywhere. Not, of course, everywhere. One circle, one place. This is Northampton's story, after all.

If this were a linear narrative we would follow Northampton, voice by voice, head to head and heart to heart, from a stopping place in a pigpen for a half-witted youth, through Ham Town to a bustling medieval town to now. But the narrative, like the town, is only linear if you want it to be, and if you expect to get a prize for getting to the end you've already lost. It's a carousel ride, not a race, a magical history tour, no more evolutionary than it is revolutionary, in which the only prizes are patterns and people and voices, severed heads and lamed feet, black dogs and crackling November flames which repeat like the suits of a deranged tarot deck.

When the book was published, in 1996, it made less impression on the world than it should have: it was a paperback original, which began, with no explanation, with the personal narrative of a half-witted man-child, at the end of the Stone Age – his mother has died, his nomadic tribe has abandoned him, he will face the evil and trickery of those smarter than he is (everyone is smarter than he is), and he will also discover love, and learn what a lie is, and the fate of the pig in the Hobman's hoghouse. He will also tell his story in the most idiosyncratic narrative since Russell Hoban's *Riddley Walker* (or, perhaps, Alan Moore's Swamp Thing story 'Pog'), using a tiny vocabulary, the present tense, and an inability to tell dreams from reality. It is not the easiest of starting points, although it is a tour de force, and it sets up all the elements that will recur through the book. The shagfoal are here, huge black dogs that run in dreams and darkness, and the hair severed from the dead head of the woman beneath the bridge, and the foot of the boy's mother protruding from her grave, and the final, heartbreaking bonfire. It is November, somewhere near the day that will come to be known as Guy Fawkes Night, when, to this day, effigies are burned on bonfires while children watch.

Some of the joy in this book lies in watching a master storyteller take the voices of the dead as his own: the nameless psychopathic girl who visits the town-tattooed Hob, with her stolen name and stolen necklace of copper, could be coiling through a Bronze Age detective story; her comeuppance is another burning on another bonfire, one unexpected and cruel and appropriate. The girl is as dangerous, and as certain of her own intelligence and superiority, as a traveling underwear salesman, who will make his own sacrificial bonfire on Guy Fawkes Night, of his car and his sad life – he talks to us in the voice of a chipper spiv, lying to us and to himself the while, and for a moment we get a glimpse of Moore as an English Jim Thompson, and the outcome, like the outcome for one of Thompson's characters, is never in any doubt. A Roman detective, here to investigate a counterfeiting ring, his brain and body being eaten by lead poisoning from the lead-lined Roman aqueducts (our word *plumber*, of course, comes from the Latin for 'one who works with lead'), learns that lead is poisoning the empire in another way. The head is that of the emperor, stamped on a circular coin. The circle will be measured and compared and found wanting.

Assume, while you read, that the history is good history. Moore's suggestion for the secret of the Templars may not be the truth (nothing in this book is true, not in the way you're thinking, even if it happened) but it fits with the facts (giving us another severed head, along with Northampton's Templar church), just as Francis Tresham's poor head gives us his history along with his life. The stories are boxes that contain mysteries – most of which are unresolved, while all solutions we are given open the door to larger problems and difficulties. Or to put it another way, *Voice of the Fire* is truth, of a kind, even if its truths are fictional and historical and magical, and so the explanations one gets are always partial and unsatisfactory, the stories, as with the stories of our lives, are unexplained and incomplete.

It is a pleasure to read, and to reread. Start where you like: the beginning and the end are both good places, but a circle begins anywhere, and so does a bonfire.

Do not trust the tales, or the town, or even the man who tells the tales. Trust only the voice of the fire.

This was my introduction to the 2003 edition of Alan Moore's *Voice of the Fire*. It was the first thing I wrote after a bout of meningitis, and I remember how scared I was to put words to paper again.

Art and Artifice by Jim Steinmeyer

O ver a decade ago, I found myself invited to a 'retreat', at which several great minds in their respective fields – futurologists, cyberneticists, musicians and suchlike – and, inexplicably, me were gathered together to discuss the future, imagine the way things would change in the years ahead. We got some stuff right and lots of things wrong. One of the other people there was Jules Fisher, who really is one of the top people in his field, that of theatrical lighting, and a former magician, and we wound up talking about magic and theater. Some months later, out of the blue, he sent me a copy of *Art and Artifice*, in its original limited-print-run form, and I am still grateful.*

There is a magic to illusion. It's the magic you got sitting in the audience watching the girl (or the donkey) vanish or fly, from watching someone walk through a wall or produce a hatful of coins from the air. Your disbelief is suspended, the natural order of things is changed, the world is, for a moment, reimagined. And that thrill is too easily punctured by explanation – someone who has just seen, and been awed by, a miracle will feel cheated and cheapened by seeing it revealed as a trick, part optical illusion,

---

* 2016 Note: One of the people at that retreat was Danny Hillis, whom I wouldn't become friends with for another two decades. Hi, Danny.

part sliding panel, part bald-faced lie. It's why magicians guard their secrets, get huffy and upset when anyone reveals anything; they don't want it to take the magic away.

But there is another magic, equally as valid, and it's the awe of understanding how something was done. The sheer giddy delight at mechanics, at the way that human intellect and imagination can be employed to dupe or trick or befuddle an audience, the intersection of science and showmanship and the power of the imagination. The way that a cliché like 'They do it with mirrors' barely begins to cover what someone like Charles Morritt actually did. It's the point where 'How it was done' becomes, not the secret of magic, but part of a different language entirely. And nobody describes that ingenuity, the delight of putting it together combined with the aesthetics of invention, better than Jim Steinmeyer.

Penn and Teller have a routine called 'Liftoff for Love,' where Teller is put into a cabinet, the cabinet is broken into sections and moved across the stage, the head section is opened to reveal Teller's head still inside, and it's reassembled again. It's the sort of illusion that used to turn up on TV when there wasn't anything else on. Then they do it again, with a transparent set, and you watch Teller shooting through trapdoors, scooting back and forth beneath the stage, popping his head up once again, like a man in a maniacal ballet, and it becomes utterly magical – the energy, the deviousness, the work that goes into the illusion is more impressive than the illusion itself.

This book is like that.

This book of essays is not a book for people who want to know How It Was Done, as much as it is a book for those who want to know Why Anyone Would Want to Do It in the First Place. It's a book about the joy of the chase. This is Steinmeyer at his best, on the trail of a long-forgotten illusion the secret of which an Edwardian magician took to his grave, figuring one clue out from the writings of someone who looked without seeing or wrote without thinking, another clue from half-an-anecdote in a book of reminiscences, taking his knowledge of the history and technology of magic, and then making the process of the illusion, the backstage stuff with half-bricks and pipes and gaffer tape, become even more magical than the illusion itself.

With *Hiding the Elephant* Steinmeyer took the public on a journey through the history of theatrical magic. *Art and Artifice* is a backstage tour; it's the perfect book for those who appreciate detective work and the thrill of the chase, those of us who are excited by the description of Devant's Mascot Moth or Morritt's Donkey and wish we could have been there then to marvel and exult and to wonder how the hell it was done. The descriptions are clear, the mysteries excellently unraveled. Steinmeyer's combination of enthusiasm and erudition is a joy.

Every now and again my copy of *Art and Artifice,* the one Jules Fisher gave me, has disappeared, which means that several times in the last decade I've discovered how very hard it is to get a new copy. (Each time I'd given up my original copy surfaced again. I have stopped wondering where it goes when it's not on my shelves. I probably wouldn't like the answer.) It's one of many reasons that I'm delighted *Art and Artifice* is being republished for a wider audience. Enjoy.

My introduction to *Art and Artifice: And Other Essays on Illusion* by Jim Steinmeyer, 2006.

The Moth: An Introduction

I was given a list of all the things the organisers wanted me to do at the PEN World Voices Festival in New York. Everything seemed straightforward except for one thing.

'What's the Moth?' I asked. It was April 2007.

'The Moth's a storytelling thing,' I was told. 'You talk about real-life things that happened to you in front of a live audience.' (There may have been other answers in human history that were as technically correct, but that missed out everything important, however offhand I cannot think what they are.)

I knew nothing of the Moth, but I agreed to tell a story. It sounded outside my area of comfort, and as such, a wise thing to do. A Moth Director, I was told, would call me.

I talked to the Moth Director on the phone a few days later, puzzled: Why was I talking about my life to someone else? And why was someone else pointing out to me what my story was about?

I didn't begin to understand what the Moth was about until I turned up for the run-through beforehand, and I met Edgar Oliver.

Edgar was one of the people who would be telling stories that night. He tells a story in this book. You get the story in these pages, but you do not get Edgar's gentleness or his openness, and you do not get the remarkable accent, which is the sort of accent that a stage-struck Transylvanian vampire might adopt in order to play Shakespeare, accompanied by elegant hand-movements that point and punctuate and elaborate on the nature of the things he is telling us about, whether Southern Gothic or New York personal. I watched Edgar tell his story in the run-through (he managed to cut about ten minutes when he told it on the stage, and it was as if I'd never heard it before) and I knew I wanted to be part of this thing, whatever it was.

I told my story (in it I was fifteen and stranded alone on Liverpool Street Station, waiting for parents who would never come), and the audience listened and laughed and winced and they clapped at the end and I felt like I'd walked through fire and been embraced and loved.

Somehow, without meaning to, I'd become part of the Moth family.

I subscribed to the Moth podcast, and every week somebody would tell me a true story that had happened to them that would, even if only slightly, change my life.

A few years later, I found myself on an ancient school bus, being driven through the American South, with a handful of storytellers, telling our stories in bars and art museums and veterans' halls and theatres. I told them about how I found a dog by the side of the road who rescued me, about my father and my son, about getting into trouble at school as an eight-year-old for telling a very rude joke I'd heard from the big boys. I watched the other storytellers telling pieces of themselves night after night: no notes, nothing memorised, always similar, always true and always, somehow, fresh.

I've visited some of the Moth 'StorySLAMs', as people who are randomly picked come up and compete for audience love and respect, I've watched the stories they tell, and told my own stories there (out of competition, before or after it's all over). I've watched people trying to tell stories fail, and I've watched them break the hearts of everyone in the room even as they inspired them.

The strange thing about Moth stories is that none of the tricks we use to make ourselves loved or respected by others work in the ways you would imagine they ought to. The tales of how clever we were, how wise, how we won, they mostly fail. The practised jokes and the witty one-liners all crash and burn up on a Moth stage.

Honesty matters. Vulnerability matters. Being open about who you were at a moment in time when you were in a difficult or an impossible place matters more than anything.

Having a place the story starts and a place it's going: that's important.

Telling your story, as honestly as you can, and leaving out the things you don't need, that's vital.

The Moth connects us, as humans. Because we all have stories. Or perhaps, because we are, as humans, already an assemblage of stories. And the gulf that exists between us as people is that when we look at each other we might see faces, skin colour, gender, race or attitudes, but we don't see, we can't see, the stories. And once we hear each other's stories we realise that the things we see as dividing us are, all too often, illusions, falsehoods: that the walls between us are in truth no thicker than scenery.

The Moth teaches us not to judge by appearances. It teaches us to listen. It reminds us to empathise.

And now, with these fifty wonderful stories, it teaches us to read.

This is an introduction for *The Moth: This Is a True Story*, 2015.

VII

MUSIC AND THE PEOPLE WHO MAKE IT

'I think that night may have lasted a thousand years, one for every ocean.'

Hi, by the Way: Tori Amos

Hi, by the way.

I met her first on a tape, and then we spoke on the phone late at night, and then one night I went to see her play piano and sing.

It was a tiny Notting Hill brasserie, and Tori had already started when I got there. She saw me come in and smiled like the lighting of a beacon, played 'Tear in Your Hand' to welcome me in. The room was almost empty, save for the owner, who was having his birthday meal in the middle of the room. Tori sang 'Happy Birthday to You', then a song she'd recently written called 'Me and a Gun', pure and dark and alone.

Later, we went off through Notting Hill and talked like old friends who are meeting for the very first time. On the empty subway platform she sang and danced and acted out the video she had made that day for 'Silent All These Years' – one moment she was a Tori in a box, spinning around, the next a small girl dancing past a piano . . .

That was several years ago.

I know Tori a little better now than I did that night, but the wonderment she inspired then has not faded with time or with familiarity.

Tori doesn't ever ring me. She sends me strange messages by other means, and I have to track her down in odd countries, negotiate my way through foreign switchboards. The last time she wanted to tell me that they served great pumpkin ice cream in the place across from the recording studio, a continent away.

She offered to save me some.

And she wanted to tell me she sings about me on *Under the Pink*. 'What do you sing?' I asked.

'"Where's Neil when you need him?" she said.

Tori is wise and witchy and wickedly innocent. What you see is what you get: a little delirium, a lot of delight. There's fairy blood inside her,* and a sense of humor that shimmers and illuminates and turns the world upside down.

She sings like an angel and rocks like a red-haired demon. She's a small miracle. She's my friend.

I don't know where I am when you need me. I hope the pumpkin ice cream doesn't melt before I find out . . .

I wrote this for the tour book for Tori Amos's *Under the Pink* tour, in 1994.

---

* I'm not saying she was born with it. She may have done something nasty to some otherwise innocent fairies in order to obtain it.

Curious Wine: Tori Amos II

R iding a train through America I'm seeing a side of the country it prefers to keep hidden: it's truly the world on the wrong side of the tracks, a world of tumbledown tar-paper shacks, abandoned cars and boarded-up buildings. Now – as I type this – I'm somewhere in North Texas, riding the train through a swamp, watching an eagle circle and the play of light through the dusty leaves. I'm listening to Tori going to Venus and back.

'Suede,' she sings, music swirling around her voice like eddies in the current of the swamp-river. 'Anybody knows you can conjure anything by the dark of the moon.' It's a song like black chocolate and woodsmoke, shimmering and remote. 'Suede,' she sings.

It's too hot outside, but winter is becoming imaginable once more. Summer is rotting in a haze like a neglected peach. The album plays over and over.

Remembering the first time I heard these songs, in early summer: I had spent the day in Dartmoor, visiting friends (Terri's Pre-Raphaelite cottage, with its magic kitchen and elegant messages written in gold on every wall; wandering the Frouds' house, made even more otherworldly by the fact that they weren't actually there, just Brian's paintings and Wendy's elfish dolls smiling and leering at you from every corner of their concertina-maze of a world). I had fetched up in Martian Studios at the end of the day like a stray puppy in need of a home.

Outside the train window now: a wall of red earth strewn with a hundred glass bottles; a seat ripped from a school bus alone under a tree; pines and willows and a vast tangle of wild honeysuckle.

'What red wine is this?' I asked Tori, that night, when the world was quiet and dark.

'I'll send you a bottle,' she said. It was a marvelous wine, gentle and wise.

Sharing secrets on the sofa: I told her of the *baku*, and the fox and the monk. She played me the new album, told me its secrets and its stories, 'Lust' and 'Bliss', apologizing for a rawness of the mix (which I believed but could not hear), and I settled back and listened.

The curious wine made me expansive. I imagined the story I would write about it: I would tell the tale of each song through descriptions of twelve imaginary albums.

It is a greatest hits album, I told her, from an alternate universe.

Of course it is, she said.

I think that night may have lasted a thousand years, one for every ocean, and at the end of it I slept on the sofa, rag-doll floppy from the fine red wine, dreaming of the glory of the eighties and wondering why I had never noticed it at the time.

Traveling still now: passing a sudden thunderstorm in the hills of New Mexico; then the stately Californian windmill fields and hills signal that the train is leaving the real America and entering the world of the imagination.

And I meant to tell you about my Happy Phantom dream, and how she smiled and said, 'I know I'm dead, but why are they making such a fuss about it!' and to talk about the way that she smiled. But we're pulling into Los Angeles now, and it's time to stop writing.

And I'm drunk on a curious wine I tasted several months ago, having traveled to Venus and back.

The introduction for Tori Amos's *To Venus and Back* tour book, 1999.

Flood: Twenty-Fifth Anniversary Edition, They Might Be Giants

Not to put too fine a point on it, I was, in my mind, already too old for music to matter, too old for an album to change me and definitely too old to buy singles. I was twenty-eight, driving to Gatwick airport when I heard 'Birdhouse in Your Soul' on the radio, and it changed my life. And this is the odd thing: I didn't listen to music radio. Then, as now, it was Radio 4, or cassette tapes. But I was listening to music radio as I drove, and 'Birdhouse in Your Soul' came on, and I made a mental note and remembered the name of the band – They Might Be Giants, just like the film, where George C. Scott thinks he is Sherlock Holmes (the title comes from a conversation about Don Quixote, who fought a windmill thinking it was a giant – and what if he was right?).

When I got to London I went straight to a record shop, and bought everything they had by They Might Be Giants (*Lincoln*, and *They Might Be Giants*). They didn't have 'Birdhouse in Your Soul'. *Flood* had not come out yet.

What I loved about They Might Be Giants was that they made stories. The words were put together in a way that left holes I needed to fill in order to know what was going on. I became, whether I liked it or not, a part of the songs.

I called Terry Pratchett, because he loved stories too, and told him that I'd found something he'd like better than chocolate. 'Shoehorn with Teeth' became the theme song of the *Good Omens* signing tour. When we were under stress, we would sing it together. We were under stress a lot.

I bought 'Birdhouse . . .' as a single, the first CD single I'd bought. There was an Ant on there too, crawling up someone's back in the nighttime.

I bought *Flood* as soon as it arrived in the shops. In a break from They Might Be Giants tradition it didn't sound like it had been recorded in someone's back room. There were guest instrumentalists, a lush sound, strange samples. It still sounded like They Might Be Giants, but this time they were bigger giants.

The songs were, for the most part, dispatches from an alternate universe, slices from stories and lives we would never quite know. That didn't stop me thinking about them, though, or making up my own tiny stories to go with them.

It was the first album to come with its own theme, for a start. The world would end, but that was all right, because this album had begun. Yes. It had 'Birdhouse in Your Soul', a song by a proud night-light who is descended from a lighthouse. It had 'Lucky Ball and Chain', which looked back on an unusual marriage.

It had 'Istanbul (Not Constantinople)', which I was sad to discover had never been performed as a sand dance by Wilson, Keppel and Betty. It had 'Dead' on it, a song about final things and the meaning of life. 'Your Racist Friend', which comes into my head whenever I find myself having a conversation with anyone who begins a sentence with 'I'm not a racist, but . . .'

It had 'Particle Man' on it, finest of all superheroes. Terry Pratchett liked 'Particle Man' so much that he put a watch with an Aeon Hand in it in one of his stories, which I thought was very unfair, because I had wanted to steal the idea for a story myself.

'Twisting' made me sad – I was certain there was a suicide in there somewhere. 'We Want a Rock' was surreal in the best sense: it only made sense if taken literally, and then it gained a dream-sense. Perhaps everybody does want a prosthetic forehead, after all.

I think that 'Someone Keeps Moving My Chair' is really called Mr Horrible, and I am afraid of the Ugliness Man.

It had 'Hearing Aid' on it. A song with an electric chair in it that somehow seemed to be filled with sweetness and gentle age.

'Minimum Wage' put visions of stampedes in my head, with the cowboys all carrying placards. 'Letterbox' was the kind of tiny horror movie in a box I loved, its lyrics all tumbly and twisted.

'Whistling in the Dark' is what we all wind up doing, after meeting people who are not unkind, but still leave scars.

'Hot Cha' never will come back. The prodigal son will remain uneaten.

'Women and Men' was an Escher drawing in my head. The lyrics unpacked to contain the lyrics, the people will cross the ocean into the jungle forever. 'Sapphire Bullets of Pure Love' is a perfect phrase, almost as beautiful as 'cellar door', and it is up on the screen in my mind in a movie of black and white and sapphire blue.

They Might Be Giants wrote a song for themselves, and it explains the band's name and everything else about them. Hold on to the merry-go-round.

We are all in a Road Movie to Berlin. Or at least, we are all in a road movie, and some of us will wind up in Berlin in 1989, if we just keep going.

And now it's the future, and *Flood* came out a long, long time ago. The floodwaters are still rising, along with the ocean levels. Some things never go out of style.

Liner notes for the twenty-fifth-anniversary release of They Might Be Giants' *Flood* LP.

Lou Reed, in Memoriam: 'The Soundtrack to My Life'

'There are certain kinds of songs you write that are just fun songs – the lyric really can't survive without the music. But for most of what I do, the idea behind it was to try and bring a novelist's eye to it, and, within the framework of rock and roll, to try to have that lyric there so somebody who enjoys being engaged on that level could have that and have the rock and roll too.' That was what Lou Reed told me in 1991.

I'm a writer. I write fiction, mostly. People ask me about my influences, and they expect me to talk about other writers of fiction, so I do. And sometimes, when I can, I put Lou Reed on the list too, and nobody ever asks what he's doing there, which is good because I don't know how to explain why a songwriter is responsible for so much of the way I view the world.

His songs were the soundtrack to my life: a quavering New York voice with little range singing songs of alienation and despair, with flashes of impossible hope, those tiny perfect days and nights we want to last forever, important because they are so finite and so few; songs filled with people, some named, some anonymous, who strut and stagger and flit and shimmy and hitchhike into the limelight and out again.

It was all about stories. The songs implied more than they told: they made me want to know more, to imagine, to tell those stories myself. Some of the stories were impossible to unpack, others, like 'The Gift', were classically constructed short stories. Each of the albums had a personality. Each of the stories had a narrative voice: often detached, numb, without judgement.

Trying to reconstruct it in my head: it wasn't even the music that sucked me in, initially, as much as it was a 1974 *NME* interview I read when I was thirteen that hooked me. The opinions, the character, the street-smarts, his loathing of the interviewer. He was in the *Sally Can't Dance* phase, drugged out, the most commercially successful and most mocked album of his career. I wanted to know who Lou Reed was, so I bought and borrowed everything I could, because the interview was about stories, and stories that would become songs.

I was a Bowie fan, which meant that I had bought or borrowed *Transformer* when I was thirteen, and then someone handed me an acetate of *Live at Max's Kansas City* and now I was a Lou Reed fan and a Velvet Underground fan. I looked for everything I could. I hunted through record shops. Lou Reed's music was the soundtrack to my teenage years.

When I was sixteen and had my first breakup with a girlfriend, I played *Berlin* over and over until my friends worried about me. Also, I walked in the rain a lot.

I was willing to sing in a punk band in 1977 because, I decided, you didn't have to be able to sing to sing. Lou did just fine with whatever voice he had. You just had to be willing to tell stories in song.

Brian Eno said that only a thousand people bought the first Velvet Underground album when it came out, but they all formed bands. That may have been true. But some of us listened to *Loaded* over and over and we wrote stories.

I'd see Lou's songs surface in the stories I read. William Gibson wrote a short story called 'Burning Chrome', which is his take on a Velvet Underground song called 'Pale Blue Eyes'. *Sandman,* the comic that made my name, would not have happened without Lou Reed. *Sandman* celebrates the marginalised, the people out on the edges, and in grace notes that run through it; partly in the huger themes: Morpheus, Dream, the eponymous Sandman, has one title that means more to me than any other. He's the Prince of Stories too, a title I stole from 'I'm Set Free' (*I've been blinded but now I can see / What in the world has happened to me? / The prince of stories who walked right by me*).

When I needed to write a *Sandman* story set in Hell I played Lou's *Metal Machine Music* (which I've described as 'four sides of tape hum on the kinds of frequencies that drive animals with particularly sensitive hearing to throw themselves off cliffs and cause blind unreasoning panic in crowds') all day for two weeks. It helped.

The things he sang about were transgressive, always on the edge of what you could say: people pointed to the mention of oral sex in 'Walk on the Wild Side', but the easy gender changes were more important in retrospect, the casual way that *Transformer* took nascent gay culture and made it mainstream.

Lou Reed's music stayed part of my life, whatever else was happening.

I named my daughter Holly after Warhol superstar Holly Woodlawn, whom I'd discovered in 'Walk on the Wild Side'. When Holly was nineteen I made her a playlist of songs she had loved as a small girl, the ones she'd remembered and the ones she'd forgotten, which led to our having the Conversation. I dragged songs from her childhood over to the playlist – 'Nothing Compares 2 U' and 'I Don't Like Mondays' and 'These Foolish Things' and then came 'Walk on the Wild Side'. 'You named me from this song, didn't you?' said Holly as the first bass notes sang. 'Yup,' I said. Lou started singing.

Holly listened to the first verse, and for the first time, actually

heard the words. "'Shaved her legs and then he was a she' . . . ?
He?'

'That's right,' I said, and bit the bullet. We were having the
Conversation. 'You were named after a drag queen in a Lou Reed
song.'

She grinned like a light going on. 'Oh, Dad. I do love you,'
she said. Then she picked up an envelope and wrote what I'd
just said down on the back, in case she forgot it. I'm not sure
that I'd ever expected the Conversation to go quite like that.

I interviewed Lou Reed in 1991, over the phone. He was in
Germany, about to go onstage. He was interested, engaged, smart.
Really smart. He'd published a collection of lyrics, with notes.
They felt like a novel.

A year or so later, I had dinner with him, with my publisher
at DC Comics. Lou wanted to make *Berlin* into a graphic novel.
He was hard work at dinner: prickly, funny, opinionated, smart
and combative: you had to prove yourself. My publisher
mentioned that she had been a friend of Warhol's and faced a
third degree from Lou to prove that she had actually been a real
friend. Before he talked to me about comics he gave me something approaching an oral examination on 1950s EC Horror
comics, and challenged me on using a phrase of his in an issue
of *Miracleman* I'd written. I told him I'd learned more about
Warhol's voice from Lou's lyrics in *Songs for Drella* than I had
from all the biographies I'd read, all the Warhol diaries, and Lou
seemed satisfied.

I had passed the exam, but wasn't interested in taking it twice
and anyway, I'd been around long enough to know that the
person isn't the art. Lou Reed, Lou told me, was a persona he
used to keep people at a distance. I was happy to keep my
distance. I went back to being a fan, happy to celebrate the
magic without the magician.

I'm sad today. Friends of his are sending me brokenhearted

e-mails. The world is darker. Lou knew about days like this, as well. 'There's a bit of magic in everything,' he told us, 'and then some loss to even things out.'

Originally published in the 28 October 2013 issue of the *Guardian*. I wrote it on the train between London and Bristol, the day after I learned Lou was dead, and I borrowed from the interview/article I did in 1991. I've now taken most of those bits out, as that article is the next thing in this book, but some sentences might seem familiar.

Waiting for the Man: Lou Reed

I

W hen I was about fourteen I found a copy of a Lou Reed lyrics book in my local bookshop. It was a cheaply bound mimeoed affair, with a stippled caricature of Lou shooting up on the flimsy cover: pirate publishing.

I wanted it so badly, but I couldn't afford it (and the police had just busted up a junior shoplifting ring at my school and I'd had to return the copy of *Lou Reed Live* that Jim Hutchins – the Artful Dodger of the fourth form – had obtained for me at a price significantly less than the record store was asking, so even that option was kind of out).

I stood and read it in the shop, typos and all. Went back for it a couple of days later, but it was gone.

I've been looking for it ever since.

II

In 1986, back when I was still a journalist, I was in the press offices of RCA, with a friend who was blagging me a copy of *Mistrial*.

'Neil wants to interview Lou Reed,' said my friend.

'Lou Reed? Jesus. I wouldn't wish that on a dog,' said his press officer. 'He's hell on interviewers. Walks out on you if you say the wrong thing. He'll probably just tell you to fuck off. Or not answer you. Or something.'

Then they went on to talk about how a few years before a young hack had begun an interview with Meatloaf by asking him if the problem was glandular and never really got much further than that.

III

It started out as an idle comment, over a lunch with an editor. I gave up journalism for fiction three years before, and mentioned that, while nothing could tempt me back, I'd always wished that I'd interviewed Lou Reed . . .

'Lou Reed?' said the editor in question, her ears pricking up. 'Well, he'll be in Europe next month. But we were already thinking of maybe asking Martin Amis to talk to him.'

But I'd volunteered and Martin Amis hadn't, and somewhere wheels were set in motion, or at least a couple of phone calls were made.

A month later the book arrived.

Between Thought and Expression: Selected Lyrics of Lou Reed. Ninety song lyrics, two poems, and two interviews – one with Václav Havel, playwright, author and president of Czechoslovakia, and the other with Hubert Selby, author of *Last Exit to Brooklyn*.

Some songs had small italic notes at the bottom of the page. Occasionally they clarified; often they infuriated.

'Kicks', a song about how murder alleviates ennui better than sex 'cause it's the final thing to do' carried the annotation 'Some of my friends were criminals', while the note for 'Home of the Brave' read, 'My college roommate and friend, Lincoln, tried to commit suicide by jumping in front of a train. He lived but lost an arm and a leg. He then tried to become a stand-up comedian. Years later he was found starved to death in his locked apartment.'

IV

I was in my local Woolworths, in the nearest dull little English town to me (which doesn't have a real record store, just a Woolworths, which is still a real improvement over a few years back, when simply possessing a compact disc in Uckfield could have got you burned as a warlock), looking for *Magic and Loss,* although I didn't seriously expect them to have it. I went through the Rs but there was just a copy of *Sally Can't Dance* with a crack running down the battered plastic of the cover.

I asked the shop assistant about it, who pointed me to the charts wall. Lou Reed's in the UK top ten?

I heard the sound of the Earth turning on mighty hinges, and of stars forming new constellations, but I wasn't going to argue. *Maybe now,* I thought, *they'll bring out the Arista albums on CD.*

My *Rock and Roll Heart* LP has been unplayable for almost a decade.

V

The first time I saw Lou Reed live I was almost sixteen. He was playing at the New Victoria, a converted London theatre which closed down a few months later. He kept stopping to tune his guitar. The audience kept cheering and yelling and shouting, 'Heroin!'

At one point he leaned in to the mike and told us all, 'Shut the fuck up. I'm trying to get this fuckin' tune right.'

At the end of the gig he told us we'd been such a crummy audience we didn't deserve an encore, and he didn't do one.

That, I decided, was a real rock and roll star.

VI

Three weeks were spent talking to WEA, Lou's record company. The interview's on. The interview's off. The interview's maybe on. It's going to be a phone interview. It's not going to be a phone interview. I'm going to be flown to Stockholm. I'm going to fly to Munich.

First thing you learn is that you've always got to wait.

Somewhere in there, at Lou's request, to prove my credentials, I handed over a pile of books and comics to Sally, the publicist at WEA. She seemed kind of impressed, so I decided not to mention that I could have been Martin Amis.

I'd seen the video of Reed's 'What's Good' at three a.m. on MTV while channel-hopping (European MTV is the only channel in the world worse than American MTV). Visually it was stunning: it looked kind of like Matt Mahurin's work, only it was in colour. I asked Sally who made the video, but she didn't know.

Days went by, and D-day was approaching fast, while we waited for word. I'm probably going to Munich. I'm almost definitely going to Munich.

I've never been to Munich. I've never met Lou Reed.

Friday, five thirty, I'm not going to Munich, and the interview's off. Cancelled. Kaput.

I went to bed for the weekend.

VII

I was fifteen and playing *Transformer* in the art room at school. My friend Marc Gregory came over, with a request. His band covered 'Perfect Day', but he'd never heard the Lou Reed original. I put it on for him. He listened for about a minute, then he turned around, puzzled, looking uncomfortable.

'He's singing flat.'

'He can't be singing flat,' I told him. 'It's his song.' Marc went off disgruntled, and I still believe I was right.

VIII

Monday morning: after it was all over, the interview was suddenly on again. Maybe.

Monday evening, I was sitting in an office in central London with a sore throat, a telephone microphone and someone else's Walkman, waiting for a possible phone call from a concert hall somewhere in Europe.

The owner of the Walkman, a music journalist, turned up to show me how to press the record button. 'Lou's meant to be a better phone interview than he is in person, anyway. I suppose he feels that he can always hang up on you,' he told me, to cheer me up.

I've always hated phone interviews. This does nothing to cheer me up.

IX

Let's put some cards on the table here. Where Lou Reed is concerned I lose all critical faculties. I like pretty much everything he's ever done (except 'Disco Mystic', on the A side of *The Bells*). I even like *Metal Machine Music*, sometimes, and that's four sides of tape hum on the kinds of frequencies that drive animals with particularly sensitive hearing to throw themselves off cliffs, and cause blind unreasoning panic in crowds.

X

It's seven thirty. The phone rings and it's Sylvia Reed. Lou's going to have to be onstage at eight p.m. Okay? No problem.
    There's a pause.
    Lou Reed's voice is charcoal-grey, detached, dry.

XI

How did you decide which song lyrics to put in the book?

Well, I've always had the view that the lyric should be able to stand alone before it gets married to music. I just got a list of all the songs, and picked out the ones I thought stood alone the best. If I even had a question about it I just took it out.

The other thing was whether it contributed to a narrative form. There's a narrative link that takes you through three decades, so they follow each other and make sense – certain themes became really apparent that you might otherwise not be so aware of.

Things like the sequence in the middle of the book, where you have a lyric for your father, your mother, your sister and your wife?

Yeah, that's an interesting little section, which actually comes from an interesting album, which had a lot of things like that on it. I hadn't really realised it until I started looking back.

That was Growing Up in Public?

Yeah. It certainly did apply.

That was one of the Arista albums. Are they ever going to release them as CDs?

I tell you, that's a really good question. I don't really have any real connection with them. In fact there's a compilation album gonna be coming out, and we had problems trying to locate the master tapes from Arista. They're corroding someplace in Pennsylvania . . .

I've been told by a secondary source that they will [be coming out] but I don't know how seriously I can take that.

I remember how badly those albums were slagged off when they came out. But in the light of the last few albums, it's seemed like the press has been reassessing them . . .

Aw . . . [laughs] I haven't seen any reassessment, to tell you the truth. I just remember getting bashed for them. But what is funny is that someone will bash them, then pick one out and say 'this one was the exception' and then another person will be bashing them and that won't be their exception, a different one'll be their exception.

I think it's possible some things are easier to view with a little distance.

Some of those albums that people say were so bad are among my favourites.

You've chosen 'The Bells' as your favourite lyric . . .

Yeah. I've always been very affected by it. And as I get older, and I get a view on the lyric a bit more, it becomes more mean-ingful to me.

So does the subject of the lyric change for you in retrospect?

Sure. Later on I find out what it was really about. Lots of times I'll think it's about one thing and as I get a little distance from it – and by distance I mean like, say, seven or eight years – it suddenly becomes very obvious to me it was about something else entirely.

It happens especially onstage. Periodically I do something older and I suddenly realise 'God – listen to what this is about. I can't believe that I said this in public.'

Some of the lyrics that you've mentioned are really incredibly personal, and pretty accurate – so obviously so that it's always kind of funny, over the years, people continuously asking me, 'Are these things based on reality?' I thought it was so obvious that they were.

You've said in the past that you started out wanting to try and bring the sensibility of the novel to the rock and roll single . . .

That was always the idea behind it. There are certain kinds of songs you write that are just fun songs – the lyric really can't survive without the music. But for most of what I do, the idea behind it was to try and bring a novelist's eye to it, and, within the framework of rock and roll, to try to have that lyric there so somebody who enjoys being engaged on that level could have that and have the rock and roll too.

Sometimes some songs take years to get right. You do it and you just know it's not right and you can't get it right so you leave it. I think you can only do your best with it and sometimes your best isn't good enough. At which point you have to give it a rest. Because then you start doing really strange things to it. And when it starts going that far astray it's time to go away from it.

Do you notice much difference between doing the public readings, and doing the concerts?

The guys aren't there: there's no band. On the other hand the humour in the lyrics is much more obvious. And some of the edge in the lyrics is also a lot more obvious . . .

I've got a new album out right now and there's a song called 'Harry's Circumcision', which you can take in a couple of ways. And one of the ways is that it's funny. I think I get classified in the black humour section . . . which I don't really think is true, myself.

Who made the video of 'What's Good'?

Isn't that something? Isn't that just something? He's so great. He's the guy who took the cover photo . . .

Matt Mahurin? It looked like his work. He really brought out the humour of the song's imagery. 'Mayonnaise soda', 'seeing eye chocolate' . . .

When I got together with Matt I was so glad he was able to do it. I said, 'Y'know, I've tried to put these really quick visual images that you can get really fast, and if we could just illustrate some of them that'd be great.' That's what he did.

It's like the storyboard for the song.

Literally. When he first sent it to me it was a storyboard . . .

It's the first video to feel like a Lou Reed song. I mean, there was that robot-ripping-its-face-off video . . .

'No Money Down'. Yeah. I thought that was really funny, that one. But yeah, as far as capturing what a song's about, this is the first one. This one actually does get it.

It adds something to the song.

That's what we thought. I mean the thing is that Matt understood it without me having to say anything, which was really great. Usually videos are pretty painful to do. But this one was actually fun. It was nice to see it realised.

   Also I didn't really have to, like, really play Lou Reed in the video – and that gets pretty tedious.

   Fifteen minutes before I'm onstage, just so you know.

Five minutes more, then?

No, I mean, you can go for the whole fifteen if you want.

Thanks. In the article on Václav Havel, you talk about the Lou Reed persona as something separate from you. Is that how you perceive it?

Well, it's something I use to keep a distance. Put it that way. But I would say it got out of control, and I've been deconstructing it. Which is really kinda funny, Neil, because I can go from this leather-jacketed street guy from New York, and then I show up and the next thing I hear is 'What are you talking about? This guy looks like an English professor.' It's actually hilarious.

Do they want to see you still shooting up onstage? Or in makeup? Or in shades and leather?

It depends what time they tagged into me. Some people are forever in the Velvet Underground thing, or the *Transformer* thing, or the *Rock N Roll Animal* thing – someplace around there. They'd like it to still be that. But I was only passing through.

It's 'You're still doing things I gave up years ago'?

[Laughs.] That's right. It is, isn't it?

Were you surprised by the commercial success of Magic and Loss?

Astonished would cover it. It's very strange. In a sense it's my dream album, because everything finally came together to where the album is finally fully realised. I got it to do what I wanted it to do, but commercial thoughts never entered into it, so I'm just stunned.

In the book, the notes at the end of the songs have a certain laconic teasing quality . . .

If by 'teasing' you mean I tell you a little bit and you would have liked to know a little bit more, then yeah. I thought it was just enough to let you know what was really happening and tie things together so you saw that there was a narrative. As though it was a novel except told in lyrics, and the little annotations were things that tied it together and gave you a little push onto the next one and also told you something that'd make you sit up for a minute. But I didn't want to go on too long with that. That'd be another book.

Are you ever going to write it?

I'm interested in writing a book. But not about me.

    [Dings and twangs in background. People seem about ready to go onstage.]

If there's one difference between the early work and the current stuff, it's in the persona of the singer. Previously Lou Reed was off on the sidelines: 'I just don't care at all', 'Makes no difference to me'. More recently there's been a willingness to be involved and affected

Yeah. I took a stance about a couple of things.

Why?

I thought I'd earned the right; that I knew enough about Life at this point, and had gone through enough where I thought stating an opinion about a thing or two would not be soapboxy or preachy but was just hard-won experience trying to communicate to other people.

    In a lot of the stuff that I wrote about there's no overt moral position, but what's being described speaks for itself and I don't think it needed me to say anything about it – I don't take a superior view or any kind of elitist view toward any of these things: it's life, and that's what we're talking about.

But over the last couple of years there has been a change, in the sense that I think I am capable of taking positions that I'm not going to change my mind about.

I think I can justify my opinions. They're hard-won and heart-felt.

You're still in rock and roll after more than thirty years. Do you ever see yourself stopping?

I just love doing it. This is like a new art form. You know, the CD, where you've got up to seventy-four minutes. It's odd to me that the last three albums all timed out at fifty-eight, fifty-nine minutes, without aiming for it.

To have, instead of fourteen or fifteen disparate songs, to have this something about one thing you can really sink your teeth into, is interesting: it might be interesting to do a two-CD set, the length of a Broadway play, I suppose.

I think on *Magic and Loss* – eventually you have to take a swing at the major themes and certainly loss and death is one of them.

They say that sex and death are all we've got to write about . . .

Those are the basic themes. There's a reason they're there, but I think every generation has to have them reinterpreted for them.

Also, while I don't understand the process in great specifics, I do understand what talent is, and what a strange thing that is, and I've been trying really hard to set up situations in which it can flourish. And that's the obligation I feel. To try to be true to the talent and make it possible for it to function.

'In dreams begin responsibilities'?

Oh sure. Absolutely. I have a dream too. And it turns out that a lot of the responsibilities involve not letting it become corrupted or compromised. Which all comes down to things you have to do in your personal life. That's why I was fascinated by talking to President Havel . . . *[Over the phone I can hear buzzers going off. It sounds like Lou ought to be onstage around now. Fifteen minutes are well up.]*

   . . . I had to ask him, 'Why didn't you leave? You could have left. You could be teaching at Columbia – you're a famous play-wright.' He said, 'I live here.'

Did that reflect your attitude to New York?

It's exactly my attitude to New York. That's why I was asking – I related to it in my own small way.
   You're being buzzed, Lou.
   Yeah.
   [He seems perfectly happy to keep them waiting. 'First thing you learn . . .']
   The thing is, I have my dream too. I'm glad my wife was there when I met President Havel, because otherwise I'd just think I dreamed it.

So where do you see the future going?

I want to take the writing further. I think that an album every three years isn't enough. I'm at the point now where I think I know what I'm doing.

As a writer?

Right. The Havel piece was hard.

Good writing ought to be hard.
You have to really want it. If you don't, it's sloppy. It's actually offensive – you'd be better off driving a truck.

   I got to run . . .

XII

Between Thought and Expression isn't a badly transcribed, pirated flimsy-covered book of the lyrics of Lou Reed. But what the hell. It'll do until one turns up.

   This was originally published in *Time Out* and reprinted in *Reflex* #26, 28 July 1992.

Afterword Afterword:
Evelyn Evelyn

The magic and the danger of fiction is this: it allows us to see through other eyes. It takes us to places we have never been, allows us to care about, worry about, laugh with, cry for, people who do not, outside of the story, exist.

There are people who think that things that happen in fiction do not really happen. These people are wrong.

*

Amanda Palmer is an outgoing, astonishingly funny, irreverent, sometimes loud, almost unembarrassable, beautiful chatty singer who plays piano as a percussion instrument. Jason Webley is a foot-stomping, freewheeling, gentle, aggressive houseboat dweller, who plays the guitar and the accordion. He always wears a hat and mostly has a beard.

Oddly enough, it was he who introduced me to Amanda Palmer, in e-mail, almost three years ago.

I heard Evelyn Evelyn before I knew anything about them. The song 'Have You Seen My Sister Evelyn?' was on my iPod, a strange ragtime encrustation, as was a song about an elephant, called 'Elephant Elephant'. The songs had crept onto my 'Stuff I Really Like That I Don't Really Know What It Is' Playlist.

I'd not been friends long with Amanda Palmer when I asked her about the Evelyn Evelyn songs.

'They are conjoined twins,' she told me. 'Jason and I met them through MySpace.'

'I thought it was you and Jason,' I said.

'No,' she said. 'Conjoined twins. They have had a hard life. But they make amazing music. They have a whole album coming out. Jason and I are producing it for them.'

'Is that true?' I asked. 'Only, on the songs on my iPod, it sounds like you and Jason singing together.'

Amanda Palmer said, 'Funny, that.'

*

I have been backstage at an Evelyn Evelyn concert. It starts out with Amanda Palmer and Jason Webley, who are two very different people.

Then they strip down. Jason shaves and puts on a bra. They make up. They put on black wigs and they clamber into a striped costume which has room for both of them. They pull it up. They put it on.

Evelyn Evelyn whisper to each other. The left-hand Evelyn seems slightly more masculine than the right-hand Evelyn. They do not meet your eyes. They are a unit. You watch them as they move, like one person. They are reluctant to walk out onto the stage.

They play two-handed piano. One of the Neville twins plays the right hand, the other plays the left hand. The same with accordion, ukulele, guitar. They play two kazoos, for they have two mouths. Only one twin needs play the snare drum and cymbals.

They sing. They relate to each other in a way they do not relate to the audience.

Amanda Palmer sings to, and talks to, and cares about, and

interacts with, her audience. Jason Webley is famous for getting his audiences magically drunk without even using alcohol.

The twins exist only for each other – they play to each other, disagree, make up, care for each other, and whisper, always whisper.

They are aware of the audience. They respond to applause. But they are not on that stage for us.

*

And people ask, as I once asked, whether Amanda Palmer and Jason Webley are actually Evelyn Evelyn.

And they are not. They are something *other*, Eva and Lynn Neville, something that exists in a make-believe space inhabited by puppets and dreams. They are no more Jason and Amanda than the Haitian *Loa,* Baron Samedi, Mistress Erzulie and the rest, are really the horses that they ride. No more than Father Christmas was only ever your dad.

*

Cynthia Von Buhler here illustrates the life of the twins.

She brings delicacy and charm to a story that contains tragedy and darkness. Her illustrations have all the simplicity of great children's illustrations, but tell a story that could only exist because adults are foolish and confused and sometimes evil. She lets the Neville sisters and their story move beyond Amanda and Jason and their music and out into the world.

Their story is hard and strange, and they have had more than their share of bad luck and tragedy. But then, the same can be said of most of us. It is one of the secrets of being human. It's not the pain that you suffer: it's how you take the pain and move on. In the case of the Neville sisters, they make art. And

so do Amanda Palmer and Jason Webley, and so does Cynthia
von Buhler.

This is the secret of Evelyn Evelyn. You can be them too.
Start reading, and you will see through their eyes, and learn to
whisper secrets to yourself in the dark.

This was the afterword to *Evelyn Evelyn: A Tragic Tale in Two Tomes*,
written by Amanda Palmer and Jason Webley, illustrated by Cynthia
von Buhler.

Who Killed Amanda Palmer

L ike you, I know exactly where I was and what I was doing when I heard Amanda Palmer had been killed. I remember the way the sunlight glittered on the water, and I remember most of all that I simply did not believe it, for it seemed impossible that Amanda Palmer (so wise and mouthy and lovely, so filled with life that it had always seemed as if she had stolen the life that rightly belonged to a dozen other people) could ever have stopped moving, stopped singing, stopped breathing. That she would never laugh that laugh again, dirty and delighted and huge, was unimaginable.

The days that followed were strange days. Rumors abounded. I met a Hells Angel in a bar in Encino who swore blind that he knew the dude who had done the job, a man who claimed to have crushed in Amanda's skull with lead piping, on behalf of a crazed ex-boyfriend.

It became a national obsession. *Who Killed Amanda Palmer* bubblegum cards were traded and traded again in schoolyards across America. I still own two of them: one shows Amanda's bullet-riddled corpse dangling from a wall; the other shows her body washed up on the shore of an unidentified lake, her face blue and puffy from the water, the claws of some crustacean pushing out from between her purple lips.

I remember the candlelight vigils, and the shrines, dozens of them, in cities all over the world, spontaneous expressions of love from people who no longer had Amanda Palmer. They lit candles and left behind telephones, scalpels, television remote controls, exotic items of underwear, plastic figurines, children's picture books, antlers, love.

'She went as she would have wanted to go,' that was what a white-faced 'Manda, one of the growing number of Amanda Palmer impersonators, told me. Much later that night, swaying and sweating, the 'Manda confided in me that he was certain that the real Amanda Palmer had been 'abducted by beings from a higher vibrational plane', and that the photographs of Amanda's death were not fakes, pasted and airbrushed in some back-alley studios, but actual photographs of the deaths of her 'sister-selves', creatures grown from Amanda Palmer's own protoplasm.

Very young children made up songs about the different ways Amanda died, killing her happily at the end of every verse, too young to understand the horror. Maybe that was how she would have wanted to go.

If you see Amanda Palmer on the street, kill her, said the graffiti under the bridge in Boston. And beneath that somebody else wrote, *That way she'll live forever.*

Neil Gaiman,

Beat and Pop Magazine, June 1965

These are the liner notes for the album *Who Killed Amanda Palmer* by Amanda Palmer, 2008, written when we barely knew each other.

VIII

ON *STARDUST* AND FAIRY TALES

*'Those of us who write fantasies for a living know that
we are doing it best when we tell the truth.'*

Once Upon a Time

O nce upon a time, back when animals spoke and rivers sang and every quest was worth going on, back when dragons still roared and maidens were beautiful and an honest young man with a good heart and a great deal of luck could always wind up with a princess and half the kingdom – back then, fairy tales were for adults.

Children listened to them and enjoyed them, but children were not the primary audience, no more than they were the intended audience of *Beowulf*, or *The Odyssey*. J. R. R. Tolkien said, in a robust and fusty analogy, that fairy tales were like the furniture in the nursery – it was not that the furniture had originally been made for children: it had once been for adults and was consigned to the nursery only when the adults grew tired of it and it became unfashionable.

Fairy tales became unfashionable for adults before children discovered them, though. Wilhelm and Jacob Grimm, to pick two writers who had a lot to do with the matter, did not set out to collect the stories that bear their name in order to entertain children. They were primarily collectors and philologists, who assembled their tales as part of a life's work that included massive volumes such as *German Legends*, *German Grammar* and *Ancient German Law*. And they were surprised when the adults who bought their collections of fairy tales to read to their children began to complain about the adult nature of the content.

The Grimms responded to market pressure and bowdlerised enthusiastically. Rapunzel no longer let it slip that she had been meeting the prince by asking the witch why her belly had swollen so badly that her clothes would not fit (a logical question, given that she would soon be giving birth to twins). By the third edition, Rapunzel tells the witch that she is lighter to pull up than the prince was, and the twins, when they turn up, turn up out of nowhere.

The stories that people had told each other to pass the long nights had become children's tales. And there, many people obviously thought, they needed to stay.

But they don't stay there. I think it's because most fairy tales, honed over the years, work so very well. They feel right. Structurally, they can be simple, but the ornamentation, the act of retelling, is often where the magic occurs. Like any form of narrative that is primarily oral in transmission, it's all in the way you tell 'em.

It's the joy of panto. Cinderella needs her ugly sisters and her transformation scene, but how we get to it changes from production to production. There are traditions of fairy tales. *The Arabian Nights* gives us one such; the elegant, courtly tales of Charles Perrault gives us a French version; the Grimm brothers a third. We encounter fairy tales as kids, in retellings or panto. We breathe them. We know how they go.

This makes them easy to parody. Monty Python's 'Happy Valley', in which princes fling themselves to their deaths for love of a princess with wooden teeth, is still my favourite send-up. The *Shrek* series parodies the Hollywood retellings of fairy tales to diminishing returns, soon making one wistful for the real thing.

A few years ago, on Father's Day, my daughters indulged me and let me show them Jean Cocteau's *La Belle et la Bête*. The girls were unimpressed. And then Belle's father entered the Beast's castle, and we watched special effects of people putting their hands through walls and film being played backwards, and I heard my daughters gasp at the magic on the screen. It was the thing itself, a story they knew well, retold with assurance and brilliance.

Sometimes the fairy-tale tradition intersects with the literary tradition. In 1924, the Irish writer and playwright Lord Dunsany wrote *The King of Elfland's Daughter*, in which the elders of the English kingdom of Eld decide they wish to be ruled by a magic lord, and in which a princess is stolen from Elfland and brought to England. In 1926, Hope Mirrlees, a member of the Bloomsbury set and a friend of T. S. Eliot, published *Lud-in-the-Mist*, a quintessentially English novel of transcendent oddness, set in a town on the borders of Fairyland, where illegal traffic in fairy fruit (like the fruit sold in Christina Rossetti's poem 'Goblin Market'), and the magic and poetry and wildness that come with the fruit from over the border, change the lives of the townsfolk forever.

Mirrlees's unique vision was influenced by English folktales and legends (Mirrlees was the partner of classicist Jane Ellen Harrison), by Christina Rossetti and by a Victorian homicidal lunatic, the painter Richard Dadd, in particular his unfinished masterwork, an obsessively detailed painting called *The Fairy-Feller's Master-Stroke* – also the subject of a radio play by Angela Carter.

With her astonishing collection of short stories *The Bloody Chamber*, Carter was the first writer I encountered who took fairy tales seriously, in the sense of not trying to explain them or to make them less or to pin them dead on paper, but to reinvigorate them. Her lycanthropic and menstrual Red Riding Hood variants were gathered together in Neil Jordan's coming-of-age fantasy film *The Company of Wolves*. She brought the same intensity to her retelling of other fairy tales, from 'Bluebeard' (a Carter favourite) to 'Puss in Boots', and then created her own perfect fairy tale in the story of Fevvers, the winged acrobat in *Nights at the Circus*.

When I was growing up, I wanted to read something that was unapologetically a fairy tale, and just as unapologetically for adults. I remember the delight with which, as a teenager, I stumbled across William Goldman's *The Princess Bride* in a North London library. It was a fairy tale with a framing story which claimed that Goldman was editing Silas Morgenstern's classic (albeit fictional) book into the form in which it was once read to him by his father, who left out the dull bits – a conceit that justified telling adults a fairy tale, and which legitimised the book by making it a retelling, as all fairy stories somehow have to be. I interviewed Goldman in the early 1980s, and he described it as his favourite of his books and the least known, a position it kept until the 1987 film of the book made it a perennial favourite.

A fairy tale, intended for adult readers. It was a form of fiction I loved and wanted to read more of. I couldn't find one on the shelves, so I decided to write one.

I started writing *Stardust* in 1994, but mentally timeslipped about seventy years to do it. The mid-1920s seemed like a time when people enjoyed writing those sorts of things, before there were fantasy shelves in the bookshops, before trilogies and books 'in the great tradition of *The Lord of the Rings*'. This, on the other hand, would be in the tradition of *Lud-in-the-Mist* and *The King of Elfland's Daughter*. All I was certain of was that nobody had written books on computers back in the 1920s, so I bought a large book of unlined pages, and the first fountain pen I had owned since my schooldays and a copy of Katharine Briggs's *Dictionary of Fairies*. I filled the pen and began.

I wanted a young man who would set out on a quest – in this case a romantic quest, for the heart of Victoria Forester, the loveliest girl in his village. The village was somewhere in England, and was called Wall, after the wall that ran beside it, a dull-looking wall in a normal-looking meadow. And on the other side of the wall was Faerie – Faerie as a place or as a quality, rather than as a posh way of spelling *fairy*. Our hero would promise to bring back a fallen star, one that had fallen on the far side of the wall.

And the star, I knew, would not, when he found it, be a lump of metallic rock. It would be a young woman with a broken leg, in a poor temper, with no desire to be dragged halfway across the world and presented to anyone's girlfriend.

On the way, we would encounter wicked witches, who would seek the star's heart to give back their youth, and seven lords (some living, some ghosts) who seek the star to confirm their inheritance. There would be obstacles of all kinds, and assistance from odd quarters. And the hero would win through, in the manner of heroes, not because he was especially wise or strong or brave, but because he had a good heart, and because it was his story.

I began to write:

There was once a young man who wished to gain his Heart's Desire.

And while that is, as beginnings go, not entirely new (for every tale about every young man there ever was or will be could start in a similar manner), there was much about this young man and what happened to him that was unusual, although even he never knew the whole of it.

The voice sounded like the voice I needed – a little stilted and old-fashioned, the voice of a fairy tale. I wanted to write a story that would feel, to the reader, like something he or she had always known. Something familiar, even if the elements were as original as I could make them.

I was fortunate in having Charles Vess, to my mind the finest fairy artist since Arthur Rackham, as the illustrator of *Stardust*, and many times I found myself writing scenes – a lion fighting a unicorn, a flying pirate ship – simply because I wanted to see how Charles would paint them. I was never disappointed.

The book came out, first in illustrated and then in unillustrated form. There seemed to be a general consensus that it was the most inconsequential of my novels. Fantasy fans, for example, wanted it to be an epic, which it took enormous pleasure in not being. Shortly after it was published, I wound up defending it to a journalist who had loved my previous novel, *Neverwhere*, particularly its social allegories. He had turned *Stardust* upside down and shaken it, looking for social allegories, and found absolutely nothing of any good purpose.

'What's it *for*?' he had asked, which is not a question you expect to be asked when you write fiction for a living.

'It's a fairy tale,' I told him. 'It's like an ice cream. It's to make you feel happy when you finish it.'

I don't think that I convinced him, not even a little bit. There was a French edition of *Stardust* some years later that contained translator's notes demonstrating that the whole of the novel was a gloss on Bunyan's *Pilgrim's Progress,* which I wish I had read at the time of the interview. I could have referred it to the journalist, even if I didn't believe a word.

Still, the people who wanted fairy tales found the book, and some of them knew what it was, and liked it for being exactly that. One of those people was filmmaker Matthew Vaughn.

I tend to be extremely protective when it comes to adaptations of my work, but I enjoyed the screenplay and I really like the film they made – which takes liberties with the plot all over the place. (I know I didn't write a pirate captain performing a can-can in drag, for a start . . .)

A star still falls, a boy still promises to bring it to his true love, there are still wicked witches and ghosts and lords (although the lords have now become princes). They even gave the story an unabashedly happy ending, which is something people tend to do when they retell fairy tales.

In *The Penguin Book of English Folktales*, we learn that

mid-twentieth-century folklorists had collected an oral story and never noticed it was actually a retelling and simplification of a strange and disturbing children's story written by the Victorian writer Lucy Clifford.

I would, of course, be happy if *Stardust* met with a similar fate, if it continued to be retold long after its author was forgotten, if people forgot that it had once been a book and began their tales of the boy who set out to find the fallen star with 'Once upon a time,' and finished with 'Happily ever after'.

A version of this was originally published in the 13 October 2007 issue of the *Guardian*. A slightly altered version was included in the programme book for the 2013 World Fantasy Convention in Brighton.

Several Things About Charles Vess

Theodor Kittelsen (1857–1914) was the greatest painter of trolls there ever was. He was a Norwegian recluse who drew and sketched water trolls and mountain trolls and strange, mad-eyed hill-sized trolls with pines growing on their backs. He lived on an island in the Norwegian Sea, two hours away by horse and (in the winter) sledge from the nearest town.

And when he heard that another artist had said that he too was going to be drawing trolls, Kittelsen is reputed to have said, 'He? Sketch trolls? He has never seen a troll in his life.'

Which makes sense, of course. The reason that Kittelsen drew such remarkable trolls was that he saw them. Just as the reason Arthur Rackham drew such sublime fairy creatures, such strange and gnarly tree-creatures, such grotesque gnomes, was that he saw them.

And the reason that Charles Vess draws such astonishing things, such beautiful things and such strange things, the reason that he draws all manner of fairy creatures and boggarts and nixies and witches and wonders so very well, is simple.

He sees them. He draws what he sees.

I have known Charles Vess for a decade (or less, I confess I've forgotten – say nine years, I guess).

This is how to spot the herbaceous or lesser spotted Charles Vess: he has an easygoing, gentle smile and he has, no kidding and in all honesty, a twinkling sort of glint in his eyes. I've seen it. His manner is quiet and reserved, and he is extremely polite. Anyone with all four of those characteristics is probably Charles Vess, assuming that he can also paint like a demon.

He likes really fine single-malt scotches. I just mention this in passing, and not to encourage anyone reading this to buy Charles a really good single-malt scotch (anything over ten years old should be fine).

I love working with Charles. It's easy.

He's a good person to spend time with. The first time we got together to talk about *The Books of Magic,* which we were going to do together, we went up to Galleon's Lap, the Enchanted Place in the Hundred Acre Wood (it's actually called Gill's Lap when you're outside of the Milne books) and just sat around in the heather up where the pine trees blow, and looked at the trees, and talked about what we were going to be doing. About rivers of blood, and the old ballads, and little houses on chicken legs. And sometimes we didn't chat at all, we just sat.

He's the finest audience in the world. When you read to him, he chuckles. Honest-to-god chuckles. When I was writing *Stardust,* at the end of each chapter I'd phone Charles up, and I'd read him what I'd written (occasionally apologizing on the way for not being able to read my own handwriting) and whenever I got to a good bit, he'd chuckle. It was wonderful.

I wound up writing things just because I wanted to see what he would paint.

Charles is someone who is doing what he loves.

He is an optimist, in the broadest sense of the word. Charles lives in a *good* world.

He's not an unrealistic optimist, though. He's sensible. When we won the World Fantasy Award for best short story, in Tucson in 1991, Charles missed it. He was playing table tennis. This is because he knew that we wouldn't win (well, it was about as likely as our being elected joint deputy Pope), so he went off to do something sensible instead. (That we won is beside the point in this anecdote.)

This summer Charles's wife, Karen, was very seriously injured in a car accident. She's spent the last several months undergoing surgery, and in rehab learning how to walk and operate her body once more.

The last time I saw Charles I asked him how he was doing.

'Mostly I'm grateful,' he said, like one of those guys in those heartwarming articles in *Reader's Digest*. Only this was for real. 'There are people in her rehab who had the same injuries as Karen who are going to spend the rest of their lives in wheelchairs. She's going to be able to walk again. We're really lucky.'

And he meant it. He is a remarkable man, in many ways.

Charles Vess lives in rural Virginia. Also he lives in Faerie. He draws what he sees.

This was originally written for the programme book for TropiCon XVII, 1998. Charles, I am glad to say, continues to twinkle. Karen Vess, I am even happier to say, made an almost complete recovery.

The King of Elfland's Daughter, Lord Dunsany

It has on occasion been a source of puzzlement to me that there are a number of otherwise sensible people, many of them old enough to know better, who maintain, perhaps from some kind of strange cultural snobbery, that William Shakespeare could not have written the plays that bear his name, and that these plays must, obviously, have been written by a member of the British aristocracy, written by some lord or earl, some grandee or other, forced to hide his literary light under a bushel.

And this is chiefly a source of puzzlement to me because the British aristocracy, while it has produced more than its share of hunters, eccentrics, farmers, warriors, diplomats, con men, heroes, robbers, politicians and monsters, has never been noted in any century or era for the production of great writers.

Edward John Moreton Drax Plunkett (1878–1957) was a hunter, and a warrior, and a chess champion, and a playwright, a teacher and many another thing besides, and he was a member of a family that could trace its lineage back to before the Norman Conquest; he was eighteenth Baron Dunsany, and he is one of the rare exceptions.

Lord Dunsany wrote small tales of imaginary gods and thieves and heroes in distant kingdoms; he wrote tall stories based in the here and now and retold, by Mr Joseph Jorkens, for whisky in

London clubs; he wrote autobiographies; he wrote fine poems and more than forty plays (at one point, reputedly, he had five plays being staged on Broadway at one time); he wrote novels of a vanished and magical Spain that never was; and he wrote *The King of Elfland's Daughter*, a fine, strange, almost forgotten novel, as too much of Dunsany's unique work is forgotten, and if this book alone were all he had written, it would have been enough.

To begin with, the writing is beautiful. Dunsany wrote his books, we are told, with a quill pen, dipping and scritching and flowing his prose over sheets of paper, and his words sing, like those of a poet who got drunk on the prose of the King James Bible, and who has still not yet become sober. Listen to Dunsany on the wonders of ink:

> . . . *how it can mark a dead man's thoughts for the wonder of later years, and tell of happenings that are gone clean away, and be a voice for us out of the dark of time, and save many a fragile thing from the pounding of heavy ages; or carry to us, over the rolling centuries, even a song from lips long dead on forgotten hills.*

For secondly, *The King of Elfland's Daughter* is a book about magic; about the perils of inviting magic into your life; about the magic that can be found in the mundane world, and the distant, fearful, changeless magic of Elfland. It is not a comforting book, neither is it an entirely comfortable one, and one comes away, at the end, unconvinced of the wisdom of the men of Erl, who wished to be ruled by a magic lord.

For thirdly, it has its feet well planted on the ground (my own favorite moments are, I think, the jam-roll that saved the child from going to Elfland, and the troll watching time pass in the pigeon-loft); it assumes that events have consequences, and that dreams and the moon matter (but cannot be trusted or relied upon), and that love, too, is important (but even a Freer of Christom should realize that the Princess of Elfland is not merely a mermaid who has forsaken the sea).

And finally, for those who feel that they need historical accuracy in their fictions, this novel contains one historically verifiable date. It is in chapter 20. But there are, I suspect, few who will have got that far in the book who will need a date to establish the veracity of the story. It is a true story, as these things go, in every way that matters.

Today, fantasy is, for better or for worse, just another genre, a place in a bookshop to find books that, too often, remind one of far too many other books (and many writers writing today would have less to say had Dunsany not said it first); it is an irony, and not entirely a pleasant one, that what should be, by definition, the most imaginative of all types of literature has become so staid, and, too often, downright unimaginative. *The King of Elfland's Daughter*, on the other hand, is a tale of pure imagination (and *bricks without straw*, as Dunsany himself pointed out, *are more easily made than imagination without memories*). Perhaps this book should come with a warning: it is not a comfortable, reassuring, by-the-numbers fantasy novel, like most of the books with elves and princes and trolls and unicorns in them, on the nearby fantasy shelves: this is the real thing. It's a rich red wine, which may come as a shock if all one has had experience of so far has been cola. So trust the book. Trust the poetry and the strangeness, and the magic of the ink, and drink it slowly.

And, for a little while, perhaps you too shall be ruled, like the men of Erl would have been, by a magic lord.

My introduction to the 1999 edition of Lord Dunsany's *The King of Elfland's Daughter*.

Lud-in-the-Mist

Hope Mirrlees only wrote one fantasy novel, but it is one of the finest in the English language.

The country of Dorimare (fundamentally English, although with Flemish and Dutch threads in the weave) expelled magic and fancy when it banished hunchbacked libertine Duke Aubrey and his court, two hundred years before our tale starts. The prosperous and illusion-free burghers of the town swear by 'toasted cheesecrumbs' as easily as by the 'Sun, Moon, Stars and the Golden Apples of the West'. Faerie has become, explicitly, obscenity.

But fairy fruit is still being smuggled over the border from Fairyland. Eating it gives strange visions and can drive people to madness and beyond. The fruit is so illegal that it cannot even be named: smugglers of fruit are punished for smuggling silk, as if the changing of the name will change the thing itself.

The mayor of Lud-in-the-Mist, Nat Chanticleer, is less prosaic than he would have others believe. His life is a fiction he subscribes to, or would like to, of a sensible life like everyone else's – and particularly like the dead that he admires. His world is a shallow thing, though, as he will soon learn: without his knowledge, his young son, Ranulph, has been fed fairy fruit.

Now the fairy world – which is also, as in all the oldest folktales, the world of the dead – begins to claim the town: a puck named Willy Wisp spirits away the lovely young ladies of Miss

Crabapple's Academy for young ladies, over the hills and far away; Chanticleer stumbles upon the fruit smugglers, and his life takes a turn for the worse; Duke Aubrey is sighted; old murders will out; and, in the end, Chanticleer must cross the Elfin Marches to rescue his son.

The book begins as a travelogue or a history, becomes a pastorale, a low comedy, a high comedy, a ghost story and a detective story. The writing is elegant, supple, effective and haunting: the author demands a great deal from her readers, which she repays many times over.

The magic of *Lud-in-the-Mist* is built from English folklore – it is not such a great step from Aubrey to Oberon, after all; Willy Wisp's 'Ho-ho-*hoh*' is Robin Goodfellow's, from a song they say Ben Jonson wrote; and it will not come as a surprise to the folklorist that old Portunus says nothing and eats live frogs. The 'lily, germander and sops in wine' song is first recorded in the seventeenth century, under the name of 'Robin Good-Fellow; or, The Hob-Goblin'.

I have seen editions of *Lud-in-the-Mist* which proclaim it to be a thinly disguised parable for the class struggle. Had it been written in the 1960s it would, I have no doubt, have been seen as a tale about mind-expansion. But it seems to me that this is, most of all, a book about reconciliation – the balancing and twining of the mundane and the miraculous. We need both, after all.

It is a little golden miracle of a book, adult, in the best sense, and, as the best fantasy should be, far from reassuring.

Originally published in the 'Curiosities' section of the *Magazine of Fantasy and Science Fiction,* July 1999.

The Thing of It Is: *Jonathan Strange & Mr Norrell*

This is a very poor introduction to *Jonathan Strange & Mr Norrell* (whose name rhymes, by the way, with *quarrel*, or with *sorrel*, the way Susanna Clarke pronounces it), and an equally meager introduction to the person of Susanna Clarke. They both deserve better. Notwithstanding, it is my story, and I shall tell it my way, which is the story of how I became aware of Susanna Clarke and of her book.

When our story begins, I was a scribbling person who made stories and such.

I moved to America from England in 1992, and I missed my friends, so I was exceedingly delighted when the post brought a large envelope from one of them, a Mr Colin Greenland. Mr Greenland had been one of the first persons I had encountered a decade earlier, when I had stumbled into the worlds of science fiction and of fantasy: an elfin gentleman with a faintly piratical air, who wrote excellent books. Inside the envelope was a letter, in which Mr Greenland explained that he had just taught a writing workshop, and that one of the writers at the workshop was a remarkable woman of great talent, and that he wished me to read her work. He enclosed an extract from a short story.

I read it, and wrote back, and demanded more.

This came as some surprise to Susanna Clarke, who had no

idea that Colin had sent me an extract from 'The Ladies of Grace Adieu'. Gamely, though, she sent me the rest of the story. I loved everything about it: the plot, the magic, the glorious way Susanna put words together, and was particularly delighted by the information in the cover letter that Susanna was writing a novel set in the world of the tale, and that it would be called *Jonathan Strange & Mr Norrell* – so delighted that I sent the story to an editor of my acquaintance. He called Susanna and asked to buy her story for an anthology he was editing.

This came, again, as some surprise to Susanna Clarke, once she had established that this was none of it a prank (for after all, it is hard enough to sell short stories in this world, but to sell your first short story when you had not even sent it to an editor borders on the unlikely, and crosses that border).

I was excited by the prospect of meeting Susanna Clarke, and when I did finally meet her it was in the company of Colin Greenland, who had, shortly after their first encounter, persuaded her to entertain his suit (an odd expression, now I come to write it down. I mean that they had become lovers and partners, not that he had removed his clothes and left them with her while she performed small puppet shows for them). From the stories of hers that I had read – Ms Clarke sent me her short stories when she wrote them, every year or so, with a note telling me she *was* still writing the novel – I was expecting someone of a fey disposition, perhaps slightly out of her own Time, and was pleasantly surprised myself to meet a sharp, smart woman with a ready smile and easy wit, who loved to talk books and authors. I took particular delight in how well she understood high and low culture, and how comfortably she went between them, seeing them (correctly, in my opinion) not as opposites to be reconciled but as different ways of addressing the same ideas.

For the next decade, people would ask me who my favorite authors were, and I would place Susanna Clarke on any lists I made, explaining that she had written short stories, only a handful but that each was a gem, that she was working on a novel, and that one day everyone would have heard of her. And by *everyone,* I meant only a small number of people, but those who counted. I assumed that the work of Susanna Clarke was a refined taste that would be too unusual and strange for the general public.

In February 2004, to my perplexity and my delight, the mail brought an advance, but finished, copy of *Jonathan Strange & Mr Norrell.* I took my daughters on holiday to the Cayman Islands and, while they romped and swam in the surf, I was hundreds of years and thousands of miles away, in Regency York and in London and on the Continent, experiencing nothing but the purest pleasure, wandering through the words and the things they brought with them, and eventually noticing that the paths and lanes of the story, with its footnotes and its fine phrases, had become a huge road, and it was taking me with it. Seven Hundred and Eighty-Two Pages, and I enjoyed every page and when the book was done I could happily have read seven hundred and eighty-two more. I loved the things she said and the things she did not say. I loved crabbed Norrell and, less feckless than he seems, Strange, and John Uskglass the Raven King, who is not in the title of the book unless he hides behind the amper-sand, but who hovers there anyhow. I loved the supporting players, and the footnotes, and the author – she is not, I am convinced, Ms Clarke, but a character in her own right, writing her book closer to Strange and Norrell's time than our own.

I wrote about the experience of reading the book in my online journal, and I wrote to Susanna's editor telling her that it was to my mind the finest work of English fantasy written in the previous seventy years. (I was thinking that the only thing it could be compared to was Hope Mirrlees's novel *Lud-in-the-Mist.* Sometimes people would ask me about Tolkien, and I would explain that I did not, and do not, think of *The Lord of the Rings* as English Fantasy but as High Fantasy.) It was a novel about the reconciliation of the mundane and the miraculous, in which the world of faerie and the world of men are, perhaps, not as divided as they appear, but might simply be different ways of addressing the same thing.

I was right about how good a book it was, and how much people would like it. I was wrong about one thing, and one thing only, in that I had thought that *Jonathan Strange & Mr Norrell* would be a book for the few – that it would touch only a handful of people, and those people deeply, and when they encountered each other they would speak of Arabella, or Stephen Black, or of Childermass or the Gentleman with the Thistle-Down Hair in the way that people talk of old acquaintances, and bonds of friendship would be formed between strangers. I daresay they do, and they are, but there are not a tiny handful of them but an army as big as Wellington's, or bigger. The book became that rare thing, a fine and wonderful book that found its readers, all across the world, and was garlanded and lauded and awarded and acclaimed.

And it is with that thought that this introduction comes to an end.

I am delighted to report, by way of postscript, that Ms Clarke has remained quite unspoiled by success, and that she is the same sharp, smart woman with the same ready wit whom I met over a decade ago, and though her hair has now turned completely white, it has done so in an elegant and stylish way which means she cuts an imposing figure on the back of book jackets. Colin Greenland, on the other hand, has become significantly less elfin as the years have gone by, but what he has lost in elvishness he has made up for in wizardliness, and now gives the vague impression that he is merely waiting for a team of hobbits to pass by in order to send them upon an adventure, although the piratical glint in his eye would cause me to think twice about

going on such an adventure were I one of those hobbits and
not, as I am, a scribbling person.

My introduction to a 2009 edition of Susanna Clarke's novel, *Jonathan
Strange & Mr Norrell.*

On Richard Dadd's *The Fairy-Feller's Master-Stroke*

Much of the Tate Gallery's Pre-Raphaelite collection is in Washington, DC, as I write this, and the Pre-Raphaelite paintings they have left have been folded into a Victorian room. I am told that when they return, it will be to a gallery organised by time period and not by artistic school. This makes sense to me.

I am in the Tate Gallery to have my photograph taken, and I am standing beside the one painting I want to talk about, early in the morning. No crowds. I tell the photographer about the history of the painting, and the painter, while getting increasingly irritated with a smudgy blotch on the glass, at the top right, and eventually I take out a cloth for cleaning off my computer's screen and I scrub vigorously at the glass until it is clean. Nobody comes and arrests me, which is, I decide, a good thing.

I am able, with no one else around, to stare at the painting until I have had my fill, but when the photographer moves me on to other places in the gallery I am still not satisfied.

There is a small plaque beside the painting, which says: *Presented by Siegfried Sassoon in memory of his friend and fellow officer Julian Dadd, a great-nephew of the artist, and of his two brothers who gave their lives in the First World War*. It has been in the Tate's collection since 1963.

Reason tells me that I would have first encountered the painting itself, the enigmatically titled *Fairy-Feller's Master-Stroke,* reproduced, pretty much full-sized, in the foldout cover of a Queen album, at the age of fourteen or thereabouts, and it made no impression upon me at all. That's one of the odd things about it. You have to see it in the flesh, paint on canvas, the real thing, which used to hang, mostly, when it wasn't travelling, in the Pre-Raphaelite room of the Tate Gallery, out of place among the grand gold-framed Pre-Raphaelite beauties, all of them so much more huge and artful than the humble fairy court standing among the daisies, for it to become real. And when you see it several things will become apparent; some immediately, some eventually.

I visited the Pre-Raphaelite room at the Tate first in my early twenties: in my teens I had loved the work of comic book artist Barry Windsor-Smith. He made no secret of his Pre-Raphaelite influences, and I wanted to see them close-up – Millais and Waterhouse and the rest. I went there, and I liked the paintings, and admired them, and decided that I did not like the work of Dante Gabriel Rossetti as much as I rather suspected Dante Gabriel Rossetti had, and the Burne-Jones picture of the ladies going downstairs made me catch my breath.

They had several Dadd paintings too, there almost by default, as if there was nowhere else to put them. I saw *The Fairy-Feller's Master-Stroke,* and I was obsessed.

When I was in my early twenties I received a copy of a book to review, of photographs mostly taken by a Victorian doctor named Diamond, of the inmates of Bedlam. Hopeless bedraggled lunatics who wring their hands as they squint at the camera, posing awkwardly for the period of time it took for the photographs to be exposed; their faces are frozen, although their hands often blur into things like the wings of doves. Portraits in madness and pain, and in only one of the photographs in the book was a man, a lunatic like the others, actually doing something.

The madman in the photograph, which was taken by Henry Hering in 1856, has a beard. He has an easel in front of him, on which he is executing an oval painting of remarkable intricacy. He stares craftily at the camera, and there is a small, fierce smile on his face. His eyes glitter. He looks squat and proud, and when, a year later, I saw, for the first time in the flesh, his masterpiece, *The Fairy-Feller's Master-Stroke,* the first thing I realised was that the white-bearded sorrowful dwarf who dominates the centre of the painting, staring out at the watcher, is Richard Dadd grown old.

The visitors to the Tate Gallery who visit the Pre-Raphaelite rooms are there for their own reasons, and are responding to something distant and melodic. The Waterhouses and the Millaises and the Burne-Joneses exert their own magic: spectators wander past the paintings, their lives enriched and made special. The Dadd, on the other hand, is a snare, and those people with a place in their soul for it – and I am one of them – are hooked. We can stand in front of that painting for, literally, hours, lost in it, puzzling over these fairies and goblins and men and women, trying to understand their size, their shape, their eccentricities. Every time you look at it you discover something, someone, you have not seen before.

Dadd knew who they were, the people in the painting. He knew their lives. He knew what they were. You know that when you see them. He wrote a poem about them, in Broadmoor, in 1865, called 'Elimination of a Picture & Its Subject – Called the Feller's Master Stroke.' That's how we know the title. He was a better painter than he ever was a poet.

If you've ever seen the painting reproduced, if you're on a journey specifically to see it, then the next thing that will surprise you is the size. It's smaller than you imagined – smaller than seems possible. There is so much to fit in, after all. The authorised Tate Gallery reproduction of *The Fairy-Feller's Master-Stroke*

I bought after seeing it the first time was almost twice the size of the picture itself, and was as unsatisfying as a photograph of a meal would be to a hungry man.

The painting is not the reproduction. The thing itself, in its frame, has a magic – in the colour, in the detail – that no photograph, no poster, no postcard, ever seems to begin to capture.

So you look at the painting, seeing every brushstroke. Every nuance of paint on the daisies.

And you can look at it for hours before you notice something else about the painting, something so big and strange and obvious you can't understand why you didn't see it at once, or why no one else has commented upon it.

It's not finished.

Much of the bottom of the painting, where the colour choices seem odd and washed out, is only outlined on the light brown of the undercoat that covers the canvas. The fawn-coloured grass that pushes the eye up to the Feller himself is fawn because Dadd – who took many years to paint it – ran out of time. He gave it away before it was done.

And there's one final thing you will know, without question, if you've seen that painting in the flesh, and it's this: he knew what he was painting. He had seen it, through those crafty eyes. He had gone on the great journey, the grandest of grand tours, and this was what he was bringing back.

Those of us who write fantasies for a living know that we are doing it best when we tell the truth. There is something that people will respond to – the True Quill, a Texan writer I met once called it. My novel *The Ocean at the End of the Lane* includes a lady on a Sussex farm who is older than the universe, and a strange flapping creature from somewhere outside space and time who comes into our young protagonist's life in the form of an evil nanny. None of it's true, except it feels right. It feels honest.

Before his madness, before the murder of his father, before the ill-fated journey to France (he was arrested on a train, when he attacked a fellow passenger, on his way to Paris to kill the emperor), Dadd's paintings are quite pretty, and perfectly ordinary: forgettable chocolate-box-cover concoctions of fairy scenes from Shakespeare. Nothing special or magical about them. Nothing that would make them last. Nothing true.

And then he went mad. Not just a little bit mad, but quite spectacularly mad; a murderous patricidal madness of demons and Egyptian gods. He spent the rest of his life locked up – first in Bedlam, later one of the first prisoners in Broadmoor – and, after a while, he began to paint, trading his paintings for favours. Gone were the chocolate-box fairies of *Come Unto These Yellow Sands*. Now there was an intensity to his paintings and drawings of fairy courts, of Bible scenes, of his fellow inmates (real or imaginary), that makes those we have such treasures. They were worked on with an intensity and single-mindedness that is, quite simply, scary.

He spent the rest of his life behind bars, locked up with the criminally insane, as criminally insane as any of them, but with a message for us from, as it were, the other side. Apart from this, his life was wasted.

Still, he left us paintings, and riddles, and one unfinished painting, which continues to obsess. Angela Carter wrote an astonishing radio play, *Come Unto These Yellow Sands*, about the painting, Dadd's life, Victorian art. I wrote a film treatment once in which the painting was a key, and came close once to organising an anthology in which each story would be about one of the witnesses to the Fairy-Feller's chestnut-smashing blow.

The mystery, like the painting, like our understanding of the painter, will always remain unfinished, or abandoned, and always ultimately remain unexplained. As Dadd himself put it, at the end of his poem, 'Elimination . . .'

But whether it be or be not so
You can afford to let this go
For nought as nothing it explains
And nothing from nothing nothing gains.

This was written for the July/August 2013 issue of *Intelligent Life* magazine, and I cannibalised an earlier introduction I had written for Mark Chadbourn's excellent novella *The Fairy Feller's Master Stroke*, 2008.

IX

MAKE GOOD ART

'Husband runs off with a politician? Make good art. Leg crushed and then eaten by mutated boa constrictor? Make good art. IRS on your trail? Make good art. Cat exploded? Make good art.'

Make Good Art

I never really expected to find myself giving advice to people graduating from an establishment of higher education. I never graduated from any such establishment. I never even started at one. I escaped from school as soon as I could, when the prospect of four more years of enforced learning before I'd become the writer I wanted to be was stifling.

I got out into the world, I wrote, and I became a better writer the more I wrote, and I wrote some more, and nobody ever seemed to mind that I was making it up as I went along, they just read what I wrote and they paid for it, or they didn't, and often they commissioned me to write something else for them.

Which has left me with a healthy respect and fondness for higher education that those of my friends and family who attended universities were cured of long ago.

Looking back, I've had a remarkable ride. I'm not sure I can call it a career, because a career implies that I had some kind of career plan, and I never did. The nearest thing I had was a list I made when I was fifteen of everything I wanted to do: to write an adult novel, a children's book, a comic, a movie; record an audiobook; write an episode of *Doctor Who* . . . and so on. I didn't have a career. I just did the next thing on the list.

So I thought I'd tell you everything I wish I'd known starting out, and a few things that, looking back on it, I suppose that I did know. And that I would also give you the best piece of advice I'd ever got, which I completely failed to follow.

First of all: when you start out on a career in the arts you have no idea what you are doing.

This is great. People who know what they are doing know the rules, and know what is possible and impossible. You do not. And you should not. The rules on what is possible and impossible in the arts were made by people who had not tested the bounds of the possible by going beyond them. And you can.

If you don't know it's impossible it's easier to do. And because nobody's done it before, they haven't made up rules to stop anyone doing that again, yet.

Secondly, if you have an idea of what you want to make, what you were put here to do, then just go and do that.

And that's much harder than it sounds and, sometimes in the end, so much easier than you might imagine. Because normally, there are things you have to do before you can get to the place you want to be. I wanted to write comics and novels and stories and films, so I became a journalist, because journalists are allowed to ask questions, and to simply go and find out how the world works, and besides, to do those things I needed to write and to write well, and I was being paid to learn how to write economically, crisply, sometimes under adverse conditions, and on time.

Sometimes the way to do what you hope to do will be clearcut, and sometimes it will be almost impossible to decide whether or not you are doing the correct thing, because you'll have to balance your goals and hopes with feeding yourself, paying debts, finding work, settling for what you can get.

Something that worked for me was imagining that where I wanted to be – an author, primarily of fiction, making good books, making good comics and supporting myself through my words – was a mountain. A distant mountain. My goal.

And I knew that as long as I kept walking towards the mountain

I would be all right. And when I truly was not sure what to do, I could stop, and think about whether it was taking me towards or away from the mountain. I said no to editorial jobs on magazines, proper jobs that would have paid proper money because I knew that, attractive though they were, for me they would have been walking away from the mountain. And if those job offers had come along earlier I might have taken them, because they still would have been closer to the mountain than I was at the time.

I learned to write by writing. I tended to do anything as long as it felt like an adventure, and to stop when it felt like work, which meant that life did not feel like work.

Thirdly, when you start off, you have to deal with the problems of failure. You need to be thick skinned, to learn that not every project will survive. A freelance life, a life in the arts, is sometimes like putting messages in bottles, on a desert island, and hoping that someone will find one of your bottles and open it and read it, and put something in a bottle that will wash its way back to you: appreciation, or a commission, or money, or love. And you have to accept that you may put out a hundred things for every bottle that winds up coming back.

The problems of failure are problems of discouragement, of hopelessness, of hunger. You want everything to happen and you want it now, and things go wrong. My first book – a piece of journalism I had done for the money, and which had already bought me an electric typewriter from the advance – should have been a bestseller. It should have paid me a lot of money. If the publisher hadn't gone into involuntary liquidation between the first print run selling out and the second printing, and before any royalties could be paid, it would have done.

And I shrugged, and I still had my electric typewriter and enough money to pay the rent for a couple of months, and I decided that I would do my best in future not to write books just for the money. If you didn't get the money, then you didn't have anything. If I did work I was proud of, and I didn't get the money, at least I'd have the work.

Every now and again, I forget that rule, and whenever I do, the universe kicks me hard and reminds me. I don't know that it's an issue for anybody but me, but it's true that nothing I did where the only reason for doing it was the money was ever worth it, except as bitter experience. Usually I didn't wind up getting the money, either. The things I did because I was excited, and wanted to see them exist in reality, have never let me down, and I've never regretted the time I spent on any of them.

The problems of failure are hard.

The problems of success can be harder, because nobody warns you about them.

The first problem of any kind of even limited success is the unshakable conviction that you are getting away with something, and that any moment now they will discover you. It's Imposter Syndrome, something my wife, Amanda, christened the Fraud Police.

In my case, I was convinced that there would be a knock on the door, and a man with a clipboard (I don't know why he carried a clipboard, in my head, but he did) would be there, to tell me it was all over, and they had caught up with me, and now I would have to go and get a real job, one that didn't consist of making things up and writing them down, and reading books I wanted to read. And then I would go away quietly and get the kind of job where you don't get to make things up any more.

The problems of success. They're real, and with luck you'll experience them. The point where you stop saying yes to everything, because now the bottles you threw in the ocean are all coming back, and have to learn to say no.

I watched my peers, and my friends, and the ones who were older than me, and watched how miserable some of them were:

I'd listen to them telling me that they couldn't envisage a world where they did what they had always wanted to do any more, because now they had to earn a certain amount every month just to keep where they were. They couldn't go and do the things that mattered, and that they had really wanted to do; and that seemed as big a tragedy as any problem of failure.

And after that, the biggest problem of success is that the world conspires to stop you doing the thing that you do, because you are successful. There was a day when I looked up and realized that I had become someone who professionally replied to e-mail, and who wrote as a hobby. I started answering fewer e-mails, and was relieved to find I was writing much more.

Fourthly, I hope you'll make mistakes. If you're making mistakes, it means you're out there doing something. And the mistakes in themselves can be useful. I once misspelled Caroline, in a letter, transposing the A and the O, and I thought, *Coraline looks like a real name . . .*

And remember that whatever discipline you are in, whether you are a musician or a photographer, a fine artist or a cartoonist, a writer, a dancer, a designer, whatever you do you have one thing that's unique. You have the ability to make art.

And for me, and for so many of the people I have known, that's been a lifesaver. The ultimate lifesaver. It gets you through good times and it gets you through the other ones.

Life is sometimes hard. Things go wrong, in life and in love and in business and in friendship and in health and in all the other ways that life can go wrong. And when things get tough, this is what you should do.

Make good art.

I'm serious. Husband runs off with a politician? Make good art. Leg crushed and then eaten by mutated boa constrictor? Make good art. IRS on your trail? Make good art. Cat exploded? Make good art. Somebody on the Internet thinks what you do is stupid or evil or it's all been done before? Make good art. Probably things will work out somehow, and eventually time will take the sting away, but that doesn't matter. Do what only you do best. Make good art.

Make it on the good days too.

And fifthly, while you are at it, make *your* art. Do the stuff that only you can do.

The urge, starting out, is to copy. And that's not a bad thing. Most of us only find our own voices after we've sounded like a lot of other people. But the one thing that you have that nobody else has is *you*. Your voice, your mind, your story, your vision. So write and draw and build and play and dance and live as only you can.

The moment that you feel that, just possibly, you're walking down the street naked, exposing too much of your heart and your mind and what exists on the inside, showing too much of yourself, that's the moment you may be starting to get it right.

The things I've done that worked the best were the things I was the least certain about, the stories where I was sure they would either work, or more likely be the kinds of embarrassing failures people would gather together and talk about until the end of time. They always had that in common: looking back at them, people explain why they were inevitable successes. While I was doing them, I had no idea.

I still don't. And where would be the fun in making something you knew was going to work?

And sometimes the things I did really didn't work. There are stories of mine that have never been reprinted. Some of them never even left the house. But I learned as much from them as I did from the things that worked.

Sixthly, I will pass on some secret freelancer knowledge. Secret knowledge is always good. And it is useful for anyone who ever plans to create art for other people, to enter a freelance world of any kind. I learned it in comics, but it applies to other fields too. And it's this:

People get hired because, somehow, they get hired. In my case I did something which these days would be easy to check, and would get me into trouble, and when I started out, in those pre-Internet days, seemed like a sensible career strategy: when I was asked by editors who I'd worked for, I lied. I listed a handful of magazines that sounded likely, and I sounded confident, and I got jobs. I then made it a point of honor to have written something for each of the magazines I'd listed to get that first job, so that I hadn't actually lied, I'd just been chronologically challenged . . . You get work however you get work.

People keep working, in a freelance world, and more and more of today's world is freelance, because their work is good, and because they are easy to get along with, and because they deliver the work on time. And you don't even need all three. Two out of three is fine. People will tolerate how unpleasant you are if your work is good and you deliver it on time. They'll forgive the lateness of the work if it's good, and if they like you. And you don't have to be as good as the others if you're on time and it's always a pleasure to hear from you.

When I agreed to give this address, I started trying to think what the best advice I'd been given over the years was.

And it came from Stephen King twenty years ago, at the height of the success of *Sandman*. I was writing a comic that people loved and were taking seriously. King had liked *Sandman* and my novel with Terry Pratchett, *Good Omens*, and he saw the madness, the long signing lines, all that, and his advice was this:

'*This is really great. You should enjoy it.*'

And I didn't. Best advice I got that I ignored. Instead I worried about it. I worried about the next deadline, the next idea, the next story. There wasn't a moment for the next fourteen or fifteen years that I wasn't writing something in my head, or wondering about it. And I didn't stop and look around and go, *This is really fun*. I wish I'd enjoyed it more. It's been an amazing ride. But there were parts of the ride I missed, because I was too worried about things going wrong, about what came next, to enjoy the bit I was on.

That was the hardest lesson for me, I think: to let go and enjoy the ride, because the ride takes you to some remarkable and unexpected places.

And here, on this platform, today, is one of those places. (I am enjoying myself immensely.)

To all today's graduates: I wish you luck. Luck is useful. Often you will discover that the harder you work, and the more wisely you work, the luckier you get. But there is luck, and it helps.

We're in a transitional world right now, if you're in any kind of artistic field, because the nature of distribution is changing, the models by which creators got their work out into the world, and got to keep a roof over their heads and buy sandwiches while they did that, are all changing. I've talked to people at the top of the food chain in publishing, in bookselling, in all those areas, and nobody knows what the landscape will look like two years from now, let alone a decade away. The distribution channels that people had built over the last century or so are in flux for print, for visual artists, for musicians, for creative people of all kinds.

Which is, on the one hand, intimidating, and on the other, immensely liberating. The rules, the assumptions, the now-we're-supposed-to's of how you get your work seen, and what you do then, are breaking down. The gatekeepers are leaving their gates. You can be as creative as you need to be to get your work seen. YouTube and the Web (and whatever comes after YouTube and the Web) can give you more people watching than television ever did. The old rules are crumbling and nobody knows what the new rules are.

So make up your own rules.

Someone asked me recently how to do something she thought was going to be difficult, in this case recording an audiobook, and I suggested she pretend that she was someone who could do it. Not pretend to do it, but pretend she was someone who could. She put up a notice to this effect on the studio wall, and she said it helped.

So be wise, because the world needs more wisdom, and if you cannot be wise, pretend to be someone who is wise, and then just behave like they would.

And now go, and make interesting mistakes, make amazing mistakes, make glorious and fantastic mistakes. Break rules. Leave the world more interesting for your being here. Make good art.

This was the commencement speech I gave at the University of the Arts in Philadelphia, 17 May 2012. It became one of the most widely distributed things I've ever done: the videos of it online have been watched many millions of times, and it is also available as a small book, designed by Chip Kidd.

X

THE VIEW FROM THE CHEAP SEATS: REAL THINGS

'I learned the poem as a boy, when Death was merely an abstract idea, one I suspected I would almost certainly manage to avoid as I grew up, for I was a clever child and Death seemed quite avoidable back then.'

The View from the Cheap Seats

There were authors grumbling about not going to the Oscars. I heard about it from friends. 'So why are *you* going?' they asked. I had written a book called *Coraline,* which director Henry Selick had transformed into a stop-motion wonderland. I'd helped Henry as much as I could through the process of turning something from a book into a film. I had endorsed the film, encouraged people to see it, mugged with buttons on an Internet trailer. I had also written a fifteen-second sequence for the Oscars, in which Coraline told an interviewer what winning an Oscar would do for her. I'd assumed that this would get me into the Oscars. It didn't. But Henry, as director, had tickets, and could decide where they would go, and one of them went to me.

My father had died on 7 March 2009. The Oscars are on 7 March 2010. I expect that it will just be another day, and it will not bother me at all, demonstrating that I do not know myself very well, because when the day arrives I am melancholy, and do not want to go to the Oscars. I want to be at home, walking in the woods with my dog, and if I could simply press a button and be there without disappointing anybody, I would.

I get dressed. A designer named Kambriel, whom I met when she had made a dress that would allow my fiancée and Jason Webley to represent conjoined twins, had offered to dress me for the Oscars, and I took her up on it. She made me a jacket and a waistcoat, and I fancy that I look pretty good in them. Best of all, I now have an answer to the people who ask 'What are you wearing to the Oscars?' And it makes Kambriel amazingly happy.

Focus Features, who distributed *Coraline,* are looking after me. The previous night they had a small reception at the Chateau Marmont for their two Oscar nominees, *Coraline* and *A Serious Man*. The partygoers were a strange mash-up of Minneapolis Jews and animators. Even more oddly, I was one of the Minneapolis Jews (or almost. I wound up comparing notes with one of the other partygoers on the St Paul paper's pulse-pounding exposé that I actually live an hour away from Minneapolis).

The best thing about the Oscars, I realised when the nominees were announced, is that *Coraline* won't win. In the year that *Up* is nominated for Best Picture, which obviously, it won't win, nothing but *Up* can win Best Animated Picture.

A limo picks me up at three p.m. and we drive to the Oscars. It's a slow drive: streets are closed off. The last civilians we see are standing on a street corner holding placards telling me that God Hates Fags, that the recent Earthquakes are God's Special Way of Hating Fags, and that the Jews Stole something, but I can't see what, as another placard is in the way.

A block before we reach the Kodak Theatre the car is searched, and then we're there and I'm tipped out onto the Red Carpet. Someone pushes a ticket into my hand, to get the car back later that night.

It's controlled chaos.

I am standing blankly, realising I have no idea what to do now, but the women look like butterflies, and there are people in the bleachers who shout as each limo draws up. Someone says, 'Neil?'

It's Deette, from Focus. 'I just came back from walking Henry through. What a nice coincidence. Would you like me to take you through?'

I would like that very much. She asks if I would like to walk past the cameras, and I say that I would, because my fiancée is in Australia and my daughters are watching on TV, and Kambriel will be happy to see her jacket on television.

We head down into the throng, behind someone in a beautiful dress. It looks like a watercolour of a dream. I have no idea who anyone is, except for Steve Carell, because he looks just like Steve Carell on television, except a tiny bit less orange.

We are scrunched together tightly as we go through metal detectors, and the beautiful watercolour dress is trodden on, and the lady wearing it is very gracious about this.

I ask Deette who's inside the dress, and she tells me it's Rachel McAdams. I want to say hello – Rachel's said nice things about me in interviews – but she's working right now. I'm not. No one wants to take my photo, or, Deette discovers, to interview me. I'm invisible.

At the bend in the red carpet we pause. I look down at Rachel McAdams's watercolour dress and wonder if I can see a footprint. Cameras flash, but not at me.

And we're into the Kodak Theatre. Someone else introduces me to the editor of *Variety*. I realise my facial recognition skills do not work when people are in tuxedos. (Except for James Cameron, whom I have now only ever seen in a tuxedo and would not recognise wearing anything else.) I tell this to the editor of *Variety*. He points to a man with a tan and a huge grin, tells me it's the mayor of Los Angeles. 'He comes to all these things,' he says. 'Why isn't he behind his desk, working?'

'Er. Because this is the biggest day in Hollywood's year?' I venture. 'And it's Sunday?'

'Well. Yes. But he still comes out for the opening of a drinks cabinet.'

I went to the Golden Globes six weeks earlier and discovered that the commercial breaks in award shows are spent in a strange form of en masse Hollywood speed-dating as people shuttle around the room trying to find friends or make deals, and assume that tonight will be much the same.

The Kodak Theatre has a ground floor and, above that, three mezzanines. My ticket is for the first mezzanine. I head, sheep-like, up the stairs. There is a crush to get in, as a disembodied voice tells us urgently that the Academy Awards will start in five minutes. I stare at the woman in front of me. She has blond hair and a face that's strangely fishlike, a scary-sweet plastic surgery face. She has old hands and a small, wrinkled husband who looks much older than her. I wonder if they started out the same age.

And we're in, with no time to spare. The lights go down and Neil Patrick Harris sings a special Oscars song. It does not seem to have a tune. Several people on Twitter who aren't sure which Neil is which congratulate me on it.

And now our hosts: Steve Martin and Alec Baldwin. They come out, they make jokes. From the first mezzanine, the timing is off, the jokes are awkward, the delivery is wooden. But it doesn't feel as if they're playing to us. I wonder if it works on television, and send the question out on Twitter. A few hundred people tell me it's just as bad on TV, twenty tell me they're enjoying it. I decide this is what Twitter is for: keeping you company when you're all alone on the mezzanine.

Best Animated Movie is the second category of the night. My fifteen seconds of *Coraline* talking to the camera go by fast. *There,* I think. *The largest audience that my words will ever have.*

Up wins.

The Oscars continue. In the audience, we cannot see what they are seeing on television at home. Somewhere below me George Clooney is grimacing at the camera, but I do not know.

Tina Fey and Robert Downey Jr present the Best Screenplay award, and are funny. I wonder if they wrote their own bit.

During the commercials the lights go down and they play music to mingle by. Roxanne does not have to put on the red light.

I head for the first mezzanine bar. I'm hungry and want to kill some time. I drink whisky. I order a chocolate brownie which turns out to be about as big as my head and the sweetest thing I've ever put in my mouth. I share it.

People are wandering up and down the stairs.

Whisky and sugar careening through my system, I defy the orders on my ticket not to photograph anything, and I Twitter a picture of the bar menu. My fiancée is sending me messages on Twitter urging me to photograph the inside of the women's toilet, something she did during the Golden Globes, but even in my sugar-addled state this seems a potentially disastrous idea. Still, I think, I should head downstairs and, in the next commercial break, say hello to Henry Selick. I walk over to the stairs. A nice young man in a suit asks me for my ticket. I show it to him. He explains that, as a resident of the first mezzanine, I am not permitted to walk downstairs and potentially bother the A-List.

I am outraged.

I am not actually outraged, but I am a bit bored and have friends downstairs.

I decide that I will persuade the inhabitants of the mezzanines to rise up as one and to storm the stairs, like in *Titanic*. They might shoot a few of us, I decide, but they cannot stop us all. We can be free; we can drink in the downstairs bar; we can mingle with Harvey Weinstein.

Someone tells me on Twitter that nobody's checking the elevators. I suspect that this might be a trap, and head back to my seat.

I have missed the tribute to horror movies.

Rachel McAdams presents an award in her beautiful, oh-so-tread-on-able dress.

For the Best Actor and Actress awards, a tableau of people who have worked with the nominees tell us how wonderful they are. I wonder if this works on television. On the stage in front of us it is painfully clumsy.

People below us are milling and chatting and schmoozing

more with every commercial break. There is an edge of panic to the disembodied announcer's voice as she orders them back to their seats.

The man in the bar who reminded me of Sean Penn turns out to have been Sean Penn. Jeff Bridges's standing ovation reaches all the way to the top mezzanine. Sandra Bullock's standing ovation only reaches the front rows of our level and stops there. Kathryn Bigelow's standing ovation covers the entire hall except, for some reason, the top right of the first mezzanine, where I am sitting, where we remain sitting and clap politely.

It all seems to be building up to a crescendo, and then Tom Hanks walks out onto the stage and tells us, with no buildup (if you exclude months of For Your Consideration campaigning) that oh, by the way, *The Hurt Locker* won Best Picture and good night. And we're out.

Up two escalators to the Governors Ball. I sit and chat to Michael Sheen, who brought his eleven-year-old daughter Lily, about the sushi dinner we had two days before, interrupted and ended by a police raid. We still have no idea why. (Next morning

it will be a front-page story on the *New York Times*. They were serving illicit whalemeat.)

I see Henry Selick. He seems relieved that Awards Season is over, and that he can get on with his life.

I feel as if I've sleepwalked invisibly through one of the most melancholy days of my life. There are glamorous parties that evening, but I don't go to any of them, preferring to sit in a hotel lobby with good friends. We talk about the Oscars.

The next morning the back page of the LA *Times* Oscar supplement is a huge panoramic photograph of the people on the red carpet. Somewhat to my surprise, I see myself standing front and centre, staring down at Rachel McAdams's beautiful watercolour dress, inspecting it for footprints.

This was originally published in the 25 March 2010 issue of the *Guardian* under the title of 'A Nobody's Guide to the Oscars'. I've restored the original title here. It wasn't about being a nobody, it was about being out on the days when you would best be at home, and melancholy.

A Wilderness of Mirrors

W*ho am I?*

It's a fine and legitimate question, one that haunted me when I was a boy. I would stare into the bathroom mirror and do my best to answer it, teasing information from my reflection, hoping for a clue. My face would be framed by the mirror: a glass shelf with toothbrushes on it beneath my face, tiled wall and frosted glass window behind me. I had too-short dark hair, one ear that stuck out from the side of my head and one ear that didn't, hazel eyes, red lips, a sprinkling of freckles across my nose.

I would stare and stare, puzzling over who I was, and what the relationship was between who I thought I was and who I really was and the face that was staring back at me. I knew I wasn't my face. If something terrible happened to me, like a fireworks accident, if I lost my face and spent my life bound in bandages like a mummy in a scary film, I'd still be me, wouldn't I? I never found an answer, not one that satisfied me. But I kept asking. I suppose I still am.

That was the first question. The second was even harder to answer. It was this: *who are we?*

And to answer it, I would open the family photo album. The photographs, black and white at the front, colour in later volumes, had been carefully stuck into the family album with photo-mounts on the corners, and handwritten notes beneath each photograph identified the subjects, and where and when the photograph had been taken. Glassine, semi-transparent paper covered each page. There was something extremely formal about the photo albums. We were never permitted to play with them unsupervised, or to remove photographs. They were, when the time was right, produced by adults from high shelves or dark cupboards, only to be put away again once we had looked at them. They were not to be played with.

This is who we are, the albums said to us, *and this is the story we are telling ourselves.*

There were the dead, grave people in uncomfortable clothes, posed in black and white. There were the living, when they were so much younger as to be different people: the old people were young people then, in ill-fitting clothes and in places we could scarcely imagine. Here assembled, formal and stiff, are grandparents and great-grandparents, uncles and aunts, weddings and engagements, silver and sepia, grey and black, and then, as time moves forward, the people and the poses drift into colour and informality, the snapshots and the holiday shots and *look!* you can recognise the wallpaper and you realise that the proud grandparents are holding a baby that was you, once upon a time. And now you are here again, in context, pondering your infancy, and the people who surrounded you, and the world from which you have come. Then you put down the photo album and go back to your life, reassured, given a frame and a place. The images of our forebears and our loved ones give us context, they tell us who we are.

For years, I believed I had visited the National Portrait Gallery, because I had been to the National Gallery. After all, there were portraits on the walls, were there not? It was not until I was a grown man that I finally wandered the corridors and spaces of the National Portrait Gallery and realised that I had never been there before. The embarrassment in my mistake was rapidly replaced by delight. I was glad I hadn't visited the Gallery as a boy: I would not have known who these people were, save for a handful of kings, and perhaps Shakespeare and Dickens. Now, it was like being handed an album of a family I knew too well.

Initially, I walked the galleries looking for the people I was familiar with – the ones whose stories I knew, the ones I wondered about, the ones I would have loved to have met. And then I moved wider, using the Gallery as a way of learning about people. Wondering, as I walked and as I stared, about the faces I passed: how they fit into the history of the country, why each person was there and not someone else in their place. The faces became a dialogue, the paintings became a conversation.

The National Portrait Gallery is the nation's family album, I realised. It gives us context. It is our way of describing ourselves and our past to ourselves, our way of interrogating and explaining and exploring who we are, inspecting our roots in a way that is more than just looking at the places from which we come. There is landscape, and there is portrait, after all, and they are ways of explaining the orientation of a sheet of paper, and they are the ways we understand who we are: the places we came from, the people we were.

For years I had loved Constable's landscapes: the clouds, which seemed so much more cloudlike than any clouds I had ever seen, and which forced me to stare at clouds and wonder if they were art, and the trees, and the way the sense of place gave continuity: the Suffolk landscape, which could have been my own Sussex lanes and skies. Now, for the first time, I saw John Constable: I did not expect him to be handsome, or so pensive. And there was something odd about his eyes: they seemed to be focused on different places. I wondered if he had a lazy eye, as my daughter did when she was young, or if it was simply the way that Ramsay Reinagle had presented him to us. I imagined what it must have been like to live inside that head, to see the world, and its clouds and skies and trees, through John Constable's strange eyes.

Some portraits were important because of who the subjects were. Others were important because of the artist. Still others were important because of the historical moment, because they were a record of their times, which are our times. Most images gain their power from the moment of intersection: painter and subject, time and history and context, ever-changing context. All come together as we walk the corridors of the National Portrait Gallery.

We look at a portrait and we begin to judge, because human beings are creatures of judgement. We judge the person being painted (a bad king? a good woman?) in the same way that we judge the artist, and occasionally we find ourselves judging them both, particularly when the subject is also the painter: Dame Laura Knight's self-portrait, a symphony in crimson and vermilion, shows the painter in perfect profile, flanked by the naked flanks of both a model and of the painting of the model. As a woman she was forbidden to attend life-drawing classes, and here she tells us that she is a woman, and she is a master at drawing from life. The technique is remarkable, the statement powerful.

Examine the Chevalier d'Eon. I mentioned him once in a story I wrote, having vaguely meant to put him into a tale: a cross-dressing spy, caught up in intrigue, royal proclamations and court cases. Legally pronounced female, apparently against his will. I knew all this, but I did not know how kind he looked. I know that if ever I write about him, this portrait, painted by Thomas Stewart after an original by Jean-Laurent Mosnier, who knew d'Eon, will change the way I tell his story.

As a writer, I find myself drawn to the writers: the Gallery's troubled portrait of the Brontë sisters is like something from a mystery novel. On the left side of the painting, Anne and Emily, jaws set and defiant, on the right side the third sister, Charlotte, her face gentler, a half-smile at the edges of her lips. The three women of glorious gothic romanticism, describers of ex-wives in attics and runaways on moors; three women who wrote of haunted figures in just-as-haunted landscapes, in a portrait painted by their mysterious and dissolute brother, who was, we realise as we stare, once himself a character in the painting, the central figure around whom the three women cluster, but who is now painted out, replaced by a pillar. Still, a ghostly shape confronts us, like an after-image, or a reflection. The painter's lack of skill somehow adds to the power of the picture: this is not a portrait by a professional. It is a story, frozen and mysterious, and there were, I have no doubt, tears and harsh words involved in Branwell's painting himself out of the portrait. (Or did someone else paint over him? Is the pillar some kind of clue to a mystery most gothic?)

I know that photographs tell us things about the photographer, but I do not wonder about the photographers in the same way that I wonder about the painters, even when they have composed their photographs as elegantly as any classical portrait. Julia Margaret Cameron's photograph of Alfred Tennyson, austere and windswept, taken on the Isle of Wight, is haunting. The background is a smudge, the hand holding a book reminds us of formal portraits of the religious, while the face is thoughtful and seems, to me at least, almost tragic. This is the man who would write 'Crossing the Bar'.

Twilight and evening bell, and after that the dark! I think. *And may there be no sadness of farewell, when I embark.*

I learned the poem as a boy, when Death was merely an abstract idea, one I suspected I would almost certainly manage to avoid as I grew up, for I was a clever child and Death seemed quite avoidable back then.

And as we come closer to now, as we come through modern (and what a beautiful, old-fashioned word that is), the paintings erupt and divide into contemporary movements and ways of seeing and of describing. Strict portraiture is given to photography, then taken back once more, and now we are in my lifetime and in the material of my life. The Brian Duffy portrait of David Bowie is as iconic as the *Aladdin Sane* record cover that I contemplated when I was twelve, certain that if I understood it and its lightning-bolt imagery, then I would understand all the waiting secrets of the adult world. Bowie's eyes are closed in the *Aladdin Sane* cover photo, but in this image, anisocoriac eyes stare, surprised, into the flash. Bowie seems more vulnerable. And, looking at an image that once symbolised all the mysteries of adulthood for me, I realise he looks so heartbreakingly young.

The joy and power of portraiture is that it freezes us in time. Before the portrait, we were younger. After it has been created we will age or we will rot. Even Marc Quinn's chilled nightmare self-portraits in liquid silicone and blood can only preserve a specific moment in time: they cannot age and die as Quinn does and will.

Ask the question, *who are we?* and the portraits give us answers of a sort.

We came from here, the old ones say. *These were our kings and queens, our wise ones and our fools.* We walk into the BP exhibition hall and they tell us who we are today: a confluence of artistic styles and approaches, of people we could pass in the streets. *We look like this, naked and clothed,* they tell us. *We are here, in this image, because a painter had something to say. Because we are all interesting. Because we cannot gaze into a mirror without being changed. Because we do not know who we are, but sometimes there is a light caught in someone's eyes, that comes close to giving us the tiniest hint of an answer.*

Perhaps it is not a portrait gallery. It is, as T. S. Eliot (hanging on the wall as a modernist scrawl of overpainted profiles) put it, a wilderness of mirrors.

If you want to know who we are, then take my hand and we will walk it together, and stare into each picture and object until, finally, we begin to see ourselves.

Originally published as an essay in the exhibition catalogue of *The BP Portrait Award, 2015.*

The Dresden Dolls: Hallowe'en 2010

I want to describe Amanda Palmer, half of art-punk cabaret-rock band The Dresden Dolls, in a way that makes her seem like something exotic, but truly, it's hard for me to think of Amanda Palmer as exotic: I know her too well. We've been friends for three years, a couple for nearly two, and engaged to be married for the best part of a year now. In that time I've seen her play gigs of all sizes and all kinds, alone or with bands, playing piano or keyboards and, sometimes, a joke that got so far out of hand it became a Radiohead covers album, the ukulele. I've seen her play grand churches and basement dive bars (once on the same night going from chapel to dive bar), watched her play a seriously genderbent Emcee in *Cabaret* and half of the pair of conjoined twin sisters known as Evelyn Evelyn.

But I'd never seen The Dresden Dolls. They went on the sort of hiatus that most bands don't come back from about a month before I met Amanda for the first time.

I'd been a lazy sort of Dresden Dolls fan before that. I had their first two major-label CDs (but didn't even notice when they released *No, Virginia*, their third). They had a few songs on my 'Stuff I Really Like' iPod playlist. I'd felt vaguely warm towards them after hearing Amanda was nice to my goddaughters Sky and Winter after a gig, and when I noticed that the Dolls put up the hatemail they had received (complete with occasional hatedrawings) on their website. I tried to see them once, in 2005, when they played Sundance, but I had a panel on animation to attend when they were on, and I watched Nellie McKay instead.

When I started going out with Amanda I asked about The Dresden Dolls. She told me it was a pity that I'd missed them. They were *so* good, she said. Brian Viglione and her, well, it was special.

I was sure it was. But then she'd talk about Brian, the other half of The Dresden Dolls (Amanda played keyboards, Brian played mostly drums and sometimes guitar), and talk about their time on the road in the way someone talks about a bad marriage she's glad she's out of: they had been together all day and every day, and for 120 minutes of that time they had made the music that made her happy, and the rest of the time they drove each other crazy. They'd sometimes been lovers, or at least, they'd had a fair amount of sex over that seven years, and they'd sometimes been friends, but mostly they'd been The Dresden Dolls, a band on the road, united in a vision of art as liberation. And then in early 2008, they weren't.

Curious, I'd watched a YouTube video from the end of their final tour. Brian talks about why it was time for them to stop: 'Why constantly fight?' he asks. 'It's not a marriage. It's a band.' Cut to Amanda: 'It's like being brother and sister and married and business partners and then put in a box where you have to see each other twenty-four hours a day,' she says. They both look tired and they look done.

But time heals. Or at least it forms scabs.

Which explains why I am standing on the balcony at Irving Plaza at Hallowe'en, at the first gig of The Dresden Dolls reunion tour, watching two young ladies, wearing mostly glitter, Hula-Hooping in the dark with glowing Hula-Hoops, watched by an audience of clowns and zombies and mad hatters and such, and

I don't actually know where the Hallowe'en costumes end and the dressing up to see The Dresden Dolls begins.

Amanda appears on the balcony to watch the support band, the Legendary Pink Dots. They were her favorite band as a teenager, gave the Dolls their first break. She's happy that they are playing to twelve hundred people who would never have seen them otherwise. She holds my hand, introduces me to the man who introduced her and Brian at a Hallowe'en party exactly a decade before, and slips back into the shadows.

The next time I see her, she's on the stage wearing a red kimono over a Hallowe'en sweater she bought in June in the Wisconsin Dells. The sweater has a scarecrow on the back. She's wearing a red military cap, and when, two songs in, she takes off the sweater and the kimono to play in skin and a black bra, she has the word LOVE written in eyeliner across her chest. Brian is dressed in a black vest, black trousers.

The first strange thing about watching the Dolls is the feeling of immediate recognition. The 'Oh, I get it. This is what the songs are meant to sound like.' As if the drumming makes sense of something, or translates it back into the language it was originally written in.

The second strange thing about the Dolls is this: it's very obviously a band that consists of two percussion players. They are two people who hit things. She hits the keys, he hits the drums.

And the third, and strangest, thing about the Dolls is that they are, when they play, quite obviously, telepathic, like a couple who can finish each other's sentences. They know each other and the songs so well that it's all there, in muscle memory and in their heads and in the subliminal cues that the rest of the world is never going to see. I'd never really got that until now. I'd puzzled over why, if the songs needed a drummer, Amanda didn't simply go and get a drummer. But drumming is only part of what Brian's doing. He's commenting, performing, panto-miming, playing, yin to Amanda's yang. It's a remarkable, virtuoso, glorious thing to see them play together.

They play 'Sex Changes'. They play 'Missed Me', and the audience are pumping their fists, zombies and superheroines and Pennywise the clown, and I think, *I've heard her play this song so many times. I've seen her cross a hall with a marching band behind her playing this song. She's done it with a full orchestra. And this is better than any of them.*

Two nights later, on the phone, after the Boston gig, she tells me how irritated she is with people who tell her that they like The Dresden Dolls better than her solo performances, and I feel guilty.

I'm starting to understand why she went on her first tour with a dance troupe, even though it guaranteed the tour would make no money, why she would go on tour as conjoined twins with Jason Webley and a single dress that fitted both of them. I can see how much of what she's been doing onstage was looking for things that replaced, not Brian, but the energy of Brian, putting something else on the stage that's more than just a girl and a keyboard.

She introduces Brian, tells off security for trying to take a fan's camera: 'We have an open photo policy.'

A change of energy: they perform Brecht/Weill's 'Pirate Jenny', and Brian acts it out as he conjures the ocean with the drum-ming. As the Black Freighter ships off to sea, and Jenny whispers that 'On it is me', the hall is perfectly quiet.

A girl shouts, 'I love you, Amanda.'

A man shouts, 'I love you, Brian.'

The Long sisters, friends of Amanda's, both made up dead, Casey with a bullet hole in her forehead, Danni's face a mess of stage blood, come and stand beside me.

'We love every single fucking one of you in this whole fucking room,' says Amanda, using her favorite intensifier.

The Dresden Dolls play Carole King's song of Maurice Sendak's 'Pierre'. The moral is 'Care', and I don't think either Brian or Amanda can stop caring for a moment: about the gig, about the other's playing, about a decade of good times and bad times and petty offenses and anger and disappointment and seven years of really, really good gigs.

Amanda goes into the chords of 'Coin-Operated Boy', a song that too often, solo, feels like a novelty song, and, played by Amanda and Brian together, it brings the house down: less of a song and more of an act of symbiosis, as they try to wrong-foot each other. It's funny and it's moving and it's like nothing else I've ever seen,

By now Amanda is a mop of hair and skin in a bra, Brian is a topless sheen of sweat and a grin. They launch into Auto-Tune the News's musical version of the 'Double Rainbow' speech, as hundreds of balloons fall, and it's as foolish as it's smart and either way it's perfectly delightful.

'The Jeep Song'. I don't think I've ever heard Amanda play this live. They grab half a dozen fans and pull them up onstage for backing vocals.

Then it's 'Sing'. If there ever was a Dresden Dolls anthem, it's this: a plea to make art, whatever the hell else you do. 'Sing for the teacher who told you that you couldn't sing,' sings Amanda. The audience sings along, and it feels important, less of a sing-along and more like communion or a credo, and we're all singing and it's Hallowe'en and I'm up on the balcony slightly drunk, thinking that this is some sort of wonderful, and Amanda's shouting, 'You motherfuckers, you'll sing someday,' and it's all so good, and I'm standing with two dead girls, and we're cheering and happy and it's one of those perfect moments that don't come along in a lifetime that often, the kind of moment you could end a movie on.

The first encore: Brian's on guitar, Amanda's now wearing a

golden bra, crawling out onto the speaker-stacks to sing 'Mein Herr' from *Cabaret*. Then a crazed, wonderful improvisation that slowly crashes into Amanda's song about parents, 'Half Jack'. 'They fuck you up, your mum and dad,' said Philip Larkin long before either of The Dresden Dolls were born, in a line that sounded like it could have swaggered out of an Amanda Palmer song, and 'Half Jack' is just all about that. Jack Palmer, Amanda's father, is up on the balcony near me, beaming proudly.

A drunk touches my shoulder and congratulates me during the flailing madness of 'Girl Anachronism'. Or I think he's congratulating me. 'How do you sleep at night?' he asks. 'It must be like catching lightning in a jar.'

And I say yes, I suppose it must be, and that I sleep just fine.

The band crashes into 'War Pigs' as a final number, and it's huge and bombastic and heartfelt, and Amanda and Brian are playing like one person with two heads and four hands, and it's all about the beat and the roar, and I watch the crowd in their lunatic, wonderful Hallowe'en costumes drink it in until the final explosive rumble of drums has faded away.

I love the gig. I love everything about it. I feel like I've been made a gift of seven years of Amanda's life, The Dresden Dolls years before I knew her. And I'm in awe of what The Dresden Dolls are, and what they do.

And when it's all over, and it's two a.m. and we are back in the hotel and the adrenaline is fading, Amanda, who has been subdued and awkward since the gig finished, starts crying, silently, uncontrollably, and I hold her, not sure what to say.

'You saw how good it was tonight?' she asks as she cries, and I tell her that, yes. I did, and for the first time it occurs to me how bad it must have got to make her leave something that meant that much to her, that made so many people happy.

Her cheeks are black with wet eye makeup and it's smearing

on the sheets and the pillow as she sobs and I hold her tight, and try with all my might to understand.

This article was written for *Spin* magazine, and originally published on their website on 5 November 2010.

Eight Views of Mount Fuji:
Beloved Demons and Anthony Martignetti

I

It's all about life.
And in the midst of whatever else we're in, it's always about life.

II

I had known Amanda Palmer for six months, and we were going on our first date. Our first date was four days long, because it was all the free time we had at the beginning of 2009 and we were giving it to each other. I had not yet met her family. I barely knew her friends.

'I want you to meet Anthony,' she said.

It was January. If I'd really known who Anthony was in her life then, if I'd known how much he'd played his part in raising her, I think I would have been nervous. I wasn't nervous. I was just pleased that she wanted to introduce me to someone that she knew.

Anthony, she told me, was her next-door neighbor. He had known her since she was a child.

He turned up in the restaurant: a tall, good-looking man who looked a decade younger than his age. He had a walking cane, an easy comfortable manner, and we talked all that evening. Anthony told me about the nine-year-old Amanda who had thrown snowballs at his window, about the teenage Amanda who had come next door when she needed to vent, about the college-age Amanda who had called him from Germany when she was lonely and knew nobody, and about rock star Amanda (it was Anthony who had named The Dresden Dolls). He asked me about me, and I answered him as honestly as I could.

Later, Amanda told me that Anthony liked me, and had told her he thought I would make a good boyfriend for her.

I had no idea how important this was, or what Anthony's approval meant at the time.

III

Life is a stream: an ongoing conversation of nature with itself, contradictory and opinionated and dangerous. And the stream is made up of births and deaths, of things that come into existence and pass away. But there is always life, and things feeding on life.

We had been married for five months. Amanda phoned me in tears from a yoga retreat in the Canary Islands, to tell me Anthony had just been diagnosed with leukemia. She flew home. Anthony began treatment. It didn't look as if there was anything real to worry about. Not then. They can treat these things.

As the next year began, Amanda recorded an album, *Theatre*

Is Evil. She started touring for it, a planned tour that would take the best part of a year.

At the end of the summer, Anthony's leukemia took a turn for the worse, and suddenly there were very real reasons to worry. He would need to go for chemo. He might not make it. We read the Wikipedia entry on the kind of leukemia Anthony had, and we learned that this was not the kind you get better from, and we were sobered and scared.

Amanda had been a touring rock musician for a decade, and took pride in never canceling gigs. She called me, and she canceled the second half of her tour to be with Anthony. We took a house in Cambridge's Harvard Square so she could be close to him.

We had a small dinner for friends, shortly after we moved in, to celebrate the birthday of Anthony's wife, Laura. Laura is very beautiful, and very gentle, and a lawyer who helps people who cannot help themselves. I cooked fish for them. Pat, Laura's mother, came, and helped me cook.

That was a year ago.

IV

Anthony had been Amanda's friend. Somewhere in there, while she and I were dating, before we were married or even engaged, he became someone I talked to when I was lost and confused and way out of my depth in the thickets of a relationship that was always like nothing I'd ever known before. I called him from Australia and texted him from a train in New Mexico. His advice was wise and practical, and often – mostly – it was right.

He stopped me overthinking things; would offer hope, always

with a matter-of-fact thread of darkness and practicality: yes, you can fix *this*, but you'll have to learn to live with *that*.

I discovered over the years to come that many of the things I treasured most about Amanda were gifts that Anthony had given her or taught her over the years of their friendship.

One night Amanda read me a story that Anthony had written, about his childhood, about food, about love. It was gripping. I asked for more.

With a mixture of nervousness and diffidence, Anthony gave me more of his stories to read: autobiographical sketches and confessionals, some funny, some dark. Each of the stories shone a light inside Anthony's skull and showed the reader the view from his past. He was nervous because I write books for a living, and he was relieved (I think) that I liked them.

I liked them very much.

I had worried that we would have nothing in common, apart from our love of Amanda. I was wrong. We both had a fascination with, and a delight in, stories. Do not give either of us gifts: give us the tale that accompanies the gift. That is what makes the gift worth having.

Ask Anthony about the walking canes I gave him The joys of the gifts are in the stories.

V

I'm thinking about all those signs we put on our walls when we were teenagers and knew that we would live forever, in order to show how tough and cynical and worldly-wise we were:

NOBODY GETS OUT OF HERE ALIVE was one of them. THE PERSON WHO DIES WITH THE MOST TOYS WINS was another. There was one of two vultures sitting on a branch that said PATIENCE MY ASS, I'M GONNA KILL SOMETHING.

And it's easy to be cynical about death when you're young. When you are young, death is an anomaly. It's not real. It only affects other people. It's a bullet you'll dodge easily. It's why young people can go into battle: they really will live forever. They know.

As you stick around, as you go around the Earth, you realize that life is an ever-narrowing conveyor belt. Slowly, inexorably, it takes us all along with it, and one by one we tumble off the sides of the conveyor belt into darkness.

A few days after Amanda decided that she was going to stop touring and be with Anthony, we heard that our friend Becca Rosenthal had died. She was twenty-seven. She was young and beautiful and filled with life and potential. She wanted to be a librarian.

Just before Christmas, our friend Jeremy Geidt went into hospital for a relatively minor operation. Jeremy was a crusty, foul-mouthed, gloriously funny actor and teacher who had come to the US in the early sixties with Peter Cook's Establishment Club. He had lived a remarkable life, which he would tell us about in booze-tinged anecdotes and perfectly deployed expletives. Jeremy spent most of the next six months in the hospital, recovering from the first operation, and dealing with a tumor in his throat. He died in August, suddenly and unexpectedly. He was old, but he relished life, chewed it like a dog with a rawhide bone.

They fall off the conveyor belt into the darkness, our friends, and we cannot talk to them any more.

In November, Anthony's friends divided up the tasks of taking him to chemo, staying with him, bringing him home again (he could not drive himself back, after all). I offered to help, but Amanda said no.

VI

I met Amanda Palmer because she wanted help in playing dead. She had been pretending to be dead in photographs for the previous fourteen years, and now she was making a whole record about it. *Who Killed Amanda Palmer,* it was called. We met and interacted because she wanted someone to write stories of her deaths.

I found the idea intriguing.

I wrote stories. I killed her over and over again in every story and poem. I even killed her on the back of the record. I wrote a dozen different Amanda Palmers before I ever knew her, each of them dying in a dozen or more inventive ways.

The deaths were inevitable. Of course, sometimes describing and thinking about death is our way of celebrating life, of feeling more alive, of grasping life tightly, licking it, tasting it, plunging our teeth into it and knowing that we are part of it. It's like sex, the tumbling into the tug and pull of the continuous stream of life. And life and sex are always tied in to death: the erection on the gallows, the final urge to procreate and live before the darkness.

We behave differently when we see the darkness looming. We become creatures of lust and fear.

Amanda pushed and helped him, and Anthony published some of his stories in a collection called *Lunatic Heroes*. He and his friends Nivi and Paul formed 3 Swallys Press to bring the book to the world. The launch event for *Lunatic Heroes*, in Lexington, Massachusetts, Anthony's hometown, was a dark event in a sold-out theater: Amanda read her introduction, and I read some of *The Ocean at the End of the Lane,* and most of all Anthony read from *Lunatic Heroes*.

I worried that he wasn't going to live much beyond the launch event.

I was scared for Laura, Anthony's wife, and scared for Amanda. I knew that any sadness I was going to feel at the loss of my friend was going to have to be put aside while I looked after Amanda, who would be broken and torn by Anthony's death.

It was going to be hard for all of us.

I felt the air from the wings of the angel of death brushing my face at that launch event, that night.

VII

Life has a sense of humor, but then again, so does death.

Laura's mother, Pat, who helped me cook when we first moved into this house, died this year of leukemia.

Anthony, to our delight, got through the chemo, and, with the help of a newly released drug, he recovered. He is in remission – for now. He beat death, as much as any of us gets to beat death. For now – it's always a transient win, that one, and the reaper can wait. She's patient, and she will be here when the last of us has gone.

Anthony no longer had leukemia; but now he had a book called *Lunatic Heroes*.

There were darker stories that Anthony had crafted from his life that had not made it into that first book. Stories of obsession and desire. Stories of loss and fear and hate. The kind of stories that need you to be brave to tell them, braver still to publish them so that other people can look inside your head and know what makes you tick, and what makes you hard, and what makes you cry, that tell you that the hardest battles are the ones you fight inside your own head, when nobody else is going to know if you won or lost or even if a battle was fought at all.

Or to put it another way, and quote the Buddha, who knew about these things,

Though one may conquer a million men in battle, yet the noblest of victors is he who conquers himself. Self-conquest is far better than the conquest of others. Not even a god, an angel, Mara or Brahma could turn that triumph back into defeat.

VIII

We win some, but we lose many. We lose a lot. We lose our friends and we lose our family. In the end we lose everything. No matter who's with us, we always die alone. When you fight your battles, whatever battles you fight, it's always going to be about life.

We leave behind two things that matter, Stephen Sondheim said, in a musical I love and Amanda doesn't, and those two things are children and art.

Anthony's children are scattered: they are the people whose lives he has influenced and helped to shape. I count my wife as one of his children. Anthony's art is here, in these pages, waiting for you, as fresh, as sharp, as painful a hundred years from now when I'm dead and Anthony's dead and Amanda's dead and everyone we know is dust and ash and bones in the ground.

This book is a gift, and, as I said, it is the tales that accompany the gift that matter: the stories that show us the joy of event, of the shaping of memories, and the joy of a life lived, as all lives are lived, both in the light and in the darkness.

These pages are gifts, from Anthony to you, and they hold the tales that accompany the gifts, from someone who has walked into the darkness and now stands in the light, ready to tell you his stories.

This was my introduction to C. Anthony Martignetti's book *Beloved Demons*. Anthony died of leukemia in June 2015, at home, surrounded by his loved ones. We were there, his friends and family, around his bed. I was holding Amanda's pregnant belly as he left us, and feeling the movements of the baby we would name after Anthony.

So Many Ways to Die in Syria Now: May 2014

We are in a metal shed in Azraq refugee camp, Jordan, sitting on a low mattress, talking to a couple who have been here since the camp opened two weeks ago. Abu Hani* is a good-looking man in his late forties who looks beaten, like an abused dog. He hangs back. His wife, Yalda, talks more than he does.

There is a water jug on the floor. It is the only water they have. We have managed to knock it over twice, and each time we apologise and feel awful, as in order to refill it there is a five-minute walk to the four taps embedded in concrete at the corner of the block. The desert air dries out the thin carpet in moments.

The couple are telling us why they left Syria. Abu Hani once owned a small supermarket, but the 'officials' who ran his town trashed it, mixed detergent into the grains and pulses and took his stock. He spent his savings restocking the shop, but when he opened again they closed him down permanently. People were killed. On the local news they would show bodies that had been found, so people could identify their relatives: one time he saw a cousin's severed head on there.

* All names of refugees have been changed.

Mostly their relatives just vanished. Yalda's brothers and cousin were on their way to deliver blood for a transfusion to their infant nephew who was having an open-heart operation when they were stopped at a roadblock, and interrogated about the blood. The three men did not arrive at the hospital and were never seen again. I did not want to ask what happened to the nephew. Her mother, Yalda tells us, has lost her mind: she goes from police station to hospital to police station, asking about her sons – the police got so tired of this they wrote 'deceased' next to their names, to make her stop coming and asking.

Abu Hani and Yalda tell us about the border crossing into Jordan, how they tried to leave their town without bribing a checkpoint officer, and how Abu Hani was taken into the office by the official and punched, kicked and jumped on in front of his wife and children for an hour and a half. All their money was taken from them. They left that checkpoint with him covered in blood, concussed, barely able to move and penniless.

'We woke up every morning glad we were alive, and went to sleep every night knowing we might not wake in the morning. There are so many ways to die in Syria now,' says Yalda. Their relatives have been imprisoned, gone missing, been murdered and killed in explosions.

The couple borrowed money from friends and the next time they went through the checkpoint, the same now-heavily-bribed officer saluted them. They reached the Jordanian border with nothing.

'I was scared of the Jordanian army on the border,' Yalda says. 'I thought, *If the uniforms on the Syrian side were so brutal . . .* But when we crossed, the Jordanian army helped us, and welcomed us with a smile.' She tells us they were given cookies and water and blankets by the army, provided by the UN Refugee Agency (UNHCR). 'I got to the camp, and I felt like a child being welcomed by its mother,' she tells me.

I have not thought of Azraq camp as welcoming until now. A ghost town that opened at the end of April, it currently holds around 4,000 people but is designed to accommodate 130,000 in its square white metal huts. It feels like the least welcoming place in the world, the only sign of life or colour or individuality is the washing we see fluttering between buildings.

Abu Hani and Yalda now both have jobs in the camp. She greets new arrivals and he works as a porter for them (although people know he has back injuries and they give him light work). They want to save enough in the camp to replace broken hearing aids for two of their four children, both of whom are deaf. They worry that if she does not hear anything, their five-year-old daughter will forget the words she already knows how to speak.

We walk to the water supply to refill the family's jerry cans and make up for what we spilled, but no water comes out. They are waiting for the supply trucks to arrive. Jordan is the fourth-driest country in the world, and every drop of water in the camps is driven there from outside boreholes.

The crisis in Syria, the unrest that became a civil war that became a nightmare, created, as all wars have created since human beings started living in villages, refugees. They left their houses, if their houses were still standing, and they went somewhere else, somewhere they might at least be safe.

More than two and a half million people have fled the country in the past two years, and more than six hundred thousand of them have gone to Jordan. The Jordanian people and government have shown exceptional generosity. There are six million people in Jordan: the Syrian refugees make up 10 per cent of the population. If Britain were to do the same proportionally, it would mean accepting about six and a half million refugees.

Syrians have come to Jordan because they speak the same language, have similar cultures and often relatives there, and because Jordan historically has taken in refugees – Palestinians,

Iraqis and Kuwaitis have all fled there over the years. Sometimes they have even gone home again.

UNHCR doesn't like camps. The money that is spent running their infrastructure is money that could be spent on more direct support to people living in their own homes. But as the towns and the cities and urban centres have filled up, with a thousand refugees coming in every night, men and women and children, camps have become a necessity. They had two weeks to open the first one, Zaatari – planned for five thousand people, it grew to hold its current population of one hundred thousand.

Before I came out here, I tried to imagine what a refugee camp would be like. It would consist of several rows of tents in a field. It would be dusty, of course, because the field was in Jordan, where it is dry, and it would be a big field, because there were a lot of refugees. I had not imagined cities. Where Azraq is a ghost city of white boxes in a flint and lava desert, Zaatari is an anarchic dusty city of tents and boxlike people-containers, in which every streetlight is covered with a wild spaghetti-tangle of wires, stealing electricity to light people's homes, charge their phones and power televisions.

Kilian Kleinschmidt, the UNHCR camp manager who is mayor to this 'city' of one hundred thousand, has resigned himself to an electricity bill of $500,000 a month, and now concentrates on putting in boxes on the lampposts that allow authorised electricians to access the power safely, and urging people to raise the wire tangles up off the ground during the rains. People move house in Zaatari by putting wheels on to repurposed fence-posts, lifting their houses onto them, and hauling them through the streets, while boys jump on and off, like a fairground ride.

I keep trying to work out how I got to Jordan. Things happen because they happen. UNHCR had noticed that when I retweeted their tweets and appeals, more people read them and acted on what they had read, so we spoke, and I linked to their sites, and read the links before I posted them. I volunteered to get more involved, and UNHCR offered to take me to a camp somewhere to show me what was happening. I agreed.

Coco Campbell from UNHCR had been to school with Georgina Chapman, the fashion designer. I wrote a short film that Georgina directed last year. Coco asked if I would find out if Georgina would be interested in coming with me to see the refugee camps and what UNHCR did, and create another story-telling project together. I asked her, and she was. Georgina brought her husband with her, film producer Harvey Weinstein, who is, in all ways, larger than life. In Azraq camp, Harvey surprises his people by wanting to be there with us and by paying absolute attention to Abu Hani and Yalda. He tells the UNHCR represent-atives that he wants to pay for the hearing aids their children need, now. They tell him it doesn't quite work like that. There is a system in place and the children will get hearing aids.

Wherever we go in the camps children flock to Georgina. She smiles at them, and they cluster around her, cling to her legs, hold her hands. 'She's like the Pied Piper,' says Harvey. We watch how, in Zaatari camp, people make lives, build a new normality as best they can. There are even shops: we eat the best baklava I have ever tasted in a bakery jerry-rigged from a container and a tent, rolled out on a metal table with a broom handle. Harvey wanders off, and I find him outside, talking with an old woman who lost her sons in the conflict, but made it to Jordan with her pregnant daughter. We ask who killed her sons, and she tells us she doesn't know.

It is a refrain we hear over and over, but we keep asking the questions, as people tell us how they came to the camps: Who bombed your house? Who shot you in the back as you drove on your motorbike to dig your children out of the rubble? Who cut off your cousin's head? Who killed your family? Who shot your son? Who cut off the food supplies? Who shot at you if you went out of your house? Who beat you up? Who broke your hand?

People shrug. They don't know. There are, as Yalda told me, so many.

Back in the improvised baklava bakery, the baker's sister is telling Georgina about her miscarriages in Syria – they would move to escape the fighting, and she would get pregnant, but each time the shelling started she would lose the baby. She is twenty-six, she wears a pink headscarf, she is very beautiful. Her husband has left her for a new wife in the camp, one who can give him children. There are so many weddings in the camp. There are people who will rent you wedding dresses, although you have to buy the wedding-night lingerie.

Everyone I talk to in the camps has a nightmare story: they stayed in Syria, going through hell, until they could take no more, and then the journey to the border, with whatever they could carry, normally just a change of clothes for the children, would be a journey across hell. They put their lives at risk, and if they arrived at the border alive, it was worth it.

I look at Azraq camp, with room for another 126,000 people, all of whom will come, most of whom will risk death to get there, and I know that is another 126,000 nightmares.

I realise I have stopped thinking about political divides, about freedom fighters or terrorists, about dictators and armies. I am thinking only of the fragility of civilisation. The lives the refugees had were our lives: they owned corner shops and sold cars, they farmed or worked in factories or owned factories or sold insurance. None of them expected to be running for their lives, leaving everything they had because they had nothing to come back to, making smuggled border crossings, walking past the dismembered corpses of other people who had tried to make the crossing but had been caught or been betrayed.

I keep going, talking to the refugees, to the people who run the camps and care for the refugees, and then, after accompanying Ayman, a Syrian volunteer nurse on his rounds, as he changes the dressings on a youth whose foot was blown off by a land mine and an eleven-year-old girl who lost half her jaw in a mortar attack that killed her father, I realise I can't think straight. All I want to do is cry. I think it is just me, but Sam, the cameraman, is crying too.

I imagine the world dividing into the people who want to feed their children, and the ones shooting at them. It is probably just an artificial divide but UNHCR is on the side of the people who want to feed their children, on the side of human dignity and respect, and it is rare that you know you have picked the right side. You are on the side of people.

This was originally published in the *Guardian,* 21 May 2014. Eighteen months later, well over four million people have fled Syria. Millions more have lost their homes, their towns, are 'internally displaced' but have not yet crossed the border out of Syria. Political solutions and humanitarian solutions are needed. The heartbreak doesn't end.

A *Slip of the Keyboard:*
Terry Pratchett

I want to tell you about my friend Terry Pratchett, and it's not easy. I'm going to tell you something you may not know.

Some people have encountered an affable man with a beard and a hat. They believe they have met Sir Terry Pratchett. They have not.

Science fiction conventions often give you someone to look after you, to make sure you get from place to place without getting lost. Some years ago I ran into someone who had once been Terry's handler at a convention in Texas. His eyes misted over at the memory of getting Terry from his panel to the book-dealers' room and back. 'What a jolly old elf Sir Terry is,' he said.

And I thought, *No. No, he's not.*

Back in February 1991, Terry and I were on a book signing tour for *Good Omens,* a book we had written together. We can tell you dozens of not-only-funny-but-also-true stories about the things that happened on that tour. Terry alludes to a few of them in this book. This story is true, but it is not one of the stories we tell.

We were in San Francisco. We had just done a stock signing in a bookshop, signing the dozen or so copies of our book they had ordered. Terry looked at the itinerary. Next stop was a radio station: we were due to have an hour-long interview on live radio. 'From the address, it's just down the street from here,' said Terry. 'And we've got half an hour. Let's walk it.'

This was a long time ago, best beloved, in the days before GPS systems and mobile phones and taxi-summoning apps and suchlike useful things that would have told us in moments that no, it would not be a few blocks to the radio station. It would be several miles, all uphill and mostly through a park.

We called the radio station as we went, whenever we passed a pay phone, to tell them that we knew we were now late for a live broadcast, and that we were, promise cross our sweaty hearts, walking as fast as we could.

I would try and say cheerful, optimistic things as we walked. Terry said nothing, in a way that made it very clear that anything I could say would probably just make things worse. I did not, ever, say, at any point on that walk, that all of this would have been avoided if we had just got the bookshop to call us a taxi. There are things you can never unsay, that you cannot say and still remain friends, and that would have been one of them.

We reached the radio station at the top of the hill, a very long way from anywhere, about forty minutes into our hour-long live interview. We arrived all sweaty and out of breath, and they were broadcasting the breaking news. A man had just started shooting people in a local McDonald's, which is not the kind of thing you want to have as your lead-in when you are now meant to talk about a funny book you've written about the end of the world and how we're all going to die.

The radio people were angry with us, too, and understandably so: it's no fun having to improvise when your guests are late. I don't think that our fifteen minutes on the air were very funny.

(I was later told that Terry and I had both been blacklisted by that San Franciscan radio station for several years, because leaving a show's hosts to burble into the dead air for forty minutes is something the Powers of Radio do not easily forget or forgive.)

Still, by the top of the hour it was all over. We went back to our hotel, and this time we took a taxi. Terry was silently furious: with himself, mostly, I suspect, and with the world that had not told him that the distance from the bookshop to the radio station was much further than it had looked on our itinerary. He sat in the back of the cab beside me white with anger, a non-directional ball of fury. I said something hoping to placate him. Perhaps I said that ah well, it had all worked out in the end, and it hadn't been the end of the world, and suggested it was time to not be angry any more.

Terry looked at me. He said, 'Do not underestimate this anger. This anger was the engine that powered *Good Omens*.'

I thought of the driven way that Terry wrote, and of the way that he drove the rest of us with him, and I knew that he was right.

There is a fury to Terry Pratchett's writing. It's the fury that was the engine that powered *Discworld,* and you will discover it here: it's the anger at the headmaster who would decide that six-year-old Terry Pratchett would never be smart enough for the Eleven-Plus exam; anger at pompous critics, and at those who think that serious is the opposite of funny; anger at his early American publishers who could not bring his books out successfully.

The anger is always there, an engine that drives. By the time this book enters its final act, and Terry learns he has a rare, early-onset form of Alzheimer's, the targets of his fury change: now he is angry with his brain and his genetics and, more than these, furious at a country that will not permit him (or others in a similarly intolerable situation) to choose the manner and the time of their passing.

And that anger, it seems to me, is about Terry's underlying sense of what is fair and what is not.

It is that sense of fairness that underlies Terry's work and his writing, and it's what drove him from school to journalism to the press office of the Central Electricity Generating Board to the position of being one of the best-loved and bestselling writers in the world.

It's the same sense of fairness that means that in this book, sometimes in the cracks, while talking of other things, he takes time to punctiliously acknowledge his influences – Alan Coren, for example, who pioneered so many of the techniques of short humor that Terry and I have filched over the years; or the glorious overstuffed heady thing that is *Brewer's Dictionary of Phrase and Fable* and its compiler, the Reverend E. Cobham Brewer, that most serendipitous of authors. Terry's *Brewer's* introduction made me smile – we would call each other up in delight whenever we discovered a book by Brewer we had not seen before ("Ere! Have you already got a copy of Brewer's *A Dictionary of Miracles: Imitative, Realistic and Dogmatic?*")

The pieces selected here cover Terry's entire writing career, from schoolboy to Knight of the Realm of Letters, and are still of a piece. Nothing has dated, save perhaps for the references to specific items of computer hardware. (I suspect that, if he has not by now donated it to a charity or a museum, Terry could tell you exactly where his Atari Portfolio is, and just how much he paid for the handcrafted add-on memory card that took its memory up to an impossibly huge one megabyte.) The authorial voice in these essays is always Terry's: genial, informed, sensible, drily amused. I suppose that, if you look quickly and are not paying attention, you might, perhaps, mistake it for jolly.

But beneath any jollity there is a foundation of fury. Terry Pratchett is not one to go gentle into any night, good or otherwise. He will rage, as he leaves, against so many things: stupidity, injustice, human foolishness and shortsightedness, not just the dying of the light, although that's here too. And, hand in hand with the anger, like an angel and a demon walking hand in hand into the sunset, there is love: for human beings, in all our fallibility; for treasured objects; for stories; and ultimately and in all things, love for human dignity.

Or to put it another way, anger is the engine that drives him, but it is the greatness of spirit that deploys that anger on the side of the angels, or better yet for all of us, the orangutans.

Terry Pratchett is not a jolly old elf at all. Not even close. He's so much more than that.

As Terry walks into the darkness much too soon, I find myself raging too: at the injustice that deprives us of – what? Another twenty or thirty books? Another shelf-full of ideas and glorious phrases and old friends and new, of stories in which people do what they really do do best, which is use their heads to get themselves out of the trouble they got into by not thinking? Another book or two like this, of journalism and agitprop and even the occasional introduction? But truly, the loss of these things does not anger me as it should. It saddens me, but I, who have seen some of them being built close up, understand that any Terry Pratchett book is a small miracle, and we already have more than might be reasonable, and it does not behoove any of us to be greedy.

I rage at the imminent loss of my friend.

And I think, *What would Terry do with this anger?*

Then I pick up my pen, and I start to write.

This was the introduction to Terry Pratchett's non-fiction collection, *A Slip of the Keyboard*, 2014. I wrote it while he was still with us, could still read it. He told me he liked it, and I was relieved. Terry died on 12 March 2015. I can't talk to him any longer. I miss my friend.

Credits

Many of the pieces appearing in this collection were first published elsewhere, permission and copyright information as follows:

Index

Abel, Jessica 317
Academy Awards (Oscars) 471–77
Acker, Kathy 194
Adams, Douglas 15, 109, 120–22, 373–78; *The Hitchhiker's Guide to the Galaxy* 120, 374, 376–78; 'Remembering Douglas Adams' 120–22; *So Long, and Thanks for All the Fish* 373–78
Adams, Neal 272–73
Addams, Charles 56
'Afterword Afterword: Evelyn Evelyn' 423–26
Agnew, Spiro 127, 128
Aladdin Sane (album) 483
Aldiss, Brian 175–82, 200, 201; *Billion Year Spree* 175, 197; *Hothouse* 175–82
Alex Award 91
Alfred Hitchcock and the Three Investigators (Arthur) 22
Alice's Adventures in Wonderland (Carroll) 73
'All Books Have Genders' 72–77
Allen, Woody 278
Allred, Michael 286
Amazing Maurice and His Educated Rodents,The (Pratchett) 109–10
America 69–71
American Gods (Gaiman) 67, 69–70, 73–77, 82, 90, 199, 364
American Library Association 304
Amis, Martin 409, 411
Amos, Tori 395–99
And to My Nephew Albert I Leave the Island What I Won off Fatty Hagan in a Poker Game (Forrest) 32, 89–90
Anderson, Brent 269
Anderson, Poul 199
Andrews, Julie 146

Angry Candy (Ellison) 129
Anno Dracula (Newman) 329
'Apt Pupil' (King) 139
Archer's Goon (Jones) 103
'Argonauts of the Air, The' (Wells) 340–41
Aristocrats, The (movie) 355
Art 459–67
Art and Artifice: And Other Essays on Illusion (Steinmeyer), Introduction to 387–89
Asimov, Isaac 32, 202
Askwith, Mark 275, 276–77
Astounding Science Fiction 346–47, 349
Astro City: Confession (Busiek), Introduction to 265–70
Austin, Alan 289–91
Author photographs 99

Bacchae, The (Euripides) 262
Bacchus 261–62
Bag of Bones (King) 140
Baker, Tom 225
Baker Street Irregulars 331
Balcombe, Florence 331
Baldwin, Alec 474
Ballard, J. G. 127, 171, 177
Banks, John 34, 34–36
Barker, Clive 154
Barks, Carl 278
Barry, Lynda 319
Batman (movie) 228
Batman: Cover to Cover 271–74
Baynes, Pauline 39, 40
Beagle, Peter S. 2, 40
Beast That Shouted Love at the Heart of the World, The (Ellison), Foreword to 123–30
Bechdel, Alison 78
'Bells, The' (song) 413, 415

Beloved Demons (Martignetti),
    Introduction to 492–500
Berger, Karen 287
Berlin (album) 404, 406
Best American Comics 2010,
    Introduction to 315–20
Best of the Spirit, The (Eisner),
    Introduction to 293–96
Bester, Alfred 189–92
Betty and Veronica 312
Between Thought and Expression:
    Selected Lyrics of Lou Reed 409–10,
    414–15, 418–20
Biard, Gérard 81
Big Time, The (Leiber) 172
Bigelow, Kathryn 476
Billion Year Spree (Aldiss) 175, 197
'Birdhouse in Your Soul' (song) 400–401
Birkin, Charles 87
Black Orchid (Gaiman and McKean) 113
Blair, Tony 231
Blish, James 176
Bloch, Robert 354
Bloody Chamber, The (Carter), 433
'Blue Cross, The' (Chesterton) 350–51
Blyberg, Will 269
Blyton, Enid 11
'Body, The' (King) 139
Bogart, Humphrey 106
Bolland, Brian 239
Bone (Smith) 275–81
'*Bone*: An Introduction, and Some
    Subsequent Thoughts' 275–81
Bookshops 31–37, 88–89
Borglum, Gutzon 123, 128
Bowie, David 404, 483
Boy Commandos 286–87
Bradbury, Ray 52, 54, 88, 183–88, 345;
    Fahrenheit 451 183–88, 324; *The*
    Martian Chronicles 32, 187; *The Silver*
    Locusts 32, 187; 'Usher II' 323–24
Brave and the Bold, The 272
'Breathing Method, The' (King) 139
Brèque, Jean-Daniel 291
Brewer, E. Cobham 511
Bride of Frankenstein (movie) 207–10
Bridges, Jeff 476
Briggs, Katharine 434
Brightfount Diaries, The (Aldiss) 176
British Fantasy Convention: (1983)
    356–57; (1985) 380
British Fantasy Society (BFS) 150
British Film Institute Journal 151
Brontë sisters 481–82
Brooker, Faith 152

Broome, John 268
Brother Power the Geek (Simon) 286
Brunner, John 177
Bug Jack Barron (Spinrad) 127
Bullock, Sandra 476
'Burning Chrome' (Gibson) 404–5
Burroughs, Edgar Rice 35
Burroughs, William 171, 199
Busiek, Kurt 265–70
'Business as Usual, During Alterations'
    (Williams) 346
'But What Has That to Do with
    Bacchus? Eddie Campbell and
    Deadface' 261–64
Byrne, Eugene 153

Cabell, James Branch 34, 35, 41, 127–28
Cale, John 113
Cameron, James 473
Cameron, Julia Margaret 482
Campbell, Coco 504
Campbell, Eddie 112, 177, 261–64, 318
Campbell, Ramsey 174, 356
Carell, Steve 473
Carnegie Medal 103, 109–10
Carpenter, John 357
Carrie (King) 12, 90, 137–38, 142, 143
Carroll, Jonathan 113
Carroll, Lewis 73, 180
Carson, Dave 356, 357
Carter, Angela 433–34, 455
'Cask of Amontillado, The' (Poe) 326
'Catastrophe, A' (Wells) 340
Central Electricity Generating Board
    107, 511
Cerebus 312
Chadbourn, Mark 456
Chambers, Robert W. 356
Chapman, Georgina 504–6
Charlie Hebdo 78–81
Chesterton, G. K. 39, 42–43, 65, 88;
    Complete Father Brown Stories 42,
    350–52
Chevalier d'Eon 481
Chicago Comics Convention (1996),
    'ashcan' tribute to Will Eisner 289–92
Chicago Humanities Festival speech
    59–68
Children: love of reading 11–14, 18;
    self-censorship of 87, 90
Children's books 82–96
China 45, 92–93
Christie, Agatha 140
Chronicles of Narnia (Lewis) 38–40
Chu's Day (Gaiman) 92–93

Cinema Macabre (Morris, ed.) 210
Cities 160–61
City Limits 151
City People Notebook (Eisner) 297–300
Claremont, Chris 258
Clarke, Arthur C. 32, 177
Clarke, Harry 327
Clarke, Susanna 202, 446–50
Cleese, John 121
Clifford, Lucy 310, 436
Climbers (Harrison) 371
Clive, Colin 208–9
Clooney, George 474
Clute, John, *Encyclopedia of Science Fiction* 108, 126, 178, 189
Cocteau, Jean 432–33
'Coin-Operated Boy' (song) 489
Colbert Report, The (TV series) 21
Cold War 185
Cole, Jack 303
Colour of Magic, The (Pratchett) 106
Come Unto These Yellow Sands (radio play) 455
Comic Book Legal Defense Fund 348
Comic Book Retailers International (CBRI) 240–41
Comic Relief 121
Comics 63, 235–320; and films 228–32, 249; illiteracy myth about 11; vs. prose 249–50
Comics and Sequential Art (Eisner) 294
Company of Wolves, The (movie) 433
Complete Father Brown Stories (Chesterton) 42, 350–52
Complete Stories and Poems of Edgar Allan Poe (Poe) 41–71
Composting 60, 179
'Concerning Dreams and Nightmares: The Dream Stories of H. P. Lovecraft' 353–58
'Cone, The' (Wells) 340
Confessions: On *Astro City* and Kurt Busiek' 265–70
Conjure Wife (Leiber) 172
Constable, John 480–81
Contract with God, A (Eisner) 293–94, 298
Contracts 254–55
Cook, Peter 496
Copyright laws 347–48
Coraline (Gaiman) 73, 82, 91, 115
Coraline (movie) 23, 471–77
Coraline (musical) 92
Coren, Alan 157, 511
Cornelius, Jerry 90

Costello, Elvis 75
Count of Monte Cristo, The (Dumas) 190
Country of the Blind and Other Stories (Wells), Introduction to 335–45
'Country of the Blind, The' (Wells) 343–44
Course of the Heart, The (Harrison) 371
'Credo' 7–8
Crompton, Richmal 108
Crumb, Robert 310, 317
'Crystal Egg, The' (Wells) 342
Cure for Cancer, A (Moorcock) 127
'Curious Wine: Tori Amos II' 397–99
Cushing, Peter 225
Cyberpunk 191–92; definition of 126

Dadd, Richard, *The Fairy-Feller's Master-Stroke* 433, 451–56
Dallas Fantasy Fair (1990) 308
Dandelion Wine (Bradbury) 188
Danse Macabre (King), 135, 329
Dark Knight Returns, The (movie) 228
Darwin, Charles 47, 337
Davidson, Avram 174, 199
Davies, Russell T. 223
Day I Swapped My Dad for Two Goldfish, The (Gaiman) 73, 91, 93, 113
Day of the Triffids, The (Wyndham) 32, 181
Daydreaming 18–19
DC Comics 113, 252, 255, 271–72, 286–87, 333, 406
Deadface (Campbell), Introduction to 261–64
Deadville Stories (Ellison) 199–90
Decimal currency 33, 89
DeFiore, Morgan 91–92
Delany, Chip 171
Delany, Samuel R. 35, 193–97; *The Einstein Intersection* 193–97; *Wonder Woman* 172
Derleth, August 354–55
Dhalgren (Delany) 35, 196
DiCrocco, Christine 4, 78
Diamond Comic Distributors speech (1993) 235–44
Diamonds Are Forever (Fleming) 32
Dick, Philip K. 199
Dickens, Charles 144, 278, 297, 348
Dickson, Dave 36, 289–90
Dictionary of Fairies (Briggs) 434
Different Seasons (King) 139
Dirk Gently's Holistic Detective Agency (Adams) 374

Disch, Thomas M. 33, 89, 199
'Disco Mystic' (song) 413
Discworld (Pratchett) 108, 510
Distributionism 352
Doctor Sleep (King) 140–41, 141, 143
Doctor Who (TV series) 223–27, 374
Doctorow, Cory, *Information Doesn't
    Want to Be Free* 346–49
Dogsbody (Jones) 103; Introduction to
    379–82
*Don't Panic: The Official Hitchhiker's
    Guide to the Galaxy Companion*
    (Gaiman) 121
'Door in the Wall, The' (Wells) 344
Doran, Colleen 304
Dorman, Sonya 171
Downey, Robert, Jr. 474
Doyle, Arthur Conan 88, 189–90, 339
Dracula (Stoker) 328–32
Dracula Tape, The (Saberhagen) 329
'Dream of Armageddon, A' (Wells)
    342–43
'Dream Quest of Unknown Kadath, The'
    (Lovecraft) 358
*Dreams of Terror and Death: The Dream
    Cycle of H. P. Lovecraft*, Introduction
    to 353–58
Dresden Dolls 219, 485–91
Duffy, Brian 483
Dumas, Alexandre 190
Dunsany, Lord, Edward Plunkett 356;
    The King of Elfland's Daughter 433,
    434, 441–43
Duplicator machines 347–48
Dutch Tulip Bubble 236–38, 301

Echo Round His Bones (Disch) 33
Eco, Umberto 357
Edmondson, G. C. 199
'Eight Views of Mount Fuji: Beloved
    Demons and Anthony Martignetti'
    492–500
Einstein, Albert 19–20
Einstein Intersection, The (Delany),
    Foreword to 193–97
Eisner, Ann 292
Eisner, Will 148, 228, 257, 291–92,
    293–96, 303, 304–5; Chicago Comics
    Convention (1996), 'ashcan' tribute
    to 304–5; *Will Eisner's New York: Life
    in the Big City* 297–300
Eisner Awards Keynote Speech (2003)
    301–6
11/22/63 (King) 138
Eliot, T. S. 433, 483

Ellison, Harlan 2, 123–30, 171, 200;
    'Banging the Drum for Harlan
    Ellison' 13–14; *The Beast That
    Shouted Love at the Heart of the
    World* 123–30
Empathy and fiction 12
'Empire of the Ants' (Wells) 344
Emshwiller, Carol 171
Encyclopedia of Science Fiction (Clute
    and Nicholls) 108, 126, 178, 189
Eno, Brian 404
Escape (magazine) 112
Escapism (escapist literature) 13, 64–65,
    86
Eshbach, Lloyd 269
Euripides 262
Evanier, Mark, *Kirby: King of Comics*,
    Introduction to 282–84
Evelyn Evelyn 423–26, 488
*Evelyn Evelyn: A Tragic Tale in Two
    Tomes* (Palmer and Webley),
    Afterword to 423–26
Evenings with Neil Gaiman 348
*Extraordinary Popular Delusions and the
    Madness of Crowds* (Mackay) 235–38
Eye of the Tyger (McCauley),
    Introduction to 223–27

Faces of Fantasy, The (Perret) 100
Fagin, Helen 51–52
Fahrenheit 451 (Bradbury) 324;
    Introduction to 183–88
Fahrenheit 451 (movie) 186
Failures 311, 461–62
Fairy Feller's Master Stroke, The
    (Chadbourn) 456
Fairy tales 64–67, 431–37; compared
    with romance books 50–51
Fairy-Feller's Master-Stroke, The (Dadd)
    433, 451–56
Family albums 478–84
Father Brown 42, 350–52
Fellowship of the Ring, The (Tolkien) 40
Female storylines 72–73
Fey, Tina 474
Finger, Bob 268
Fire and Hemlock (Jones) 103
'Fireman,The' (Bradbury) 186
Fisher, Jules 387, 389
Fleming, Ian 32
Fletcher, Jo 150
Flood (album), liner notes 400–402
Flying Inn, The (Chesterton) 43
Focus Features 472–73
Forbidden Planet 36, 201

Forrest, David 89–90
Fortunately, the Milk (Gaiman) 93
'Four Bookshops' 31–37
Fourth World 282–83
Fox, Gardner 268
Frankenstein (Shelley) 175
Fraser, George MacDonald 363
Free speech 7–8, 79
Freedom and libraries 14
Freelancer life 464–65
'Fritz Leiber: The Short Stories' 171–75
From Hell (Moore) 255–56, 263, 383
'From the Days of Future Past: *The*
   Country of the Blind and Other
   Stories, by H. G. Wells' 335–45
Fry, Stephen 230

Gaiman, David 26, 125, 148, 471
Gaiman, Holly 12, 90, 129, 148, 405–6,
   432–33
Gaiman, Maddy 104, 207–8, 312,
   432–33
Gaiman, Michael 1–2, 21, 28
Galvin, Cathy 135
'Garden, The' (Marvell) 175
'Gardener, The' (Kipling) 334
Gardening 45, 60
Garland, Lorraine 23–24
Garner, Alan 88
Geidt, Jeremy 496
Gender and books 72–77
Genre fiction 47–50, 52–53
'Geoff Notkin: Meteorite Man' 147–49
Ghastly Beyond Belief (Newman and
   Gaiman, eds.) 151–52, 202
Ghost stories 55–58
Ghosts in the Machines: Some
   Hallowe'en Thoughts' 54–58
Gibbons, Dave 228, 296
Gibbs, A. Hamilton 128
Gibson, William 189; 'Burning Chrome'
   404–5; *Neuromancer* 193
'Gift, The' (song) 404
Gilbert, W. S. 40
Gilliam, Terry 213, 214, 308
GK's Weekly 351
Golden Globes 473–74, 475
Goldman, William 434
Gone with the Wind (Mitchell) 51–52
'Gonna Roll the Bones' (Leiber) 196
'Good Comics and Tulips: A Speech'
   235–44
Good Omens (Pratchett and Gaiman)
   108–9, 465, 508, 510
Google 14–15, 45, 78, 365

Goosebumps (Stine) 90
Gotti, John 137
Grandenetti, Jerry 286
Gravett, Paul 112
Graveyard Book, The (Gaiman) 21, 23,
   24–25, 27–29
Graveyards 27–28
Gray, Nicholas Stuart 22
Great Cow Race, The (Smith) 275, 276,
   281
Green Mile, The (King) 144
Greenland, Colin 446–47, 449–50
Gregory, Marc 412
Grimm Brothers 276, 431–32
Grisham, John 127
Gulliver's Travels (Swift) 73
Gumshoe (Thompson) 156–59
Gursky, Steve 240–41

'Half Jack' (song) 490
Hallowe'en 54–58, 486–87
Happiest Days of Your Life, The (play)
   85–86
Hard Candy (movie) 220
Hard Core: Power, Pleasure and the
   'Frenzy of the Visible' (Williams) 48–49
Harris, Neil Patrick 474
Harrison, Jane Ellen 433
Harrison, M. John 367–72
'Harry's Circumcision' (song) 416
Hartnell, William 225
Harvey Awards Keynote Speech (2004)
   307–14
Harvey Comics 294
'Have You Seen My Sister Evelyn?'
   (song) 423
Havel, Václav 400, 410, 411
Hayden, Teresa Nielsen 47
'Hearing Aid' (song) 402
Heavenly Breakfast (Delany) 195
Heifetz, Merrilee 23–24, 91
Heinlein, Robert 176, 193, 269
Hellbound Heart, The (Barker) 154
Hellraiser (movie) 154
Helplessness 87, 94
Henson, Brian 215
Henson, Jim 211, 212
Henson, Lisa 211, 215, 219
Herbert, Frank 199, 200
Hering, Henry 453
Hernandez, Jaime and Koko 292
Herriman, George 303, 310
'Hi, by the Way: Tori Amos' 395–96
Hiding the Elephant (Steinmeyer) 389
Hill, Joe (Joe King) 136, 140, 143

Hillis, Danny 387n
Hillyer, Ed 263
Hitchhiker: A Biography of Douglas Adams (Simpson), Foreword to 120–22
Hitchhiker's Guide to the Galaxy, The (Adams) 120, 374, 376–78
Hitchhiker's Guide to the Galaxy, The (movie) 375
Hitchhiker's Guide to the Galaxy, The (radio series) 374
Hoban, Russell 384
Hobbit, The (Tolkien) 40
'Home of the Brave' (song) 409–10
'Hop-Frog' (Poe) 323
Horatio Stubbs Saga (Aldiss) 177
'Hot Cha' (song) 402
Hothouse (Aldiss), Introduction to 175–82
'How Dare You: On America, and Writing About It' 69–71
'How to Read Gene Wolfe' 117–19
Howard, Robert E. 173, 354
Hubbard, L. Ron 269
Hugo Award 176, 181
Hurt Locker, The (movie) 476
Hutchins, Jim 408

I, Robot (Asimov) 32
'I Have No Mouth and I Must Scream' (Ellison) 125
Iceland 75
'I'm Set Free' (song) 405
Imagination 18–19
Imagine (magazine) 151
Immigrant experience 70
'In the Abyss' (Wells) 341
In Viriconium (Harrison) 370, 371
Infantino, Carmine 272, 274
Information Doesn't Want to Be Free: Laws for the Internet Age (Doctorow) 346–49
Information glut 14–15
Intelligent Life (magazine) 456
International Conference on the Fantastic in the Arts, keynote speech (2013) 44–53
Interzone 150–51
Invisible Man, The (Wells) 335–36
Irving, Henry 331
Island of Dr. Moreau, The (Wells) 336
Ismayilova, Khadija 79
'Istanbul (Not Constantinople)' (song) 400–401

Jack the Ripper 153, 255–56

Jacket, The (movie) 219–20
James, John 362–66
Jaworczyn, Stefan 153
'Jeep Song, The' (song) 489
Jeff Smith: Bone and Beyond (Filipi) 275–81
Jillette, Penn 221, 388
Jim Henson Company 211–12, 214–16, 230
Jimmy Corrigan (Ware) 303
Jonathan Strange & Mr. Norrell (Clarke), Introduction to 446–50
Jones, Chuck 276
Jones, Diana Wynne: *Dogsbody* 103, 379–82; 'Reflections: On Diana Wynne Jones' 101–5
Jones, Steve 358
Jones, Terry 214
Jordan, Neil 433
Jordan, UNHCR camps 501–7
Jorkens, Joseph 441–42
Joyland (King) 137, 140
Jungle Book, The (Kipling) 28
Jurgen, A Comedy of Justice (Cabell) 34

Kahn, Jenette 287
Kambriel 471–72, 473
Kane, Bob 255, 273–74, 300
Karloff, Boris 207–10
Keeler, Harry Stephen 287
Kelly, Walt 276, 279
'Kicks' (song) 409
King, Carole 489
King, Naomi 143
King, Owen 136, 143
King, Stephen 2, 129, 334, 357, 465; *Carrie* 12, 90, 137–38, 142, 143; 'On Stephen King' 135–46; *'Salem's Lot* 137–38, 143, 329
King, Tabitha 136–38, 141–42, 143, 146
King Foundation 139
King of Elfland's Daughter, The (Dunsany) 433, 434, 441–43
Kipling, Rudyard 28, 333–34
Kirby, Jack 268, 282–88
Kirby, Ronald William 'Josh' 115
Kirby: King of Comics (Evanier), Introduction to 282–84
Kittelsen, Theodor 438
Kleinschmidt, Kilian 503
Klinger, Les 331
Knight, Laura 481
Knockabout Comics 80–81
Kraków University 51
Krazy Kat (Herriman) 310

Krigstein, Bernie 303
Kryptonite Kid, The 266, 267
Kupferberg, Tuli 171
Kurtzman, Harvey 148, 307–8

La Belle et la Bête (movie) 432–33
Labyrinth (movie) 211, 212, 214
Lafferty, R. A. 34, 36, 171, 174
Lanchester, Elsa 207–10
Landau, Yair 219
Larkin, Philip 490
Last Exit to Brooklyn (Selby) 409
Laumer, Keith 199
Layer Cake (movie) 218–19
Le Guin, Ursula K. 2, 88
League of Extraordinary Gentlemen, The
    (movie) 229, 231
Lee, Stan 268, 282
Legendary Pink Dots 487
Leiber, Fritz 171–75, 196, 354
Lemon, Denis 80–81
L'Engle, Madeleine 25
Levitz, Paul 255
Lewis, C.S. 13, 32, 38–40, 43, 73, 86,
    103
Lewis, Matthew 'Monk' 273
Lexton, Maria 162
Librarians 14, 22–23, 30, 304
Libraries 9–10, 13–20, 21–23
Liefeld, Rob 258, 259
Life, the Universe and Everything
    (Adams) 374
'Ligeia' (Poe) 324, 327
Light (Harrison) 371
Lion, the Witch and the Wardrobe, The
    (Lewis) 38
Literacy 10, 11, 16, 19, 20
Little Nemo (McCay) 310
Lloyd, David 231
Lloyd, John 121, 374
Loaded (album) 404
Locus 45
Look Magazine, 'Sundance Diary'
    218–22
'Lord of the Dynamos, The' (Wells)
    339–40
Lord of the Rings, The (Tolkien) 2,
    40–42, 448–49
'Lou Reed, in Memoriam: 'The
    Soundtrack to My Life'' 403–22
Lovecraft, H. P. 2, 174, 353–58
'Lucky Ball and Chain' (song) 401
Lud-in-the-Mist (Mirrlees) 433, 434,
    444–45, 448
Lugosi, Bela 329

Lumley, Brian 356
Lunatic Heroes (Martignetti) 497, 498

McAdams, Rachel 473, 475, 477
McCauley, Paul, Eye of the Tyger 223–27
McCay, Winsor 303, 310
McCloud, Scott 268, 300, 317
MacDonald, John D. 138, 145
McIntosh, J. T. 87
Mackay, Charles 235–38
McKay, Nellie 486
McKean, Clare 113, 114
McKean, Dave 250, 258–59; MirrorMask
    (movie) 211–22, 230, 232; 'On Dave
    McKean' 112–16
Madden, Matt 317
'Made in USA' (McIntosh) 87
Magazine of Fantasy and Science Fiction
    445
Magic (magicians) 387–89
Magic and Loss (album) 410, 418, 420
Mahurin, Matt 417
Major, John 127
'Make Good Art' 459–67
Male storylines 72–73, 76–77
'Man Who Could Work Miracles, The'
    (Wells) 342
'Man Who Rowed Christopher
    Columbus Ashore, The' (Ellison)
    129–30
Man Who Was Thursday, The
    (Chesterton) 42, 351
Mandeville, John 178
Manhattan 160
Marder, Larry 240
Marquee Club (London) 163
Martian Chronicles, The (Bradbury), 32,
    187
Martignetti, Anthony 492–500
Martignetti, Laura 494, 498
Martin, George R. R. 266
Martin, J. P. 22, 88
Martin, Steve 474
Marvell, Andrew 175
'Masque of the Red Death, The' (Poe)
    324, 326
Maus (Spiegelman) 228, 296, 302
Mayer, Robert, Superfolks 266
Mehta, Sonny 375, 377
Melville, Herman, Moby-Dick 267,
    275–76
Merril, Judith 171–72
Metal Machine Music (album) 405,
    413
Meteorites 148–49

Milford Writers' Workshop 101
Milholland, Randy 313
Miller, Frank 228, 232, 239, 258, 303
'Minimum Wage' (song) 402
Mirrlees, Hope, *Lud-in-the-Mist* 433, 434, 444–45, 448
MirrorMask (movie) 211–22, 230, 232; Sundance diary 218–22
MirrorMask: The Illustrated Film Script of the Motion Picture 211–17
Misery (King) 140
Mistakes 311
Mistrial (album) 408
Mitchell, Margaret 140; *Gone with the Wind* 51–52
Moby-Dick; or, The Whale (Melville) 267, 275–76
Monk, The (Lewis) 273
Monstrous Regiment (Pratchett) 110
Moorcock, Michael 88, 90, 177, 370; *A Cure for Cancer* 127; *Stormbringer* 171
Moore, Alan 228, 239, 255–56, 258, 302–3, 310, 383–86; *From Hell* 255–56, 263, 383; *Supreme* 267; *V for Vendetta* 230–31; *Voice of the Fire* 383–86
Morris, Mark 210
Morrison, Grant 310
Morritt, Charles 388
Mosnier, Jean-Laurent 481
Moth, The: This Is a True Story, Introduction for 390–92
'Moth, The' (Wells) 340
Motion of Light in Water, The (Delany) 195
Movies 207–22; 'A View from the Cheap Seats' 471–77; and comics 228–32, 249
Mr. Punch (Gaiman and McKean) 113
Mugnier, Arthur 62
Music 395–428; copyright laws 347–48
Musicals compared with pornographic films 48–49
Muth, Jon 250
MythCon 35, 38–43; Guest of Honour Speech (2004) 38–43
Myths 59–68

Nancarrow, Conlon 113
Napoleon of Notting Hill, The (Chesterton) 42–43
Napster 347
National Book Foundation 140
National Portrait Gallery 478–83

'Nature of the Infection, The: Some Thoughts on *Doctor Who*' 223–27
Nebula Awards speech (2005) 198–203
Negotiations 254–55
Neuromancer (Gibson) 193
Neverwhere (Gaiman) 72, 436
Neverwhere (TV series) 226, 249
'New Accelerator, The' (Wells) 343
New Annotated Dracula (Stoker), Introduction to 328–32
New Statesman 81
New Wave: definition of 126–27
New Worlds (magazine) 126, 177
New Yorker (magazine) 23, 126, 317
New York's Village Halloween Parade 56
Newbery Medal Speech (2009) 21–30
Newman, Kim 150–55, 226, 329
Newton, Isaac 310
Nicholls, Peter 382; *Encyclopedia of Science Fiction*, 108, 126, 178, 189
Night Watch (Pratchett) 110
Nightmare Movies (Newman) 151
1984 (Orwell) 193
Niven, Larry 266
'No Money Down' (song) 417
'Nobody's Guide to the Oscars, A' 471–77
Non-Stop (Aldiss) 178
Norse sagas 364–65
Not for All the Gold in Ireland (James) 363, 365–66
Notkin, Geoff 147–49, 291
Notkin, Sam 147, 148
Nova (Delany) 35, 196

Ocean at the End of the Lane, The (Gaiman) 94–95, 454–55
Of Time, and Gully Foyle: Alfred Bester and *The Stars My Destination*' 189–92
Of Worlds Beyond (Eshbach, ed.) 269
Oliver, Edgar 390–91
'On Dave McKean' 112–16
'On *The 13 Clocks* by James Thurber' 359–61
'On *Viriconium*: Some Notes Toward an Introduction' 367–72
'Once Upon a Time' 431–37
Organisation for Economic Co-operation and Development 16
Original Dr. Shade and Other Stories, The (Newman), Introduction to 150–55
Original Plays (Gilbert) 40
Orpheus 194–95

Orwell, George 189, 193
Oscars 471–77
Outrageous Tales from the Old Testament (comic) 80
Outsider and Others, The (Lovecraft) 355

Pace that Kills, The (Roberts/Bevan) 269
Palmer, Amanda 92, 462; and Anthony Martignetti 492–98; The Dresden Dolls 485–91; Evelyn Evelyn 423–26, 488; *Who Killed Amanda Palmer* (album) 427–28, 497
Pan Book of Horror Stories 32, 88
Pan Books 375
Pangborn, Edgar 525
'Particle Man' (song), 401
Pastel City, The (Harrison) 367–68, 369–70
'Patricia's Profession' (Newman) 151
Peace (Wolfe) 118
Peace and Love Corporation 153–54
Peak, Bob 258–59
'Pedestrian, The' (Bradbury) 186
PEN Awards 78–81
PEN World Voices Festival (2007) 390
Penn, Sean 476
'Perfect Day' (song) 412
Perkins, Geoffrey 121
Perrault, Charles 64–65, 432
Perret, Patti 100
Pertwee, Jon 225
Photographs of authors 99–100
'Pickman's Model' (Lovecraft) 358
Pilgrim's Progress, The (Bunyan) 436
'Plattner Story, The' (Wells) 341
Plus Books 34–35
Poe, Edgar Allan 32, 323–27
Poe, John Allan 326
Pop, Iggy 283
Pornographic films compared with musicals 48–49
'Pornography of Genre, or the Genre of Pornography, The' 44–53
Portraiture 479–84
Pratchett, Terry 106–11, 400–401; *A Slip of the Keyboard* 508–13; 'Terry Pratchett: An Appreciation' 106–11
Price, Vincent 324–25
Princess Bride, The (Goldman) 434
Prison industry 10
Prisoners of Gravity (TV series) 277
'Problem with Susan, The' (Gaiman) 43
ProCon speech (1997) 245–60
Provenza, Paul 221
PS (magazine) 298

Quinn, Marc 483
Quinn, Seabury 354

Rackham, Arthur 435, 438
Radomsko Ghetto 51–52
Rat Race, The (Bester) 191
Rathbone, Basil 324
'Raven, The' (Poe) 325
Raw Power (album) 283
'Ray Bradbury, *Fahrenheit 451* and What Science Fiction Is and Does' 183–88
ReaderCon 11 program book (1999) 13–14
Readers: as collaborators 45–46; obligation to 18
Reading 9–20
Reading Agency Lecture (2013) 9–20
Rebecca (du Maurier) 140
Red Riding Hood 65, 433
Reed, Kit 171
Reed, Lou 120, 147, 403–22
Reed, Sylvia 413
Reflections (Jones), Foreword to 101–5
Reinventing Comics (McCloud) 317
'Remarkable Case of Davidson's Eyes, The' (Wells) 340
'Remembering Douglas Adams' 120–22
Report on Probability A (Aldiss) 177
Restaurant at the End of the Universe, The (Adams) 374
Return of the King, The (Tolkien) 41
Return of the Shadow, The (Tolkien) 41
Revolt in 2100 (Heinlein) 193
Rex, Adam 92
Riddell, Chris 8
Riddley Walker (Hoban) 384
Roadmarks (Zelazny) 36
Robinson, James 163
Rock Bottom Remainders 136
Rock Star: Adventures of a Meteorite Man (Notkin), Introduction to 147–49
Rodriguez, Robert 232
Rose for Ecclesiastes, A (Zelazny) 35
Rosenthal, Becca 496
Roshell, John 269
Ross, Alex 269
Rossetti, Christina 433
Rossetti, Dante Gabriel 452
Rowling, J. K. 110
Rudyard Kipling's Tales of Horror and Fantasy (Jones), Introduction To 333–34
Russell, Eric Frank 177
Russell, P. Craig 250

Saberhagen, Fred 329
Sailor's Girl, The (movie) 221
'*Salem's Lot* (King) 137–38, 143, 329
'Samuel R. Delany and *The Einstein Intersection*' 193–97
San Diego Comic Convention 232
Sandman (Gaiman) 61–62, 63, 69, 72, 114, 245, 247, 405, 465
Sandman (movie project) 249
Sandman (Simon and Kirby) 285–86, 287
Satire 110
Saturday Night Live (TV series) 120
Schmidt, Eric 14–15
School of Visual Arts (New York City) 148, 291, 299
Schwartz, Lew Sayre 271, 274
Science fiction, misconceptions about 193–94
Scott, George C. 400
Screwtape Letters, The (Lewis) 32, 39
'Sea Raiders, The' (Wells) 341–42
Searle, Ronald 360
Selby, Hubert 409
Selected Stories (Leiber), Introduction to 171–75
Self-censorship of children 87, 90
Selick, Henry 471–72, 475, 477
Sendak, Maurice 489
Serious Man, A (movie) 472
Set, The (Newman) 151
Sexes and books 72–77
SF12 (Merril, ed.) 171–72
Shadows over Innsmouth (Jones, ed.) 358
Shakespeare, William 441
Shatterday (Ellison) 125–26, 128–29
Shawshank Redemption (King) 139
Sheen, Michael 476
Shelf Life: Fantastic Stories Celebrating Bookstores (Ketter, ed.) 31–37
Shelley, Mary 175, 208
Shining, The (King) 141
'Shoehorn with Teeth' (song) 401
Siegel, Jerry 255, 268
Signal to Noise (Gaiman and McKean) 113
Signal to Noise (radio drama) 247
Silver Locusts, The (Bradbury) 32, 187
Silverberg, Robert 356
Sim, Dave 239, 251, 277, 312
Simak, Clifford D. 199
SimCity 2000 160–61
Simon, Brett 221
Simon, Joe 284, 285–88

Simon and Kirby Superheroes, Introduction to 285–88
Simont, Marc 360
Simpson, M. J., *Hitchhiker: A Biography of Douglas Adams* 122
Sin City (movie) 232
Sinatra, Nancy 136
Sinclair, Alex 269
Sinclair, Iain 113
'Sing' (song) 489
'Six to Six' 162–67
Slip of the Keyboard, A (Pratchett), Introduction to 508–13
'Slip Under the Microscope, A' (Wells) 341
Smash! 271
Smith, Cordwainer 370
Smith, Jeff 251, 275–81, 304, 312; *Bone* 275–81, 312
Smoke and Mirrors (Gaiman) 66n
So Long, and Thanks for All the Fish (Adams), Introduction to 373–78
'So Many Ways to Die in Syria Now: 2014' 501–7
Soho (London) 163–66
'Some Reflections on Myth (With Several Digressions onto Gardening, Comics and Fairy Tales)' 59–68
'Some Strangeness in the Proportion: The Exquisite Beauties of Edgar Allan Poe' 323–27
Son of Dracula (movie) 329
Sondheim, Stephen 113, 499
Soundings (Gibbs) 128
Space Voyager (magazine) 106, 123
Speculative fiction 110, 183–86, 189–90, 193, 201
Spiegelman, Art 78, 79, 148, 228, 300, 303, 304
Spin (magazine), 'The Dresden Dolls: Hallowe'en 2010' 485–91
Spinrad, Norman 127, 266
Spirit (comics) 289–96
Spirit, The (Eisner) 228, 293–96, 298, 299–300
Sprang, Dick 271, 274
Stalking the Nightmare (Ellison) 129
'Star, The' (Wells) 342
'Star Pit, The' (Delany) 171
Stardust (Gaiman) 72–73, 88, 434–37
Stardust (movie), 435
Stars My Destination, The (Bester), Introduction to 189–92
Steel, Danielle 140
Stein, Gertrude 131

Steinmeyer, Jim 387–89
Stern, Howard 128
Stewart, Thomas 481
Stine, R. L. 11, 12, 90
Stoker, Bram, *Dracula* 328–32
Stooges, the 283
Stoppard, Tom 79
Storey, Margaret 22, 88
Storm of Wings, A (Harrison) 370
Stormbringer (Moorcock) 171
'Story of the Late Mr. Elvesham, The' (Wells) 341
'Story of the Stone Age, A' (Wells) 342
Stranger in a Strange Land (Heinlein) 176
'Study in Scarlet, A' (Doyle) 323
Sturgeon's Law 47
'Suede' (song) 397
Sundance 218–22
Sunday Times 239–40; 'On Stephen King' 135–46
Superfolks (Mayer), 266
Superheroes, lineage of 265–68
Supreme (Moore) 267
Švankmajer, Jan 113
Swamp Thing 273, 286
Swift, Jonathan 73
Sword of Sorcery (Leiber) 172
Swords of Lankhmar, The (Leiber) 172
Syria 501–7

Tales of Mystery and Imagination (Poe), 327
Tales of the Norsemen 59
Tan, Amy 136
Tate Gallery 451–56
'Telling Lies for a Living... And Why We Do It' 21–30
'Tell-Tale Heart, The' (Poe) 324, 326
Tennyson, Alfred 482
'Terry Pratchett: An Appreciation' 106–11
Thatcher, Margaret 371
Theatre Is Evil (album) 493–94
'These Are Not Our Faces' 99–100
Thesiger, Ernest 208–9
Thespis 261
They Might Be Giants 400–402
They Might Be Giants (movie) 400
'Thing of It Is, The: *Jonathan Strange and Mr. Norrell*,' 446–50
13 Clocks, The (Thurber) 359–61
Thomas, Theodore 199
Thompson, Jim 385
Thompson, Josiah, *Gumshoe* 156–59

'Three Authors: On Lewis, Tolkien and Chesterton' 38–43
Thurber, James, *The 13 Clocks* 359–61
Tiger! Tiger! (Bester) 190, 193
Time Bandits (movie) 213
Time Machine, The (Wells) 336
Time Out (magazine): 'Six to Six' 162–67; 'Waiting for the Man: Lou Reed' 408–22
To Venus and Back (tour book) 397–99
Tolkien, Christopher 41
Tolkien, J.R.R. 2, 40–42, 43, 88, 103, 110, 431; *The Lord of the Rings* 2, 40–42, 448–49
'Tolkien's Magic Ring' (Beagle) 2, 40
Torchia, Joseph 266
Tragedy 261–63
Transformer (album) 404, 405, 412, 418
Trevino, Rose 24
Trillion Year Spree (Aldiss) 175
Trouble on Triton (Delany) 194
Troughton, Patrick 224–25
Truffaut, Francois 186
'Truth About Pyecraft, The' (Wells) 343
Tulip mania 236–38, 301
'Twisting' (song) 401

UN Refugee Agency (UNHCR) 501–7
'Under the Knife' (Wells) 341
Under the Pink (tour book) 395–96
University of the Arts Commencement Speech (2012) 459–67
Up (movie) 472, 474
'Usher II' (Bradbury) 323–24
Utterly Utterly Merry Comic Relief Christmas Book (Adams) 121

V for Vendetta (movie) 231
Vance, Jack 36, 370
Vaughn, Matthew 218–19, 435
Velvet Underground 149, 404–5, 418
Verne, Jules 335
Vess, Charles 250, 435, 438–40
Vess, Karen 440
Victorians 12, 104, 331
Victor/Victoria (musical) 146
'View from the Cheap Seats, The' 471–77
Viglione, Brian 486–90
Violent Cases (Gaiman and McKean) 112
Viriconium (Harrison), Introduction to 367–72
Voice of the Fire (Moore), Introduction to 383–86
Von Buhler, Cynthia 425, 426
Vonnegut, Kurt 145

Votan (James) 362–66
Votan and Other Novels (James),
    Introduction to 362–66
Voyage of the Dawn Treader, The (Lewis)
    38

Wagner, Karl Edward 356, 357
'Waiting for the Man: Lou Reed' 408–22
'Walk on the Wild Side' (song) 405–6
Wallace, Edgar 42, 88
Wandrei, Donald 355
War Games, The (TV series) 224–25
'War Pigs' (song) 490
Ware, Chris 303
Warhol, Andy 405, 406
Warrior (magazine) 231
Watchmen (movie) 228, 266, 296
'We Want a Rock' (song) 401–2
Webley, Jason 423–26, 488
Webster, John 325
Webster, Miss 124–25, 128
Wein, Len 273
Weinstein, Harvey 475, 504
Weird Tales 354
Weller, Mr. 45
Welles, Orson 228, 229
Wellman, Manly Wade 354
Wells, H. G. 176, 335–45
W.H. Smith Bookshop 31
Whale, James 210
'What the [Very Bad Swearword] Is a
    Children's Book, Anyway?', 82–96
'What's Good' (song) 411, 416–17
Wheatley, Dennis 32, 42, 88
'When the World Screamed' (Doyle) 339
'Whistling in the Dark' (song) 402
White, James 199
Who Killed Amanda Palmer (album)
    427–28, 497
'Why Our Future Depends on Libraries,
    Reading and Daydreaming' 9–20
'Wild Asses of the Devil, The' (Wells)
    344
Wild Cards (Martin, ed.) 266
Wilde, Oscar 331

'Wilderness of Mirrors, A' 478–84
Wilhelm, Kate 199
Wilkins' Tooth (Jones) 380
*Will Eisner's New York: Life in the Big
    City*, Introduction to 297–300
William (Crompton) 108
Williams, Alan D. 139
Williams, Linda, *Hard Core* 48–49
Williams, Ralph 346
Wilmington Bookshop 33–34
Wilson, Colin 357
Wind Through the Keyhole, The (King)
    140, 143–44
Windsor-Smith, Barry 452
'Winter Flies, The' (Leiber) 171–72
'Witch's Headstone, The' (Gaiman)
    28
Wolfe, Gene 77, 99, 199, 356
Wolves in the Walls, The (Gaiman and
    McKean) 115–16
'Women and Men' (song) 402
Woodlawn, Holly 405–6
World Fantasy Award (1991) 438–40
World Fantasy Convention program
    book (2002) 112–16
World Horror Convention program book
    (2002) 117–19
World Science Fiction Convention
    speech (2004) 106–11
Wrightson, Bernie 258, 273
Wrinkle in Time, A (L'Engle) 25
Writing exercises 257–58
Written contracts 254–55
Wyndham, John, *The Day of the Triffids*
    32, 181

YALSA (Young Adult Library Services
    Association) 91
Young Frankenstein (movie) 209
'Your Racist Friend' (song) 401

Zelazny, Roger 34, 35, 36, 127, 200
Zemeckis, Robert 229
Zena Sutherland Lecture (2012) 82–96
Zulli, Michael 248